Social Movements in an Organizational Society

Mayer N. Zald and
John D. McCarthy

Introduction by William A. Gamson

Social movements are collections of individuals and groups striving for social and individual change. In *Social Movements in an Organizational Society*, Zald and McCarthy and their collaborators offer a detailed analysis of the process involved when individuals and groups are mobilized for collective action. The common thread that unites the various essays is the treatment of social movement activity as purposeful behavior. Three of the essays are new to this volume.

The authors explore five major themes: First, they present their resource mobilization theory, focusing on the resources, manpower, money, and media attention that social movements must collect from supporters. They examine problems that confront all organizations, including economic and political pressures. They analyze the social movement industry—conflicting segments that compete and cooperate systematically. They detail the social movement-like phenomena that occur within large-scale organizations. Finally, they explore the structure and process of social movements in different societies and the future of social movements.

Zald and McCarthy and their collaborators provide a coherent and integrated approach to a major facet of modern society. Social movement phenomena are major agents of social change and they raise many of the agenda items of our public life. This volume dissects how they are made and why they succeed and fail.

SOCIAL MOVEMENTS IN AN ORGANIZATIONAL SOCIETY

SOCIAL MOVEMENTS IN AN ORGANIZATIONAL SOCIETY

Collected Essays

Edited by

MAYER N. ZALD

and

JOHN D. McCARTHY

Transaction Books
New Brunswick (U.S.A.) and Oxford (U.K.)

Library of Congress Catalog Number: 86-11398
ISBN: 0-88738-119-7
Printed in the United States of America

Library of Congress Cataloging in Publication Data

Social movements in an organizational society.

   Bibliography: p.
   Includes index.
   1. Social movements.   2. Social structure.   3. Social
history.   I. Zald, Mayer N.   II. McCarthy, John D.
(John David), 1940-
HN13.S652   1986   303.4′84   86-11398
ISBN 0-88738-119-7

Contents

List of Tables and Figures

Tables

Figures

Acknowledgments

We are indebted to several publishers for permission to reprint articles previously published, as follows.

The University of Chicago Press is acknowledged for permission to reprint:
"Resource Mobilization and Social Movements: A Partial Theory," *American Journal of Sociology* 82, 6 (May 1977):1212-41.
"Organizational Intellectuals and the Criticism of Society," *Social Service Review* 49, 3 (September 1975):344-62.
"Social Movements in Organizations: Coup D'Etat Bureaucratic Insurgency and Mass Movement," *American Journal of Sociology* 83, 4 (January 1978):823-61.

University of North Carolina Press is acknowledged for permission to reprint:
"Aspects of Racial Integration in the Methodist Church: Sources of Resistance to Organizational Policy," *Social Forces* 45, 2 (December 1966):225-65.
"Social Movement Organizations: Growth, Decay and Change," *Social Forces* 44, 3 (March 1966):327-40.

Administrative Science Quarterly is acknowledged for permission to reprint:
"From Evangelism to General Service: On the Transformation and Character of the YMCA," *Administrative Science Quarterly* 8, 2 (September 1963):214-34.

JAI Press is acknowledged for permission to reprint:
"Social Movement Industries: Cooperation and Conflict Amongst Social Movement Organizations," in Louis Kriesberg, ed., *Research in Social Movements, Conflict and Change* 3 (1980).

Religious Research Association is acknowledged for permission to reprint:

"Theological Crucibles: Social Movements in and of Religion," *Review of Religious Research* 23, 4 (June 1982):317-31. It is published here in substantially revised form.

Society for the Scientific Study of Social Problems is acknowledged for permission to reprint:
"From Pressure Group to Social Movement: Efforts to Promote Use of Nuclear Power," *Social Problems* 30, 2 (December 1982):144-56.

ABLEX Publishing is acknowledged for permission to reprint:
"The Political Economy of Social Movement Sectors," in G. Suttles and M.N. Zald, eds., *The Challenge of Social Control: Citizenship and Institution Building in Modern Society: Essays in Honor of Morris Janowitz* (Norwood, N.J., 1985).

Introduction

The idea that organizations act as carriers of social movements is now commonplace in political sociology. It wasn't always thus. Twenty years ago, when Mayer Zald and Roberta Ash (now Garner) wrote "Social Movement Organizations," the idea did not fit well with the dominant way of framing social movements.

Obviously, those who studied social movements were aware of the numerous organizations that dotted their ebb and flow. But these organizations were seen more as excrescence than as the essence of the movement. Charisma gets routinized, the iron march of oligarchs follows the freewheeling and spontaneous expression of the masses, bureaucracy marches on. But it was the contrast between the solidity of bureaucratic organization and the fluidity of social movements that most observers saw then.

Zald and his various collaborators, particularly John McCarthy, have helped us to see it differently. Rather than seeing organization and movement as contrasting phenomena, they taught us to see them as embedded. And, in the twenty years since "Social Movement Organizations," they have demonstrated the fecundity of their alternative.

Zald and McCarthy represent one major tributary to a stream of revisionist thinking on social movements generally referred to as "resource mobilization" theory. The common theme that unites the various tributaries is the treatment of social movement activity as purposeful behavior. But each major tributary has its own special emphasis, calling our attention to different aspects of social movements. This introduction will try to assess both the special contribution and the lacunae in the particular tributary represented here.

McCarthy and Zald gave the mainstream the label that has stuck: "resource mobilization." There is irony in this because their special contribution doesn't really focus much on resources. The concept itself—the soft underbelly of the theory—is never given more than passing attention in any of the papers here. But then other resource mobilization theorists have not done much better with this decidedly mushy concept.

What Zald and his collaborators call our attention to are not resources

1

themselves and how they are used but how they are acquired and organized. Theirs is the *organizational* tributary in two senses: (1) they focus our attention on interaction between social movement organizations (SMOs) and a variety of other organizations—other SMOs in the same movement, countermovement organizations, and authorities; (2) they, and here John McCarthy's influence is especially strong, focus us on organizational infrastructure—the unglamorous nuts and bolts of social movement activity. Each of these contributions is worth examining in some detail.

Organizational Interaction

Zald brought to the study of social movements a political economy and open systems view of organizations. Organizations, in this view, live in a changing environment to which they must adapt to survive. They adapt in order to continue the flow of resources required for organizational maintenance and growth. Power relations within an organization and other internal processes are dramatically affected by the position of individuals and organizational subunits in the regulation and control of this resource flow.

Applying this perspective to the study of SMOs required Zald to explore the organizational environment. "Environment," it turns out, is a poor way of thinking of the issue, since it suggests an active organization in a passive world. The world of SMOs is populated with other purposeful actors who are deliberately trying to influence, control, or even destroy it. This is more than a problem of analyzing adjustment to a turbulent environment. It calls for an analysis of interaction between an SMO and other organizations.

What are the other types? First, there are competitors for the same resource base. This already is an insight because these other SMOs frequently have the same or very similar goals. Two organizations that want pretty much the same changes could easily be thought of as natural allies rather than competitors. Indeed, there are many instances of effective alliances of groups with shared sympathies within the same social movement.

But resources are scarce and, when one views SMOs as organizations, cooperation is no more inherent than competition. There is a natural tension in the relationship among like-minded SMOs that may be played out in different ways at different times. Zald and McCarthy push the economic analogy, seeing where it will lead them. One can think of all those SMOs who are seeking similar goals as forming a particular social movement industry (SMI). The tension between competition and cooperation is present in this industry just as it is in more conventional, economic ones.

They quite profitably raise the level of analysis from organization to industry. This leads to fruitful questions comparing one SMI with another and to the theoretical necessity of positioning any given SMO within its particular industry. They find SMOs seeking special market niches by "product" differentiation. The product here may be an innovative tactic that promises special efficacy, a particular vision and line of action with a special appeal for one part of the constituency, or anything else that distinguishes an SMO from its competitors. Product differentiation allows an SMO to capture a particular market segment and to maintain itself by establishing a stable niche from which it may compete for new markets.

This analysis also suggests comparisons between different SMIs. Some are growth industries, others are stable or declining. The state of the industry will have systematic effects on the balance between competition and cooperation among the SMOs within it. In a shrinking industry, competition will be most acute; in a growth industry, it will be muted.

SMOs don't merely or primarily interact with other SMOs with similar goals. Much of their interaction is with antagonists—either authorities who control the decisions which they want to influence or countermovements that oppose the changes they are promoting. Much work from a resource mobilization perspective has emphasized this interaction between SMOs and the authorities who are targets of change. Zald and his collaborators have not made this aspect of organizational interaction the most central part of their agenda, but they address it at several points. "Social Movement Industries," for example, shows how the means of social control that authorities use affect interaction within an SMI.

Their agenda does include a close look at the interaction between movements and countermovements. Zald and Useem examine the tango between movement and countermovement on nuclear power and the complicated triadic relationship with authorities. McCarthy looks at pro-choice and pro-life SMOs on the abortion issue. Finally, in this essay Zald and Useem attempt a general theoretical statement on movement and countermovement relations.

Of course, social movement industries are different from economic ones. Zald and his collaborators are well aware of this, but they tend to highlight similarities. Not much is made of the fact that many American industries are regulated, subject to antitrust laws and to restrictions on cooperative pricing and other coordinated action "in restraint of trade." SMOs are not so regulated, but they are subject to many other forms of social control that are unheard of for economic industries. Not much is made of the differences between a merger of two hierarchical corporations and two voluntary associations. Unlike the former, the latter are constrained by the possibility of mass defections and factional splits should a proposed merger offend large numbers of SMO supporters.

Zald and his collaborators wisely treat the conditions under which cooperative or competitive modes will dominate relations in a social movement industry as an empirical question—one for which they supply hypotheses and theoretical arguments. But they do not fully exploit the features of SMIs that make them a very special kind of industry.

Perhaps this fact explains why their agenda has not included the interaction of SMOs with third parties of various sorts, particularly with media organizations. This interaction seems an equally natural extension of their general program and one that fits especially well with their strong emphasis on the professionalization of social movement activity. Yet, you will find no essays in this collection that address movement-media relations. It is unfinished business in the analysis of SMO interaction with other organizations.

Their alternative agenda has been to extend the analogy to economic organizations in a macrodirection. Just as there is a financial sector or a service sector comprising several industries, there is a social movement sector. Here the unit of comparative analysis becomes the society.

One can then ask, as Garner and Zald do, a number of provocative questions about the nature of the social movement sector in different societies. First, there is the obvious matter of size—the sector is bigger in some societies than others and at different times in the same society. But size is only the beginning of what a proper theory must explain.

Garner and Zald offer us a much richer explicandum. They ask about the conditions under which working-class movements will be more or less unified into a single industry or differentiated; when life style and identity SMIs will flourish; how politicized the social movement sector will be.

It is a considerable achievement to set our mind on these questions. I don't mean to belittle their answers, which are thoughtful and sophisticated. But their biggest contribution is their implicit invitation to students of social movements to join them in pursuing this agenda. Exciting research possibilities fall from the paragraphs like so many petals, waiting to be picked up by Ph.D. candidates in search of a dissertation—or, for that matter, by established scholars.

Organizational Infrastructure

The second major contribution of this tributary is an emphasis on organizational infrastructure. Resource mobilization theory generally views social movement activity as a craft, requiring practical knowledge to perform. Zald and McCarthy focus particular attention on the routine organization of this craft and the various structures that support it.

McCarthy's essay "Pro-Life and Pro-Choice Mobilization: Infrastructure Deficits and New Technologies" is an especially good illustration of the fruits of this attention. It has been known for some time that, although pro-choice and pro-life SMIs have about equal pools of adherents, the pro-life groups have had more success in mobilizing resources from their pool. One plausible explanation that has been offered is the greater intensity of pro-life sentiments, but the evidence for this is weak.

It is the infrastructure of the two SMIs, McCarthy suggests, that can better account for the difference in translating sentiments into resources. There are different types of infrastructures, some more easily usable than others for social movement activity. Pro-life groups have benefited greatly (as did civil rights groups) by their ability to use the infrastructure of traditional religious organizations. These traditional structures were unavailable to pro-choice groups, forcing them to rely on the "thin" infrastructures of professional social movement organizations. This state of affairs means, especially, a reliance on mass mailing lists, which can be conceived of as "very weak communication networks along which information and resources may pass." We are led, in this analysis, to look closely at the extent to which a social movement industry creates its own, special purpose infrastructure or adapts existing societal structures to its purposes—and the important consequences of these different paths.

They also provide a clearer rationale for a building stage in the history of a movement. Opportunities will arise, generally in unpredictable fashion, and there may be long periods in which no effective action is possible. Rather than viewing such interim periods as waiting time, McCarthy and Zald have us see them as opportunities of a different sort. It is not a new idea—Lenin adumbrated it in "What Is to Be Done?"—but they flesh out the idea of infrastructure in ways that can and should inform the efforts of community organizers in quiet times.

Several of the essays here call our attention to one important modern technique—the use of direct mailing to adherents whose SMO membership consists of nothing more than paying annual dues, responding to occasional emergency appeals, and receiving a newsletter. They seem to have missed another, quite contrasting organizational form—the affinity group.

The affinity group structure is reticular and decentralized, composed of many small, loosely linked cells. It reflects the insight that people enter into many social movement activities in social molecules, with friends and acquaintances, rather than as atomized individuals. It was used as a self-conscious organizational form by the anti–Vietnam War movement in the early 1970s and by the Clamshell Alliance and other antinuclear power groups in the mid-1970s, and it is used by groups opposed to intervention in Central America today. There have been earlier versions of cell-like structures, particularly among underground groups, but there are many new and unanalyzed features in this latest version. With such a strong emphasis on forms of organization, it is something of a surprise that this particular structure has not made it onto the Zald agenda.

In spite of such omissions, the organizational tributary represented here has contributed greatly to increasing our awareness of the complex organizational life underlying social movement activity—and the role of movement activity in formal organizations. Resource mobilization theory has benefited substantially by dropping the sharp contrast between movements and organizations and adopting the embedded approach represented here.

The Missing Parts

There is a good-natured eclecticism in many of these essays and the authors seem ready to include whatever one might suggest. But any frame calls our attention to certain aspects and distracts us from others. This one has its blindspots.

One of them is cultural. We are not directed to the ways in which SMOs compete with ideologies and condensing symbols, or of their uneasy dance with the mass media and other actors in the consciousness industry. What they give us is heavily institutional and organizational, with little about norms, values, and political discourse. When Garner and Zald try to explain the nature of the social movement sector, cultural differences between countries take a back seat to global markets and their differential impact. When Zald tries to predict the future of social movements, he looks to the negative externalities of industrial production, not to cultural trends. From political economy, they borrow much; from political culture, hardly at all.

Nor is there any concern with the social psychology of resource mobilization. There is little here of loyalty, commitment, solidarity, consciousness, or the role of face-to-face interaction. The meanings that participants give to their involvements in collective action are made to seem largely irrelevant.

Zald and McCarthy believe that discontent has been given entirely too much attention in the past. They tell us that there has been "too much focus on the life situation of the oppressed." Yes, there are grievances, but they are ubiquitous and explain little or nothing, in their view. This debunking quality is at its purest in "The Trend of Social Movements in America," where they offer us a kind of Parkinson's Law of social movements. "The definition of grievances," they write, "will expand to meet the funds and support personnel available." They point to the "distinct possibility that professional SMOs create rather than mobilize grievances" and claim that it is "entirely likely" that creating the appearance of grievances "will bear no relationship to any pre-existing grievance structure."

Organizational needs, not hearts and minds, is their keynote. What is important about people is not their sentiments or the meanings they give the world, but whether they have discretionary time and money to spend on social movements. College students at elite schools have a lot of both, and, hence, form a central constituency for a number of different social movement industries. So do middle-class professionals of various sorts, making them a "conscience constituency" for a large number of causes.

Most resource mobilization theory operates from the assumption that it is the aggrieved population that will provide the critical resources for collective action. Further, there is a strong emphasis on issues of powerlessness and lack of representation as metagrievances, underlying manifest movement goals.

The essays here challenge such notions. The unrepresented are no real problem when a large conscience constituency exists. Zald reminds us that "children, whales, and dogs are the object of concern of foundations, voluntary associations, professional groups, and professional schools."

In reacting against the "hearts and minds" approach to social movements, Zald and his collaborators would have resource mobilization theory throw out the baby with the bath. Yes, outside groups of white liberals provided supporting resources to the civil rights movement, but as Aldon Morris and Douglas McAdam have demonstrated, indigenous resources and traditional black infrastructures provided the solid foundation for the southern civil rights movement.

Yes, the amount of spare time and money one has is important, and professional social movement organizations relying on direct mail appeals are an important phenomenon worth noting. Movements are not all *Sturm und Drang*. But let us not be becalmed by the Reagan era into another end-of-ideology error. Unruliness has been part of the history of social movements in America and elsewhere. Participants frequently take risks of getting arrested, losing their jobs, getting injured or killed. One doesn't take such risks lightly, and it is still necessary to understand hearts and minds and emergent processes, not merely bureaucratic ones.

In the end, incompleteness is no serious fault, since others can provide the complementary perspectives. If resource mobilization theory is itself viewed as a small industry within sociology, Zald and his collaborators have a distinctive product with its own important niche. No student of social movements can afford to ignore the organizational processes highlighted here so effectively. It is fitting and convenient to have this product available, for the first time, in one neat package.

WILLIAM A. GAMSON

PART I
RESOURCE MOBILIZATION THEORY

Introduction

In the last two decades the study of social movements has undergone a profound change. On the one hand, it is now closer to political sociology than before. On the other hand, its concerns are now more distant from the analysis of certain traditional collective behavior foci such as fads, fashions, and panics than earlier. Where social movement participation was commonly analyzed as spontaneous and enthusiastic, and, by some analysts, out of the ordinary, it is now mostly analyzed as a form of rational, normal behavior, subject to the decision-making constraints of all behavior. This transformation has occurred as the study of social movements has shifted from one embodied mostly in textbooks toward one based more in journals and research monographs; it has become more rigorous in method and in theoretical analysis. The substantive transformation of the social movement analysis of collective action and protest has been systematically described by Morris and Herring (1985). Let us try to situate our work within this general transformation.

The transformation of social movement theory rests upon a recognition that the mobilization of resources (labor, materials, and money) for collective action is problematic. Unlike some early statements of relative deprivation theory, which were quite popular during the 1960s and against which we reacted, mobilization is assumed to have costs as well as benefits. Relative deprivation theory ignored the costs of participation, focusing centrally upon grievances. Similarly, despite earlier group interest theory in political science, it is no longer assumed that the existence of an interest automatically leads to organized action in defense of that interest. There are organizing costs in defending interests. And if the interests lead to the quest for collective good, many individuals may choose a free ride.

There are several variants of what we have called resource mobilization theory. They differ from one another primarily in their main emphases. Some analysts focus more directly than we do upon the relation of collective action to the interest underlying broad changes in work and political structure (i.e., Charles Tilly). Others put more emphasis upon the analysis of the linkages among individuals, the mobilization of individuals through preexisting structures, and the microsituational determinants of participation (i.e., Anthony Oberschall). Still others focus upon the political process aspects of mobilization, noting how opportunities for social movement action are created by regime weakness and instability on the one hand, as well as regime support on the other (i.e., Doug McAdam).

Our own work has four features that make it a distinct version among the resource mobilization family of approaches. Of course, these features have been a source of debate and discussion among proponents of one or another of these variants as well as between resource mobilization theorists and their critics. This criticism of approaches has made for a lively intellectual scene in the thinking and research on social movements recently.

First, since we began we have been concerned with the carriers of social movements (SMOs)—the organizations such as the National Association for the Advancement of Colored People (NAACP), Common Cause, Students for a Democratic Society (SDS), and the National Organization of Women (NOW). These organizations attempt to gather in individuals and groups, to develop tactics and strategies, and in the process are subject to organizational transformation. This focus has set us apart from those who use events and chains of interaction between authorities and partisans as units of analysis.

Second, our work has been closely tied to our concern with the fate of social movements in modern America. It has assumed an organizational society in which much activity is coordinated through limited-purpose voluntary associations. Although resource mobilization and social change efforts may be activated through communal, class, and religious institutions, our work has assumed that formal organizational entities were a key component of analysis. As a result we have drawn extensively upon the particularly American empirical study of complex organizations. Some have suggested that our approach is less generalizable to other settings as a consequence.

Third, we have assumed that the technologies available to movements change as technology in the broader society changes. The development of mass television and of direct-mail fund raising are part and parcel of modern American society. They have important consequences for the structure and tactics of groups seeking social change. Indeed, in the extreme case, they lead to the development of professional movement organizations (PMOs) where social change entrepreneurs may have most tenuous ties to a "membership" through the mails. Some have been reticent to think of these groups as falling within the purview of social movement analysis, but we have been particularly loose in the empirical boundaries we have established around social movement organizations—sometimes coming perilously close to groups many would call "pressure groups."

Finally, our work assumes that collective action is supported by and occurs in institutional settings. Social movement activities not only result in the lobbying of Congress and marching in the streets, but also penetrate formal religious groups. Factions and individuals may attempt to take over their organizations. There are social movement-like phenomena within organizations. On the other hand, churches and other kinds of organizations may facilitate and encourage attempts to bring about social change. Thus, analysis of the infrastructural supports of social movements is given central attention.

Each of these features of our approach is treated in the sections that follow. The first section consists of our most general statement of resource mobilization theory. It sketches the components of an approach to understanding the dynamics of social movements that takes the mobilization of people, money, and materials as problematic. It introduces several concepts, such as a social movement industry, infrastructure, and the social movement sector, that will be amplified in later sections of the volume. Our earliest statement of the approach, less theoretically formal and more densely empirical, *The Trend of Social Movements in America: Professionalization and Resource Mobilization*, is reprinted in the appendix to the volume.

1

Resource Mobilization and Social Movements: A Partial Theory

John D. McCarthy and *Mayer N. Zald*

Past analysis of social movements and social movement organizations has normally assumed a close link between the frustrations or grievances of a collectivity of actors and the growth and decline of movement activity. Questioning the theoretical centrality of this assumption directs social movement analysis from its heavy emphasis upon the social psychology of social movement participants; it can then be more easily integrated with structural theories of social process. This chapter presents a set of concepts and related propositions drawn from a resource mobilization perspective. It emphasizes the variety and sources of resources; the relationship of social movements to the media, authorities, and other parties, and the interaction among movement organizations. Propositions are developed to explain social movement activity at several levels of inclusiveness—the social movement sector, the social movement industry, and the social movement organization.

For quite some time a hiatus existed in the study of social movements in the United States. In the course of activism leaders of movements here and abroad attempted to enunciate general principles concerning movement tactics and strategy and the dilemmas that arise in overcoming hostile environments. Such leaders as Mao, Lenin, Saul Alinsky, and Martin Luther King attempted in turn to develop principles and guidelines for action. The theories of activists stress problems of mobilization, the manufacture of discontent, tactical choices, and the infrastructure of society and movements necesssary for success. At the same time sociologists, with their emphasis upon structural strain, generalized belief, and deprivation, largely have ignored the ongoing problems and strategic dilemmas of social movements.

Recently a number of social scientists have begun to articulate an approach to social movements, here called the resource mobilization approach, that begins to take seriously many of the questions that have concerned social movement leaders and practical theorists. Without attempting to produce handbooks for social change (or its suppression), the new approach deals in general terms with the dynamics and tactics of social movement growth, decline, and change. As such, it provides a corrective to the practical theorists, who naturally are most concerned with justifying their own tactical choices, and it also adds realism, power, and depth to the truncated research on and analysis of social movements offered by many social scientists.

The resource mobilization approach emphasizes both societal support and constraint of social movement phenomena. It examines the variety of resources that must be mobilized, the linkages of social movements to other groups, the dependence of movements upon external support for success, and the tactics used by authorities to control or incorporate movements. The shift in emphasis is evident in much of the work published recently in this area (J. Wilson, 1973; Tilly, 1973, 1975; Tilly, Tilly, and Tilly, 1975; Gamson, 1975; Oberschall, 1973; Lipsky, 1968; Downs, 1972; McCarthy and Zald, 1973). The new approach depends more upon political sociology and economic theories than upon the social psychology of collective behavior.[1]

This chapter presents a set of concepts and propositions that articulate the resource mobilization approach. It is a partial theory because it takes as given, as constants, certain components of a complete theory. The propositions are heavily based upon the American case, so that the impact of societal differences in development and political structure on social movements is unexplored, as are differences in levels and types of mass communication of the left, ignoring, for the most part, organizations of the right.

The main body of the chapter defines our central concepts and presents illustrative hypotheses about the social movement sector (SMS), social movement industries (SMI), and social movement organizations (SMO). However, since we view this approach as a departure from the main tradition in social movement analysis, it will be useful first to clarify what we see as the limits of that tradition.

Perspectives Emphasizing Deprivation and Beliefs

Without question the three most influential approaches to an understanding of social movement phenomena for American sociologists during the past decade are those of Gurr (1970), Turner and Killian (1972), and Smelser (1963).[2] They differ in a number of respects. But, most important, they have in common strong assumptions that shared grievances and generalized beliefs (loose ideologies) about the causes and possible means of reducing grievances are important preconditions for the emergence of a social movement in a collectivity. An increase in the extent or intensity of grievances or deprivation and the development of ideology occur prior to the emergence of social movement phenomena. Each of these perspectives holds that discontent produced by some combination of structural conditions is a necessary if not sufficient condition to an account of the rise of any specific social movement phenomenon. Each, as well, holds that before collective action is possible within a collectivity a generalized belief (or ideological justification) is necessary concerning at least the causes of the discontent and, under certain conditions, the modes of redress. Much of the empirical work that has followed and drawn upon these perspectives has emphasized even more heavily the importance of understanding the grievances and deprivation of participants. (Indeed, scholars following Gurr, Smelser, and Turner and Killian often ignore structural factors, even though the authors mentioned have been sensitive to broader structural and societal influences, as have some others.)[3]

Recent empirical work, however, has led us to doubt the assumption of a close link between preexisting discontent and generalized beliefs in the rise of social movement phenomena.[4] A number of studies have shown little or no support for expected relationships between objective or subjective deprivation and the outbreak of movement phenomena and willingness to participate in collective action (Snyder and Tilly, 1972; Mueller, 1972; Bowen et al., 1968; Crawford and Naditch, 1970). Other studies have failed to support the expectation of a generalized belief prior to outbreaks of collective behavior episodes or initial movement involvement (Quarantelli and Hundley, 1975; Marx, 1970; Stallings, 1973). Partially as a result of such evidence, in discussing revolution and collective violence Charles Tilly is led to argue that these phenomena flow directly out of a population's central political processes instead of expressing momentarily heightened diffuse strains and discontents within a population (Tilly, 1973).

Moreover, the heavy focus upon the psychological state of the mass of potential movement supporters within a collectivity has been accompanied by a lack of emphasis upon the processes by which persons and institutions from outside of the collectivity under consideration become involved; for instance, northern white liberals in the southern civil rights movement, or Soviets and Cubans in Angola. Although earlier perspectives do not exclude the possibilities of such involvement on the part of outsiders, they do not include such processes as central and enduring phenomena to be used in accounting for social movement behavior.

The ambiguous evidence of some of the research on deprivation, relative deprivation, and generalized belief has led us to search for a perspective

and a set of assumptions that lessen the prevailing emphasis upon grievances. We want to move from a strong assumption about the centrality of
deprivation and grievances to a weak one, which makes them a component—indeed, sometimes a secondary component—in the generation of
social movements.

We are willing to assume (Turner and Killian [1972] call the assumption
extreme) "that there is always enough discontent in any society to supply
the grass-roots support for a movement if the movement is effectively
organized and has at its disposal the power and resources of some established elite group" (p. 251). For some purposes we go even further: grievances and discontent may be defined, created, and manipulated by issue
entrepreneurs and organizations.

We adopt a weak assumption not only because of the negative evidence
(already mentioned) concerning the stronger one but also because in some
cases recent experience supports the weaker one. For instance, the senior
citizens who were mobilized into groups to lobby for Medicare were
brought into groups only after legislation was before Congress and the
American Medical Association had claimed that senior citizens were not
complaining about the medical care available to them (Rose, 1967). Senior
citizens were organized into groups through the efforts of a lobbying group
created by the AFL-CIO. No doubt the elderly needed money for medical
care. However, what is important is that the organization did not develop
directly from that grievance but very indirectly through the moves of actors
in the political system. Entertaining a weak assumption leads directly to an
emphasis upon mobilization processes. Our concern is the search for analytic tools to account adequately for the processes.

Resource Mobilization

The resource mobilization perspective adopts as one of its underlying
problems Olson's (1965) challenge: since social movements deliver collective goods, few individuals will "on their own" bear the costs of working to
obtain them. Explaining collective behavior requires detailed attention to
the selection of incentives, cost-reducing mechanisms or structures, and
career benefits that lead to collective behavior (see, especially, Oberschall,
1973).

Several emphases are central to the perspective as it has developed.[5]
First, study of the aggregation of resources (money and labor) is crucial to
an understanding of social movement activity. Because resources are necessary for engagement in social conflict, they must be aggregated for collective purposes. Second, resource aggregation requires some minimal form
of organization, and hence, implicitly or explicitly, we focus more directly

upon social movement organizations than those working within the traditional perspective do. Third, in accounting for a movement's successes and failures one finds an explicit recognition of the crucial importance of involvement on the part of individuals and organizations from outside the collectivity a social movement represents. Fourth, an explicit, if crude, supply-and-demand model is sometimes applied to the flow of resources toward and away from specific social movements. Finally, there is a sensitivity to the importance of costs and rewards in explaining individual and organizational involvement in social movement activity. Costs and rewards are centrally affected by the structure of society and the activities of authorities.

We can summarize the emerging perspective by contrasting it with the traditional one as follows:

Support base

Traditional. Social movements are based upon aggrieved populations that provide the necessary resources and labor. Although case studies may mention external supports, they are not incorporated as central analytic components.

Resource Mobilization. Social movements may or may not be based upon the grievances of the presumed beneficiaries. Conscience constituents, individual and organizational, may provide major sources of support. And in some cases supporters—those who provide money, facilities, and even labor—may have no commitment to the values that underlie specific movements.

Strategy and Tactics

Traditional. Social movement leaders use bargaining, persuasion, or violence to influence authorities to change. Choices of tactics depend upon prior history of relations with authorities, relative success of previous encounters, and ideology. Tactics are also influenced by the oligarchization and institutionalization of organizational life.

Resource Mobilization. The concern with interaction between movements and authorities is accepted, but it is also noted that social movement organizations have a number of strategic tasks. These include mobilizing supporters, neutralizing and/or transforming mass and elite publics into sympathizers, and achieving change in targets. Dilemmas occur in the choice of tactics, since what may achieve one aim may conflict with behavior aimed at achieving another. Moreover, tactics are influenced by interorganizational competition and cooperation.

Relation to Larger Society

Traditional. Case studies have emphasized the effects of the environment upon movement organizations, especially with respect to goal change, but have ignored, for the most part, ways in which such movement organizations can utilize the environment for their own purposes (see Perrow, 1972). This situation has probably been largely a result of the lack of comparative organizational focus inherent in case studies. In analytical studies emphasis is upon the extent of hostility or toleration in the larger society. Society and culture are treated as descriptive historical context.

Resource Mobilization. Society provides the infrastructure that social movement industries and other industries utilize. The aspects utilized include communication media and expense, levels of affluence, degree of access to institutional centers, preexisting networks, and occupational structure and growth.

Theoretical Elements

Having sketched the emerging perspective, our task now is to present a more precise statement of it. In this section we offer our most general concepts and definitions. Concepts of narrower range are presented in following sections.

A *social movement* is a set of opinions and beliefs in a population representing preferences for changing some elements of the social structure or reward distribution, or both, of a society.[6] A *countermovement* is a set of opinions and beliefs in a population opposed to a social movement. As is clear, we view social movements as nothing more than preference structures directed toward social change, very similar to what political sociologists would term *issue cleavages*. (Indeed, the process we are exploring resembles what political scientists term *interest aggregation*, except that we are concerned with the margins of the political system rather than with existing party structures.)

The distribution of preference structures can be approached in several ways. Who holds the beliefs? How intensely are they held? In order to predict the likelihood of preferences being translated into collective action, the mobilization perspective focuses upon the preexisting organization and integration of those segments of a population that share preferences. Oberschall (1973) has presented an important synthesis of past work on the preexisting organization of preference structures, emphasizing the opportunities and costs for expression of preferences for movement leaders and followers. Social movements whose related populations are highly organized internally (either communally or associationally) are more likely than are others to spawn organized forms.

A *social movement organization* (SMO) is a complex, or formal, organization that identifies its goals with the preferences of a social movement or a countermovement and attempts to implement those goals.[7] If we think of the recent civil rights movement in these terms, the social movement contained a large portion of the population that held preferences for change aimed at "justice for black Americans" and a number of SMOs such as the Student Non-Violent Coordinating Committee (SNCC), the Congress of Racial Equality (CORE), the National Association for the Advancement of Colored People (NAACP), and Southern Christian Leadership Conference (SCLC). These SMOs represented and shaped the broadly held preferences and diverse subpreferences of the social movement.

All SMOs that have as their goal the attainment of the broadest preferences of a social movement constitute a *social movement industry* (SMI)—the organizational analogue of a social movement. A conception paralleling that of SMI, used by Von Eschen, Kirk, and Pinard (1971), the "organizational substructure of disorderly politics," has aided them in analyzing the civil rights movement in Baltimore. They demonstrate that many of the participants in a 1961 demonstration sponsored by the local chapter of CORE were also involved in the NAACP, the SCLC, Americans for Democratic Action (ADA), or the Young People's Socialist Alliance (YPSA). These organizations either were primarily concerned with goals similar to those of CORE or included such goals as subsets of broader ranges of social change goals. (The concept employed by Von Eschen et al. is somewhat broader than ours, however, as will be seen below.)

Definitions of the central term, *social movement* (SM), typically have included both elements of preference and organized action for change. Analytically separating these components by distinguishing between an SM and an SMI has several advantages. First, it emphasizes that SMs are never fully mobilized. Second, it focuses explicitly upon the organizational component of activity. Third, it recognizes explicitly that SMs are typically represented by more than one SMO. Finally, the distinction allows the possibility of an account of the rise and fall of SMIs that is not fully dependent upon the size of an SM or the intensity of the preferences within it.

Our definitions of SM, SMI, and SMO are intended to be inclusive of the phenomena analysts have included in the past. The SMs can encompass narrow or broad preferences, millenarian and evangelistic preferences, and withdrawal preferences. Organizations may represent any of these preferences.

The definition of SMI parallels the concept of industry in economics. Note that economists, too, are confronted with the difficulty of selecting broader or narrower criteria for including firms (SMOs) within an industry (SMI). For example, one may define a furniture industry, a sitting-furniture industry, or a chair industry. Close substitutability of product usage and, therefore, demand interdependence is the theoretical basis for defining industry boundaries. Economists use the *Census of Manufacturers* classifications, which are not strictly based on demand interdependence. For instance, on the one hand various types of steel are treated as one industry, though the types (rolled, flat, wire) are not substitutable. On the other hand, some products are classified separately (e.g., beet sugar, cane sugar) when they are almost completely substitutable (Bain, 1959, pp. 111-18).

Given our task, the question becomes how to group SMOs into SMIs. This is a difficult problem because particular SMOs may be broad or narrow in stated target goals. In any set of empirical circumstances the analyst must decide how narrowly to define industry boundaries. For instance, one may speak of the SMI that aims at liberalized alterations in laws, practices, and public opinion concerning abortion. This SMI would include a number of SMOs. But these SMOs may also be considered part of the broader SMI commonly referred to as the "women's liberation movement," or they could be part of the "population control movement." In the same way, the pre-1965 civil rights movement could be considered part of the broader civil liberties movement.

Economists have dealt with this difficulty by developing categories of broader inclusiveness, sometimes called *sectors*. Even this convention, however, does not confront the difficulties of allocating firms (SMOs) that are conglomerates, those that produce products across industries and even across sectors. In modern America there are a number of SMOs that may be thought of as conglomerates in that they span, in their goals, more narrowly defined SMIs. Common Cause, the American Friends Service Committee (AFSC), and the Fellowship of Reconciliation (FOR) are best treated in these terms as each pursues a wide variety of organizational goals that can only with difficulty be contained within even broadly defined SMIs.[8] The *social movement sector* (SMS) consists of all SMIs in a society no matter to which SM they are attached. (The importance of this distinction will become apparent below.)

Let us now turn to the resource mobilization task of an SMO. Each SMO has a set of *target goals*, a set of preferred changes toward which it claims to be working. Such goals may be broad or narrow, and they are the characteristics of SMOs that link them conceptually with particular SMs and SMIs. The SMOs must possess resources, however few and of whatever type, in order to work toward goal achievement. Individuals and other organizations control resources, which can include legitimacy, money, facilities, and labor.

Although similar organizations vary tremendously in the efficiency with which they translate resources into action (see Katz, 1974), the amount of activity directed toward goal accomplishment is crudely a function of the resources controlled by an organization. Some organizations may depend heavily upon volunteer labor, while others may depend upon purchased labor. In any case, resources must be controlled or mobilized before action is possible.

From the point of view of an SMO the individuals and organizations that exist in a society may be categorized along a number of dimensions. For the appropriate SM there are adherents and nonadherents. *Adherents* are those individuals and organizations that believe in the goals of the movement. The *constituents* of an SMO are those providing resources for it.

At one level the resource mobilization task is primarily that of converting adherents into constituents and maintaining constituent involvement. However, at another level the task may be seen as turning nonadherents into adherents. Ralph Turner (1970) uses the term *bystander public* to denote those nonadherents who are not opponents of the SM and its SMOs but who merely witness social movement activity. It is useful to distinguish constituents, adherents, bystander publics, and opponents along several other dimensions. One refers to the size of the resource pool controlled, and we shall use the terms *mass* and *elite* to describe crudely this dimension. Mass constituents, adherents, bystander publics, and opponents are those individuals and groups controlling very limited resource pools. The most limited resource pool individuals can control is their own time and labor. Elites are those who control larger resource pools.[9]

Each of these groups may also be distinguished by whether it will benefit directly from the accomplishment of SMO goals. Some bystander publics, for instance, may benefit directly from the accomplishment of organizational goals, even though they are not adherents of the appropriate SM. To mention a specific example, women who oppose the preferences of the women's liberation movement or have no relevant preferences might benefit from expanded job opportunities for women pursued by women's groups. Those who would benefit directly from SMO goal accomplishment we shall call *potential beneficiaries.*[10]

In approaching the task of mobilizing resources an SMO may focus its attention upon adherents who are potential beneficiaries and/or attempt to convert bystander publics who are potential beneficiaries into adherents. It may also expand its target goals in order to enlarge its potential beneficiary group. Many SMOs attempt to present their goal accomplishments in terms of broader potential benefits for ever-wider groupings of citizens through notions of a better society, and so on (secondary benefits). Finally, an SMO may attempt to mobilize as adherents those who are not potential beneficiaries. *Conscience adherents* are individuals and groups who are part of the appropriate SM but do not stand to benefit directly from SMO goal accomplishment. *Conscience constituents* are direct supporters of an SMO who do not stand to benefit directly from its success in goal accomplishment.[11]

William Gamson (1975) makes essentially the same distinction, calling groups with goals aimed at helping nonconstituents *universalistic* and those whose beneficiaries and constituents are identical, *nonuniversalistic*. Gamson concludes, however, that this distinction is not theoretically important, since SMOs with either type of constituents have identical problems in binding them to the organization. It is not more "irrational," in Olson's sense, to seek change in someone else's behalf than in one's own, and in both cases commitment must be gained by other means than purposive incentives. The evidence presented by Gamson suggests that this dimension does not bear much relationship to SMO success in goal accomplishment or in the attainment of legitimacy. We argue below, however, that the distinction should be maintained: it summarizes important attachments and social characteristics of constituents. The problems of SMOs with regard to binding beneficiary and conscience constituents to the organization are different, not with regard to the stakes of individual involvement relative to goal accomplishment (the Olson problem) but with regard to the way constituents are linked to each other and to other SMOs, organizations, and social institutions (see also J. Q. Wilson, 1973).

An SMO's potential for resource mobilization is also affected by authorities and the delegated agents of social control (e.g., the police). While authorities and agents of control groups do not typically become constituents of SMOs, their ability to frustrate (normally termed *social control*) or to enable resource mobilization are of crucial importance. Their action affects the readiness of bystanders, adherents, and constituents to alter their own status and commitment. And they themselves may become adherents and constituents. Because they do not always act in concert, Marx (1974) makes a strong case that authorities and delegated agents of control need to be analyzed separately.

The partitioning of groups into mass or elite and conscience or beneficiary bystander publics, adherents, constituents, and opponents allows us to describe more systematically the resource mobilization styles and dilemmas of specific SMOs. It may be, of course, to the advantage of an SMO to turn bystander publics into adherents. But since SMO resources are normally quite limited, decisions must be made concerning the allocation of these resources, and converting bystander publics may not aid in the development of additional resources. Such choices have implications for the internal organization of an SMO and the potential size of the resource pool that can ultimately be mobilized. For instance, an SMO that has a mass beneficiary base and concentrates its resource mobilization efforts toward mass beneficiary adherents is likely to restrict severely the amount of resources it can raise. Elsewhere (McCarthy and Zald, 1973) we have termed an SMO focusing upon beneficiary adherents for resources a *classical SMO*. Organizations that direct resource appeals primarily toward conscience adherents tend to utilize few constituents for organizational labor, and we have termed such organizations *professional SMOs.*

Another pattern of resource mobilization and goal accomplishment can be identified from the writings of Lipsky (1968) and Bailis (1974). It depends upon the interactions among beneficiary constituency, conscience adherents, and authorities. Typical of this pattern is an SMO with a mass beneficiary constituency that would profit from goal accomplishment (for instance, the Massachusetts Welfare Rights Organization) but that has few resources. Protest strategies draw attention and resources from conscience adherents to the SMO fighting on behalf of such mass groups and may also lead conscience elites to legitimate the SMO to authorities. As a result of a similar pattern, migrant farmworkers benefited from the transformation of authorities into adherents (Jenkins and Perrow, 1977).

But an SMO does not have complete freedom of choice in making the sorts of decisions to which we have alluded. Such choices are constrained by a number of factors, including the preexisting organization of various segments of the SM, the size and diversity of the SMI of which it is a part, and the competitive position of the SMS (McCarthy and Zald, 1974; Zald and McCarthy, 1974). Also, of course, the ability of any SMO to garner resources is shaped by important events such as war, broad economic trends, and natural disasters.

The Elements Applied: Illustrative Hypotheses

Let us proceed to state hypotheses about the interrelations among the social structure, the SMS, SMIs, and SMOs. Occasionally, we introduce specifying concepts. Because the levels of analysis overlap, the subheadings below should be viewed as rough organizing devices rather than analytic categories.

Resources, the SMS, and the Growth of SMIs

Over time, the relative size of the SMS in any society may vary significantly. In general it will bear a relationship to the amount of wealth in a society. Hence:

Hypothesis 1: As the amount of discretionary resources of mass and elite publics increases, the absolute and relative amount of resources available to the SMS increases.

This hypothesis is more of an orienting postulate than a directly testable hypothesis, but it is central to our perspective. And some related supporting evidence can be given.

By *discretionary resources* we mean time and money that can easily be reallocated, the opposite of fixed and enduring commitments of time and money. In any society the SMS must compete with other sectors and industries for the resources of the population. For most of the population the allocation of resources to SMOs is of lower priority than allocation to basic material needs such as food and shelter. It is well known that the proportion of income going to food and shelter is higher for low-income families, while the proportion of income going to savings and recreation increases among high-income families (Samuelson, 1964). The SMOs compete for resources with entertainment, voluntary associations, and organized religion and politics.

There is cross-sectional evidence that the higher the income, the larger the average gift to charitable activities and the greater the proportion of total income given (see Morgan, Dye, and Hybels, 1975; U.S. Treasury Department, 1965). Moreover, Morgan et al. (1975) show that (1) the higher the education, the more likely the giving of time, and (2) people who give more time to volunteer activities also give more money. As the total amount of resources increases, the total amount available to the SMS can be expected to increase, even if the sector does not increase its relative share of the resource pool. However, as discretionary resources increase relative to total societal resources, the SMS can be expected to gain a larger proportional share (see U.S. Treasury [1965], which shows a long-term secular increase in charitable giving). This argument is based upon our belief that, except in times of crisis, the SMS is a low-priority competitor for available resources—it benefits from the satiation of other wants.[12]

Of course, the validity of this hypothesis depends upon a *ceteris paribus* proviso. What might the other factors be? First, the existing infrastructure, what Smelser (1963) terms *structural conduciveness*, should affect the total growth of the SMS. Means of communication, transportation, political freedoms, and the extent of repression by agents of social control, all of which may affect the costs for any individual or organization allocating resources to the SMS, serve as constraints on or facilitators of the use of resources for social movement purposes. Also, the technologies available for resource accumulation should affect the ability of SMOs within the sector to mobilize resources. For instance, the advent of mass-mailing techniques in the United States has dramatically affected the ability of the SMS to compete with local advertising in offering a product to consumers. The organization of the SMIs will support or hinder the growth of the sector as additional resources become available. The greater the range of SMOs, the more different "taste" preferences can be transformed into constituents.

Hypothesis 2: The greater the absolute amount of resources available to the SMS, the greater the likelihood that new SMIs and SMOs will develop to compete for these resources.

This and the previous proposition contain the essence of our earlier analysis (McCarthy and Zald, 1973). That study accounts in part for the proliferation in SMOs and SMIs in the 1960s in the United States by demonstrating both the relative and the absolute increases of resources available to the SMS. The major sources of increase in financial resources were charitable giving among mass and elite adherents, as well as government, church, foundation, and business giving among organizational adherents.

These two propositions attempt to account for the total growth of the SMS. They ignore variations in the taste for change over time. They imply nothing about which SMI will reap the benefits of sector expansion. Nor do they imply what types of SMOs will lead the growth of an expanding SMI. They explicitly ignore the relationship between the size of the SMS and the intensities of preferences within an SM.

Parallel hypotheses could be stated for the relationship of resources among different categories of SM adherents and SM growth. For instance:

Hypothesis 3: Regardless of the resources available to potential beneficiary adherents, the larger the amount of resources available to conscience adherents the more likely the development of SMOs and SMIs that respond to preferences for change.

The importance of this hypothesis in our scheme hinges upon the growing role of conscience constituents in American social movements. First, the greater the discretionary wealth controlled by individuals and organizations the more likely it is that some of that wealth will be made available to causes beyond the direct self-interest of the contributor. An individual (or an organization) with large amounts of discretionary resources may allocate resources to personal comfort and to the advancement of some group of which he or she is not a member. Second, those who control the largest share of discretionary resources in any society are also those least likely to feel discontent concerning their own circumstances.[13]

In a sense, Hypothesis 3 turns Olson (1965) on his head. Though it may be individually irrational for any individual to join an SMO that already fights on behalf of his preferences, the existence of an SM made up of well-heeled adherents calls out to the entrepreneur of the cause to attempt to form a viable organization (cf. Salisbury, 1969). To the extent to which SM beneficiary adherents lack resources, SMO support, if it can be mobilized, is likely to become heavily dependent upon conscience constituents.

This argument is also important in understanding the critique of interest-group pluralism as a valid description of modern America.[14] Many collectivities with serious objective deprivations, and even with preexisting preferences for change, have been highly underrepresented by social movement organizations. These SMOs tend to be very limited in their control of discretionary resources. It is only when resources can be garnered from conscience adherents that viable SMOs can be fielded to shape and represent the preferences of such collectivities.

Organization Structure and Resource Mobilization

How do the competitive position of the SMS, processes within an SMI, and the structure of an SMO influence the task of resource mobilization? Some aspects of these questions have been treated by Zald and Ash (1966). To discuss SMOs in detail we need to introduce assumptions about relevant SMO processes and structures.

Assume that SMOs operate like any other organization (J. Q. Wilson, 1973), and consequently, once formed, they operate as though organizational survival were the primary goal. Only if survival is insured can other goals be pursued. Second, assume that the costs and rewards of involvement can account for individual participation in SMOs and that, especially, selective incentives are important, since they tend to raise the rewards for involvement.[15] Gamson (1975) and Bailis (1974) provide impressive evidence that selective material incentives operate to bind individuals to SMOs and, hence, serve to provide continuous involvement and thus resource mobilization.

For a number of reasons the term *member* has been avoided here. Most important, membership implies very different levels of organized involvement in different SMOs. The distinction between inclusive and exclusive SMOs has been utilized in the past to indicate intensity of organizational involvement (Zald and Ash, 1966), but intensity of involvement actually includes several dimensions, usefully separated. Let us attempt to partition constituent involvement in any SMO. First there is the *cadre*, the individuals who are involved in the decision-making processes of the organization. Cadre members may devote most of their time to matters of the organization or only part of their time. Those who receive compensation, however meager, and devote full time to the organization, we term *professional cadre*; those who devote full time to the organization but are not involved in central decision-making processes, we term *professional staff*; those who intermittently give time to organizational tasks, not at the cadre level, we term *workers*. (Remember, constituents are those who give either time or money.)

A *transitory team* is composed of workers assembled for a specific task, short in duration. Transitory teams are typically led by cadre members. Members of transitory teams and cadre have more extensive involvement than other segments of an SMO constituency. What distinguishes these constituents from others is that they are directly linked to the organization through tasks—they are involved directly in the affairs of the SMO. Since involvement of this sort occurs in small, face-to-face groups, workers, whether through transitory teams or through continuous task involvement, can be expected to receive solidary incentives from such involvement—selective benefits of a nonmaterial sort.

Federated and Isolated Structure

An SMO that desires to pursue its goals in more than a local environment may attempt to mobilize resources directly from adherents or to develop federated chapters in different local areas. Federation serves to organize constituents into small local units. The SMOs that develop in this manner may deal with constituents directly, as well as through chapters or only through chapters. But many SMOs do not develop chapters but deal directly with constituents, usually through the mails or through traveling field staff. The important point is that constituents in nonfederated SMOs do not normally meet in face-to-face interaction with other constituents and hence cannot be bound to the SMOs through solidary selective incentives. We term these constituents *isolated constituents*.

Federation may occur in two ways. One strategy assigns professional staff the task of developing chapters out of isolated adherents or constituents. To some extent SDS and CORE (Sale, 1973; Meier and Rudwick, 1973) utilized this approach during the 1960s. Common Cause seems to have used it recently. Another strategy relies upon preexisting nonmovement local groups that have heavy concentrations of adherents or isolated constituents (Gerlach and Hines, 1970). This latter style, termed *group mobilization* by Oberschall (1973), was typical of several waves of recruitment by the Ku Klux Klan (Lipset and Rabb, 1970). Federation developing out of preexisting groups can occur quite rapidly, whereas organizing unattached individuals probably requires more time and resources. To the extent that it utilized mass involvement in the South, the SCLC operated through preexisting groups. We have argued elsewhere (McCarthy and Zald, 1973) that nonfederated SMOs dealing with isolated constituents accounted for much of the SMS growth during the burst of SMO activity during the decade of the 1960s.

Empirically, SMOs will combine elements of the two major organizational forms we have identified here. The manner in which the organization garners the bulk of its resources should be used to characterize it during any time period. For instance, CORE would be deemed federated until the early 1960s, nonfederated at its peak during the early 1960s, and then federated again (Meier and Rudwick, 1973). It maintained a set of federated chapters during this entire period, but during the interim period its major resource flow was provided by isolated conscience constituents.

Hypothesis 4: The more an SMO is dependent upon isolated constituents, the less stable will be the flow of resources to the SMO.

Because isolated constituents are little involved in the affairs of the SMO, support from them depends far more upon industry and organizational (and counterindustry and counterorganizational) advertising than does support from constituents who are involved on a face-to-face basis with others. Advertising and media attention provide information about the dire consequences stemming from failure to attain target goals, the extent of goal accomplishment, and the importance of the particular SMO for such accomplishment.

Strickland and Johnston's (1970) analysis of issue elasticity is useful in understanding isolated constituent involvement in SM activities. At any time a number of target goals are offered to isolated adherents to any SM by one or more SMOs (and by other SMIs). Isolated adherents may choose to become constituents by allocating resources to one or another SMO according to the goals propounded. The SMOs within any SMI will tend to compete with one another for the resources of these isolated adherents. If they allocate resources, but remain isolated, their ties to the SMO remain tenuous. To the extent that any individual is an adherent to more than one SM, various SMIs will also be competing for these resources.

Treating SMO target goals as products, then, and adherence as demand, we can apply a simple economic model to this competitive process. Demand may be elastic, and its elasticity is likely to be heavily dependent upon SMO advertising. Products may be substitutable across SMIs. For example, while various SMOs may compete for resources from isolated adherents to the "justice for black Americans" SM, SMOs representing the "justice for American women" SM may be competing for the same resources (to the extent that these two SMs have overlapping adherent pools). Some adherents may have a high and inelastic demand curve for an SMO or SMI; others' demand curves may show great elasticity.

This state of affairs suggests that effective advertising campaigns may convince isolated adherents with high-issue elasticity to switch SMOs or SMIs, or both. Issue elasticity relates to what Downs (1972) terms *issue attention cycles*. These apparent cycles, he observes, include the stages of a problem discovered, dramatic increases in adherence as advertising alerts potential adherents, attempts at problem solution, lack of success of such attempts, and a rapid decline in adherence and advertising. Isolated adherents may purchase a target goal product when offered but can be expected to base decisions about future purchases upon their conception of product quality. Tullock (1966) has argued that the consumption of such products is vicarious, not direct; thus, perceived product quality is not necessarily related to actual goal accomplishment. Much publicity is dependent upon an SMO's ability to induce the media to give free attention, because most SMOs cannot actually afford the high cost of national advertising. They do, however, use direct-mail advertising. The point is that the media mediate in large measure between isolated constituents and SMOs.

Perceived lack of success in goal accomplishment by an SMO may lead an individual to switch to SMOs with alternative strategies or, to the extent that products are substitutable, to switch to those with other target goals. It must be noted, however, that there is also an element of product loyalty in this process. Some isolated constituents may continue to purchase the product (to support an SMO) unaware of how effective or ineffective it may be.

One could treat individual SMO loyalty in the same way as political party loyalty is treated by political sociologists, but most SMOs do not command such stable loyalties from large numbers of people. Certain long-lasting SMOs, the NAACP and the AFSC, for instance, may command stable loyalties, and the process of socializing youth into SMO loyalty could be expected to be similar to that of socialization into party loyalty (Converse, 1969). This process, however, most probably occurs not among isolated constituents, but among those who are linked in more direct fashion to SMOs.

Advertising by SMOs recognizes that isolated constituents have no direct way of evaluating the product purchased; therefore, it may stress the amount of goal accomplishment available to the isolated constituent for each dollar expended. The AFSC, for instance, informs isolated potential constituents in its mass mailings that its overhead costs are among the lowest of any comparable organization, and hence the proportion of each donation used for goal accomplishment is higher; the findings of an outside consulting firm that evaluated the organization support this claim (Jonas, 1971). Within an industry SMO products are normally differentiated by conceptions of the extremity of solutions required (Killian, 1972) and by strategies of goal accomplishment (passive resistance, strikes, etc.). When products are not differentiated in either of these ways, we can expect differentiation in terms of efficiency.

These considerations lead to a subsidiary proposition:

Hypothesis 4a: The more dependent an SMO is upon isolated constituents, the greater the share of its resources that will be allocated to advertising.

As indicated, SMO advertising can take the form of mailed material that demonstrates the good works of the organization. Media bargaining (Hubbard, 1968; Lipsky, 1968; Turner, 1969) can also be conceptualized as SMO advertising. By staging events that will possibly be "newsworthy," by attending to the needs of news organizations, and by cultivating representatives of the media, SMOs may manipulate media coverage of their activities more or less successfully.[16] Some kind of information flow to isolated constituents including positive evaluation is absolutely essential for SMOs dependent upon them.

The foregoing reasoning, combined with Hypotheses 1 and 2, leads us to another related proposition:

Hypothesis 4b: The more an SMO depends upon isolated constituents to maintain a resource flow, the more its shifts in resource flow resemble the patterns of consumer expenditures for expendable and marginal goods.

Stated differently, the hypothesis holds that if an SMO is linked to its major source of constituent financial support through the advertising of its products, isolated constituents will balance off their contributions with other marginal expenditures. Time of year, state of checkbook, mood, and product arousal value will influence such decision making.

The more attractive the target goal (product) upon which such a solicitation is based, the more likely that isolated adherents will become isolated constituents. Consequently, SMOs depending heavily upon such resource mobilization techniques must resort to slick packaging and convoluted appeal to self-interest in order to make their products more attractive. This should be especially true within competitive SMIs. The behavior in the early 1970s of environmental groups, which depend heavily upon isolated constituents, appears to illustrate this point. Many of those SMOs took credit for stalling the Alaskan pipeline and attempted to link that issue to personal self-interest and preferences in their direct-mail advertising. Slick packaging is evident in the high quality of printing and the heavy use of photogravure.

Another technique advertisers utilize to appeal to isolated adherents is the linking of names of important people to the organization, thereby developing and maintaining an image of credibility (Perrow, 1970). In the same way that famous actors, sports heroes, and retired politicians endorse consumer products, other well-known personalities are called upon to endorse SMO products: Jane Fonda and Dr. Spock were to the peace movement and Robert Redford is to the environmental movement what Joe Namath is to pantyhose and William Miller is to American Express Company credit cards.

The development of local chapters helps bind constituents to SMOs through networks of friendships and interpersonal control.[17] But note the following:

Hypothesis 5: An SMO that attempts to link both conscience and beneficiary constituents to the organization through federated chapter structures, and hence solidarity incentives, is likely to have high levels of tension and conflict.

Social movement analysts who have focused upon what we have termed *conscience constituency participation* normally call it outsider involvement. Von Eschen et al. (1969), for instance, show that for a local direct action civil rights organization involvement on the part of geographical outsiders (both conscience and beneficiary) created pronounced internal conflict in the organization. Marx and Useem (1971) have examined the record of the recent civil rights movement, the abolitionist movement, and the movement to abolish untouchability in India. In these movements, "outsiders were much more prone to be active in other causes or to shift their allegiances from movement to movement" (p. 102). Ross (1975) has argued the importance of friendship ties based upon geographical and generational lines to the internal conflict of SDS. The more unlike one another workers are, the less likely there is to be organizational unity, and the more likely it is that separate clique structures will form. If conscience constituents are more likely to be active in other SMOs and to be adherents of more than one SM, we would expect their involvement to be less conscious.

Now the earlier discussion of conscience and beneficiary constituents can be combined with the analysis of SMI and SMO processes. First, conscience constituents are more likely to control larger resource pools. Individuals with more resources exhibit concerns less directly connected with their own material interests. Consequently, conscience constituents are more likely to be adherents to more than one SMO and more than one SMI.[18] Though they may provide the resources for an SMO at some point, they are likely to have conflicting loyalties.

This situation provides an account for why SMO leaders have been skeptical of the involvement of conscience constituents—intellectuals in labor unions, males in the women's liberation movement, whites in the civil rights movements. Conscience constituents are fickle because they have wide-ranging concerns. They may be even more fickle if they are isolated constituents—they are less likely to violate personal loyalties by switching priority concerns. But organizations that attempt to involve them in face-to-face efforts may have to suffer the consequences of the differences in backgrounds and outside involvements from those of beneficiary constituents. On the one hand, involving only conscience constituents in federated chapters, which might be a method of avoiding such conflict, forces the SMO to pay the price of legitimacy—how can an SMO speak for a beneficiary group when it does not have any beneficiary constituents? On the other hand, depending exclusively upon mass beneficiary constituents reduces the potential size of the resource pool that can be used for goal accomplishment.

The involvement of conscience and beneficiary constituents may lead not only to interpersonal tensions, but also to tactical dilemmas. Meier and Rudwick (1976) document the extent to which the question whether the NAACP should use black or white lawyers to fight its legal battles has been a continuous one. Especially in the early days, the symbolic value of using black lawyers conflicted sharply with the better training and courtroom effectiveness of white lawyers. W. E. B. Dubois came out on the side of courtroom effectiveness.

Rates of Resource Fluctuation and SMO Adaptation

We have focused thus far upon the development of resource flows to SMOs, primarily in terms of how they link themselves to their constituents and the size of the resource pool controlled by constituents. What are the implications of larger or smaller resource flows for the fate of SMOs, for careers in social movements, and for the use of different types of constituencies?

An interesting question concerns the staying power of new and older entries into an SMI. Consider the following proposition:

Hypothesis 6: Older, established SMOs are more likely than newer SMOs to persist throughout the cycle of SMI growth and decline.

This state of affairs is similar to the advantage of early entry for a firm in an industry: A structure in place when demand increases improves the likelihood of capturing a share of the market. Stinchcombe (1965, p. 148) points out that "as a general rule, a higher proportion of new organizations fail than old. This is particularly true of new organizational *forms*, so that *if an alternative requires new organization*, it has to be much more beneficial than the old before the flow of benefits compensates for the relative weakness of the newer social structure." All the liabilities of new organizational forms that Stinchcombe elaborates—new roles to be learned, temporary inefficiency of structuring, heavy reliance upon social relations among strangers, and the lack of stable ties to those who might use the organization's services—beset new organizations of established forms as well, if to a lesser degree.[19] Moreover, a history of accomplishment is an important asset, and, as Gamson (1975) shows for his sample of SMOs, longevity provides an edge in the attainment of legitimacy. Older organizations have available higher degrees of professional sophistication, existing ties to constituents, and experience in fund-raising procedures. Thus, as factors conducive to action based upon SM preferences develop, older SMOs are more able to use advertising to reach isolated adherents, even though new SMOs may of course benefit from the experience of older ones. The NAACP, for instance, already had a fund-raising structure aimed at isolated adherents before the increase in demand for civil rights goals increased in the 1960s. And CORE had the advantage of a professional staff member who was committed to the development of such techniques, but it took time for him to convince the decision makers of the organization to pursue such resource mobilization tactics (Meier and Rudwick, 1973). Newer SMOs may capture a share of the isolated constituent market, but they will be disadvantaged at least until they establish a clear image of themselves and a structure to capitalize upon it. J. Q. Wilson (1973) cogently argues that competition between SMOs for resources occurs between organizations offering the most similar products, not between those for which competition in goal accomplishment produces conflict. Since SMOs within the same SMI compete with one another for resources, they are led to differentiate themselves from one another. The prior existence of skilled personnel and preexisting images are advantages in this process. In the same way that name recognition is useful to political candidates it is useful to SMOs when issue campaigns occur.

Hypothesis 7: The more competitive an SMI (a function of the number and size of the existing SMOs), the more likely it is that new SMOs will offer narrow goals and strategies.

We have alluded to the process of product differentiation. As the competition within any SMI increases, the pressure to specialize intensifies. The decision of George Wiley (Martin, 1971, 1974) to present the National Welfare Rights Organization as an organization aimed at winning rights for black welfare recipients was apparently made partially as a result of the preexisting turf understanding of other civil rights organizations.

Hypothesis 8: The larger the income flow to an SMO, the more likely that cadre and staff are professional and the larger these groups are.

This proposition flows directly from an economic support model. It is obvious that the more money available to an organization, the more full-time personnel it will be able to hire. Though this is not a necessary outcome, we assume that SMOs will be confronted with the diverse problems of organizational maintenance, and as resource flows increase these will become more complex. As in any large organization, task complexity requires specialization. Specialization is especially necessary in modern America, where the legal requirements of functioning necessitate experienced technicians at a number of points in both resource mobilization and attempts to bring influence to bear. The need for skills in lobbying, accounting, and fund raising leads to professionalization.

It is not that SMOs with small resource flows do not recognize the importance of diverse organizational tasks. In them, a small professional cadre may be required to fulfill a diverse range of tasks such as liaison work with other organizations, advertising, accounting, and membership service. Large resource flows allow these functions to be treated as specialties, though organizations of moderate size may have problems of premature specialization. Economies of scale should be reached only at appropriate levels of growth. In CORE we have a good example of this process: early specialization required constant organizational reshuffling in order to combine functions and staff members in what seemed to be the most efficient manner (Meier and Rudwick, 1973).

Hypothesis 9: The larger the SMS and the larger the specific SMI, the more likely it is that SM careers will develop.

An SM career is a sequence of professional staff and cadre positions held by adherents in a number of SMOs or supportive institutions, or both. Such a career need not require continuous connection with an SMI, though the larger the SMI the more likely such continuous involvement ought to be. Supportive institutions might be universities, church bodies, labor unions, governmental agencies, and the like (Zald and McCarthy, 1975). Moreover, target institutions sometimes develop positions for SM cadres, such as human-relations councils in local governments. Corporations have affirmative-action offices and antitrust lawyers.

When the SMI is large, the likelihood of SMI careers is greater simply because the opportunity for continuous employment is greater, regardless of the success or failure of any specific SMO. Though many of the skills developed by individuals in such careers (public relations, for instance) may be usefully applied in different SMIs, our impression is that individuals typically move between SMIs that have similar goals and hence have overlapping constituencies. Although we might find individuals moving between civil rights and labor SMOs, we would be unlikely to find movement from civil rights SMOs to fundamentalist, anticommunist ones. (But it should be remembered that communists have become anticommunists, and that an antiwar activist such as Rennie Davis later took an active role in the transcendental meditation movement.) The relevant base for SMO careers, then, is usually SMIs or interrelated SMIs.

Funding strategies affect not only careers but also the use of beneficiary constituents and workers.

Hypothesis 10: The more an SMO is funded by isolated constituents, the more likely that beneficiary constituent workers are recruited for strategic purposes rather than for organizational work.

This proposition is central to the strategy of the professional SMO. It leads to considering the mobilization of beneficiary constituent workers as a rational tool for attempts to wield influence, rather than as an important source of organizational resources. Earlier we mentioned the creation of senior citizen groups for purposes of bargaining by the AFL-CIO in the Medicare fight. The use of some poor people for strategic purposes by the Hunger Commission, a professional SMO, also illustrates the point (Brown, 1970). Also germane is the fact that of the groups in Gamson's study (1975), none that were heavily dependent upon outside sponsors provided selective material incentives for constituents. Binding beneficiary constituents to an SMO with incentives is not so important to an organization that does not need them in order to maintain a resource flow.

Much of this discussion has been framed in terms of discretionary money, but discretionary time is also of importance.

Hypothesis 11: The more an SMO is made up of workers with discretionary time at their disposal, the more readily it can develop transitory teams..

The ability to concentrate large numbers of constituents and adherents is highly useful for SMOs in certain situations, such as demonstrations. But the occupational characteristics of constituents and adherents are crucial to an understanding of how an SMO or a coalition of SMOs is able to produce such concentrations. Producing large numbers can be used to impress bystanders, authorities, and opponents. In some nations (particularly authoritarian ones) authorities may, through control over employers or control of the work schedules of governmental employees, be able to produce large concentrations at will. But SMOs typically do not exercise such control; hence, it is the preexisting control adherents and constituents exercise over their own work schedules that shapes the possibility of concentration. The same mechanisms operate in peasant societies where the possibilities of concerted action are shaped by planting and harvesting schedules.

In modern society discretion over work schedules tends to be related to larger pools of discretionary income, allowing travel to distant sites as well. The discretion of constituents over work schedules, then, may be seen as a potential organizational resource useful in mounting short bursts of organizational activity. Students, college professors, and other professionals, for instance, probably find a three-day trip to Washington for a demonstration easier to bear than wage workers do. The March on Washington in support of the war in Vietnam, headed by the Rev. Carl McIntire, was poorly attended. For the reasons enumerated above, many of the adherents to which he appeals were probably unable to attend such a demonstration.[20]

Conclusion

The resource mobilization model we have described here emphasizes the interaction between resource availability, the preexisting organization of preference structures, and entrepreneurial attempts to meet preference demand. We have emphasized how these processes seem to operate in the modern American context. Different historical circumstances and patterns of preexisting infrastructures of adherency will affect the strategies of SMO entrepreneurial activity in other times and places. Our emphasis, however, seems to be useful in accounting for parallel activity in different historical contexts, including peasant societies, and in explaining the processes of growth and decline in withdrawal movements as well.

The history of the Bolshevik SMO (Wolfe, 1955) shows how important stable resource flows are to the competitive position of an SMO. The Bolsheviks captured the resource flow to the Russian Social Revolutionary movement and, at certain points in their history, depended heavily upon isolated conscience constituents. Free media are probably necessary to mass isolated constituent involvement in resource flows, so isolated adherents with control over large resource pools are probably more important to SMI growth in societies without mass media. Leites and Wolf (1970) make a similar analysis of the revolutionary SMI in its relationship to the constant rewards of participation by the peasants in Vietnam. Of course, the extent of discretionary resources varies considerably between that case and the modern American case, but so did the ability of authorities to intervene in the manipulation of costs and rewards of individual involvement in the revolutionary SMO. The flow of resources from outside South Vietnam was important in the SMO's ability to manipulate these costs and rewards. Extranational involvement in the American SMS seems almost nonexistent.

Moreover, Oberschall (1973) has shown how important communal associations may be for facilitating mobilization in tribal and peasant societies. Although the number of SMOs and hence the size of the SMI may be smaller in peasant societies, resource mobilization and SM facilitation by societal infrastructure issues are just as important.

Withdrawal movements are typically characterized primarily by the way in which constituents are bound to the SMO (Kanter, 1972). But SMOs in withdrawal SMs also encounter difficulties in developing stable resource flows, and they use a variety of strategies similar to those of other SMOs in response to their difficulties. The recent behavior of the Unification Church of America (led by the Reverend Sun Myung Moon) in the United States illustrates processes close to those we have focused upon for modern reform movements: heavy use of advertising and emphasis upon stable resource flows in order to augment the development of federated constituencies. The Father Divine Peace Mission (Cantril, 1941) utilized rather different strategies of resource mobilization, including a heavier dependence upon the constituents themselves, but the importance of maintaining flows for continued viability was recognized in both of these withdrawal movements.

Our attempt has been to develop a partial theory; we have only alluded to, or treated as constant, important variables: the interaction of authorities, SMOs, and bystander publics; the dynamics of media involvement; the relationship between SMO workers and authorities; the impact of industry structure; the dilemmas of tactics. Yet, in spite of the limitations of this brief statement of the resource mobilization perspective, it offers important new insights into the understanding of social movement phenomena and can be applied more generally.

Notes

For critical, helpful, and insightful remarks upon an earlier version of this chapter we are indebted to Gary Long, Anthony Oberschall, Anthony Orum, Kathy Pearce, Jack Seidman, and Benjamin Walter. This line of research and the preparation of the manuscript were supported by the Vanderbilt University Research Council.

1. One reflection of this change has been discussion of the appropriateness of including the study of social movements within the social psychology section of the American Sociological Association (see the *Critical Mass Bulletin*, 1973-74). The issue is whether social movements research should consist largely of individual social psychological analysis (e.g., value, attitudes, and grievances of participants).
2. We are responding here to the dominant focus. Some analysts, most notably

Rudolf Heberle (1951, 1968) among U.S.-based sociologists, have viewed social movements from a distinctly structural perspective. Of course, structural approaches have remained dominant in Europe.

3. For example, see Levy (1970). For an early attempt to move beyond a simple grievance model, see Morrison (1971): this article attempts to explain recruitment in social movement organizations rather than the attitudes of movement support of isolated individuals. Gurr's own empirical studies have led him to emphasize institutional-structural factors more heavily, because he has found that the structural characteristics of dissident groups are important factors in accounting for both violent and nonviolent civil strife (Gurr, 1972).

4. For a full and balanced review of research and theory about social movements during the past decade, see Marx and Wood (1975).

5. Other contributors to the research mobilization perspective, aside from those already noted, are James Q. Wilson (1973), Breton and Breton (1969), Leites and Wolf (1970), Etzioni (1968), Jenkins and Perrow (1977), Salisbury (1969), Strickland and Johnston (1970), and Tullock (1966).

6. There is by no means a clear consensus on the definition of the crucial term *social movement*. We employ an inclusive definition for two reasons. First, by doing so, we link our work to as much past work as possible. Second, there are important theoretical reasons that will be discussed below. Our definition of *social movement* allows the possibility that a social movement will not be represented by any organized groups but also allows for organizations that do not represent social movements at formation. Most earlier definitions have included both preferences and organizational factors. See Wilkinson (1971) for an extensive survey of definitions of *social movement*.

7. Making the distinction between a social movement (SM) and a social movement organization (SMO) raises the question of the relevance of the vast literature developed by political scientists on the subject of interest groups. Is an SMO an interest group? Interest group theorists often blur the distinction between the representative organization and the interest group (e.g., the AMA and doctors) (see Wootton [1970] for an extended discussion). Whereas political scientists usually focus upon interest groups' organizations and not the groups themselves, sociologists largely have focused upon social movements rather than upon social movement organizations. Though we are not fully satisfied with Lowi's (1971) distinction between the two terms, we will employ it for a lack of a better one. Lowi maintains that an SMO that becomes highly institutionalized and routinizes stable ties with a governmental agency is an interest group. This way of approaching the problem, of course, flows from Lowi's distinctive view of the functioning of pluralistic politics.

8. Although we can easily label the SMs these organizations relate to—political reform and peace, for instance—the diffuseness of their goals and the range of their concern seem to bring them closer to representing what Blumer (1946) calls *general movements*. Blumer's notion of general movements (as contrasted with specific ones) implies widespread appeal and attendant trends in culture and lifestyle, however, and the general peace-humanitarian organizations do not appear to generate such appeal today. In any case, Blumer's distinction is an early attempt to distinguish movements along dimensions of specificity of goals. (See Halloron's [1971] treatment of Common Cause, Jonas's [1971] treatment of the AFSC, and Hentoff's [1963] treatment of FOR for analyses of the wide range of goals pursued by these SMOs.)

9. Of course, the size of the resource pool controlled by an individual or an organization that might be allocated to an SMO is a dimension. We dichotomize the dimension only for purposes of discussion, and the appropriate cutting point will vary from situation to situation.

10. A potential beneficiary group has normally been termed an interest group. The distinction between beneficiaries and adherents recognizes that interests and preferences may not coincide.

11. We have borrowed this term from Harrington (1968, p. 291), who uses it to refer to middle-class liberals who have demonstrated strong sympathies for the interests of underdog groups. Our use broadens the meaning of the term.

12. The recent resource mobilization difficulties of the consumer movement as prosperity wanes provide support for these arguments. (See Morris [1975] for extensive evidence of the fund-raising difficulties of consumer groups—especially professional SMOs—and the resulting organizational difficulties, and Pombeiro [1975] and the *New York Times* [1974] for similar material on a wide range of SMOs.)

13. Stouffer (1955) showed that among Americans the wealthier experienced fewest personal worries, though they were more concerned than the poorer with the problems beyond their immediate experience. In the United States wealth is positively related to happiness in general (Bradburn and Caplovitz, 1964). Cantril (1965) used a ladder technique to have respondents place themselves with respect to their closeness to "the best possible life." He shows that upper economic groups in a number of nations place their present circumstances closest to full satisfaction. Important for our analysis, when asked a similar question about their satisfaction with the nation, American respondents who were wealthy were no more satisfied than their counterparts.

14. For a review and statement of the critique, see Connolly (1969).

15. See Clark and Wilson (1961), J. Q. Wilson (1973), and Zald and Jacobs (1976), for a discussion of various types of incentives.

16. See *Organizer's Manual Collective* (1971) for a review of media manipulation techniques. The many "how to do it" books vary in their sophistication and comprehensiveness. Several others worthy of note are Kahn (1970), Walzer (1971), and Ross (1973).

17. Orum and Wilson (1975), and Freeman (1975) discuss the role of preexisting solidarity relations in SMO mobilization.

18. The empirical pattern of such ideological overlapping in choices of SMO and SMI provides a very different way of distinguishing SMIs from the one we have chosen. Ideological coherence is unusual, of course. See Campbell et al. (1960) for an empirical treatment of this problem, and Miller and Levitin (1976) for a more recent demonstration with regard to what has been termed the "new left" ideology. Even though conscience constituent involvement in an SMO or SMI may not imply involvement in another SMO or SMI through preexisting ideological coherence, any involvement increases the likelihood of adherence to another SM.

19. Stinchcombe's (1965) attempt to isolate the factors related to the rate of organizational formation in a society is quite similar to our own. He maintains that (1) new ways of doing things (technologies), (2) the belief on the part of organizational entrepreneurs that new organizations will have staying power, (3) a belief in direct benefits flowing from new technologies, (4) resource availability, and (5) the belief that opponents will not defeat organizing attempts are impor-

tant factors in understanding the rate of organizational formation. Our analysis has stressed the first and fourth factors, but our formulation recognizes the importance of the other factors.

20. See Cicchetti et al. (1971) for an empirical demonstration of the costs of attendance and their effects upon recruitment patterns in an antiwar demonstration. For a study showing the minor importance of ideological commitment relative to structural and preorganizational factors for the McIntire-organized march, see Lin (1974-75).

PART II
THE INFRASTRUCTURE OF MOVEMENTS

Introduction

Social movements are not created outside of the traditions and institutional bases of the larger society in which they are nested. Instead, the cadre and networks of adherents and activists grow out of, build upon, and use the repertoires of action, the institutional forms and physical facilities of the larger society.

Resource mobilization analysts approach the problem of the combination of resources at two levels. In its entrepreneurial mode—the point of view of the organizer—the analysis emphasizes how social movement organizations and cadre combine money, materials, people, and technology into strategic and tactical action. The entrepreneurial mode of analysis includes both the rational-economic assumptions and formal organizational thrusts of our approach. At another level, the approach analyses the infrastructural supports provided to SMOs, SMIs, and the SMS by the social structure of the society or the societal segment in which the social movement is largely nested. The infrastructure is the set of social relations, roles, and facilities that are generally available to people in a society or societal segment. The infrastructure is available to societal participants generally, not just to the carriers of a social movement. But the existence or absence of infrastructural options and supports shapes the course of a movement, just as the course of a river is shaped by the geological base of a river bed. The infrastructure of the economy is the set of general resources and institutions that make specialized economic activity, the production of specific goods and services, possible. Such items as the state of the labor force are generalized resources affecting the production decisions and possibilities and specific costs to firms. Similarly, the social movement's societal segment provides generalized skills, traditions, and processes that may provide a fertile or lean social base to social-change attempts. The three essays in this section explore aspects of the infrastructures available to social movements.

In the first essay, "Pro-Life and Pro-Choice Mobilization," John D. McCarthy examines the institutional bases available through time to the anti-abortion (pro-life) and pro-abortion (pro-choice) movements. The mobilization levels of the two sides cannot be easily explained by the distribution of public opinion on the issue. He argues that the support of

45

the Catholic Church and the consistency between the established positions of the church and the movement made available networks that were easily exploited by the pro-life forces, especially in their earlier stages of action. And Protestant congregations, especially fundamentalist ones, provided an important basis of support later. On the other hand, the pro-choice groups were based upon adherents with fewer appropriately dense networks. Mc-Carthy argues, consequently, that the pro-choice movement suffered from an infrastructural deficit. For them, professional movement organizations, using technology to capitalize on weak networks and loose affiliations, have been the most successful form of mobilization.

In the second essay, "Religious Groups as Crucibles of Social Movements," we address three general issues concerning religious groups. First, we note that religious institutions are central repositories and are centrally concerned with ideas about the relations of people to each other, about how life should be lived, and about the moral basis of society. Thus, religious organizations provide a continuing ground for debate about social change, and hence social movement issues. Religious leaders and adherents attempt to define justice and moral relations for the broader society. Moreover, the specific associational form of religious organization at the local and central levels provide generalized resources such as meeting places, communication networks, age-graded associations, and the like, which can be utilized by social movement cadre. They provide dense nodal points for mobilization.

Second, it is argued that understanding the transactions within the world-system of nations is crucial to a full treatment of how religious groups may participate, facilitate, and constrain social change actions. Trans-national religious identities and organizations lead to the transportation of social movement forms, resources, and ideas through the system of nations. This flow generally moves from the core nations outwards through a variety of missionary action forms. Also world-system relations create new bases of grievances throughout the world which, mediated through local social structures, may generate social change activities.

The third general point in the essay is that religious groups are particularly vulnerable to internal social movement processes because coercive and utilitarian sanctions are less widely available within them. As a result, purposive incentives play a larger role. The general issue of social movement processes within organizations will be treated more directly in Part III. Here, the implications of these processes within religious groups for social movement processes are the central focus.

In the final essay in this section, "Organizational Intellectuals and the Criticism of Society," we argue that much of the current discussion of the role of intellectuals as critics of social arrangements misses a central point.

We do have a larger "new class" of social critics, but not only because we have a larger cadre of well-educated professionals. Compared to earlier times, many organizations in government and in the private sector provide career settings for professionals and other employees that allow them to act upon their social-change commitments. Whereas life as a permanent activist is possible only to the very rich or those willing to suffer poverty in less affluent societies, ours provides a range of career options compatible with social-change activities. The great wealth of our nation surely marks it off from earlier nations in this regard. Since the essay was written before the rise of the "New Right" and during the heyday of the "New Left," it focuses primarily upon such niches for those with leftist commitments. But organizational careers for committed activists are extensively available on the Right as well as the Left, though it is clear that the career opportunities compatible with any set of convictions vary over time. There is little doubt, however, that the societal infrastructures which promote some form of intellectual criticism and advocacy in America is much larger than that in poorer societies with fewer voluntary associations and special-purpose organizations.

2

Pro-Life and Pro-Choice Mobilization: Infrastructure Deficits and New Technologies

John D. McCarthy

Washington, D.C., January 23, 1982
On the ninth anniversary of the Supreme Court decision that legalized abortion, demonstrators marched here today to support a legislative campaign to reverse that ruling. Antiabortion leaders met with President Reagan, who reiterated his longstanding personal opposition to abortion. But they said that the President had not promised to give the abortion issue a high priority or to use his political muscle to push an antiabortion bill through Congress.

For all its problems, the antiabortion movement seems stronger today than at any time since the Supreme Court handed down its landmark ruling in the case of *Roe* vs. *Wade* in 1973. This strength was demonstrated by the long line of marchers, estimated by the local police at 25,000, who paraded past the White House waving antiabortion banners and chanting slogans such as "Life, life, life!"

Last month, a Senate subcommittee approved a constitutional amendment [the "Hatch" amendment] that would validate the 1973 decision and the full Judiciary committee will probably send it to the Senate floor sometime this spring.

Those who favor abortion rights consider the Hatch amendment "a very real threat," in the words of Marguerite Beck-Rex, spokesman [sic] for the National Abortion Rights Action League. Accordingly, the league announced today a $500,000 advertising campaign aimed at generating public opposition to the Hatch bill and public support for candidates they support in next fall's election.

"It's really important for us to sound the alarm, to call our supporters to arms," said Miss Beck-Rex. "We know there's a pro-choice majority out there, but we have to get them involved."

Since the Supreme Court decision, she added, opponents of abortion have "felt more intensely" about the issue than many voters who favor legal abortion, and as a result opponents have had a stronger impact on the political

49

process. The aim of the new advertising campaign is to convince lawmakers that they will pay a political price if they support restrictions on abortions. (Roberts, 1982, pp. 1,10)

The above account following the 1982 annual "March for Life" provides a snapshot of some of the contrasting forms of contention of the pro-life and pro-choice movements—marches versus advertising campaigns. The two movements have occupied my attention for several years, and I want to briefly summarize what are, in my view, several important differences between them. My purpose however, is not to thoroughly analyze these movements, but to use what I know of them as grist for a more general consideration of the role of social infrastructures in social movement mobilization. Most analysts now agree that social infrastructures facilitate the effective mobilization of public opinion preferences for change. Those public opinion preference structures that are organized neatly along pre-existing infrastructural dimensions can, under certain circumstances, lead to social movements of the traditional grass-roots form. Such has been the case with the pro-life movement. But many public opinion preference clusters do not so neatly articulate with infrastructural dimensions. Such is the case with the pro-choice movement. Its relative lack of usable social infrastructures compared with the pro-life movement leads it to depend far more heavily upon modern mobilization technologies in order to aggregate people and resources. This is my central argument. What follows is the development of its details and implications.

Abortion Attitudes and Movement Structure

Let me begin by briefly describing in broad outline the size and make-up of the adherent pools from which these two movements may draw constituents and the structure of the two social movement industries that have been developed out of the pools in the recent period. The routinization of modern survey research and the subsequent regular national surveys of opinion on social issues allow us to chart with some confidence the national preference structure on the question of abortion. Indeed, the literature on abortion attitudes has become quite large. We can draw several generalizations from this wealth of information (Granberg and Granberg, 1980; Jaffe et al., 1981; McIntosh et al., 1979; Singh and Leahy, 1978; Tatalovich and Daynes, 1981; Tedrow and Mahoney, 1979), that would appear to hold for the most recent period (1975-82).[1]

First, with some rather minor exceptions, the size and make-up of the pro-life and pro-choice adherent pools have remained relatively stable during the recent period. Second, it is clear that a large proportion of the population in recent years (40 percent) approves of the relatively unrestricted availability of abortion and that the vast majority of the population approves of its availability if the life of the woman is seriously threatened (90 percent). Third, "the abortion issue is an intense political issue for only a small minority of people—and they are about evenly split between opponents and proponents" (Jaffe et al., 1981, p. 100). This is reflected in small proportions of self-proclaimed single-issue voters[2] and in the fact that when asked to rank a series of policy issues, respondents rarely rank the abortion issue as very high in importance. Fourth, an analysis of a national survey that asked respondents whether they would describe themselves as "pro-choice" or "right-to-life" find 41 percent choosing the former and 43 percent the latter self-identification (Mitchell, 1981). Fifth, religious preference is not a good predictor of abortion attitude, but religious attendance is one of the best predictors among almost all religious groups. The more one attends religious services, the more restrictive one's abortion attitudes. Political party preference and liberal-conservative self-description are not good predictors of abortion attitudes, but level of formal education is one of the best predictors—as one might expect, the more education, the less restrictive one's attitudes, with the most highly educated the least restrictive by large margins.[3]

This evidence portrays more than large enough pools of potential activists available to contending movements around the issue of abortion, and gives us a bit of a feel for where the two pools are located socially. The two movements bicker incessantly about such poll results, each focusing upon question wordings that tip the numbers of supporters in their own favor, but my reading of the evidence convinces me that neither movement commands more than a minimal majority of potential support, nor have they during the recent period. Remember that we come to this conclusion with extensive public-opinion survey evidence.

But assume that we have not seen the survey evidence. If we observe the social movement activity around the abortion issue, how will we read the shape of the preference structures? First, it is clear, as I will attempt to show, that there are far more people involved and they are more deeply involved on the pro-life side than on the pro-choice side. This has not always been the case, but has been so since at least 1975. Let me focus upon the structure of the two social movement industries since 1975—the shape of the modern social movement industries postdates the 1973 Supreme Court decision in *Roe* vs. *Wade*, which reversed a long period of tight restrictions upon the legal availability of abortion.

Kathy Pearce, who has generated an impressively detailed description of the organizational structures of the two movements, says: "Pro-life has a wider array of organizations with different kinds of organizational structure, and has more single issue organizations" (1982a). There is a dense and extensive local organizational structure that is embodied in "Right-to-Life" committees. "These committees are organized throughout the country at the national, state and local levels. They claim a membership of around 11 million divided into some 1,500 chapters, with an operating budget of $1.3 million" (Tatalovich and Daynes, 1981, pp. 159-60).

> The National Right to Life Committee (NRTLC) is an umbrella organization for numerous local groups that are in turn linked into state organizations. . . . March for Life, Inc. has a Washington, D.C. office and draws on other pro-life groups once a year . . . Americans United for Life (AUL) is a non-membership group of legal experts; the ad hoc Committee in Defense of Life is a newsletter producing organization that solicits annual dues and additional contributions through mass mailings; the American Life Lobby (ALL) is a group based in Washington, D.C. that has many small pro-life groups and church congregations as members; the Life Amendment Political Action Committee (LAPAC) is a direct mail, political action committee; and the Catholic Church and its network of dioceses, of state conferences, parochial schools, and lay organizations, and the central bureaucracy in Washington, the National Conference of Catholic Bishops (NCCB) and the United States Catholic Conference (USCC), are involved in many ways; and the fundamentalist television broadcasters and their viewer-contributors, particularly Jerry Fallwell's Moral Majority are active, as is the Mormon Church. (Pearce, 1982a, p. II,3)

On the other hand, Pearce says,

> There are fewer pro-choice organizations, and membership growth [in the movement] has been within the established organizations. The most active and largest of these organizations have a similar structure: a national office, and affiliated groups throughout the states, and also a large proportion of isolated members who pay dues and receive newsletters, but who are, beyond that not actively involved. One of these organizations, the National Abortion Rights Action League (NARAL) is a single issue organization, while other active organizations, the American Civil Liberties Union (ACLU), Planned Parenthood (PP) and the National Organization of Women (NOW) make abortion rights one among their range of issues. (Pearce, 1982a, p. II, 2)

While those groups on the pro-life side that are multi-issue are primarily organized religious groups, the multi-issue pro-choice groups link the abortion issue to the population/fertility control social movement; to the feminist social movement industry; to the professional associations of doctors and nurses and others in the health field, and through the National Abortion Federation (NAF) which is the abortion providers association.

This sketch should not be taken to imply that there is no grass-roots activity on the part of pro-choice advocates. There is such activity. Nor is it intended to deny the extensive proclaimed support for pro-choice among liberal Protestant denominations and many health and professional associations. The sketch is designed to point up the contrast between the two social movement industries, the collection of organized groups which focus primarily upon the abortion issue. It can be safely said that pro-life is more dense in numbers, more grass-roots in nature, more variegated in organizational form, and more widely populated with single-issue groups than is pro-choice (see Johnston and Gray, 1983, for a similar sketch).

Now contrast what we know about the attitude structures consistent with the two movements and self-identification with them through survey evidence with the evidence drawn from the above observations of actual social movement behavior. The two relatively stable and equivalently sized preference structures seem to be transformed into direct movement activity at quite different rates. Why? The spokesperson for the National Abortion Rights Action League (NARAL), Ms. Beck-Rex cited above, suggested that pro-life supporters are more intense in their feelings. I do not believe this explanation to be consistent with the preference structure evidence, though the forms of activity that are typical on the two sides suggests greater intensity and wider use of unorthodox tactics on the part of the pro-life movement.[4] The answer lies primarily, I think, in the contrasting infrastructural patterns of mobilization from the two pools of potential supporters. In the case of pro-life, traditional infrastructural patterns of mobilization are central, while in pro-choice, modern technologies of mobilization are more prominent. Let me expand a bit upon this claim before I seek to spell out its general implications.

The density and extensiveness of the pro-life mobilization is importantly the result of the leadership by the hierarchy of the American Catholic Church and the consequent widespread availability to activists of the structures of the church and its community organizations. This is the conclusion of a number of observers of the recent pro-life movement (Tatalovich and Daynes, 1981; Jaffe et al., 1981), and is consistent with two forms of evidence. First, one could cite various forms of involvement by the church itself. These include the direct involvement of Bishops, the support by national committees of the church, the use of communication channels of the church, the direct involvement of local groups such as the Knights of Columbus, and the use of Catholic schools for indoctrination and mobilization for pro-life. Second, evidence based upon survey of pro-life activists supports the conclusion indirectly. Though Protestant church attenders are almost as pro-life in sentiment as Catholic attenders, the vast majority of pro-life activists seem to be Catholic. While approximately 25 percent of the American population is Catholic, one national survey of National Right to Life Committees (Granberg and Denny, 1982; Granberg,

1981) showed 70 percent of the membership to be Catholic, while a survey of the South Dakota Right-to-Life Committee showed 85 percent of its membership to be Catholic (Pearce, 1982b). This evidence supports the more recent findings of social movement researchers that structural location is a more important determinant of mobilization than is sentiment or ideology (Snow et al., 1980). The implication of this understanding will be explored further below.

On the other side, the largest and most influential single-issue membership group in the "pro-choice" movement is the National Abortion Rights Action League, which was organized in 1969. It was originally called the National Association for the Repeal of Abortion Laws in New York by its organizers, including, importantly, philanthropist Stewart Mott (Lader, 1973). Though not initially a professional social movement organization (SMO) (McCarthy and Zald, 1973), it can now be characterized as one since it depends primarily upon a large membership that relates to the organization primarily through the mail. Its membership grew from approximately 100,000 in 1980 to 175,000 in August, 1982 (Peterson, 1982b). It employs a national office staff and uses volunteers in its Washington office. It has organized forty state affiliates and has attempted to generate greater grass-roots action along with its primary tactics of lobbying at the federal level and advertising. There are some quite active local affiliates, though this is not the rule. The organization continually solicits new members through large mailings. The organization also purchases newspaper advertisements and radio spots to both alert supporters and to canvas potential new members. The only other national single-issue, pro-choice organizations of any strength are the Religious Coalition for Abortion Rights (RCAR), which is not a membership organization, and the National Abortion Federation (NAF), which has abortion providers as primary members.

My sketch, then, has these two movements with about equal-sized potential pools of activists, but very different rates and types of mobilization. Pro-life mobilization is heavily dependent upon the infrastructure of the Catholic church and, increasingly, Protestant denominations, while pro-choice mobilization depends importantly on the newer advertising and mass-mail technologies. The pattern is not restricted to these contending movements, either. It seems to characterize well the movements around the gun-control issue with gun clubs, manufacturers, and sales outlets serving traditional infrastructural purposes for the pro-gun movement and professional social movement organizations representing the pro-gun-control sentiment. The pro-gun mobilization depends upon social infrastructures and is importantly facilitated by the heavy use of modern technology by the National Rifle Association (Kohn, 1981). The pro-gun-control movement, however, consists almost exclusively of professional SMOs, most notably Handgun Control, Inc., a direct-mail organization. Yet the dispassionate reviews of the survey evidence on the gun-control issue shows large pools of supporters on both sides of it (Wright et al., 1983; Wright, 1981; Schuman and Presser, 1981). This has led many analysts (i.e., Wright, 1981) to puzzle over the lack of mobilization around gun-control sentiment not unlike that presented here on the pro-choice movement. I raise this case primarily to put the pro-choice movement into perspective. Pro-gun-control is an almost pure case of a sentiment pool mobilized exclusively through professional SMOs. While dependent on this technology, the pro-choice movement represents a mixed case.

While some analysts perceive a close relationship between public opinion preferences and social policy outcomes partly mediated through normal political processes and sometimes as the result of social movement activity (see Burstein, 1981), the sketch I have offered here poses the following question: What are the conditions under which the existence of a large sentiment pool cannot be easily translated into normal political activity or grass-roots social movement activity?[5] Since social infrastructures have been seen as so important for the emergence of such social movement activity, my search for constraining conditions naturally leads me to their lack—what I will call infrastructural deficits. Of course, I recognize the crucial importance of other facilitating conditions of successful mobilization such as effective ideological packages, political opportunity, and, of course, resources, but I will ignore these factors here. Let me briefly review the common understanding of the importance of social infrastructures for social movement emergence prior to exploring an infrastructural deficit account of nonmobilization.

Social Infrastructure

There has emerged a "post–mass society theory" consensus around the importance of preexisting social infrastructures for the mobilization of social movements. Close observation of the civil rights movement (Von Eschen, Kirk, and Pinard, 1971; McAdam, 1982; Morris, 1984), the feminist movement (Freeman, 1975), the Farmer's Alliance (Schwartz, 1976), a third party (Pinard, 1971), neighborhood organizing (Boyte, 1980), as well as more general treatments of social movements (Oberschall, 1973; Turner and Killian, 1972; Jenkins, 1979; Snow et al., 1980; Fireman and Gamson, 1981) agree that preexisting relations among social movement supporters make social movement mobilization far more likely and less costly in human effort and material resources. These networks of interrelationships must, of course, be usable, or, as some say, cooptable. This means, as the latter term implies, that they can be put to purposes other than those for which they were originally intended. Such networks of relations should also be more than casual—the more solidary the relations, generally, the more useful. There are a wide variety of terms used to capture the dimensions of social structure upon which social movement organizations and social movement activity can build (catness and netness, preexisting ties, communication networks, secondary relations, indigenous organizational strength), which I have called social infrastructures. The diversity of descriptive terminology reflects, to some extent, the wide variety of social structural linkages that have been used for social movement mobilization and, to some extent, the wide variety of social structure linkages that can be emphasized in attempting to characterize societies.

The social infrastructures of religious groups have been, and remain, in the United States, fertile territory for social movement mobilization. So, too, have relations generated at the workplace and through work, and, lately, at the welfare place (Piven and Cloward, 1977; Bailis, 1974; West, 1981). Also, lately, colleges and universities and the many networks of relations developed there have served as bases for mobilization. Voluntary associations of many kinds, too, have served social movement mobilization functions as the earlier pluralist theorists observed that they did.

Attempting to imagine the usable infrastructural map of a society leads also to thinking about its changing nature. We know, for instance, that church membership has been in rather consistent decline lately among the liberal Protestant denominations (Hoge and Roozen, 1979). It might be suggested that the internal problems created by membership decline for these religious bodies has been partially responsible for their recent pulling back from the facilitation of social movement activity, but the case of the Catholic Church belies such a straightforward explanation. It, too, has experienced membership declines in the recent period, one which also has witnessed extensive facilitation of social movement activity on the abortion and the peace issues. The structure of the Catholic Church, of course, makes many of its clergy less directly dependent upon membership trends. Those Protestant Church bodies that have experienced growth, the fundamentalists groups, have, on the other hand, been fertile ground for a number of recent social movements.

The traditional role of local political party structures in incorporating and mobilizing emergent sentiment pools in the United States appears to have atrophied. Polsby (1983) blames party reforms for this, and says:

> Party is increasingly a label for masses of individual voters who pick among various candidates in primary elections as they would among alternatives marketed by the mass media. Achieving financial support through mass

mailings and through the public purse has displaced in importance the mobilizing of well-heeled backers and the seeking of alliances with territorially
identifiable interest groups and state party organizations. (pp. 132-33)

So, apparently, the lack of incentives in these new arrangements mean that
party structures are less usable infrastructures for the mobilization of sentiment than they had been historically.

The occupational structure has changed rather dramatically over the last
several decades, and this, too, can be expected to have implications for the
shape, extent, and location of social movement mobilization. Labor
unions have experienced membership declines and professional employment has increased with concomitant increases in professional associational membership. The structures of relationships that these two forms of
occupational association produce can be expected to be quite different in
their mobilization dynamics. Many labor unions have consistently engaged
in the direct support of social movement activity as well as having provided
usable infrastructures for SMO mobilization. Professional associations, on
the other hand, appear more reticent to get involved in social issues that
range very far afield of their "claimed expertise," though they are certainly
active in their own direct self-interest. Though symbolic support for social
movement activities is not uncommon, making directly available the resources and infrastructural networks to SMOs, which has been typical of
labor unions and church bodies, seems rare among professional associations. It seems reasonable to conclude that this reticence is the result of the
need to protect the legitimacy that such associations gain by successfully
making claims to narrow technical expertise. This is not unlike the structure of motives that led many craft unions generally to avoid involvement
in broader social issues. Whether new employment structures (large hospitals, government agencies, etc.) will lead to the undermining of typical craft
professionalism and the emergence of a potentially more aggressive industrial type of professionalism remains to be seen. Those who posit the rise of
a "new class" (see Bruce-Briggs, 1979) see the growth of newer professions
as fueling social movement activity, as have some of the resource mobilization analysts (McCarthy and Zald, 1973). The new class theorists, for the
most part, however, argue from preference structures to outcomes ignoring
social movement mechanisms such as infrastructures. The argument made
here suggests that "professionalism" may inhibit the use of some of the
potentially most fruitful infrastructures of the attitudinally activist new
class.

The growth in size and complexity of large employing bureaucracies can
be expected to produce social infrastructures that can serve social movement mobilization functions within them (Zald and Berger, 1978; Wein-

stein, 1979), if not without. That social movement–like activities are rife within such organizational settings is responsible, in part, for the plausibility of political bargaining models of their functioning (cf. Pfeffer, 1978). Involvement in social movement activities within these organizations, however, is likely to reduce the amount of activity without, other things being equal. The success or failure of such activity within organizations may indirectly affect the outside world, but such activity can be expected to have few such consequences normally.

Charles Tilly (1978) has outlined the dimensions of an analytic census of social infrastructure categories, but there exists no adequate substantive census of them.[6] The results of such a systematic census could be juxtaposed to the sentiment census evidence which is, or could be, produced by opinion polling. Such a matrix would show some sentiments coherently clustered along infrastructural dimensions, some sentiments showing very little clustering along infrastructural lines and many intermediate patterns. We can imagine the first situation where all of those who favor some change are linked to one another through preexisting solidary relations and the second where few who so believe are linked to one another. This second is the condition I call a social infrastructural deficit—widespread sentiment exists favoring or opposing a social change, but the lack of available infrastructures inhibits the mobilization of the sentiment.

If we apply the key elements of this analysis to the pro-choice sentiment on the abortion issue, we can map the sentiments against key infrastructural dimensions. We should, therefore, be able to predict where pro-choice sentiments could potentially become mobilized through preexisting groups, and, conversely, where not. Remember, religious structures are unavailable because religious apathy predicts pro-choice views. As I noted earlier, pro-choice sentiment is concentrated among the highly educated, but this individual characteristic doesn't tell us much about the institutional locations where the highly educated congregate. Interestingly enough, university settings have not served well as pro-choice mobilization sites, though admittedly this period has been one of general quiescence on college and university campuses.

Certain professional occupations are quite solidly pro-choice in sentiment—especially health and human service groups. Indeed, in the earlier period of contention, before the 1973 Supreme Court ruling, professional associations were more prominent, partly because the general level of mobilization was low. Professional associations have all along pretty well restricted their involvement to public support and a bit of technical and legal assistance. This sort of support was quite important to the pro-choice movement when the issue was being pursued in state legislatures with little or no opposition (see Steinhoff and Diamond, 1977). It is of far less note, I think, when a vital and variegated grass-roots opposition is in the field. The full-scale commitment of the organizational structures and resources of supportive professional associations is quite rare in comparison with the level of commitment we find for religious groups in the pro-life movement. I believe that the scale of the commitment of such resources is constrained by the self-interested necessity of professional groups to maintain their uncontested claims of narrow technical legitimacy. Committing resources in contests on issues peripheral to these claims or, in this case, a politically controversial issue, threatens to undermine such claims. Thus, attempts to get more fully involved led by sentimental factions within professional associations are always strongly, and generally successfully, resisted by core professional groups. As a result, then, the infrastructures that appear to hold the most potential for pro-choice mobilization are only weakly available for cooptation. This is my account, then, of the pro-choice infrastructural deficit.[7]

So what is to be done in the face of infrastructural deficits? One strategy is to await a more propitious historical moment (Wilson and Orum, 1974). Another is to begin to build social infrastructures—generating social connections among the like-minded—that can be exploited sometime in the future[8] for social movement activity. A third is to attempt to aggregate the like-minded but unlinked adherents into organizational vehicles explicitly designed for social movement activity (SMOs). It is this third approach that characterizes the new social movement technocrats. Their technologies are well suited to the problems of social infrastructural deficits.

Thin Infrastructures

When an infrastructural deficit exists, now, it can be known. Previously such deficits were only suspected or claimed by social movement leaders. Systematic survey research reveals the existence of unmobilized sentiment pools.[9] Earlier, Blumer (1948) argued against their importance without naming them, suggesting that public opinion only exists in its representations—unless activated it is socially irrelevant. But now such deficits serve as the raw material for social movement entrepreneurs and technological innovators. Rather than traditional forms of social infrastructures, thin infrastructures serve as the basis for the formation of professional social movement organizations. These thin structures consist of lists of names and addresses that have been gathered initially for other purposes. These lists can be characterized as very weak communication networks along which information and resources may pass. The social infrastructures that have drawn the attention of analysts have been based upon face-to-face interaction. These thin infrastructures are not.

The keystone of the new technologies for aggregating the disconnected but likeminded is direct mail. This and derivative technologies depend upon cost-effective communication with sentimental supporters. Preexisting lists with high proportions of supporters are sought. If such lists (or media targets) consist of numerous supporters and these are appealed to in ways that effectively stimulate their sentiments, some proportion of them can be expected to write a check and, thereby, reciprocally activate the thin communication channel. Cost-effectiveness is determined by the rates of response to such appeals, and, hence, partially, the proportion of preexisting supporters on the lists. The quality of these thin infrastructures, then, that is most important is rate of return, not solidarity and cooptability as with traditional infrastructures. Individuals are connected to the soliciting social movement organization, as we shall see below, individually, rather than in preexisting groups. These lists are generated in a wide number of ways—through magazine subscription lists, from other social movement organization membership lists, from political campaign lists, from the files of private mailing firms, and from demographically targeted geographical areas. The process can be described as mining for sentimental homogeneity.

Once an individual has responded, he or she becomes eligible for emergency appeals to stimulated sentiments. A membership survey of NARAL showed that 30 percent of the members gave more than the then standard $15 membership fee (Mitchell, McCarthy, and Pearce, 1979).[10] Some large proportion of the additional giving stemmed from such emergency appeals. The timing of these appeals can be elegantly coordinated with legislative and movement struggles—witness the appeal onslaught that came from the National Organization of Women (NOW) during the final death rattle of the Equal Rights Amendment (Peterson, 1982a).[11] Telephone contacts can, and do, allow even more perfectly timed appeals to those who, based on past experience, are known to be likely to contribute.

The culling[12] of lists of names to produce SMO members, and, then, the most supportive and hence cost-effective members, requires a period of time. The process requires several rounds of mailings and remailings to those who initially respond (Sabato, 1981). The procedures are well suited to issues that find a well-educated and well-heeled sentimental constituency for which little SMO representation exists. Fifty-five percent of the NARAL members, for instance, had at least some graduate training. The technologies can also be used, however, to gather resources from the more traditional thick infrastructures, and are widely used in such cases. The pro-life movement utilizes these technologies quite effectively building upon the thick grass-roots infrastructures that have been formed. Pearce's survey of the South Dakota Right to Life Committee (1982b) shows that 16.2 percent of the members of this grass-roots local group also belong to the National Right to Life Committee, 21.58 percent belong to Life Amendment Political Action Committee, and 8.3 percent belong to the American Life Lobby, all of which are primarily direct-mail SMOs. Here, however, the organizations built by these technologies are part of a variegated movement industry rather, as with pro-choice, the center piece of the industry.

Many of these professional social movement organizations spend reasonably large percentages of their resources upon advertising, including newspaper, radio, and, sometimes, television. Advertising can be seen to function in a number of ways for these organizations. First, it increases name recognition for the organization. Second, it heightens the sense of threat among supporters concerning the success of the opposition. It is almost never the case that such advertising does not dwell on the opposition threats. Third, it creates small numbers of names of persons who have taken it upon themselves to respond for whom barriers to response are greater than usual. The importance of media coverage for the mobilization of resources has been highlighted in the past (McCarthy and Zald, 1973, 1977), but such accounts stressed attempts by social movement leaders to win unpaid coverage. The perils associated with such attempts are illustrated in Gitlin's analysis of Students for a Democratic Society (1979), which shows the relative lack of control by that SMO over relevant media frames. Since these direct-mail organizations buy advertising, they should be less vulnerable to media imposed frames of their positions and activities.

The social history of the use of these interlinked technologies for social movement purposes remains to be written. The use has been evolving for some time and professionalization has begun in earnest with a professional association of practitioners of direct-mail, associated publications, and even an educational foundation to encourage the development of appropriate educational attention to the technologies. Its technological side is advancing rapidly with the integration of computers that can dial culled telephone numbers for solicitors who then read emergency appeal messages off a video screen to the listening sentimental supporters. The appeal is not unlikely to include some reference to yesterday's national news broadcast. The results of this transaction can be entered into the computer and stored for further action. Credit cards are preferred.[13] In these ways SMOs can be created and SMO resources aggregated through thin infrastructures.

Membership and Activity in Direct-Mail Professional SMOs

"Professional social movements" exist in several forms (McCarthy and Zald, 1973). The variety I have been discussing here, the direct-mail professional SMO, has proved, I think, to be the heartiest of them. This is so, I think, because the form is based upon a highly profitable marketing mechanism. In spite of its widespread application and the number of professional SMOs it has spawned, neither its technologies nor the organizational form have been well examined by social analysts.[14]

The suspicion that member commitment to this organizational form is weak, no matter the sentimental fit, seems confirmed. McFarland (1976) reports a study of Common Cause members which shows that 79 percent of them disagreed that they would like to be more active in the organization if given the opportunity. Remember, being active in such an organization generally means no more than sending a contribution and receiving the newsletter. Our NARAL survey showed that only 13 percent of the members belonged to local affiliates, and 60 percent said they didn't want to join one or didn't know if they were interested in doing so. Forty-eight percent of the NARAL members agreed, also, with the statement, "I don't really think of myself as a member of NARAL, the money I send is just a contribution." Robert Mitchell finds 58 percent of a sample of the membership of the Environmental Defense Fund (EDF), an environmental professional SMO agreeing with the same statement. Goodwin and Mitchell (1984) report that attachment to the organization is inversely proportional to the percentage of direct-mail joiners for five environmental organizations. When we asked NARAL members how many of their friends belonged to the organization, 77 percent didn't know—strongly suggesting that they did not talk with their friends about their membership in the organization, and this is consistent with the fact that 67 percent had encouraged no friends to join the organization.

So these organizations are built out of thin infrastructures, and they create weak commitments to themselves in spite of their regular contacts through the mails, and, sometimes, over the telephone with their members. This weak membership form is reflected in rather high rates of turnover of membership in these SMOs. This fact encourages the constant mining for new members through the available thin infrastructures.

Recruiting with these technologies, however, seems to have the effect of producing startling sentimental homogeneity among SMO members compared with traditional, thick, infrastructural SMO formation. Our survey of NARAL members, for instance, showed them to concentrate almost exclusively in the least restrictive response categories (Mitchell, McCarthy, and Pearce, 1979), while surveys of pro-life activists (Granberg, 1981; Granberg and Denny, 1982; Pearce, 1982) show them to be far more heterogeneous in their attitudes toward the conditions for the availability of abortion. Goodwin and Mitchell (1983) report that direct-mail joiners of five environmental groups are substantially more extreme in their view than social network joiners, consistent with the evidence from the pro-life and pro-choice movements.

One might ask why a direct-mail SMO couldn't link its likeminded members with one another in local areas in order to generate grass-roots organizational strength. It should not be surprising, however, given the weak commitment we observe to these organizations, to find that such efforts have been relatively unsuccessful when tried.[15] NARAL attempted to create such groups earlier without notable success. Increased effort, however, seems to have yielded greater success in the face of vital grass-roots pro-life action. But to dwell upon such failures is to be bound by past understandings and diverts attention from the technologies used by these organizations to activate members and supporters.

These techniques include asking members through direct appeals to take action—usually contacting a legislator, and, also, targeted mixed media appeals (television and radio spots as well as newspaper ads) asking supporters to take action—again, usually in contacting a legislator. Each of these appeals also typically includes solicitation of resources. Of course, members can be expected to be more likely to act when asked than nonmembers and media blitzs, as they are called, can be expected to activate some small proportion of those sentimental supporters who are exposed to the exhortation. In this way, through increasingly thin infrastructural connections, very small segments of large sentiment pools can be fleetingly and individually activated. An example will illustrate this process. On August 17, 1982 the U.S. Senate began consideration of the abortion issue. On the same day, I received in the mail an emergency appeal from NARAL. It asked me for a donation for a media blitz to counteract the forces supporting a Helms Bill and a Hatch Amendment. It also encouraged me to contact the Senate majority and minority leaders and my senators. Planned Parenthood also alerted its 30,000 members. Press reports (Peterson, 1982b) indicate that this encouragement succeeded for the first time in producing a greater volume of pro-choice than pro-life mail to a number of senators. These blips of activity are utilized by professional staff lobbyists in their contention with the opposing movement industry.

Conclusion

I have argued here that known infrastructural deficits allow the application of new technologies. Some observers have concluded that the membership in direct-mail professional SMOs that results is an "ersatz" form of participation that has driven out more meaningful forms—read grass-roots participation (Topulsky, 1974; Sinclair, 1982). This is one among a number of theoretical possibilities, however. These minimal forms of activism could also replace declines in more traditional forms of participation, could substitute for their lack, or, finally, could supplement these forms. In the case of the pro-life movement, it seems clear that these forms supplement more traditional forms, and if this case is typical probably increase the total volume of participation.

My portrayal of the pro-choice sentiment pool as suffering from an infrastructural deficit favors the view that this new form of participation substitutes for the lack of more traditional forms. When pro-choice was the movement, rather than the countermovement, before the 1973 Supreme Court decision, it was not, with the exception of a few areas (notably New York), a vital grass-roots movement. Its sentiment base has been quite large for as long as we have systematic survey evidence on the issue. Its few victories, however, were won against minimal opposition (Steinhoff and Diamond, 1977). Whether the newer forms drive out or replace more traditional forms depends upon demonstrating their decline and the relative time order of these and the increases in the newer forms in specified sentimental arenas—both very difficult descriptive empirical tasks.

Finally, let me say that the action taken by a NARAL member responding to an emergency appeal is certainly not extra-legal or unorthodox. Indeed, it is only collective in a very restricted sense. As well, the facilitators and perpetrators of these actions can rarely be considered outside of the polity. These are the three criteria most widely used to characterize collective action as social movement action. Rigidly applying them to these activities would exclude the forms from our view as analysts of social movements. To do so, however, would seriously undermine our ability to understand the pro-choice/pro-life battle I have been following. The new technologies have complicated traditional forms of contention.

Notes

I wish to thank Kathy Pearce and Robert Cameron Mitchell for the many hours of fruitful discussion on these topics and the extensive analyses they have both made available to me on these questions. Thanks also to Gene Weinstein and Doug McAdam for helping me sharpen the arguments. Doug McAdam, Clark McPhail, Joane Nagel, and Mayer Zald all made valuable comments on an earlier version of this manuscript, which was presented at the annual meetings of the American Sociological Association in 1982.

1. See Blake (1971) for the earlier period.
2. This pattern does not appear to hold for pro-life and pro-choice activists (Granberg, 1981), but more about this below.
3. This pattern seems to hold also when one compares pro-life and pro-choice activists. The former are substantially more likely to attend religious services and to have less formal education than the latter (cf. Granberg and Denny, 1982; Granberg, 1981; Mitchell, McCarthy, and Pearce, 1979; Pearce, 1982a).

4. But see Blake and Del Pinal (1981) for an attempt to account for the different rates of activism directly with attitudinal differentials between the two pools of adherents. They argue that the pro-choice supporters are less intense in their preferences. It is, nevertheless, the case that most of the intense pro-choice supporters are not mobilized, and, as we shall see below, the mobilized pro-life supporters are more "wobbly" in their views on abortion than are the mobilized pro-choice supporters.

5. Remember that abortion sentiment is not well predicted by political party preference. This fact translates into a lack of clustering of abortion attitudes along political party structures, and has led Speaker of the House Thomas P. O'Neill to call the issue a "plague on the House" (Jaffe, Lindheim, and Lee, 1981, p. 149). As the issue has been adopted by the Reagan administration, however, the correlation between abortion attitude and party preference can be expected to improve.

6. Analysts of social movements have not addressed themselves much lately to the search for *the* key infrastructural dimension along which group conflict can be expected to turn for the new era, but see Tourraine (1981) for an exception.

7. Of course, the lack of grass-roots mobilization on the part of pro-choice supporters could be, and probably is, partially the result of other important factors. These include the lack of political opportunity—the period of the strong pro-life mobilization (1975 to the present) has seen pro-life presidents in office almost entirely. Also, ideology is important—the pro-life forces link their actions to the sanctity of human life, while the pro-choice forces utilize First Amendment and "civil liberties" symbolism, which appears to command far less widespread legitimacy.

8. See McAdam (1982) for an account of the institution building phase that preceded and facilitated the civil rights movement.

9. The sample of sentiments from the potential range for which systematic public opinion polling evidence exists is, in fact, quite narrow. As a result, large sentiment pools may remain unknown, and hence unexploited by the new entrepreneurs. For instance, on the nuclear freeze issue, Matt Reese, a modern political operative, says, "It's a strong issue whose birth was secret. I didn't see it coming" (Clymer, 1982, p. 1). The new technocrats of citizen involvement are unlikely to see grass-roots movements coming, I would surmise.

10. In May 1978 we mailed a survey to 1,000 NARAL members asking a variety of questions about their recruitment, involvement, and attachment to the organization, along with questions about their general political participation. Fifty-nine percent of the questionnaires were returned in completed form. The evidence reported here and below is drawn from the responses to that survey.

11. I have ignored the widespread use of these technologies for raising funds for political action committees (PACs). Each of these direct-mail SMOs can now be expected to operate a PAC arm which raises money to be funneled into the political campaigns of supporters. A full analysis of this class of SMOs would require taking these structures seriously into account.

12. "Culling" is a term which is widely used in the industry. The term carries both the meanings of putting aside the choice and putting aside the inferior. The British colloquial usage is "to dupe or fool."

13. See Hadden and Swann (1981) on the use of these technologies by the Fundamentalist Protestant groups. They seem particularly adept at integrating them with television programming.

14. There are, however, several exceptions, including McFarland (1976, 1984), Troyer, (1980), and Sabato (1981).
15. See McFarland (1976) and Frankel (1979) for reviews of such an attempt by Common Cause and its ironical consequences.

3

Religious Groups as Crucibles of Social Movements

Mayer N. Zald and John D. McCarthy

Scan the "religion page" of any metropolitan newspaper in the United States. Alongside reports of ministers arriving and departing, of church-related social events, of special services, and of new buildings dedicated or planned, one cannot fail to notice coverage of the involvement of religious groups in a variety of controversial issues. Recently there have been reports of resolutions by many national religious bodies pertaining to nuclear disarmament. There have been reports of bitter contests among factions of Southern Baptists over the election of a national leader. There have been reports of extensive involvement by many church groups in the affairs of Central American nations. There have been persistent reports of controversy over the appropriateness of female clergy. And much attention has been focused upon the Catholic Bishops' Pastoral Letter on economic issues.

But news reinforcing the centrality of religious groups to broader social and political processes has not been restricted to the "religious pages." An effective religious coalition lobbying against the Reagan administration's attempts to aid the overthrow of the Sandinista regime in Nicaragua is front-page news. So, too, is continuing coverage of the role of the Catholic Church as the major institutional base of dissent as well as a moderating force on that dissent in Poland. And a series of events in the Middle East continue to highlight the importance of the Islamic resurgence to political and social currents there. The vigorous involvement of evangelical fundamentalists has been "news" ever since Jimmy Carter was elected president in 1976. Finally, "Liberation Theology" has become the subject of serious debate as it comes under attack from Rome and is seen as an important basis for a wide variety of forms of dissent in Latin America.

Over the last several decades, in the face of this "news," sociology has generally ignored the relevance of religious beliefs and institutions to broader social processes. While many classical sociologists were centrally interested in these issues—Durkheim, Weber, Troeltch, and H. Richard Niebuhr—their concerns have not occupied the disciplinary mainstream in the recent period. This in spite of a lively and productive band of sociologists of religion laboring in their somewhat isolated scholarly vineyards. The sociology of religion seemed anachronistic to many in what was described as an increasingly secularized society. If as many sociologists and others believed, science, technology, and modernism led to both the death of God and a decline in church attendance, why study a declining set of beliefs and institutions?

But the events of world and American politics surely indicate the strength of religiously related institutions. Moreover, national and international politics aside, into the vessels of religions and the religious have been poured the competing and contrasting wines of cultural and moral aspiration. Just as sociologists have been led by events to recognize the endurance of ethnic cleavages (see Olzak, 1983), so too have they been forced to rethink the endurance and viability of religious institutions. Understanding the dynamics of change in religious organizations and the interplay of religion and religious change within the larger society thus reasserts itself as a prime topic for both scholarly and policy research. As will become evident below, it has particular relevance to social movement analysis and research.

In particular, we wish to understand the important role of religious beliefs and institutions in the emergence and growth of social movements in the United States. Such a focus is appropriate in the United States, because here, as in many Third World nations and Poland, but in contrast with modern West European nations, religious beliefs are central for a large proportion of the citizens and large numbers of them act upon these beliefs through personal involvement in religious groups and regular ritual gatherings. This fact has important implications for understanding social movements in America when contrasted to movements in Western Europe.

For instance, in 1976, 86 percent of the adult American population professed to hold religious beliefs "very important" or "fairly important" in their lives. This compares with an equivalent 59 percent of British adults, 55 percent of French adults, and 47 percent of West German adults (Gallup, 1976). And while in a typical week, 41 percent of adult Americans attend church services, only 15 percent of the British, 12 percent of the French, and 20 percent of the West German citizens do so (Princeton Religious Research Center, 1982). Church membership is the most common form of voluntary associational membership for Americans, and "church-affiliated" organizational participation appears to have been growing in the most recent period.

This exceptional American pattern of religious belief and participation means that religious structures are centrally important to understanding the emergence and growth of many American social movements. Religious groups are fertile soil for social movement birth and growth because they are face-to-face groups that are constituted around some commonly held beliefs (Collins, 1982). The solidarity, enthusiasm, and potential conflict that can characterize such groups makes them ideal vehicles for social movement purposes if they can be appropriated. Unrelated to the content of their theological beliefs, religious groups vary in their willingness to become involved in worldly pursuits. Recent experiences with black fundamentalists (Nelson, 1979) and white evangelicals (Wuthnow, 1983) suggest that groups may very quickly move from a position of strong aversion to involvement in worldly pursuits to a deep involvement. Theological principles are apparently not a very reliable guide to such involvement. Short-term shifts in social movement activism on the part of religious groups appear to be far more the result of alterations in the availability of religious infrastructures than of changes in religious values (see Wood and Hughes, 1983; Mueller, 1983). In any case, structures of religious participation may, and often do, serve as the infrastructural bases for social movement activity. Such activity may be built directly out of coalitions of congregations, as with the Moral Majority (Liebman, 1983; Cable, 1984), or through the development of newly organized groups based upon preexisting religious structures as with some segments of the pro-life movement.

Beyond the grass-roots mobilization potential of established religious groups, the fertile religious soil of the United States continues to result in the emergence of waves of new religious groups. It is these groups that have been, by many, included in the analysis of social movements since the groups represent a common emergent form of collective action. Beyond adding to the store of institutional structures in "civil society," however, these groups increasingly are constrained from adopting "retreatist" stances and, hence, are important to understanding modern social movement processes.

Both established religious institutions and the new emergent ones show extensive amounts of dissent and conflict within themselves. These processes allow the analysis of social movement processes within organizations, an important pursuit in itself. But they also allow attempts to understand the interaction between these processes and social movement processes outside of the organizations.

Finally, religious groups and religious movements may be transnational. In order to understand how these forms operate in the emergence and growth of social movements we must acknowledge this fact and begin to think about how world-system processes may impinge upon national, local, and within-organizational social movement processes.

This chapter will proceed at three distinct but intertwined levels. First, we will discuss how movements may be more or less based upon religious groups. Here movements and SMOs will be our units of analysis. Then we will address social movements within religious groups examining the forces that create social movements and political conflict *within* religious organizations, and, here, our unit of analysis will be the religious group. Finally, we will discuss the interplay of social movements and religious movements within the context of a global system of nations. In particular we are interested in the relation of religious organizations and personnel to changing intergroup and international relations as they relate to social movement processes. Throughout we will rely upon the insights of a resource mobilization perspective toward social movement processes. We will, secondarily, be attentive to the insights of a political economy perspective toward organizations, the social and political processes of statemaking, and a world-systems perspective.

Facilitation by Established Religious Groups

Religious groups if so disposed may become important facilitators for the emergence and growth of social movements. Resource mobilization perspectives have stressed that resources and the structures of everyday life are important to understanding social movement processes, and the behavior of religious groups in this regard offer extensive illustrations of the point. Rather than stressing the role of religious belief in such facilitation, which was common earlier (i.e., Lipset and Rabb, 1970), we stress how religious institutional structures may affect social movement trajectories. Evidence supporting the utility of our approach has accumulated for recent "New Right" groups. So, Mueller (1983) finds, using surveys of national public opinion, there is no conservative trend on feminist issues during the 1970s in spite of the growing, organized antifeminist action. And, conversely, Wood and Hughes (1983) find that the strong attitudinal support for "New Right" issues that has become manifest in recent SMO activity can be shown to have been a stable reservoir of support over the last several decades.

Religious groups may help facilitate social movement activity by lending the preexisting groups' structures to movements, by direct support of movements through the flow of money and personnel, and through the maintenance of "halfway houses" that may serve as repositories of social movement skills, tactics, and visions that may be lent to emergent social movements.

Infrastructures

We use the term *infrastructure* to refer to the preexisting structures of organization and communication that characterize cohesive, ongoing, face-to-face groups. Outside of economic infrastructures of the same form, religious structures represent an important portion of the civil society in the United States. This is why they have served as such an important facet of social movement mobilization through the late nineteenth and throughout the twentieth century here, being central to the abolition movement, the prohibition movement, early Ku Klux Klan mobilization, the civil rights movement, and the recent Moral Majority.

The prototype use of such structures is by local religious units becoming direct parts of social movement activities. So, for instance, in the southern civil rights movement, many local congregations became directly involved as congregations in the various activities of the movement (Morris, 1984; McAdam, 1982). Local religious units were important as building blocks for community campaigns as well as the bases for building formal SMO units such as the Congress on Racial Equality. This pattern also characterizes the grass-roots segment of the Moral Majority, according to Liebman (1983), where a large, independent Baptist church coalition serves as the carrying structure of the state-level movement organization. This same pattern characterized local congregational support of the Anti-Saloon League, an important SMO of the prohibition movement where "between 1905 and 1915 the number of churches cooperating with the league increased from 19,000 to 40,000" (Engelman, 1979, p. 11). So, too, was it common during the second resurgence of the Ku Klux Klan where it was not uncommon for preachers to turn over their pulpits for an appeal for membership from a traveling Kleagle (Alexander, 1965; Jackson, 1967; Chalmers, 1965). The pattern seems to be well demonstrated within the recent "Creationist" movement, which has aimed, locally, to alter public school curricula (Nelkin, 1982).

The other common form of the infrastructural use of religious groups is the development of formal SMOs that depend, at least at their formation, upon the religious group, but which are made up of independent, separate, structures. This was the pattern for many CORE and NAACP chapters that grew out of local congregations during the civil rights movement in the South. It is also the typical pattern for Right-to-Life SMOs that have grown out of local Catholic parishes recently. Jaffe and his colleagues say in this regard:

> This relationship differs on the national and local levels: the Church frequently is directly involved in local RTL activities. The Catholic hierarchy and national RTL organizations are more circumspect in their connections. ... Local Catholic churches provide RTL groups with physical facilities, supplies, fund-raising help, and volunteer workers. In many states with effective RTL movements, seemingly distinct Church and RTL structures mask

what in reality is a unified organizational effort. (Jaffe, Lindheim, and Lee, 1981, p. 74)

The structures of association of religious groups are usable if they are cooptable, in Jo Freeman's terms (Freeman, 1975). This requires at a minimum some consensus among members of a congregation that a social movement is worthy of support and a local leader who is willing to commit institutional and membership support. The ability of the local minister to be protected from outside retaliation is important in understanding such support. In this regard McAdam (1982) argues that the growth of large urban congregations before the rise of the southern civil-rights movement was important in providing more independence to ministers who wished to actively support the movement. The choice of generating new, separate, organizational vehicles based upon religious infrastructures seems best understood as a tactic to avoid criticism and buffer the potentials of social control that might be aimed, otherwise, directly at the religious group itself. A front group might initially be the appropriate concept for understanding this form, but these vehicles may take on lives of their own over time.

The widespread use of local religious group infrastructures seems to have been most typical of established groups with more congregational structures. The freedom of action that characterizes local units in such structures allows diffuse responsibility and the other attendant advantages of decentralized, reticulate, and segmented structures analyzed by Gerlach and Hine (1970). Protestant denominations with Episcopal structures and the Catholic Church in the United States have not been as likely to be the basis for mass social movements based upon local units; though the recent experience of the Catholic Church in the Right-to-Life movement suggests the possibilities that exist if the central authorities choose to commit the church and its infrastructural and other resources to the founding or continuing support of an emergent social movement.

Direct Provision of Discretionary Resources

We have elsewhere discussed (chapter 1 and appendix) in some detail the direct provision of personnel and material resources to social movements by church groups in the recent experience. There was, for instance, an extensive flow of resources from religious groups to many organizations of the civil rights movement as well as to the Farmworkers movement (Taylor, 1975; Jenkins and Perrow, 1977). Such flows are also characteristic of the Right-to-Life movement (Jaffe, Lindheim, and Lee, 1981) and the Nuclear Freeze movement (Garfinkle, 1984; van Voorst, 1983) where facilities, donations, and the loan of religious personnel are common.

The Mormons, the Catholic Bishops, and other religious groups have recently directly aided in the development of a number of "pro-family" groups such as the United Families of America, the American Family Institute, and the Pro-Family Forum (Conover and Gray, 1983).

The example of the International Peace Council (IKV) founded by the churches in the Netherlands is worth noting in some detail. Klandermans describes this group:

> The IKV was founded by the churches in the Netherlands in 1966. The initial emphasis lay on encouraging discussion in the churches about issues relating to peace and security. In the early years, the rallying point was the annual peace week, when it was expected that the parishes would devote their attention to questions of peace. Local IKV groups then sprang up in many Dutch communities, to take care of the organization of peace week. . . . One of the keys to the success of the peace movement in the Netherlands is the IKV and the way in which the organization is put to use in mobilizing resistance against cruise missiles. At its inception in 1966, a loose, informal structure was chosen. The council itself is comprised of 25 representatives of the participating churches. There is also a modest secretariat: 10 staff members worked there during 1983. The basis of the organization is the local IKV groups, some of which have been working since the IKV was founded. There are presently 430 such groups. . . . Local IKV groups have three tasks: reflection, organizing action aimed at the local population, and supporting activities of the national IKV. (1984, pp. 9-10)

This structure was central in mobilizing one out of every 25 Dutch inhabitants in a demonstration against installation of U.S. cruise missiles in October of 1983.

While movement appropriation of infrastructures seems most typical of the congregational structures, the loan of personnel and the direct provision of more fungible resources seems typical of the more centralized structures. The more centralized denominations, of course, are more likely to have surpluses that may be allocated to social movement purposes. But the pattern is certainly not unknown among congregational groups. Cable's recent account of the Pennsylvanians for a Biblical Morality (1984), for instance, describes a number of local congregations contributing to a central state office in order to hire a full-time lobbyist for the state Moral Majority organization to lobby for related causes. Here a professional social movement organization is constructed out of the resources provided by many local congregations.

Halfway Houses

"A movement halfway house is an established group or organization that is only partially integrated into the larger society because its participants are actively involved in efforts to bring about a desired change in society. ... What is distinctive about movement halfway houses is their relative isolation from the larger society and the absence of a mass base" (Morris, 1984, p. 139). Such institutions may serve as repositories of information about past movements, strategy and tactics, inspiration, and leadership. They are distinctive also in that many of them survive short-term fluctuations of social movement cycles and, finally, that many of them receive crucial support from established religious groups. Let us briefly describe three religiously based halfway houses: the Fellowship of Reconciliation (FOR), the American Friends Service Committee (AFSC), and the Catholic worker movement. Each of these groups have survived many waves of movement activity and served important training and support functions for specific SMOs through these cycles.

Founded in the early twentieth century in the United States, FOR has remained one of the major pacifist organizations. Throughout this period it has had very close ties with a variety of religious groups, particularly the historic "Peace Churches" (see Wittner, 1984). It has been most closely associated with A. J. Muste, who was a major figure in its activities through its most active periods (Hentoff, 1963; Robinson, 1981). Serving as a storehouse of information about pacifism and nonviolence, the organization has been important in supporting and aiding a variety of other SMOs including The National Committee for a Sane Nuclear Policy (SANE), the Committee for Nonviolent Action (CNVA), CORE, the March on Washington Movement (MOWM), the Church Peace Mission (CPM), the Student Peace Union (SPU) and, now, the Nuclear Freeze movement (Garfinkle, 1984). The organization has lacked a mass base, but worked diligently to provide support and encouragement for emergent social movements consistent with its religious pacifist approach. It has worked consistently toward the development of alliances between SMOs of emergent social movements. FOR is embedded in a variety of relations with mainline Protestant denominations and the Mennonites, Friends, and Brethren, the historic peace churches, which is where its consistent, if meager, support has always originated.

The American Friends Service Committee occupies a somewhat similar position as a movement halfway house: "The AFSC was founded in Philadelphia in the spring of 1917 to provide a channel of alternative service for young Quakers who objected to the draft as a matter of conscience" (Jonas, 1981, p. 85). "In the fiscal year of 1969, the committee spent $7,002,041 around the world, and employed some 600 people (only one-third of whom were professing Quakers)" (p. 86). The committee has engaged in a wide variety of activities during its history, including the aid of noncombatants in deadly conflicts, community development, and, especially important from our perspective here, the development, encouragement, and aid of a variety of social movement organizations in the United States that are consistent with the general pacifist orientation of the AFSC. Groups and collective actions which they have touched in these ways include the National Tenants Organization, the Southern Christian Leadership Conference, the National Mobilization Committee to end the War in Vietnam, and the Poor People's Campaign. The committee provided training to antinuclear activists who wished to use nonviolent tactics in protesting nuclear powerplants. It has provided organizing skills to a wide variety of groups and organizations. It is probably one of the most diversified of religiously supported halfway houses in the social movement sector.

Finally, the Catholic Worker is something akin to these two halfway houses within the American Catholic Church (Miller, 1974). This movement was begun in 1932 by Dorthy Day and Peter Maurin, though it has been most closely associated since then with Day's name. It remains active through a number of loosely affiliated hospitality houses around the United States that simultaneously feed the hungry in soup kitchens and serve as the base for many peace and social welfare activists. The movement has been incredibly decentralized, knit together over the years by a newspaper, the *Catholic Worker*, and communications and travel between various hospitality houses. People affiliated with Catholic Worker groups were linked through the years to a variety of groups such as the Catholic Radical Alliance, the Committee of Catholics to fight Anti-semitism, and the Catholic Peace Fellowship. Some of its local heroes, such as Ammon Hennacy of the Salt Lake City Hospitality House, were themselves, for years, available repositories of tactics and inspiration for antiwar activity for generations of Americans. Though never well supported, the diverse Catholic Worker affiliated hospitality houses normally have depended upon a minority of the local Catholic community for rather meager voluntary support, and, especially, upon dedicated, voluntary labor.

Religious institutions of learning can also to some extent serve similar functions to movement halfway houses in retaining knowledge and an unpopular stance toward certain issues that allow aid and comfort to newly emergent movements from institutional religious sources. Some of the "liberal" seminaries may serve such purposes, as will, certainly in the future, some of the newer "New Religious Right" seminaries.

In these various ways, then, religious institutions may serve to facilitate social movement processes. At a minimum, efficient facilitation requires some belief consensus consistent with the social movement groups soliciting church support. But such consensus is certainly not enough to guarantee extensive facilitation efforts. We have seen cycles of involvement and withdrawal of such support through the last three decades which cannot be fully explained by changes in a basic belief consensus. These cycles are partly shaped by processes within religious groups, which we discuss later.

Our rough survey of the forms of facilitation through a number of social movements suggests a crude correspondence between the organizational structures of established national religious groups and their typical form of facilitation when it is forthcoming. Congregational structures seem most likely to provide infrastructural support to emergent social movements. This may entail money and labor power at the local level, but is typically limited in amounts. Episcopal structures are more likely to provide money and personnel from their central coffers since they gather greater pools of resources from the local units and have them to be allocated. If we look at the social movements with extensive mass bases of the recent period, however (i.e., civil rights, antiwar, pro-life), we are likely to see all forms of facilitation being used simultaneously.

A Note on New Religious Movements

The study of the emergence and transformation of social movements owes much to Weber's early formulations, and, it will be recalled, religious movements were a special focus of the analyses he carried out. But later conceptions of social movements stressed the distinction between withdrawal movements and those movements that actively attempted to change some elements of the broader social or political environment. For instance, Aberle (1966) used the category of redemptive movements, or those aimed exclusively at changing individuals, for special analysis. And Turner and Killian (1957) used the term *cult* to designate a movement that makes only demands upon the behavior of its members, "making no effort to promote acceptance of such a program in the society. . . . To the degree to which collectivities proselytize as a means toward changing society, they become true social movements" (p. 309). Employing such categories led scholars to separate many emergent religious groups into the withdrawal category for special analysis.

This approach may have made empirical and substantive sense in earlier periods, but, in postindustrial settings effective withdrawal from the field by newly emergent religious groups is an increasingly difficult path to follow. In recent American experience, for instance, many newly emergent religious groups have found themselves in protracted conflict with the representatives of many organized sectors of their environments. As a consequence, many new religious groups come to adopt social change goals directed toward external social and political arrangements as a matter of simple survival, if not ideological choice. And the general pattern has implications for understanding social movement processes.

During the recent past many new religious groups have appeared on the scene in the United States, including the Unification Church, Nichiren Shoshu, Hare Krishna, Divine Light Mission, Children of God, and the like. The activities of these newly emergent groups have inspired extensive analysis that illuminates social movement processes. First, these groups help to maintain open space in "civil society" by the reaffirming boundaries around the category of "religious group." Second, since being categorized as a religious group has tax and legal advantages in the United States, many emergent social movement organizations may attempt to be religious groups, thereby blurring the boundary between the emergent religious group and the emergent social movement group. Third, these groups have inspired many countermovement actions. Consequently, the analysis of many of these movements carried out by social scientists has become more directly tied to the mainstream of social movement analysis.

Thomas Robbins (1984), in a masterful analysis of the litigation surrounding these new religious groups, makes the following argument. The state has grown extensively in the recent period and, hence, "public authority increasingly regulates all manner of nonreligious organizations in the United States" (p. 47). The historic privileges and exemptions enjoyed by religious groups give them some freedom from this authority. But modern established religious groups have become increasingly specialized so that emergent religious groups attempting to offer a full range of services (i.e., education, mental health, etc.) provoke the wrath of the representatives of organized sectors. Such an analysis leads Robbins to understand the strong attacks from legitimate quarters that have confronted the new religious groups as well as the tendency of many newer movements to attempt to be included under the religious label.

To carry the analysis further, even though established religious groups were critical of the newer groups earlier, they have lately made some common cause with the groups when some of their longstanding privileges have been threatened. Thus, when the Reverend Sun Myung Moon appealed his tax fraud conviction to the Supreme Court, many mainline religious groups supported his appeal since they did not relish losing their ability to shield their financial dealings from government intervention. Many of these groups have recently joined the Coalition for Religious Freedom, a Unification Church–sponsored group.

So the tension and conflict that results from the emergence of such groups reaffirms the civil space for religious groups, and, thereby, retains the likelihood that the United States will continue to spawn such groups. It also means that many emergent groups will attempt to fit themselves into the religious category. Two such groups that have run into difficulties doing so lately are worth a brief review. They are the Church of Scientology and

Synanon. Both of these groups have gone through major internal changes during their growth. Each, originally, made no claim to religious status. Each has had to confront the Internal Revenue Service over its claims, since, if the claims are not accepted, the groups' revenues must be more closely monitored by the IRS, and they are open to a variety of other regulatory actions at both the state and federal levels.

Synanon began as a drug-counseling operation (Yablonsky, 1965). It went through a stage of mass recruitment where a variety of individuals who were not necessarily drug dependent were brought into regular group therapy sessions. Ultimately, it developed into a full-time cadre of committed followers. During the later phase the group regularly professed to be a religious group (Mitchell, Mitchell, and Ofshe, 1980). It encountered serious problems, however, from the California attorney general's Charitable Trust Division. The category "charitable organization" also enjoys somewhat protected status on the American scene, though not as privileged as that of a religious group.

The Church of Scientology was founded in 1951 by L. Ron Hubbard. An outside observer might classify the movement as a mental health/self-help group. "In his early writings, Scientology's founder, L. Ron Hubbard, referred to his philosophy as a science. In 1952 he organized Scientology for the practice of that science. But in 1955 the group incorporated as a religion. In the certificate of incorporation for the Founding Church of Scientology in the District of Columbia, the group said the Founding Church was to "act as a parent church for the religious faith known as 'Scientology' and to act as a church for the religious worship of the faith" (Stoner and Parke, 1977, p. 89). In an extensive and bitter series of encounters since the founding, this group has fought for its religious self-designation against attacks by the IRS and others. These two groups illustrate concerted attempts by emergent SMOs to get under the religious tent.

The growth of new religious movements has spawned a series of counteractions by those affected or threatened by these groups. But as Bromley and Shupe (1981) point out in their analysis of the new groups and their critics, of the "three institutions most directly affected by the rise of the new religions—family, church and government—it is the family that has been the backbone of the anticult crusade" (p. 205). The major anticult groups are made up of parents surrounded by a series of entrepreneurs who call themselves deprogramers. "It is these parent groups who have appealed to the churches for support, petitioned the government for action, and flooded the media with stories of brainwashing and enslavement" (p. 206).

The phenomenon of new religious groups in the recent period has had several implications, then, for social movement analysis. The changed circumstances of the density of state penetration means that, even though much space remains in civil society, new religious groups will find themselves to be at least reactive social movements (Tilly, 1973). This brings their study back into concert with studies of a wide variety of proactive social movements. It has meant in practice that the sociologists of religion studying these movements and other social movement scholars are increasingly coming to speak similar languages and employ similar conceptual tools of analysis.

Social Movements Within Religious Groups

Thus far we have proceeded as if no conflict occurs within religious groups as they pursue social movement activity, serve as the bases for such action, or note the rise of competitors on the horizon. Even the most cursory examination of church histories, however, leads us to be aware that these activities have often been accompanied by bitter struggles. Though struggles between contending factions within religious groups need not be related directly to social movement activity in the larger society, often they are. Church authorities may lead the battle for the development of new, "progressive," understandings and find resistance among traditionalists; heresy trials may occur, though the heretics may be the progenitors of ideas accepted as reasonable generations later; schisms occur; and mass insurgencies occur. How are we to understand these internal conflicts and what have they to do with understanding social movement processes in modern society?

There is, in fact, a substantial body of literature that deals with internal conflict within Protestant denominations. Sociologists of religion, such as Jeffrey Hadden, James R. Wood, Peter Takayama, and Dean R. Hoge have examined conflict, especially as it has related to policies toward racial integration and civil-rights issues. Robert Adams (1970) has written an impressive, though largely unknown, dissertation on heresy trials in American Protestant seminaries, and Kurtz (1983) and Talar (1979) have written on the heresy of modernism in the Catholic Church. We will use these and other studies of conflict and social movement activity within religious groups as we develop several themes. First, we will summarize the, by now, standard organizational model that can be used for understanding conflict within religious organizations. Then we will briefly expand upon how the perspective developed by Zald and Berger (chapter 8) for analyzing social movements within any organization may help to understand these phenomenon within religious groups. Finally, we will come back to the theme of the interaction of these processes with social movement processes in the wider society.

Organizational Theory and Conflict Within Churches

There are many competing theories or approaches to the study of organizations. Organizations can be thought of as closed, optimizing systems (what is sometimes called the machine model of organizations); they can be thought of in cybernetic terms, as coordination devices for the attainment of human potential, as barriers to self-actualization, as approximations to the Weberian bureaucratic ideal-type. Each of these approaches will help us understand something about organizations. Certainly, a central process of the last two centuries—the long march of the bureaucrats—has affected churches as forms of social organization. So the development of offices, administration of routine functions, record keeping, and limited discretion have affected churches as it has the new religious groups mentioned above. The growth of central records, of church pension programs, of publishing houses, of staff professionals dealing with issues as diverse as church architecture, fund raising, Sunday School administration, and curriculum planning obviously present a source of tension and strain between amateur and professional as well as between local autonomy and central church authority.

Yet none of these models or approaches, it seems, is as powerful in explaining and understanding within-church conflicts as the open or natural systems model of organizations, which sees the organization as a bounded group of individuals harnessed together by incentives and commitments to a relatively small set of goals (some of which may be conflicting), yet open to new pressures from the environment as it both obtains and gives back resources to that environment and, simultaneously, attempts to affect its internal constituent parts and its environment. The political economy approach, which is a variant of open-systems models, focuses upon what we consider the most important aspects of organizational structure and process.

Very schematically, the political economy approach examines the governance-control structures and problems and the task-production system of organizations. Organizations may be analyzed in terms of their external political connections and problems, the gaining of legitimation and support of authorities and external power centers, and their external economic structures and processes—labor markets, financial resource flows, competition, and so on. Internally, organizations vary in their constitutions, power structures, processes of succession, and mechanisms of control (budgets, decision centers, etc.). They also vary in their internal economies, technologies, division of labor, and problems of transforming raw materials (Zald, 1980a, 1980b; Wamsley and Zald, 1973).

Peter Takayama and James R. Wood have employed open-systems theoretical perspectives and their own versions of a political economy approach to analyze conflict, rebellion, and social control within Protestant denominations (see Wood and Zald, 1966; Wood, 1970; Takayama and Cannon, 1979; Takayama and Darrell, 1979; Takayama, 1980). Let us examine some of the structural dimensions that emerge from these accounts.

Congregational versus Episcopal Polity Structure. Essentially a measure of the centralization or dispersion of power and control in religious organizations, this dimension is not a very subtle measure; for many detailed purposes of understanding church policies, it misses additional dimensions of power relations within churches. Yet for many comparative analyses it is extremely robust. We employed it above in our analyses of the facilitation of social movements by religious groups. It includes a number of more specific dimensions of church polity—the authoritative control of church buildings, the appointment of clergy, the readiness to follow central authority policy decisions, and the self-perceived power of church authorities to act upon their own. The processes of policy choice differ substantially between congregational and episcopal church structures. When the central bodies within episcopal structures make a choice, it goes a long way toward committing the constituents. This is not so in congregational structures where local control predominates.

Autonomy-Vulnerability. Denominations and churches develop many differentiated agencies. Unlike the divisions of corporations, which are fully disposable by corporate boards, these differentiated agencies have complex constitutional linkages to the larger church or denomination. The Society of Jesus is part of the Roman Catholic Church, but it has operated with great autonomy over long periods. The Lutheran seminary operated by the Missouri Lutheran Synod, on the other hand, was highly vulnerable to the intervention of the Synod's president, Mr. Preus. The degree of autonomy is affected by funding sources, by buffering mechanisms in the selection of personnel and in the review of organizational performance, as well as by the visibility and measurability of agency performance.

Incentive Balances. Every organization varies in its mix of incentives. Church organizations may offer material incentives (wages, business contacts), but fundamentally they rely upon purposive and solidary (or communal) incentives. Purposive incentives include moral incentives and social redemption. Solidary incentives include the social and communal sense of association with like-minded people. These various kinds of incentives tend to cluster at different organizational locations. Professionals and deeply committed cadres are most likely to be motivated by purposive incentives (and material necessities); solidarity incentives are more likely to dominate among laypersons in local congregations. The matter is obviously more complicated than this, but an understanding of incentive balances is important for understanding why conflict takes place, who initiates it, how it is dealt with, and who wins and loses.

Since solidary incentives are so important in maintaining member commitment, especially in Protestant denominations, there is a temptation for ministers in local congregations to avoid conflict if they believe there is dissensus on an important issue.

Environmental Relations. Conflict within churches is affected by relations with the external environment through several mechanisms, the importation of preferences, interorganizational relations, and the demography of growth and decline. First, conflict in the larger society and concern about various aspects of social change may be imported into the organization through the interests and value preferences of either lay members and/or the professional staff. The issue of homogeneity and heterogeneity is important *within* congregations in understanding church conflict at the local level and between congregations at the denominational or pan-congregational level. In particular, and most dramatically, those denominations that spanned the North/South regional divide in the United States have faced tremendous conflict when abolitionist and civil-rights issues emerged and penetrated churches.

To the extent that religious groups are not sealed off from the larger society through insulating organizational and communal structures, it may be difficult to avoid involvement in broader societal issues. Dean Hoge remarks in conclusion to his study of conflict within a variety of Protestant denominations: "In recent history there have been two kinds of divisions: those over theological questions and those over social questions. The former were found mostly in the theologically conservative denominations and the latter in the liberal denominations" (p. 119). Wuthnow (1984) sees expanding educational opportunities in the larger society as key to these divisions when he says, "The net result of the sixties, therefore, was to create a new basis of social division along educational lines, a division which cut through established religious organizations and set the stage for movements and countermovements which would realign religious loyalties" (p. 23). Conflicts over the role of gender and sexual preference, as well, have been recently imported into many religious groups (see White, 1981, on the issue of the feminist issue within the Church of Christ of the Latter Day Saints).

Second, environmental relations affect internal church politics through interorganizational relations. Denominations sometimes join inter-denominational coalitions and organizations. The grounds for joining may be theological, ecumenical, more practical (as with economies of scale or the benefits of coordination for everything from pension management to missionary activity), or some variety of these. But once joined, the actions of the coalition partners and the interdenominational organization can rebound back and commit the denomination to activities it might have chosen to avoid, which can create internal conflict. Many denominations have found themselves in these straits as a result of actions of the World Council of Churches.

Finally, trends in the broader society may affect church groups through the effect they have upon the growth or decline in numbers of both clergy and lay members. During the recent period, for instance, the American Catholic Church has experienced major declines in the number of priests and seminarians while some Protestant denominations have experienced rapid growth in both (Hoge, Potvin, and Ferry, 1984). Fundamentalist Protestant denominations have been growing at the same time that Liberal Protestant denominations and the Catholic Church have been losing members. These broader demographic trends can be expected to have some effect upon conflict within the groups. The recently increasing autonomy and assertiveness of women's orders in the Catholic Church seems to be importantly affected by these trends. The average age of these women has been increasing and they are becoming more scarce. The increased dependence of the institution on the labor of this more mature group has been associated with their gaining more autonomy. The recent aggressiveness of fundamentalist groups and the reticence of liberal Protestant groups to engage in outside social movement activity, it could be argued, are indirectly related to their recent distinctive demographic trends.

Much of the above discussion is based upon the work of Wood, Takayama, and Hoge and relies, either directly or indirectly, upon an open system political-economy model of organizations. It is based upon systematic and comparative research. We now know, then, a bit about the sources of conflict in Protestant denominations, but we have not explicated the forms of conflict or the social movement processes in any systematic manner. Stated another way, we have introduced some independent variables but not focused upon the dependent variables. There are many potential forms of social movement phenomena in organizations. They range from coup d'état and the small insurgency to mass movement and organizational civil war. Let us describe, briefly, these forms and then apply them to an understanding of movements in religious organizations.

Social Movements in Organizations

Students of social movements in society have used a variety of labels and dimensions to differentiate them from one another. We noted above, for instance, the distinction between withdrawal movements and those aiming at social change. It is obvious that a general strike, the closing down of all services and industrial activity in a community or nation, is different from a wildcat strike in a single plant. It differs in the number of participants, the amount of coordination and organization necessary, its likely direction, and so on. A major part of social movements analysis concerns its *scope*. Three common dimensions of scope are (1) breadth, or number of participants; (2) duration, or the length of time that participants are engaged in collective action; and (3) intensity, the severity-cost dimension of collective actions. As is obvious, each of these vary somewhat from the others and, itself, can be decomposed. The number of participants may expand or contract; duration can consist of one long action or more sporadic events (contrast the plant with many, brief wildcat strikes with one that has a lengthy authorized one); intensity can include acts of violence and/or property destruction, or it can be limited to symbolic acts such as carrying signs.

Social movements differ in their *location* in the social structure. Those people lower in the stratification order have command of different resources and are mobilizable through different tactics than those at the top. A middle-class pressure group differs from a working-class group in its access to authorities, in the financial resources it controls, and in the stock of tactics that it commands. And an unemployed urban group will differ from a working-class group in its potential forms of social organization, tactics, and resources.

Finally, collective actions differ in their *goals*—are the participants and/or cadre committed to revolutionizing the system by effecting a massive transfer of power? Or are their goals merely to change specific policies such as the duties on silk stockings? Or the goals may be diffuse, yet fail to call for system transformation. The goals may call for the transformation of one sector of policy (i.e., tax reform) or a changed policy toward a single group (i.e., the transformation of policy toward native Americans).

It should be apparent that this same range of social movement activity in the larger society may also be found within organizations. Some conflicts in organizations consist of small-scale insurrections, as when a small number of members of a denomination insist upon using altered ritual formats; others lead to heresy trials; still others may lead to a coup d'état as the head of a seminary or denomination is successfully removed; and a very few result in mass movements such as the Charismatic movement in the American Catholic Church or the Liberation Theology movement within the Latin American Catholic Church.

Zald and Berger (chapter 8) have attempted to develop this analogy more systematically. Several comments are in order, however, before we attempt to draw out the more explicit implications for social movements within religious organizations. First, a major dimension of analysis has to be the distribution of power balance between authorities and dissidents. If the authorities can easily expel members, then subordinates may be wary of participating in collective action. Second, organizations exist within society, and the relative ability to appeal to the resources controlled by external groups are important. The courts, the police, stockholders, and the media may become actors in such conflicts. Finally, we must remember that these movements within organizations may be parts of broader social movements, generated as much by conditions and changes in the larger society as by events within the organization under scrutiny. Workers may be protesting the actions of a single company, but they may also be part of a larger attempt to transform industrial society; students may be protesting food in their dormitory, but may also be part of a larger antiwar movement. Women may be protesting the sexist policies of a given religious group, but their effects are nested in a larger, ongoing, feminist movement. The extent to which the movement within a church is part of a broader movement affects the nature of the battle, the resources available, the tactics of struggle, and the potential outcomes.

What, then, are some of the most pervasive forms of social-movement–like conflicts to be found in religious organizations? We shall discuss three: succession conflicts, heresy, and mass movements, recognizing that these are a restricted sample of the forms that could be analyzed.

Succession Processes. Organizations, like states, develop institutionalized succession systems. These systems reflect constitutional norms, realities of the institutionalization of power, and the rights to participate in the choice of key officers. There are three aspects of succession and removal that may develop social-movement–like phenomena around them: (1) the system for selection and removal, (2) the criteria for office-holding, and (3) specific incumbents of leadership positions.

Succession systems institutionalize powerful actors' and groups' conceptions of appropriate choices and choice procedures. The institutionalized system may be modified by later generations in an incremental fashion, reflecting newer perceptions of rights; or the old selection system may be radically altered in the midst of a large-scale mobilization. Weber noted the difficulties of succession in charismatic sects where rules of choice have not yet been institutionalized. The annointed new leader can expect to face contending factions as has characterized the recent experience of the Nation of Islam after Elijah Muhammed's death. But established groups have more highly institutionalized systems of succession, and they are most likely to be overturned by elite movements.

Insurgency and Heresy. In any organization, single individuals or small groups may attack the policies or practices of leaders. They may intend to disobey or disagree or they may intend to change the organization. We call hidden instances of this conspiracy, but when authorities come to know of such behavior they may attempt to eliminate it. In some cases authorities may accept the disagreement, but oppose an insurgency upon which it is based. There is not a clear demarcation between insurgencies and mass movements. It depends importantly upon the number of people involved and the breadth of change demanded. Insurgencies may lead to mass movements. When they are effectively circumscribed and blunted through social control within religious groups, they are often called heresies.

Let us briefly describe two studies of heresies. Robert Adams (1970) examined ten heresy trials in American Protestant seminaries. The trials were set in three kinds of seminaries—what he calls movement seminaries, denominational seminaries, and univerity seminaries. The trials occurred in the context of theological change—from traditional to more progressive. They also occurred in the context of a changing professional and scholarly orientation of the seminary. The three types of seminaries differed in their control structures and the extent to which their constituents—benefactors, board members, ministers—were buffered by the seminary and also possessed progressive theological perspectives. Adam's account focused heavily upon the changes that resulted from these trials in the various seminaries. A common pattern was that the accusers won the battle—the trial—but lost the war. Not long after the battle, the theological position that had been under attack was well represented at the seminary.

Lester Kurtz (1983; Lyng and Kurtz, 1985) has investigated the "Crisis of Modernism" in the Catholic Church as a social movement within an organization. His analysis suggests that modern theological currents began to be incorporated by a disparate group of lay and clerical Catholic theologians after the turn of the century. Though many of these scholars had contact with one another, they were, at least initially, not at all a coherent group and by no means an insurgency. But they were seen as a threatening group by the social control authorities of the Vatican who brought sanctions to bear upon many of them. As a consequence, Kurtz argues, this widespread band of scholars came to resemble an insurgent movement. As they were branded a heretical movement by the church authorities they tended to become one and were severely repressed.

These examples suggest the rich historical record that is available for detailed analyses of social movements within religious groups and organizations. Functionaries of the more established religious organizations in the modern period are compulsive about recording the details of these squabbles. Even earlier, as the work of Le Roi Ladurie (1979) suggests, religious authorities were highly likely to leave historical traces of their attempts to justify their social-control activities.

Mass Movements and Schisms. When fairly large and open insurrection meets opposition, it may withdraw and form a new organization. We call this a schism. Various church structures deal differently with such a state of affairs. The Catholic Church is replete with "Orders," some of which can be thought of as coopted insurgencies. The political status of "order" provides the possibility of subgroups able to direct energies toward certain objectives with some autonomy from the regional control structure of the church. Of course, Protestantism represents the greatest schism in the history of the Roman Catholic Church. But Protestant religious groups have shown tendencies to be far more schismatic than their Roman forebearers.

Two recent mass movements within the Catholic Church deserve brief note: the spread of the Charismatic renewal in the United States and the development of Liberation Theology in Latin America. The Charismatic Renewal is a widespread, grass-roots movement within the American Catholic Church (Neitz, 1981; Bord and Faulkner, 1983). It originated, as far as one can tell, in several dissident Catholic academic communities. The movement is best known for its tendency to encourage members to "speak in tongues," but more than anything else, it represents an emergent and local Pentecostal movement within Catholicism. It has grown very extensively, but local church authorities were encouraged to accommodate the movement, and if not without conflict and tension it has been accepted as an integral part of local parish activities. As a result, this movement has not become a schism. The common impression of a rigid nonaccommodating hierarchy, then, does not do justice to understanding the structure of the modern American Catholic Church in light of its recent experience with this grass-roots movement. It should also be noted that a similar wave of charismatic activity spread through the American Church in the late 1800s and was, in a very similar fashion accommodated and its insurgency potential, hence, blunted (Neitz, 1981).

The second movement is "Liberation Theology." This movement is regionally based in a number of Latin American countries. It has been promulgated by a group of theologians as a series of ideas, but it has programmatic and institutional consequences. As one consequence, Vatican authorities are now in the process of attempting to curtail the activities of its practitioners. It, too, can be viewed as an insurgent movement whose ideas serve to empower the lower participants in the Roman church to challenge the common practices of state authorities appointed to make policy decisions. So, one version of this theology suggests "Christian-Marxist dialogue" (see Lane, 1984), a tactic unlikely to find favor in Rome. The outcome of this mass movement in the International Catholic Church is difficult to project at the moment, though sanctions, defections, and censorship have begun to be common occurrences.

Conclusion. There is no question that the notion of social movement processes within religious groupings can be a useful tool to understanding conflict within these groups. Understanding something of groups' structure and incentive balances may reveal why episcopal forms seem to yield extensive dissidence, but relatively little defection (Hirschman, 1970). It is the congregational form that seems to produce the vitality of newer religious groups.

But we are interested here, also, in understanding how these processes affect social movement processes in the larger society. Let us conclude this section with several observations on how these internal processes, sometimes affected by external processes, may affect larger social movement processes. First, dissidents within religious groups may find local sustenance for their activities in broader social movement actions. So while religious groups may serve as infrastructures for broader social movement action, minority dissident factions within local religious groups may be important cells in broader movements even if they cannot convince the majority of their congregation to support them. Second, local factions may triumph and produce general support for their broader social movement activities within their local communities of believers. Third, schisms may occur that produce new religious groups that enter the loose turf of modern American "civil society." Fourth, factional disputes within religious groups may provide useful sites that those engaging in broader based collective action may find useful in their struggles.

In any case, it is clear that little systematic assessment has been carried out of the relationships between social movement processes *within* religious groups and their interaction with broader social movement processes in the larger society. Since religious institutions provide both the infrastructural support and direct leaderships of so many modern movements, scholars ignore these processes at their peril.

World Systems Relations, Social and Religious Movements

During the last decade, Wendell Wilkie's catch phrase of the 1940s, "one world," has become a cornerstone of sociological and historical analysis. The key to such analysis has become how classes and nations relate to one another during the global growth and transformation of capitalism, industries, and political systems. In the works of Immanuel Wallerstein, Samir Amin, Andre Gunder Frank, John Meyer, Michael Hannan, Michael Hechter, and others, local social structures, class relations, and encompassing broader political forms are treated as intertwined with systemic properties of the spread of capitalism itself. Yet as Chirot and Hall (1982) argue, these approaches generally ignore cultural forms and structures and the neglect of these factors is quite clear when one focuses upon religion. Nor do these theories have much to say about the long toleration and support of free-thinking intellectuals within core nations. In this section we will, briefly, summarize dominant themes from the various world system approaches and then discuss how these ideas illuminate our central questions of religious facilitation of social movements, emergent religious movements, and social movements within religious groups.

World systems theories argue that "core" nations, those that dominate and lead capitalist world production, exhibit different internal social structure than do "peripheral" and "semiperipheral" nations. These latter types of nations are either caught up in resource extraction with core nations or in mixed forms of exploitation and mediation with other types. Of course, peripheral nations are poorer and weak. The politics and social processes that occur in the core nations will spill over in ways that have impacts upon the peripheral nations. Immigration policies, customs, licensing arrangements, industrial development, educational policies—all of these and more can be understood in relation to the position of a nation in the world economic system. The most comprehensive statements of the approach (Wallerstein, 1974, 1980) seek to account for broad historical patterns of growth and decline of national dominance in the world system. So an early peripheral nation, the United States, may become a core nation. Holland and Spain were leading core nations at one historical point, Britain, France, and Germany at others, and the United States and Japan rose in position later.

But one does not have to subscribe to one or another historical interpretation of the rise and fall of nations to appreciate the usefulness of the idea of a global system of nations for analyses of social process in the recent period. There is no question that a hierarchy of nations exists, and that much intercourse occurs outside of diplomatic channels. Let us focus upon a few insights of the world systems theorists that can be useful to dealing with the questions we have addressed here.

First, it is clear that core nations exploit the natural and human resources of noncore nations. This insight directs one's attention to the inequalities of wealth and power between core and noncore nations. In the same way that capitalists may seek to exploit labor in peripheral nations, so, too, may movement entrepreneurs, religious missionaries, and bourgeois zealots seek to mobilize peripheral labor in their ideological and institutional behalf.

Second, it is clear that core nations may use semiperipheral nations in attempts to deflect the anger and revolutionary activities of peripheral national groups such as the American policies toward Brazil and Iran, as Wallerstein has suggested (1980). Such use of semiperipheral nations has the potential consequences of producing countermovements among them which challenge the cultural dominance of the core nations. Such has, apparently occurred with the growth of the "Islamic fundamentalism" in Iran and "Liberation Theology" across Latin American nations.

Third, the insight of world-system analysts that the bourgeoisie are a world class, solidary across national boundaries, has implications for understanding international religious processes. Religious groups are also, solidary across international boundaries providing a central identity for many individuals that transcends national identity. It is also the case that religious groups have been central to the growth of capitalism, and some even argue that the "Western state . . . developed in part as a project under the aegis of the now invisible universal Western Church and was legitimated by broad cultural mechanisms" (Thomas and Meyer, 1984). The freedom of maneuver that is provided to religious groups within most core nations also characterizes their freedom to travel and engage in wide varieties of activities outside of their core national boundaries.

Let us discuss several cases that relate to our general argument here. First let us look at the International Federation for Family Life Promotion (IFFLP). "IFFLP was created in 1974 in Washington, D.C., following an international symposium on NFP convened by the Human Life Foundation. Beginning as an association of delegates from 14 countries, IFFLP has grown in the last 10 years to become a thriving international nongovernmental association of over 60 countries with some 120 members, who have a primary interest in the promotion of natural family planning" (Lanctôf et al, 1984, p. 10). Members in this instance are member groups at the national level who in turn have individual members. The IFFLP has encouraged the growth of grass-root groups to encourage natural family planning through support from the AID, Catholic Relief Services of the United States, the United Nations Fund for Population Activities, and others. The movement has been encouraged in the United States by the National Council of Catholic Bishops Pro-Life Committee and in many countries by elements of the local Catholic hierarchy. This case illustrates very clearly how religious groups may facilitate social movement activities throughout the world system of nations through cross-national religious institutions. It also shows how these movements are sponsored at the core of the system and then disseminated to noncore nations. In fact, IFFLP has thus far devoted extensive efforts at peripheral nations, exactly those nations that have been the focus of more technically modern family planning activities through a series of programs sponsored heavily by core nations, particularly the United States. So in the same way that core Catholic groups have facilitated reproductive related social movement activities in the United States, their efforts can facilitate other versions of such activities throughout the world system.

Let us take another example. This is the activities of FOR (Fellowship of

Reconciliation) that we mentioned, again, above in connection with religious facilitation of movements in the American context. FOR has, for many years, sponsored missionary activities in Latin American and Central American nations in hopes of encouraging indigenous peace movements in these nations. Augusto Sandino, for instance, the leader of the first Sandinista movement, was aided in some of his efforts by FOR-sponsored missionaries. These missionaries were almost exclusively Protestant and, for obvious reasons, made rather little headway in predominantly Catholic countries attempting to gain support for their pacifist messages. But more recently, these missionary outposts throughout Latin America have served as the infrastructural bases for the development of an organization named Servicio Paz y Justicia. This group is most closely associated with the name of Adolfo Perez Esquivel, who received the Nobel Peace Prize in 1980 for his activities in attempting to defend human rights and disseminate pacifist teachings throughout Latin America at great risk to himself. Here we have a case of a very small core nation "halfway house" that, also, spreads its activities throughout the system of nations. Poor by American standards, its committed missionaries may labor unnoticed for decades in peripheral nations awaiting the propitious moment (see Ready, Tyson, and Pagnucco, 1985). In fact, Servicio has received funding from a variety of West European peace church sources during the recent period.

Next, let us think about some of the new religious groups that we discussed above. The Unification Church, Hare Krishna, and the Rajneeschies all originated in the persons of citizens of peripheral nations, yet they choose to proselytize in core nations, and now heavily base their activities in the United States. But from this base they have attempted to penetrate other core nations, particularly Canada and West European nations. In these examples we see representatives of peripheral religious traditions successfully penetrating the core with its extensive freedoms and then their attempts to extend activities into less dominant core nations. So the development of new religious groups can usefully be thought of in the context of world-systems nations, though little analysis has been accomplished along these lines.

Finally, let us focus upon Liberation Theology again. While we thought of this movement as one within a church above, we can also conceive of it within the context of the world system of nations. In this case we see it quite differently, and this view adds to our earlier understanding of the movement. It is also the peripheral movement and, led by semiperipheral nations, it provides a justification for challenging the core religious understandings of the relations between church and state. So as the Vatican formally separated itself from Italian political structures in the late twentieth century, the church expects that its Latin American priests will appreciate the separation of church and state in the core understanding of such an idea. The view from the core makes the appropriateness of such an understanding obvious, but the view from the periphery suggests otherwise. So the Jesuit, Robert Drinan, accepted the Vatican order to resign political office at the core, the United States Congress, while the Maryknoll priest, Miguel d'Esccoto, refuses to be bound by the order in the peripheral nation of Nicaragua.

There are other ways of applying world-system notions to an understanding of emergent religious groups across nations. Robert Wuthnow (1980) has recently attempted to show how seemingly discrete groups of religious phenomena can be understood by linking them to world-system processes. We cannot do justice to his rich analysis here, but let us touch upon the highlights of his argument.

Wuthnow discusses revitalization movements, reformation movements, religious militance, counterreform, religious accommodation, and sectarianism. He begins from a position that well summarizes the traditional sociology of religion position on the relations of social change to religion. "Groups whose lives have been intruded upon by the expanding world-economy have sought refuge in the security of religion. Rising cadres have legitimated their new status with religious creeds. Basic changes in the structure of the world order have characteristically produced, and in turn been nurtured by exceptional outpourings of religious activity" (p. 57). Accounting for the timing of religious movements at the national level has always perplexed sociologists of religion, but Wuthnow believes that the timing is partially the result of changing structures of the world economy, the nature of core-periphery relations and the extent of conflict between center and periphery. He states that "three kinds of periods have in particular given rise to intense religious activity: (a) periods in which the dominant world order has expanded rapidly to the point of producing strain in the basic institutions linking together core and periphery areas; (b) periods of overt polarization and conflict between core and periphery; and (c) periods in which newly stabilized patterns of world order are being reconstituted" (p. 59). Populations, classes, and their elites have different power and rising and falling status as they stand in relation to the world order. They define their problems and shape their religious orientations, at least in part, in terms of their relation to the underlying world economy.

How does this framework help explain the specific kinds of religious expression listed above? Revitalization movements are attempts to collectively restore or reconstruct patterns of life that have been rapidly disrupted or threatened. The main varieties include nativistic movements (purifying from alien customs or persons), revivalistic movements (recreating simpler styles of life), cargo cults, millenarian movements, and messianic movements. Wuthnow notes that social disruption does not automatically lead to these movements. Natural disasters and the devastation of war, for instance, are not accompanied by revitalistic movements. Instead, Wuthnow argues, they are most likely to occur when the changing world economy leads local elites to be less integrated and dependent upon the local population. For instance, he agues that the Anabaptists emerged as the local elites (territorial landlords and city magistrates of the German states) because of their greater power and opportunities, abrogated traditional relations of peasants to the land and of contractual relations. He further argues that the diversity of vitalistic forms is related to the disparate nature of local customs and social structure and the way the expanding world economy impacts upon the local structure. "For example, revitalistic movements that stress individual salvation and piety, such as early Methodism, have been more common where individuals have been displaced from traditional groups and incorporated separately into new economic contexts. In contrast, cargo cults and nativistic movements have been more likely where whole groups have been collectively displaced, as among North American Indians" (p. 62). Moreover, the evolution of revitalization relates to the kind of expansion that has been experienced. Where commercial expansion has been accompanied by settlement colonies, revitalization movements have tended to be short-lived because of the reorganization or extinction of native populations. Where expansion has occurred through the incorporation of domestic lower classes into new occupational roles, these movements have generally evolved into established religious organizations.

Wuthnow argues that there have been three major ideological reformations since the inception of the modern world order: the Protestant Reformation, the Enlightenment, and the growth of Marxism. Each institutionalized a fundamental redefinition of ultimate reality. He argues that each of these reformations has been carried by rising elites in peripheral areas during periods of rapid expansion in the world system. The distinctive ideological coherence of each global reformation inhered in its opposition to the sacred assumptions underlying the prevailing world order—church as harlot, mercantilist protection as inimical to national wealth, bourgeois culture as false consciousness.

We could continue with Wuthnow's argument: for instance, he argues that counterreformations occur among institutional representatives in core areas undergoing polarization; religious militance occurs in peripheral areas when the core powers are weakened and unable to crush these revolutionary organizational forms; religious accommodation occurs where a new order is being institutionalized; and sectarianism where a group's powers are declining in relation to a newly institutionalized world order. His analysis is provocative and in the main quite convincing.

Though Wuthnow is cautious in his application of this perspective, and regularly notes the importance of local economic and structural contexts, the argument underplays the organization and mobilization of groups. The recent theoretical traditions upon which we have been drawing above, the resource mobilization perspective on collective action and the world-system perspective, both lead toward a focus directly upon the mechanisms that process local level grievances. Let us state the issue starkly: Two nations or groups equally affected by relations with the activities of core nations and their representatives will differ in their responses depending upon the structure of their local associations, institutions, access to resources, and the like. Thus, the mobilization or spread of cargo cults, for instance, depends not only upon the amount of disruption created by local relations with the core (the grievance base), but also upon local associational forms, relations between types of nations in the world system, and so on. So, while native American groups were directly affected by the growth of capitalist expansion in the United States, it was those groups that had remained tribal in structure of land holding, contrasted to those who had been divided into capitalist nuclear family land-holding patterns, who adopted the "Ghost Dance" (Landsman, 1979). It is this revitalization movement that is seen, normally, as a direct response to core-inspired disorganization. The disruption of peripheral groups will not automatically lead to the generation of revitalistic movements.

The growth of religious movements in peripheral nations, as well, can expect to find support for religious freedom from mechanisms generated by the established religious groups of the core nations. So, religious repression in the periphery is a constant theme of established religious groups in core nations. So, too, is a series of mechanisms designed to aid aspiring groups of all kinds, including religious groups, that have been developed at the supra-national level (Nagel and Olzak, 1982). These mechanisms, it should be clear, however, are normally sponsored and supported by groups within core nations in order to aid their allies in noncore nations.

We have explored ways in which a world-systems perspective might help us understand the basic questions we have raised in this chapter. We can show how groups and institutions in core nations are important in understanding the development of new religious movements in noncore nations. We can also demonstrate how religious groups are important in generating support for social movement activities in noncore nations. It is most important to understand that the resource crumbs of core religious groups may be greatly useful to those attempting to create social change in poor, peripheral nations. Finally, we have shown how relations between nations in the world systems are important in understanding some of the social movements that occur within religious groups.

Conclusion

Our scope has been broad. We have used a diverse palette to sketch the interplay of social movements and religious institutions. First, we examined the role of religious organizations, personnel, and theological concerns in facilitating and creating ongoing social movements and countermovements. We then examined conflict within religious denominations, using both a political-economy and social movement analysis to show how change occurs within religious groups. The changes and conflicts within denominations feed back upon and are part of social movements in the larger society. Finally, we argued that nesting the analysis of religious change in a larger world-systems context would be illuminating at two levels: on the one hand, the changing structure of the world political economy impinges upon groups and elites, leading to changes in religious expression; on the other hand, religious organizations and personnel participate in the international trade, meaning they are carriers of religious values, political values, and ideology.

By this time it is clear that the study of social movements from a resource mobilization perspective and the study of the transformation of and within religion have much to offer to each other. There are many exciting topics that we have barely touched upon. Why do some religious structures have higher rates of schisms than others? How is heresy and dissent treated in different religions? When do religious groups switch from pietistic and withdrawal modes to participatory modes? What kinds of political and movement involvement by religious organizations lead to backlash and the emergence of countermovements within denominations? Both the sociology of religion and the sociology of social movements can be invigorated by continuing this interchange.

Note

An earlier version of this essay was delivered by Mayer N. Zald as the 1981 H. Paul Douglas Lecture to the Religious Research Association and was subsequently published in the *Review of Religious Research* under the title "Theological Crucibles: Social Movements in and of Religion." This essay was adapted especially for this volume.

4

Organizational Intellectuals and the Criticism of Society

Mayer N. Zald and *John D. McCarthy*

"Intellectuals are those who create, distribute and apply culture."[1] People who are passionately attached to symbols as well as people who are trained in their use and manipulation are commonly termed intellectuals. The term demonstrates a useful ambiguity. It may be applied only to those who are on the creative edge, the elite symbolic innovators in ideology, philosophy, art, and criticism. Or, in our usage, the term can be used more broadly to apply to those who use as well as create abstract symbol systems. Within this broad stratum, one can contrast those intellectuals who use ideas in primarily a consummatory fashion, for "play," with those who use ideas to justify and criticize existing social arrangements. It is with intellectual as social justifier or critic that we are mainly concerned.

How does this species of the intellectual differ from the professional? For us the professional uses symbols to perform specific tasks. Some professionals are also intellectual critics, or justifiers, either of the society at large or of specific institutional-professional arrangements.

There can be little doubt that intellectuals are more likely to be organizationally attached today than they were just forty years ago. Nor is there any doubt that intellectuals have recently played an important role in criticizing American social structure and in advocating social change. What requires interpretation and analysis is how institutionally employed intellectuals can criticize social arrangements. What are the emerging trends of Western and modern society that support the growth of the intellectual class and shape the direction of criticism? We present a set of interrelated propositions that explain the recent growth of the stratum of organizationally attached intellectual critics, its dominant orientations, and the institutional supports and constraints under which it must operate.

This ground has been previously illuminated by Joseph Schumpeter and C. Wright Mills. During the Second World War, Joseph Schumpeter wrote:

"Capitalism subsidizes a vested interest in social unrest" (1947, p. 146). First, bourgeois-capitalist classes have an interest in establishing and maintaining institutions of freedom. In preserving their own freedom of actions, institutions of liberty, a free press and free speech, are established. In establishing institutions to preserve their own freedom of action, the bourgeoisie inevitably also open the door to criticism of their own social order.

Second, and the point of our departure, Schumpeter (1947, p. 152) thought that capitalist societies are marked by "the vigorous expansion of the educational apparatus and particularly the facilities of higher education." The essence of this education is rationalism. Because the short-run performance of social arrangements diverges from the publicly espoused values that are used to justify them, such an educational apparatus is bound to produce criticism of the functioning of the capitalist order. Further, the greater supply of professional and quasi-professional intellectuals is likely to produce situations where individuals are dissatisfied with their work conditions and hence become generally discontented. Schumpeter (1947, p. 150) predicts, further, high levels of unemployment from time to time for intellectuals. This he believes will produce great social unrest among them. In some societies these critics might be repressed, but, believes Schumpeter, these critical intellectuals find some protection in a capitalist order, since "in defending the intellectuals as a group—not of course every individual—the bourgeoisie defends itself and its scheme of life."

Schumpeter focuses primarily on the climate of dissent produced by these factors. In passing he also examines the employment of some of these dissident intellectuals as staff members, writers, and advisors to politicians and government employees. In so doing he alludes to how the intellectuals' hostility to the social system is translated into social change and public policy in ways other than through public criticisms and debate.

Schumpeter was writing after the Great Depression. His picture of the dissent- and change-producing nature of the organization of capitalist society must have rung hollow to C. Wright Mills as he wrote *White Collar* (1951). Just a few years later Mills believed that the postwar American intellectual had "little or none of that resentment and hostility that arose in many European intellectual circles between the wars" (1951, p. 157). It was not the critical orientation of modern intellectuals which impressed Mills but their subservience. Concluding his study, Mills (1947, p. 353) remarked, "there is no probability of the new middle-classes [including intellectuals] forming or inaugurating or leading any political movement." Mills came to this conclusion from his perception of the structural changes in American society. Increasing numbers of intellectually equipped individuals worked within large bureaucratic settings. Since these bureaucracies are hierarchically organized, Mills argued that intellectuals came to serve those who hired them by justifying the status quo. He concluded his discussion of intellectuals by saying, "The social developments centered upon the rise of bureaucracies and the ideological developments centered upon the continual demands for new justifications have coincided: together they increasingly determine the social position and ideological posture of the intellectual."[2] For Mills the decline of *free* intellectuals meant the decline of criticism of the present social arrangements.

The trends he outlined have continued apace—a quickening of social criticism was seen before 1970, much of it emanating from the source Mills had written off as hopeless as a source of criticism: intellectuals in bureaucratic settings. Although grounded in his observation of postwar intellectuals, Mills's analysis did not pay enough attention to historical variations in the institutional support of intellectuals and intellectual dissent. In the American case, as long as we have had modern universities (at least since 1900), university-based intellectuals, faculty, and students have been one of the main bases for the continuing criticism of society.[3] Moreover, the growth of intellectual criticism is occurring outside as well as inside the university, and we need to examine where Mills went wrong. The increasing institutionalization of the intellectual stratum and the possibility of its increasing criticism of the status quo call out for some explanation.

One way of accounting for the increased criticism recently emanating from intellectuals is to point to the increasing distance that developed between them and the men of power over the issue of the Vietnam war. Lewis Coser (1970, p. xvi), for instance, says: "Any future sociology of American intellectuals will have to consider the Viet Nam protests as one of the most profound watersheds in the history of American intellectuals." Though the war protests demonstrated to many intellectuals how they could combine their work situation with value-infused criticism, we believe that the critical nature of modern American intellectuals has more enduring sources than the divisiveness of the Vietnam War. Moreover, to avoid a purely historicist interpretation, we must cast the unique Vietnam experience in a more general structural conceptualization.

Our analysis is guided by three broad postulates: First, the increasing criticism of social arrangements on the part of modern intellectuals has cultural and structural roots in the growth of higher education and the emerging socially oriented professions and occupations. Second, the amount of expression of criticism at any point in time is related to the ebb and flow of political cycles and the formation of the political identities of intellectuals. Third, trends and events in the larger society intersect with trends and changes in specific professional and institutional settings and with the career orientations of intellectuals to support or constrain the expression of dissent and criticism.

In discussing the first two postulates, we present our elaboration of Schumpeter's insights. We examine the sweeping forces of societal change, the shape, size, and perspectives of the intellectual classes. In our discussion of the intersection of societal institutions and careers, we present our modification of the Millsian position. We sketch how the organizational intellectual is constrained or *supported* by specific organizational settings.

Growth and Orientation of the Organizational Intellectual Stratum

To understand the situation of modern intellectuals, it is necessary to examine the master trends affecting their growth and common perspective.[4] This involves a brief analysis of trends in the growth of higher education, the changing shape of the labor force, and orientations of the educated.

Transformation of Higher Education

The growth of modern society is everywhere accompanied by an expansion of literacy, but also by an expansion of higher education. In all Western nations a larger proportion of the population now receives higher education than two decades ago.

Moreover, university systems have been under pressure to transform their access and their offerings (Trow, 1972). Ben-David (1963-64, pp. 247-53) has documented the declining ratio of medical and law degrees to total graduates in Western society. One of the largest sections of growth has been the social sciences. In the 1960-61 academic year, 15.4 percent of all B.A. and first professional degrees were in the social sciences; by 1970-71, 24 percent of B.A. and first professional degrees were in these fields in the United States (Reitman and Greene, 1972, p. 150).

The phenomenal growth in advanced degrees (M.A.'s and Ph.D.'s) granted in the humanities and social sciences in the 1960-70 decade is probably a better index to the growth of the organizational intellectual stratum. While there were 59,460 master's degrees granted in 1959-60, there were 179,940 such degrees granted in 1970-71. Similarly, 5,132 Ph.D.'s were granted in the humanities and social sciences in 1959-60 and 17,350 in 1970-71 (Reitman and Greene, 1972, Tables 134, 135).

The Service Society

Not only do we have a population of which increasing proportions attend college and receive advanced degrees, especially in social science, but the educated work in organizations and we have become a service society. Kornhauser (1962), Zald (1971), and Moore (1967) have shown that the professions that have grown the most in the United States are those whose members are most likely to be employed in large-scale organizations. Fuchs (1968) has documented the extent to which the service sector has grown most rapidly.

Singelmann and Browning (1973) have noted the heterogeneity of the service sector and have provided us with a most informative reclassification of it. They make a distinction between what they call goods services (e.g., financing, insurance, business services, advertising), social services (e.g., education, medical and health, charity and religious, and government), and personal services (e.g., domestics and food service, beauticians and barbers). Examining these categories in the United States for a thirty-year period (1940-70), they find a doubling of the percentage of the labor force in goods services (from 4.6 to 9.2 percent), a doubling of the percentage of the labor force in social services (from 10.6 to 20.6 percent), and a 30 percent decline in persons employed in personal services (from 13.9 to 9.9 percent). Within the social services, personnel employed in education have risen from 3.5 percent of the total labor force to 8 percent, whereas government employment has risen from 3.9 to 5.5 percent of the total labor force. (It is worth noting that the largest part of the growth in government employment has not been in federal but in state and local government [Zald, 1971]).

Some might argue that these data are only partially relevant to our argument. After all, schoolteachers and government employees are not necessarily intellectuals. Of course. But these sectors include the educated and the more literate. To the extent that they are trained in the humanities and social sciences, they are educated in disciplines that examine the human condition and social arrangements. They provide an audience for creative, dissenting intellectuals in the media, they are taught by liberal professors, and many of them are organizational intellectuals themselves.

The Orientations of the Educated

Richard Hofstadter (1963) tells us that for the present century American intellectuals have been predominantly progressive, liberal, and leftist. This observation, combined with the consistent positive relationship between education and Republican voting (usually taken as an index of conservatism or support for the status quo), at first appears puzzling.[5] But modern intellectuals, especially the creative edge, are not only well educated but highly educated. Moreover, there is tremendous variation in political beliefs among the highly educated.

First, let us examine the relationship between voting and education.

There appears to be a nonlinear relationship between Republican voting and education. On the basis of a national probability sample taken in the weeks preceeding the 1964 presidential election, Selznick and Steinberg (1969, pp. 216-25) show steady increases in Republican support from those who have finished only grade school up to those who have finished college. Those who have earned postgraduate degrees, however, are less likely to have preferred the Republican candidate than are those with bachelor degrees.

More important are differences by discipline and profession. Although we possess no systematic evidence for different highly educated professions, data are available for professors. Those disciplines that contribute to the training of students who enter the social service sector are the most politically Left and are certainly far more to the Left politically than the highly educated or professionals generally. Based on data from a mail questionnaire study, Table 1 shows the average Democratic vote between 1948 and 1956 and a conservatism score (made up of questions about social policy change) for college professors in a number of disciplines. The differences presented between disciplines are striking, and, according to Spaulding and Turner, "cannot be explained in terms of the measured background factors and environmental conditions" (1968, p. 262).

More recent data gathered by the Carnegie Commission on Higher Education and presented by Lipset and Ladd (1970, pp. 49-51, 106) support the results of Spaulding and Turner. Table 2 shows the political self-appraisal of professors by field, and again the social sciences are far to the Left. We assume that students in disciplines mirror their professors. They select ideologically compatible disciplines and are reinforced in their views by their professors and their peers (Kenniston, 1968).

There is also direct evidence that college students have become more leftist. Lipset and Ladd (1971, p. 112), after reviewing survey evidence on the political attitudes of several generations of college students, concluded: "In short, the historical slope of political attitudes among American college generations has been toward a more liberal position over time. So, even if the generation after 1960 becomes more moderate, it, like earlier ones, is still likely to end up at a point further to the 'left' than its predecessors and to the 'right' of its successors."

In any case we can conclude that the well educated are more likely today to hold values consistent with social-change advocacy. Lipset and Ladd recognize the effects of this leftward movement in terms highly relevant to our discussion:

> As the students of this college "generation" have graduated and entered the junior ranks of the professions, the media, business, government, even aca-

TABLE 4.1

Democratic Affiliation, Democratic Vote, and Conservatism Index for a Sample of College Professors, by Discipline*

Discipline	Democratic Affiliation	Democratic Vote (1948–56)	Conservatism Index**
Philosophers..........	79%	79%	9%
Sociologists..........	78	83	12
Political scientists...	74	72	10
Historians............	72	73	17
Psychologists.........	70	68	26
Botanists.............	50	39	51
Geologists............	35	33	61
Mathematicians........	29	30	54
Engineers.............	27	21	66

Source. – Charles B. Spaulding and Henry A. Turner, "Political
    Orientation and Field Specialization among College
    Professors." Sociology of Education 41(1968): 263.

*These data were gathered by mailed questionnaires from a sample of
   of the professional association directory for each discipline.
**These scores here are the percentages who were high on the
   Conservatism Index. The index was made up of a number of closed
   questions dealing with governmental obligation and involvement
   in social problems.

TABLE 4.2

Political Self-Appraisal of the Faculty and 1968 Support for Nixon, by Field of Study

Field of Study	Left or Liberal	Conservative	Nixon Support
Social sciences (N=6,845).........	71%	11%	19%
Humanities (N=9,546).............	62	17	23
Fine arts (N=3,732).............	52	22	36
Education (N=3,277).............	41	27	40
Physical sciences (N=7,599).....	44	26	38
Biological sciences (N=4,403)..	44	27	40
Business (N=2,080).............	33	36	53
Engineering (N=4,165).........	29	41	60
Agriculture (N=1,348).........	18	50	61

Source. - S.M. Lipset and Carl Everett Ladd, Jr., "...And What Professors Think," <u>Psychology Today</u> 4(1970): 49-51, 106.

deme itself, it would appear that they have brought to these occupational environments a deep concern for egalitarian, populist, and often strongly radical principles. Young journalists press for advocacy rather than "objective reporting"; new physicians support socialized medicine; architects demand plans which "serve the people"; young academics want "relevance," i.e., radical social positions in their teaching and research. (1971, p. 100)

So the increasing importance of higher education in modern society combined with the increasing proportional size and importance of the "liberal" social sciences is likely to produce a change-oriented perspective among a larger segment of the professionals. The thrust of this evidence suggests this is likely to be a continuing phenomenon.

To the extent that other Western societies follow the American patterns in growth of higher education and the development of social service occupations, we would expect a parallel growth in the potentially intellectual strata. Increasing proportions of youth in other modern societies are receiving high education. But there is less evidence that their occupational structures are closely paralleling ours. Singelmann (1974) has shown, for instance, that the relative growth of the service sector in countries such as West Germany and France has been far slower than in the United States. We would expect, then, fewer organizational intellectuals in these societies.

There is no necessity that organizational intellectuals be dissenters. The stratum may grow only to produce greater volumes of support and justification for the existing regime. We do not argue that critical values necessarily result from a growth of the organizational intellectual stratum. To the extent to which newly educated intellectuals are inculcated with dominant regime ideologies, we would expect support to predominate over criticism. Given the inculcation of critical values, and the growth of professions based on these values, the structural constraints and encouragements to an airing of these values become an important object of study.

Political Structure and Social Movements

The basic transformation of the educational background of intellectuals and the organizational settings in which they are employed occurs within limits set by the political structure and culture. Within these limits the ebb and flow of politics and social movements affect the political identification of generations and the costs and benefits of overt political engagement.

It is apparent that the more centralized and all-encompassing the state, the more it controls both inculcation of critical perspectives and opportunities to express them. Highly centralized states directly control the curricula of schools and socializing institutions. Moreover, to a greater or lesser degree the state can control the media of communication and the institutional settings in which intellectuals are employed.

The degree of concentration of power sets potential limits to the degree of expression of dissent, but nations with similar concentrations of power may vary in their cultural traditions and protection of dissent. As John Roche (1963) notes, the growth of stronger national institutions in America was accompanied by institutional protection of individual liberties. Both within and without government the rights of expression and dissent have been expanded. Moreover, intellectual traditions need not emphasize freedom to criticize; they may emphasize regime justification or contemplation, yea-saying instead of nay-saying, self-criticism instead of societal criticism.

Both regime concentration and cultural norms interact with the ebb and flow of domestic political expression. Over time, regimes vary in both their openness to political and social criticism and the direction of that criticism. Societies may experience cycles of reform and social movement vitality.

Where movements of criticism and reform are restricted to narrow elite circles, we would not expect such movements to have broad impact on the identities of generations or on careers and occupational choices of intellectuals. On the other hand, where the cycles of reform involve numerous institutions and extensive mobilization of intellectuals, both identities and careers may be affected (Lipset and Dobson, 1972).

After 1930 in America, Left-leaning intellectuals were shaped by the Depression, by the rise of labor unions, and by the rise of fascism. Fighting in the Spanish Civil War can be seen as an early version of Mississippi Summer. If, during the Great Depression, one tried to act out one's values in a career (rather than merely being a value sympathizer), one entered the labor movement or joined a New Deal agency. During the Depression, if one were a Left-leaning lawyer, one developed a practice in labor law; after 1966, one entered poverty law or consumer law.

Social movements shape the identities of organizational intellectuals in two ways. First, they provide experiences that affect attitudes and perspectives during the period when activist intellectuals are making basic career choices. Second, if the movements are successful, new organizations and programs, leading to new career opportunities, are created because of their demands.

A recent study of forty students who took part in the activities sponsored by the Southern Christian Leadership Conference in the Deep South during the height of the civil rights movement ("freedom summer") shows both how a social movement experience may lead to future social-change–linked employment and the variety of such employment opportunities. Interviewed four years after the summer experience, the students "included a girl who worked with neighborhood legal aid centers in poverty areas, two members of church related service organizations, a Head Start teacher, three other teachers who were committed to working in ghetto schools, and a part-time politician who spent his off hours lecturing to churches and other groups on civil rights and the black revolution" (Demerath et al., 1971, p. 176). Also included were a law student planning a career in civil liberties cases, a teacher at a small college speaking widely against the war and advising black students, and a teacher at a black school who in her spare time organized welfare mothers, worked for Eugene McCarthy, and attempted to stop a freeway being put through a black community.[6]

When social movements affect governmental and private allocations of funds and the development of new institutional programs, new careers and occupational opportunities are opened or old ones redefined. Ministers, social workers, YMCA secretaries, lawyers, economists, ecologists, political scientists, sociologists, educators, doctors, nurses, urban planners, public housing administrators, and business managers are all potential recruits to new governmental and private programs. The consumer movement, the ecology movement, the antipoverty movement—each creates a set of positions in pressure groups, government, universities, and other agencies. The war on poverty led to a redefinition of community organization practice. These governmental and private programs become the institutional embodiment of social movement goals.

It is enormously difficult to estimate the number of organizational intellectuals at any one time. And *over time* the number will vary as supports for programs and movement values change. Nevertheless, it should be possible to estimate their numbers systematically. For instance, in any large city how many ministers are employed in church-related social activist positions? How many serve on boards of action programs? What are the numbers of positions in church administrative bodies that are related to social-change programs? How many social workers engage in new forms of advocacy or radical community organization? How many poverty lawyers are there? What proportion of their time is involved in delivery of services rather than class action or legislative lobbying? What are the orientations of Housing and Urban Development (HUD) administrators? How many see themselves as guerilla administrators?

Warren (1973, pp. 355-63) reports that agencies running community action programs in eight cities he studied employed 4,536 people and 596 were employed by the Model Cities program. At the professional level, he reports, these two programs employed 186 educators, 35 social workers, 91 community organizers, 28 lawyers, 63 researchers, 27 accountants, 51 administrators, 25 city planners, 42 nurses, and 19 sociologists. Warren goes on to note that the Model Cities and community action agency personnel were matched by a similarly large number of personnel in federal, regional, state, and local agencies. This is a specific example of how a social movement and politically related change effort (the war on poverty) created new occupational positions embodying change goals and utilizing, to some extent, organizational intellectuals.[7]

The Microprocess: Organizational and Career Opportunities as Supports for Change

The broad macroprocesses discussed above become microprocesses as specific institutional settings are expanded or contracted, as the political process interacts with budgetary decisions in government and other agencies to shape career options in organizations and occupations and to encourage commitment to change or to the status quo. Now we discuss two aspects of the microprocess. First, we sketch the differences between organizational settings in social movements, private organizations, and governmental agencies as they affect the advocacy potential of organizational intellectuals. Second, we examine the effects of career orientations on the maintenance of and commitment to critical dissent.

In the discussion that follows it would have been better to present systematic trend evidence in support of many of the arguments. We have found it extremely difficult, however, to map the changing matrix of occupations, organizations, and careers as this matrix bears upon our arguments. This difficulty, we believe, is the result of the rapid growth of both new organizations and associated new professional roles and careers, which, as yet, has not been well described in its important parts.[8]

Organizational Settings

Intellectuals hold positions in three major types of settings: social movement organizations, private organizations not formally connected to social movements, and governmental agencies. Each type of setting is subject to different sets of pressures and constraints. Some organizational intellectuals engage in work that is directly related to their social-change commitment, others engage in work which is peripheral to their social-change commitment, but may, by virtue of the autonomy of their position, be more or less free to engage in social-change advocacy. So, for instance, a community health center staff member may devote much of his time to political organizing to stop the building of a freeway through the center's service area. Of course, most organizational intellectuals are far less free to engage in social-change advocacy than this individual. A narrower use of institutional position might involve the frequent use of institutional facilities such as copying machines, telephones, secretarial assistance, meeting space, and the like.

Social Movement Organizations

Some organizational intellectuals may pursue their commitment to social change by taking full-time positions in social movement organizations. Obviously, if the individual's change goals are compatible with those of the organization, such a position allows a high degree of freedom, but social movement organizations respond to the ebb and flow of sentiments and support in relevant constituencies (Zald and Ash, 1966, pp. 327-40; McCarthy and Zald, 1973). Some social movement organizations are repressed and coerced by government. In those cases the organizational intellectuals pursuing movement goals may run the risk of jail and intimidation. But where government controls are relaxed, weak, or ineffectual, the social movement usually provides a market forum for the pursuit of goals: if the organization anticipates the support bases correctly, it flourishes and the individual's sense of efficacy thrives. On the other hand, in the face of a played-out issue-attention cycle (Downs, 1972, pp. 38-50) or a declining resource base, the organizational intellectual may be left without support for a cherished ideology and program.

Private Organizations

These provide a range of options for organizational intellectuals. Where the goals of the private organization are consonant with a movement and the organizational resource base is fractionated and secure, organizational intellectuals may be able to pursue goals and societal change long after social movement organizations and governmental agencies prove to be inhospitable settings. Private organizations such as trade unions, churches, foundations, universities, or liberal law firms may provide a stable base for the organizational intellectual. Even where organizational goals are relatively neutral with respect to the goals of the organizational intellectual (as in universities), if work schedules are flexible or if the professional routines are seen as consonant with other professional activities, private organizations may support criticism of societal arrangements and alternative societal policies. For example, doctors attached to university hospitals may pursue change in health delivery systems as part of their professional interests. Or social work professors may urge reform of the welfare system.

Of course, private organizations may be hostile to change. In such a case the organizational intellectual may experience isolation and pursue cherished goals under the possibility of being discovered. The separation of social-change advocacy and organizational pursuits may become a necessity.

Private organizations vary in their insulation from external pressure. They may be penetrable by government and other antichange forces. Thus, a radical schoolteacher who teaches in a town where the board of education opposes his goals may soon be unemployed. Even if the school board wishes to protect the radical teacher, its vulnerability to pressures from the city council or other agencies may lead it to discipline the change-oriented professional.

Governmental Agencies

Governmental agencies vary in the extent to which their missions can be used by organizational intellectuals. First, some governmental programs can be eliminated or changed if they are too radical for either the legislative or executive branches (Donovan, 1970). Second, even if a program is maintained and funded, its aims and goals can be shifted to the extent that legislatures or executives can control the appointment of executives, the definition of programs, and the amount of monies allocated. As social movements become institutionalized in governmental agencies, we of course expect them to make their peace with controlling bodies and agencies.

Nevertheless, especially where the interpretation of mission is open to administrative discretion, the employees of agencies can continue to promote social-change goals. If the political executive is highly opposed to those goals, then a concerted war will take place against the agency and its personnel. But it is a mistake to assume that a change in the executive or in the legislature automatically means a transformation in the extent to which professionals in these agencies continue to pursue their own definition of the situation. It is apparent that agency traditions, executive cadre, and alliances with outside groups can protect an agency from even the most determined executive (Wamsley and Zald, 1973). Moreover, at any point in time different departments of the executive branch (for instance, the Department of Agriculture and HEW) may support different views of the world.[9]

In some agencies, organizational intellectuals will be "guerrilla administrators" attempting to change status-quo–oriented agencies toward their own definitions of proper public policy, or individually pursuing their own conception of the goals of the agency. In other cases the agency itself may be the leading edge of social change.

But dissent is not revolutionary activity and rhetoric. At the same time that modern institutions provide the opportunity for dissent, they shape and narrow that dissent. Both inside and outside the university, reform rhetoric and activity are the accepted mode. Revolutionary rhetoric rarely finds wide acceptance. Organizational attachment requires the moderation of dissent, and those intellectuals who violate this norm find themselves at odds with the very institutions that allow widespread reform dissent. In this sense Mills is correct: radical dissent is unlikely among organizationally attached intellectuals. However, even here we can modify Mills: when a large number of organizational intellectuals hold critical values, an audience is available for the products of more radical, less organizationally attached, intellectuals and activists. Consumption of their products and financial support for their activities become more likely.

In summary, social movement organizations, private organizations, and governmental agencies vary in the support and insulation from control they provide to organizational intellectuals. With widespread social movement activity, the organizational intellectual may ride a crest of reform. But even as society retreats from the high tide of social movement commitment, it provides niches for the promotion of social change. These niches are important to careers and career choices.

Professions and Career Orientations

Just as organizational settings vary in their support of change orientations, so too do professions. The cultural traditions of professions vary in legitimation of and compatibility with social criticism. For instance, in some societies medical doctors may be an elite cultural group deeply involved in politics and general cultural affairs (as in Latin America), while in other societies medical doctors may be technocrats relatively neutral to political life. Some professions, such as accounting or dentistry, give much less scope to social action activities than others, such as the ministry or social work. Moreover, in the natural history of professions there will be phases in which the search for legitimation or the internal processes of change encourage or discourage criticism of institutional and societal arrangements (Bucher and Strauss, 1961, pp. 324-34; Becker and Strauss, 1956, pp. 253-63).

Professions also differ in their assumptions about the relations of means to ends, their prescriptions for change. Lawyers are trained to see the world differently from economists. And a lawyer and an economist equally committed to ameliorating poverty will be very different in the tactics they choose, the programs they see as having payoff, and the skills that they bring to any program. The particular melding that takes place is partly shaped by individual values, generational political perspectives, and professional training; but it is also affected by situational factors, institutional settings, and career opportunities.

Large variations in career patterns are available to organizational intellectuals. For instance, within the class of lawyers committed to ameliorating poverty there may be those for whom it represents a marginal career choice made out of career opportunism. Degrees of commitment, perceptions of self, and perceptions of long-range career goals will intersect with societal supports and organizational supports to affect critical perspectives and programmatic commitment.

Professional careers that include heavy components of social-change advocacy are not as highly institutionalized as more traditional careers in terms of training, career steps, and the existence of professional associations. Nevertheless, the availability of organizational supports and strong individual commitments to change allow some intellectuals to develop fairly stable careers of social-change advocacy. One of the goals of many of the "radical caucuses" that developed in the social service professional associations during the period of the war on poverty and anti-Vietnam protests was an attempt to redirect professional service toward social-change advocacy.

Two career types deserve special mention. These are the "occupational altruist" (Krause, 1971) and the "program professional" (Wilensky, 1956). "By the term 'occupational altruist' we mean the action by members of an occupational group itself to change the way in which it deals with have and have-not groups" (Krause, 1971, p. 98). "Occupational altruists . . . work to transform the goals of their particular field from service to the haves to an increased pattern of service to the have-nots" (Krause, 1971, p. 344).

For this group social-change advocacy is primarily within the profession. The program professional is concerned less with changing the nature of the service of his own professional group. He develops a strong competency in some particular social policy area, such as public assistance or race relations. By virtue of professional competence, he may move in and out of government agencies, private agencies, community organizations, foundations, and universities. Social-change advocacy and professional duties are directly tied. The commitment is to specific programs and policy changes rather than to any specific occupation or organizational setting.

The ability to transfer skills and credentials from one setting to another is an important characteristic of organizational intellectuals. The "program professional" depends on this ability. But in some cases organizational intellectuals have transferable skills and low commitment to movement goals. Thus, when social movements are highly institutionalized, such as the antitrust section of the Department of Justice, professionals may work and gain experience in the Justice Department and then, when a better job comes along, work for the corporations that the Justice Department is supposed to control! Here a person uses skills learned in a social-movement–related setting to pursue antimovement goals. On the other hand, some skills may be sharply limited to the particular setting with which the organizational intellectual has identified. For instance, we suspect that community organizers with ethnic backgrounds are fairly restricted in their career options. Or program professionals may be missionaries with deep commitment to the program and have transferable skills, with low commitments to particular organizations. They may be able to switch from movement to movement as issue-attention cycles change (McCarthy and Zald, 1973), or they may be able to move from social movement organizations to private organizations, such as universities, and then again out into newly developed social movement organizations.

When organizational intellectuals are deeply committed to social change but have transferable skills, we would expect them to be the fellow travelers of the next generation. As they succeed in establishing themselves in activities marginally related to social movements, they become the financial base for the next movement that touches their intellectual commitments. The "occupational altruist," on the other hand, exhibits greater commitment to a standard occupational career and the possibilities inherent in its changed service. Analysis of career orientations and career options may be critical for examining the maintenance of the hidden remnant. It may account for the continuing intellectual ferment and criticism in specific program sectors.

Conclusion: The Self-Regulating Society and the Future of Intellectual Criticism

The growth of the intellectual stratum must be seen as the result of the transformation of higher education and the professionalization processes in modern society. This process, combined with the relative degree of autonomy provided by many modern organizational settings and the growth of organizations specifically addressed to social change, allows a segment of the larger intellectual stratum, the organizational intellectuals, a measure of freedom to engage in critical dissent. Mills saw the bureaucratization of the intellectual leading to a decline in intellectual criticism. Surely Schumpeter is closer to the mark than Mills, however. Schumpeter saw the outlines of this growing stratum but did not anticipate the directions of the transformation of higher education and the occupational structure or the possibilities provided by complex organizations. Rather than an image of modern America *allowing* its intellectuals freedom to dissent, we believe that modern social structure actually encourages reform dissent.

Is this state of affairs inevitable in modern industrial society? Is it an outgrowth of economic and technological trends that could not have resulted in other possibilities? Two points need to be addressed: the determinants of the orientations of the intellectual class and the determinants of its expansion. Briefly, must the intellectuals necessarily be critics? The answer is "No." They may be justifiers: they may, if bound to the elites, develop sophisticated managerial ideologies, and they may be conservators of the societal ideology. Although the trend in the United States has been for intellectuals to be on the Left, some segments have been conservative. And political events and cycles may shift the direction of dissent for several generations.

By the Reagan era it had become clear that the neoconservatives and conservatives had expanded their organizational base and their role in the arena of ideas and politics. One can argue whether the American population had become significantly more conservative after 1970. Philip Auclaire's (1984) analysis of attitudinal trend data suggests that there is little evidence that the American population's opinion had become significantly more conservative, at least concerning social welfare expenditures. It is clear that the population elected a conservative president, but the meaning of that election for shifts in mass ideology is not clear. However, there is no doubt that a new organizational and institutional support base for conservatism had developed. Himmelstein and Zald (1984) have documented the extent to which foundations supported by the Coors, Pew, Scaife, and Richardson families had financed the research and writings of scholars and intellectuals at such organizations as the Heritage Foundation, the American Enterprise Institute, and so on. With an avowed agenda of supporting capitalism and discrediting the writings of new class intellectuals, the new group of conservative intellectuals use the same means and are dependent upon the same kinds of institutional support as the Left organizational intellectuals. The rising tide of support for conservative intellectuals coupled with the secular trends of shifting involvements from public to private action (Hirschman, 1982) go far to explain the changing rhetoric of the public arena.

Finally, is the expansion of the intellectual class inevitable? We believe not. In modern society, governments can control in some measure the shape of the occupational pyramid. Where the means of central economic control have been perfected, where governmental allocations and subsidies are an increasing part of the economic system, governmental actions become a determinant of the stratification system, of the career opportunities for professionals.[10]

The basis of the stratification system is obviously related to technology and stages of industrialization. But because modern societies differ in political structure, in cultural tradition, and in institutional commitments, they also differ in the size and orientation of key groups. A society need not encourage its critical classes. Even as we move into a postbourgeois society, as capitalism in its classical sense loses its hold, political systems differ enough so that social-change perspectives may be encouraged in one society and contained in another. Societies with parallel underlying economic structures may encourage very different intellectual strata to emerge and sustain themselves. Though capitalist and even postcapitalist societies may provide some freedom for intellectual dissent, we see no reason why the opportunity structure of dissent for the organizational intellectual stratum must *inevitably* expand.

Notes

1. Seymour Martin Lipset (1960). See the following for a variety of definitions of intellectuals: Lipset; Edward Shils (1971); C. Wright Mills (1951); Lewis A. Coser (1970).
2. Joseph A. Schumpeter (1947, p. 156). See also C. Wright Mills (1962, pp. 292-304). In this essay, Mills, in 1944, lays down generally the same thesis when he says of the intellectual: "The material basis of his initiative and intellectual freedom is no longer in his hands. Some intellectuals feel these processes in their work. They know more than they say and they are powerless and afraid" (p. 297).
3. Late in his career, observing dissent in university settings by young intellectuals, Mills (1962, pp. 247-59) rethought his pessimism. Nevertheless, his earlier analysis did not anticipate increasing dissent.
4. Our interest here is to trace the common situation of organizational intellectuals; thus we do not address the question of conflicts between structurally distinct groups of intellectuals. Of course, such conflicts exist, and many freer, literary intellectuals would not accept our inclusion of most social scientists in the stratum of intellectuals, let alone our inclusion of the less well-trained intellectuals. See Bennett M. Berger (1957, pp. 275-90).
5. Of course, the puzzle vanishes if we take the term "intellectual" to mean "creative intellectual," as Hofstadter does. The puzzle exists only with a broad use of the term. S. M. Lipset and R. B. Dobson (1972, pp. 137-98) review the evidence for the Left-leaning propensities of creative intellectuals, especially among the professoriate at elite institutions.
6. See also James Fendrich and Alison T. Tarleau (1973, pp. 245-53). It is impossible to separate self-selection from experiential effects in this and the Demerath et al. study.
7. Recent market conditions which have slowed the demand for labor in this sector do not negate the longer-term trend of growth.
8. For exceptions, see Robert J. S. Ross (1975), and Irwin Epstein (1970, pp. 155-63). Both studies examine the relationships between social movements external to professions and career variety and change within a profession.
9. See Robert C. Wood (1970, pp. 39-51) for a discussion of this issue. He maintains that lower-level policymaking in governmental agencies is the result of a lack of clear program guidelines and the absence of firm and competent leadership. Wood recognizes that lower-level policymaking may in some cases be quite antithetical to either congressional or executive wishes.

PART III
PROCESSES OF
ORGANIZATIONAL CHANGE

Introduction

One of the distinctive features of our approach has been its emphasis upon the organizational carriers, the social movement organizations (SMOs) that aggregate preferences for change. Before the crystallization of the resource mobilization perspective, Mayer Zald's writings focused upon the transformation of SMOs.

The transformation of social movement organizations has been a historic interest of students of social movements and social change. Max Weber's discussion of the routinization of charisma, Roberto Michels' analysis of the processes of oligarchization, and numerous sociologists' analyses of the goal displacement process stemmed from a concern with how the original spirit and commitment of social movements was vitiated and transformed.

The three chapters in this section, written before the development of resource mobilization theory, employed a form of institutional analysis developed by Philip Selznick. Selznick's approach was an early attempt to view organizations whole, to analyze organizations as congeries of groups brought together in complex systems and nested in environments that supported or challenged different organizational structures and tendencies. Mayer Zald and Roberta Ash Garner used this approach to challenge linear, natural history approaches to the transformation of SMOs. They argued, as had Alvin Gouldner, that the pessimistic assumption that SMOs always become oligarchical, conservative, and bureaucratic was a metaphysical pathos. Instead, sometimes organizational processes, such as oligarchization, lead to greater radicalism, rather than conservatism. Moreover, the swings of social movement cycles in the larger society may create pressures on older, staid SMOs to become more radical and innovative.

Resource mobilization (RM) theory leads one to recast some of the terms of Zald and Garner's analyses. For instance, they emphasized membership commitment and routinization. But RM theory downplays the importance of formal membership criteria in favor of a more realistic notion of sympathizers, adherents, and constituents. Adherents and constituents may provide a variety of resources; yet they may not be formal members. And much of social movement activity is made up of transitory teams, loosely pulled together by cadre and network leaders. Nevertheless, aside from this qualification, Zald and Garner's analysis holds up well, twenty years after it was originally published. (It is reprinted here without revision.)

The analysis of the YMCA, co-authored by Mayer Zald and Patricia Denton, shows how an organization that was founded as part of evangelical revivalism developed a stable base of accommodation to the larger society. It is, in a sense, a documentation of the goal displacement process.

On the other hand, the essay "Social Movement Industries: Competition and Conflict Among SMOs," stems directly from the logic of the resource mobilization approach. Our version of resource mobilization theory steps off from an economic analogy: social movement industries and the competition and cooperation among industry components. Of course, the contributors to the sociology of complex organizations had discussed interorganizational relations previously, and we have drawn heavily upon that literature. So the use of an economic framework allows us to incorporate insights from both the sociology of organizations and from industrial economics. We believe we go beyond the sociology of complex organizations because economists stress industrial concentration—monopoly, oligopoly, and the relationship of competitors to market leaders in a way that sociologists have not. Our essay here is one of the few organizational-focused attempts to force the analysis of social movements away from the stress upon the single leading organization in a movement industry. Our approach emphasizes that all of the SMOs of a social movement industry must be seen as part of an interacting field.

5

Social Movement Organizations: Growth, Decay, and Change

Mayer N. Zald and *Roberta Ash Garner*

Social movements manifest themselves in part through a wide range of organizations. These organizations are subject to a range of internal and external pressures that affect their viability, their internal structure and processes, and their ultimate success in attaining goals.

The dominant line of approach to the sociological study of the transformation of social movement organizations (hereafter referred to as MOs) has been the institutionalization and goal displacement model of organizational transformation. This model, which stems from Weber, (Gerth, and Mills 1946) and Michels (1949) takes the following line of analysis: as an MO attains an economic and social base in the society, as the original charismatic leadership is replaced, a bureaucratic structure emerges and a general accommodation to the society occurs (see Chapin and Tsouderos, 1956). The participants in this structure have a stake in preserving the organization, regardless of its ability to attain goals. Analytically there are three types of changes involved in this process; empirically they are often fused. The three types of change are goal transformation, a shift to organizational maintenance, and oligarchization.

Goal transformation may take several forms, including the diffusion of goals in which a pragmatic leadership replaces unattainable goals with diffuse goals, so that the organization can pursue a broader range of targets (Zald and Denton, 1963). However, according to the Weber-Michels model, whatever the form of goal transformation, it is always in the direction of greater conservatism (the accommodation of organization goals to the dominant societal consensus).

Organizational maintenance is a special form of goal transformation in which the primary activity of the organization becomes the maintenance of membership, funds, and other requirements of organizational existence. It, too, is accompanied by conservatism, for the original goals must be

121

accommodated to societal norms in order to avoid conflicts that could threaten the organization's viability.

Oligarchization may be defined as the concentration of power, in the Weberian sense, in the hands of a minority of the organization's members. (For our purposes, bureaucratization is that form of oligarchization that stresses a hierarchy of offices and prescribed rules for conducting affairs.) Of course, some MOs begin with a relatively oligarchical structure and de-oligarchization may occur. But the Michels part of the model treats mainly of the movement from democratic decision structures—a situation of dispersed power, to centralization and oligarchy. (This process is typically evaluated as morally wrong and as a prelude to member apathy and organizational conservatism.)

This line of sociological analysis has a distinguished place in the literature, if only for its imaginative concepts—goal displacement, iron law of oligarchy, routinization of charisma, and the like. Nevertheless, as a statement on the transformation of (social) movement organizations it is incomplete. There are a variety of other transformation processes that take place including coalitions with other organizations, organizational disappearance, factional splits, increased rather than decreased radicalism, and the like. And in fact, the Weber-Michels model[1] can be subsumed under a more general approach to movement organizations that specifies the conditions under which alternative transformation processes take place.

An essay in theoretical synthesis, here we attempt to specify some of the major factors influencing the direction of MOs and to provide illustrative propositions. Each section contains several of these, but only a few propositions and predictions that summarize and sharpen the argument will be listed and set off.

We follow the general sociological approach to organizations most explicity stated by Selznick (1948) and often called organizational or institutional analysis. The approach can be applied to any kind of association or organization, not just those with bureaucratic structures. Briefly, large-scale organizations are seen as a collection of groups harnessed together by incentives of various kinds to pursue relatively explicit goals. Both the ends and means of subgroups may conflict with those established by the authoritative elements in the organization; there may be conflict over the distribution of power and rewards within the organization. Organizations exist in a changing environment to which they must adapt. Adaptation to the environment may itself require changes in goals and in the internal arrangement of the organization. This view of organizations treats goals as problematic, and as changing in response to both internal and external pressures. It is especially useful for the study of MOs precisely because it focuses on conflict, environmental forces, and the ebb and flow of organizational viability.[2]

Our first task is to define the analytic characteristics of movement organizations: How does an MO differ from other complex or formal organizations? A social movement is a purposive and collective attempt of a number of people to change individuals or societal institutions and structures. Although the organizations through which social movements can manifest themselves may have bureaucratic features, analytically they differ from "full-blown" bureaucratic organizations in two ways. First, they have goals aimed at changing the society and its members; they wish to restructure society or individuals, not to provide it or them with a regular service (as is typical of bureaucracies). For example, proselytizing and usually messianic religious groups, melioristic political organizations, and conspiratorial parties are movement organizations by our definition. Goals aimed at change subject movement organizations to vicissitudes that many other types of organization avoid. For instance, if the society changes in the direction of the MOs goals, the organization's reason for being no longer exists. On the other hand, its goals of change may incur great hostility and repressive action in the society.

Second (and related to the goals of change), MOs are characterized by an incentive structure in which purposive incentives predominate.[3] While some short-run material incentives may be used, the dominant incentives offered are purposive, with solidary incentives playing a secondary role. Organizations that rely on purposive incentives often have the problem of maintaining membership commitment and participation, for the values represented by the MO's goals must be deeply held in order for the organization to command time and loyalty in the face of the competition of work and the demands of family and friends.[4]

As we have noted, the Weber-Michels model predicts changes in goals (conservatism and organizational maintenance) and in structure (oligarchization). Although we will comment on the latter aspect of organizational change, we focus more on the transformation of and the interplay of goals and structure. On this point we challenge the Weber-Michels model by limiting its predictions to certain types of MOs, and by suggesting conditions under which alternatives are possible.

In this chapter we first discuss the relation of movement organizations to the environment in which they exist—both the society at large and more narrowly the social movement of which they are a manifestation. The ebb and flow of sentiments, the results of success and failure in attaining goals, and the problems of coordination and cooperation among movement organizations are treated. The purpose of the first section is to show how the transformation of MOs is conditioned or determined by factors outside of itself. The second, briefer, section focuses to a greater extent on internal processes related to goals and commitment. There we discuss two topics, the causes of factionalism and schismogenesis and the relation of leadership to organizational transformation.

Environment and Organization

The environment of MOs consists of two major segments. One segment is the broader social movement, which consists of potential supporters— members and financial backers and other movement-organizations. The people who identify with the movement represent the potential support base for the organization. The other major segment of the environment is the society in which the social movement exists. The larger society may contain the target structures or norms which the movement organization wishes to change; but even in cases where the MO's goal is to change individuals, members or not, the larger society affects the MO because the attitudes and norms of the larger society affect the readiness of movement sympathizers to become members, and the readiness of members to participate fully.

There are at least three interrelated aspects of the environment of MOs that critically affect both their growth and transformation. Changing conditions in the society increase or decrease the potential support base of an MO; there is an ebb and flow of supporting sentiments. Second, the society may change in the direction of organizational goals, or events may clearly indicate that goals will not be attained; the possibilities of success or failure sharply influence member and potential member sentiments and attachments. Third, MOs exist in an environment with other organizations aimed at rather similar goals. Similarity of goals causes an uneasy alliance but also creates the conditions for interorganizational competition.

The Ebb and Flow of Sentiments

Any MO is dependent on the readiness for mobilization of potential supporters. This readiness is dependent on the ebb and flow of sentiments toward an organization, which in turn is a function of at least two major variables: (1) the extent to which there are large numbers of people who feel the MO's goals and means are in harmony with their own; and (2) the extent to which groups and organizations in the larger society feel neutral toward, reject, or accept the legitimacy and value of the social movement and its organizational manifestations. The attitudes in the larger society toward the movement and the MO condition the readiness of potential supporters to become actual supporters.

The difference between the ebb and flow of sentiment for a *social movement* and for a given MO has important consequences for organizational growth. Under some conditions there may be a strong sentiment base—at the same time that there is strong hostility to a particular organization in the society. "Front" organizations are attempts to capitalize on such a situation. The dimensions are partially independent. The ideal condition for organizational growth is obviously a strong sentiment base with low societal hostility towards the movement or its MOs. Periods of great religious revival are characterized by this condition. On the other hand, the more interesting case may be when there is a weak sentiment base or no or low societal interest. A petulant stance and organizational decline as in the Women's Christian Temperance Union may be the consequence.[5]

The processes of change predicted by the Weber-Michels model are thus affected by the organization's relations to its environment. Organizational maintenance and other forms of goal transformation are the outcomes of a struggle to maintain membership in the face of changes in the larger society. The changes in the society that threaten the MO's viability may be either favorable (the goal is achieved and the MO seems to lose its *raison d'etre*) or unfavorable (widespread hostility arises).

However, the ebb and flow of sentiment does not effect organizational transformation at equal rates in all MOs. Two dimensions of movement organization mediate the extent to which MOs are affected by the ebb and flow of sentiments: (1) the extent of membership requirements, both initial and continuing, and (2) the extent to which operative goals are oriented to change of member or individual behavior rather than oriented to societal change. These two dimensions are related to the defining characteristics and recurring problematic foci of MOs stated earlier. Variability in them means that MOs can take a broad variety of organizational forms.

Membership Requirements. The "inclusive" organization requires minimum levels of initial commitment—a pledge of general support without specific duties, a short indoctrination period, or none at all. On the other hand, the "exclusive" organization is likely to hold the new recruit in a long "novitiate" period, to require the recruit to subject himself to organization discipline and orders, and to draw from those having the heaviest initial commitments. When such an organization also has societal goals of changing society it may be called a vanguard party.

Inclusive and exclusive MOs differ not only in recruitment procedures and requirements, but they also differ in the amount of participation required. The inclusive MO typically requires little activity from its members—they can belong to other organizations and groups unselfconsciously, and their behavior is not as permeated by organization goals, policies, and tactics. On the other hand, the exclusive organization not only requires that a greater amount of energy and time be spent in movement affairs, but it more extensively permeates all sections of the member's life, including activities with nonmembers. Any single MO may have attributes of both the inclusive and exclusive organization; even the inclusive movement must have some central cadre.

The ebb and flow of sentiments in the society more markedly affect the inclusive than the exclusive organization. For example, membership figures compiled by Mike Muench (1961) indicate that the Socialist party had a more rapid decline in membership than the Socialist Worker's party during the McCarthy era, and a more rapid rise following the Irish peril. This despite the fact that the SWP's ideology was more left-wing and more subject to charges of un-Americanism. (The Communist party had an exclusive orientation and declined greatly, but it was under heavier and more direct attack than the other two.)

The inclusive MO's membership declines and rises faster than that of the exclusive's because competing values and attitudes are more readily mobilized in the inclusive organization. While members of both organizations may have similar goals, the members of inclusive organizations are more likely to be subjected to conflicts in the face of threats or in the face of competing social movements that appeal to other values. Their allegiances to other groups and values lead them to rather switch than fight.

Changing Individual and Member Behavior Versus Changing Society.[6] In many ways, as has often been noted, the religious sect and the vanguard party have much in common and, in our terms, are both exclusive organizations. The separation from other roles or positions, the total allegiance and discipline, the messianic vision are parallel phenomena. But a key distinction is their strategy for attaining fundamental goals: What are they trying to accomplish in the here and now? Some MOs, especially those with religious affiliations, have as operative goals the changing of individuals.[7] As such, they *may be* less threatening to dominant values and other institutions. At least to the extent that operative goals are restricted to membership proselytization and are not relevant to control of institutional centers, to political action, or to central societal norms, counterpressures are less likely to be brought to bear on them. Furthermore, the commitment of members in this type of movement organization is less dependent on the external success of the organization. Commitment is based to a greater extent on solidary and/or expressive incentives than on purposive incentives.

Of course, the growth of religious sects is related to the ebb and flow of sentiment in the society. But it is possible that once recruits are gained, the organization can maintain its members. First, focusing on member change, the sect may threaten the society less, calling forth fewer punishments for belonging. (In a theocratic state, however, the religious sect would be a direct challenge to the larger society.) Second, if the sect is not milleniastic, it is not subject to the problems of success and failure in the environment. Therefore, the rate of attrition is likely to be a function of the life careers of members rather than of wide swings in societal attitudes affecting members. Third, the organization that attempts to change individuals, especially its own members, is less constrained by the definitions of reality of the broader society.

Proposition 1: The size of the organizational potential support base, the amount of societal interest in the social movement and its MOs, and the direction of that interest (favorable, neutral, or hostile) directly affect the ability of the organization to survive and/or grow.

Proposition 2: The more insulated an organization is by exclusive membership requirements and goals aimed at changing individuals, the less susceptible it is to pressures for organizational maintenance or general goal transformation.

Interorganizational Competition: The Press to Left and Right

Thus far our discussion of the ebb and flow of sentiment has been presented as if within a social movement there was consensus on goals and tactics. However, there may be many definitions of proper goals and tactics and these may shift over time. Competition among MOs for support requires them to be responsive to these differences and to shifts in sentiment towards goals and tactics. It is our thesis that these shifts are a major determinant of the transformation of organizational goals.

The major thrust of the iron law of oligarchy deals with the internal bureaucratization of MOs; officials gain a vested interest in maintaining their positions and in having a stable and nonconflictive relation to the society. In the process of accommodating to the society, the goals of the MO become watered down. Over time, the prediction runs, MOs shift to moderate goals or even to goals of maintaining the status quo. But the competition for support among movement organizations leads to shifts in goals which may be towards the center, but *which may also be towards the extremes.*

In *An Economic Theory of Democracy,* Anthony Downs (1957, pp. 115-27) argues that in a two-party, issue-oriented political system, there are strong pressures to make the difference between parties minimal. If the parties are relatively well balanced, movement away from the center of the distribution of attitudes by one party means loss of votes to the other party and, therefore, loss of the election. The competition is for election, not directly for long-range goals. Only if there are large pools of abstaining and alienated voters at the extremes, does a movement away from the center promise greater support than a movement towards the center. The notion of the distribution of sentiments in social movements permits an analysis similar to that of Downs.

This analysis uses as its example the case of the civil rights movement. Consider the situation before the Supreme Court's school desegregation ruling in 1954. The goals and tactics of the Urban League and the NAACP were in agreement with most active supporters of the movement. However, the number of actives was relatively small, and there were large segments of the potential supporters who were not active at all—college and high school students, working-class Negroes (in both the North and South), and the clergy. After 1954 and especially after the Montgomery bus strike in 1958, the sentiment base of the movement changed—there was an increased readiness for mobilization of potential adherents, adherents expected more rapid change in a wider range of areas, and tactics acceptable to adherents became more militant. Furthermore, new or previously marginal organizations, such as CORE and SNCC, began to compete for support of the enlarged potential support base. As a response both to the new opportunities for change presented by the society *and* the competition from other organizations, the stance of such organizations as the NAACP and the National Urban League became more radical. Failure to respond to these pressures would have led to either a smaller relative support base and/or a less prominent role in the leadership of the civil rights movement.

This analysis is, of course, too simple. It ignores cleavages within movements; for instance, in the case of the civil rights movement differences in sentiment can be found between financial backers and between members of the same organizations, between class groups and generations. Furthermore, it ignores the polarization processes whereby the growth of intense attitudes on the Left generates a large number of people with intense attitudes on the Right. Lastly, it ignores the very complex problem of the competition and interaction of organizations with different primary goals that draw from the same pool of supporters—for instance, SANE, NAACP, and ACLU. Nevertheless, the essential point is clear.

Proposition 3: Goal and tactic transformation of MO is directly tied to the ebb and flow of sentiments within a social movement. The interorganizational competition for support leads to a transformation of goals and tactics.

Failure and Success in Achieving Goals[8]

The first problem of MOs is to gain support. But, an MO, like any organization, must have a payoff to its supporters. Aside from the joys of participation, its major payoff is in the nature of a promise; its goals or at least some of them must appear to have a reasonable chance of attainment. In a sense, the perfectly stable MO that avoided problems of organizational transformation, goal displacement, and the like would be one which over time always seemed to be getting closer to its goal without quite attaining it.

An MO succeeds when its objective is attained; an MO is becalmed when, after achieving some growth and stability, its goals are still relevant to the society but its chances of success have become dim; an MO fails when the society has decisively rejected the goals of the organization and the MO as an instrument is discredited. Although the sources of the change in MO status differ in the three cases, in all three cases incentives to participate decline and the survival of the organization is threatened. Survival depends, partially, on the ability of the MO to muster solidary, material, or secondary goal incentives.

Success

There are various kinds of movement success. At the very least, one must distinguish between the actual attainment of goals and the assumption of power assumed to be a prerequisite to attaining goals. The analysis of the transformation of the MO ends when it or the movement it represents accedes to power; at that point, analytic concepts applicable to party structure and governmental bureaucracy become more relevant. The operating dilemmas of MOs that have assumed power have been well described by S. M. Lipset (1950). The organization in power is limited by its coalition dependencies—its links to other organizations; it is limited by a range of variables outside of its control, such as the general state of world economy; it is limited by lack of experience and competence, by its dependency on the holdover office holders; and whereas incentives were earlier of a purposive and idealistic sort, now material incentives become the rule of the day—the organization loses its romantic idealism.

But what happens when the goals of the MO are actually reached; what happens when a law is enacted, a disease is eradicated (for instance, women get suffrage, the threat of infantile paralysis is drasticallly reduced), or social conditions change, thus eliminating the ostensible purpose of the organization? Two major outcomes are possible: new goals can be established maintaining the organization or the MO can go out of existence.

The establishment of new goals to perpetuate the organization is more likely to occur if: (1) the MO has its own member and fund-raising support base, or (2) there are solidary of short-run material incentives that bind members to each other or to the organization. In order to continue obtaining such rewards, the members support a new goal. It must be noted that lacking such support, the organization leaders cannot maintain the organization. It is not the existence of bureaucratic structure and office holders per se that guarantees continuance, if the rank and file or the contributors do not share the desire to continue the organization.

In some cases, however, solidary and material incentives alone become sufficient to hold the allegiance of some of the members. This is the extreme case of a shift to organizational maintenance. Such an organization can hardly be classified as a part of social movement, since it has abandoned both defining characteristics—purposive incentives and change goals. The remains of the Townsend movement represent such an ex-MO. The New Deal and old-age pensions cut away much of its programs and goals. But its solidary incentives, minimal membership requirements, and material resources from the sale of geriatric products allowed it to maintain itself, albeit at a minimum level of functioning (Messinger, 1955).

Several propositions about the relation of organizational change to success follow:

Proposition 4: MOs created by other organizations are more likely to go out of existence following success than MOs with their own linkages to individual supporters.

Proposition 5: MOs with relatively specific goals are more likely to vanish following success than organizations with broad general goals.

Proposition 6: MOs that aim to change individuals and employ solidary incentives are less likely to vanish than are MOs with goals aimed at changing society and employing mainly purposive incentives.

Proposition 7: Inclusive organizations are likely to fade away faster than exclusive organizations; the latter are more likely to take on new goals.

(These predictions apply to the failing as well as to the successful MO.)

The Movement Becalmed

Many MOs do not represent either successes or failures. They have been able to build and maintain a support base; they have waged campaigns that have influenced the course of events; and they have gained some positions of power. In short, they have created or found a niche for themselves in the organizational world but their growth has slowed down or ceased. Members do not expect attainment of goals in the near future, and the emotional fervor of the movement is subdued. As in the case of the successful organization, it is the existence of extra-purposive incentives that is a fundamental condition for maintaining the organization.

However, the goals of the MO are still somewhat relevant to society. Thus, the organization is able to maintain purposive commitment and avoids losing all of its purposively oriented members to competing causes.

It is such a becalmed movement that is most susceptible to processes predicted by the Weber-Michels model. First, the lack of any major successes produces periodic bouts of apathy among the members. Membership is maintained, but attrition takes place over time and no new blood is attracted. Second, leadership becomes complacent, resting on its control of material incentives. The leaders' control over access to such material rewards increases their power, perhaps to the point of oligarchization. Third, the leaders become more conservative, because the pursuit of the MO's initially more radical goals might endanger the organizations' occupation of secure niches by provoking societal and, perhaps, members' hostility, consequently endangering the power of the leaders and their access to material rewards.

Proposition 8: A becalmed movement is most likely to follow the Weber-Michels model because its dependence on and control of material incentives allows oligarchization and conservatism to take place.

Failure

Where the successful organization loses members because it has nothing to do, the failing MO loses members because they no longer believe their goals can be achieved with that instrument. The leadership cadre may attempt to redefine goals and to define external reality as favorable to the organization; nevertheless members are usually not fully shielded from societal reality and have independent checks on the possibility of attaining goals.

An MO may also fail because its legitimacy as an instrument may be discredited. Discreditation may happen rapidly or may take several years. Central to the discreditation process is the MO's inability to maintain legitimacy even in the eyes of its supporters. Discreditation comes because of organizational tactics employed in the pursuit of goals. For instance, many moderate organizations have lost support when they appeared to accept support from extremist groups. The consequences of failure are not discussed by scholars using the Weber-Michels model.

One consequence of the failure of an MO is the search for new instruments. Where the member leaving a successful movement may either search for new goals and social movements or lapse in quiescence, different alternatives seem to be open to members leaving the failing organization: either they search for a more radical means to achieve their goals within the movement, decrease the importance of their goals, or change the focus of discontent. A Mertonian analysis of anomie might be relevant to this point.

Interaction Among Movement Organizations

Under some conditions the tactics of an MO in attempting to succeed or avoid failure involve it in direct interaction and coordination with other organizations from the same social movement. Above we discussed competition among MOs, but our analysis did not focus on direct interaction and exchange. Here, in our last topic under the heading of the relation of MOs to their environment, we discuss of mergers and other aspects of inter-MO relations. Such relations could be treated as an organizational outcome. But we are chiefly concerned with how interaction affects member commitment and ultimately the goals of the involved organizations.

We distinguish three types of interaction: cooperation, coalition, and merger. Typically, cooperation between MOs is limited. Except during full-scale revolutions or total movement activities, MOs do not engage in a complex division of labor. It occurs primarily in situations where special competencies are required for legislative lobbying or legal work, and a simple symbiotic relationship may develop that does not lead to transformation in either organization.

More interesting are the creation of coalitions and mergers (Duverger, pp. 281-351) for here the interaction may lead to new organizational identities, changes in the membership base, and changes in goals. The coalition pools resources and coordinates plans, while keeping distinct organizational identities. It will take place if it promises greater facilities, financial aid, or attainment of goals. Thus, coalitions are more likely when MOs appear to be close to the goal than at other times, for then the costs of investing in the coalition seem small in comparison with the potential benefits.[9]

Some coalitions resemble mergers in that only one organization retains an identity. However, within the MO the old MOs retain identities and allegiances. Such coalition-mergers are most likely to take place when there is one indivisible position or reward at stake (e.g., one governor or president can be elected, one law is required).

Each organization then may have a distinct role in the overall plan of attack. The coalesced organization is ruled through a committee or umbrella organization. Such an organization may be riven by factional positional jockeying if the leadership is not fully committed to the coalition. Furthermore, not all MOs are equally capable of mergers or coalitions. The level of outgroup distrust and the unlikelihood of shared perspectives make it difficult for an exclusive MO to participate in mergers or coalitions.

A merger or coalition leads to a search for a common denominator to which both parties can agree. The more conservative party to the merger finds itself with more radical goals and vice versa. The goals of the more conservative party can remain nearly the same only if both organizations are trying to persuade a broader and even more conservative public.[10]

A true merger leads to the suppression of previous organizational identities. Because of the likelihood that the basic stance of the MOs involved will change, a true merger does not necessarily broaden the support base for its program. The more conservative members of the conservative partner and the more radical members of the radical partner may find that the goals (or tactics) of the newly formed organization are no longer congenial. Both extremes drop away. Furthermore, now only one organization speaks for the movement, whereas before several voices clamored for change. The merging of movement organizations may make the movement appear smaller from the outside.

Since true mergers may have such potentially drastic effects on the support base, it is possible that they only occur when the leadership of one or both MOs feel their cause is lost, there is growing apathy, or the like. Then the merger appears as a way of preserving some vestige of vitality.[11]

Proposition 9: Inclusive MOs are more likely than exclusive MOs to participate in coalitions and mergers.

Proposition 10: Coalitions are most likely to occur if the coalition is more likely to achieve goals or lead to a larger resource base—when success is close or when one indivisible goal or position is at stake.

Internal Processes and Organizational Transformation

All of the topics discussed in the previous section have dealt with the effects of external events or problems on the growth and change of movement organizations. However, external events are not the only causes of change. Emerging bureaucratic structures, internal ideological factions, leadership styles, and other, essentially internal factors, also cause organizational transformation. Here we focus on MO factions and on leadership changes.

When discussing external factors the task of separating dependent from independent variables was relatively simple. The effects of the environment are mediated through membership recruitment, requirements, and incentives, or through the organizational structure, and ultimately affect goals. But here we deal with the influence of internal variables on each other; the cause and effect sequences cease to be analytically (much less empirically) distinct; vicious circles as well as causal chains are possible. Consequently we can no longer so clearly distinguish goals as our dependent variable. However, we still offer alternatives to the Weber-Michels model and point to a broader range of organizational outcomes.

Factions and Splits

Schismogenesis and factionalization have received but little attention from sociologists.[12] A faction is an identifiable subgroup opposed to other subgroups; a split occurs when a faction leaves an MO. There are two major internal preconditions for splits and the development of factions: heterogeneity of social base and the doctrinal basis of authority.

The role of heterogeneity in creating conditions for organizational splitting needs little discussion. H. Richard Niebuhr's (1929) discussion of the role of class and ethnic factions in denominationalism remains the classic statement of the need for internal homogeneity in an MO with no ultimate and accepted internal authority. Consciousness of kind and the solidary incentives gained from homogeneity lead to the development of schisms.

What is true for religious sects and denominations is also true for political MOs. The early history of the American Communist party, as described by Theodore Draper (1957), was marked by fights based on disputes between the Left and the Right and connected to the European (particularly, Dutch, Lettish, and German) versus American base of the party. In this case, factions within the party were only finally suppressed by the use of the great external authority and legitimacy of the true revolutionaries, the Bolsheviks.

Factions and schisms occur not only because of the heterogeneity of an MO's support base, but also because of concern with doctrinal purity. MOs concerned with questions of ultimate ideological truth and with theoretical matters are more likely to split than MOs linked to bread and butter issues. It is not concern with ideology per se that is central to this proposition, but rather that ideological concerns lead to questioning the bases of organizational authority and the behavior of the leadership. Miller (1963) has argued that the difference between Catholic sects that remained in the church and those which left depended on the acceptance of the ultimate authority of the Word as revealed in the Bible, and interpreted by the Fathers of the Church, versus the word of contemporary church authorities: The Montanists of second-century Phrygia and the Feeneyites of twentieth-century Boston both rested their authority on the former and left the church, whereas St. Francis bowed to the latter.

Unless the nonreligious movement organization possesses the prestige of success and material incentives, as did the Bolsheviks in relation to the American Communist party, the bases for authority are difficult to establish. In this respect, the inclusive organization with its looser criteria of affiliation and of doctrinal orthodoxy is more split-resistant than the exclusive organization. The inclusive organization retains its factions while the exclusive organization spews them forth. Given internal dissension, it may be that the inclusive organization retains its support base, but is crippled in its capacity for concerted action. Splitting, of course, leads to a decrease in membership in the orginal movement organization. For a short period of time, at least, it leads to higher internal consistency and consensus. As such, it may also transform organizational goals away from a conservative or organizational maintenance position, for the remaining remnant is not encumbered by the need to compromise.

Proposition 11: The less the short-run chances of attaining goals, the more solidary incentives act to separate the organization into homogeneous subgroups—ethnic, class, and generational.[13] *As a corollary, to the extent that a becalmed or failing MO is heterogeneous and must rely heavily on solidary incentives, the more likely it is to be beset by factionalism.*

Proposition 12: The more the ideology of the MO leads to a questioning of the basis of authority, the greater the likelihood of factions and splitting.

Proposition 13: Exclusive organizations are more likely than inclusive organizations to be beset by schisms.

Leadership and Movement Transformation

Initially we suggested that the Weber-Michels model is a subcase of a more general set of concepts explaining MO transformation. Using such concepts as the ebb and flow of sentiments, potential and actual support base, membership requirements, incentives, and goals, we have attempted to explain a number of organizational processes. In simplified terms, the Weber-Michels model predicts changes in organizations stemming from changes in leadership positions and leadership behavior; it also predicts what organizational changes lead to changes in organizational behavior. If our more general approach is to be of value, it must be able to deal with the same problems.

Analysis of leadership phenomena are an even more crucial aspect of the study of an MO than of other large-scale organizations. Because the situation of the MO is unstable, because the organization has few material incentives under its control, and because of the nonroutinized nature of its tasks, the success or failure of the MO can be highly dependent on the qualities and commitment of the leadership cadre and the tactics they use (Blumer and Lee, 1955). Three aspects of leader-organization relations are discussed: the organizational transformation following the demise of a founding father, the factors affecting the commitment of leaders to goals, and the consequences for the organization of differences in leadership style.

The Replacement of Charisma

Following the death of a charismatic leader, several changes in an MO can be expected. But the more bureaucratized the MO the less the replacement of a leader causes organizational transformation. Three kinds of change are likely in the less bureaucratized MOs.

First, there is likely to be a decline in membership and in audience as those drop away whose commitment was more to the man than to the organizational goal and sentiment base. Furthermore, we would expect the outer circle of those who were weakly committed to drop away first.

Secondly, the death of a charismatic leader can lead to factionalization. The divergent tendencies of subgroups and the power struggles of lieutenants may have only been suppressed by the authority of the leader. His "word" now becomes one ideological base for intraorganization debate as the factions seek their place in the distribution of reward and the definition of goals and tactics (Lipset, 1960, pp. 412-16).

Finally, there occurs the professionalization of the executive core and the increased attempts to rationalize the administrative structure of the organization that is heir to the charismatic leader's own organization. The routinization of charisma is not only an institutionalization and rationalization of the goals and guiding myths of the organization but also a change in the incentive base of the organization—from gratifications related to the mythic stature of the leader and the opportunity to participate with him to the gratifications afforded by the performance of ritual and participation in a moral cause. Rationalization also produces a routinization of material incentives.[14]

Proposition 14: Routinization of charisma is likely to conservatize the dominant core of the movement organization while simultaneously producing increasingly radical splinter groups.

Goal Commitment of Leaders

More relevant to the Michels argument than the problems discussed above are the organizational changes attendant on officers' increased attachment to their offices and perquisites. While attachment to office may lead leaders to be more interested in organizational maintenance than pursuit of goals, organizational maintenance seems to displace radical goals following the creation of a bureaucratic structure only under three prerequisite conditions: (1) a base of support independent of membership sentiment; in labor unions the payroll checkoff insures a constant flow of funds and permits the leadership to remain in office and to replace the original goals of the MO (the union) by the goal of clinging to their own relatively lucrative offices. (2) The commitment of leaders (and followers) to other goals—to social position, to a stable life, to a family (as Jesus Christ recognized); leadership concern with the maximization of non-MO goals is a major cause of decline in intensity in any organization (Gouldner, 1947). (3) The co-optation of leaders by other groups with subsequent transformation of goals; co-optation is the most extreme result of what Gusfield terms "articulating leadership." The growth of "statesmanship" in labor unions is one example of articulating leadership producing changes in goals and tactics of an MO (Gusfield, 1966).

However, none of these three conditions is in itself sufficient to produce a long-range change in goals or tactics. A necessary precondition for leaders to become concerned with organizational maintenance is a change in member sentiment—a growing lack of interest.

Under some conditions, however, a decline in member interest may actually allow a movement to grow more radical. As members permit other concerns to tempt them away from the MO, they insist less on their right to participate in decision making. The decision-making apparatus of the organization thus falls into the hands of the persons with the greatest commitment to the movement goals. In some cases, these persons actually form a cadre of professional organizers. As the MO becomes oligarchical, contrary to Michels, it may become *more* rather than less radical in its goals.[15]

Proposition 15: If a leadership cadre is committed to radical goals to a greater extent than the membership-at-large, member apathy and oligarchical tendencies lead to greater rather than less radicalism.

Leadership Style

Gusfield (1966) distinguishes between the articulation function of leaders and the mobilizing function. In brief, mobilization refers to reaffirming the goals and values of the organization and building member commitment to the goals, while articulation means linking the organization and its tactics to those of other organizations and to the larger society. There is an almost inherent dualism and conflict between these roles, for mobilization requires a heightening of the ideological uniqueness of the MO and the absolute quality of its goals, while articulation often requires the uniqueness of the organization to be toned down and an adoption of the tactics of compromise. In the simple interpretation of the Weber-Michels model, mobilization is followed by articulating leadership style. And at a much later date, when organizational needs changed, more articulation followed the retirement of a mobilizing leader.

Not only is the notion of a simple and inevitable progression from mobilizing to articulating a false notion of leadership transformation, but different kinds of MOs make different demands on leaders. For instance, the exclusive organization is restricted in its possibilities of articulation.

Proposition 16: An exclusive organization is almost certain to have a leadership that focuses on mobilizing membership for tasks, while the inclusive organization is readier to accept an articulating leadership style.

Proposition 17: The MO oriented to individual change is likely to have a leadership focused on mobilizing sentiments, not articulating with the larger society. Organizations oriented to changing the larger society are more likely to require both styles of leadership, depending on the stage of their struggle.

Conclusions: The Relation of Goals and Structure

While there is often an association between growing institutionalization and bureaucratization *and* conservatism, there is no evidence that this is a *necessary* association. Instead it is a function of the cases examined and the frame of reference with which scholars have approached the study of social movement organization. In particular, many of the studies of movement organization have been conducted out of a "metaphysical pathos" of the social democratic Left (Gouldner, 1955). Left-leaning scholars have noted that the radical organizations of their youth have changed their goals and structure. The concepts they employed or which "caught on" both summarized the movement's trend *and* implied the emotional evaluation of the trend. In this chapter we have attempted to work out of a relatively neutral frame of reference to account for organizational transformation. Furthermore, we have used a fairly general approach and set of concepts which, we think, allow us to examine the transformation of any MO, whatsoever.

To briefly recapitulate, we have examined the impact of a number of internal and external processes on the transformation of MOs. By examining the ebb and flow of sentiments and incentives available to organizations and interrelating these with the structural requirements for membership and the nature of organizational goals, two crucial analytic factors, we have made predictions about how different movement organizations will grow and decline and in what direction their goals will change. We have paid less attention to the internal authority structure, although it would be relatively easy to incorporate such analysis into our framework. We see one of the main advantages of our approach as raising to the center of sociological analysis a number of phenomena that have only rarely been at the center.

For instance, the problems of mergers, of factions and schisms, of alternating leadership styles, and of interorganizational competition all deserve greater attention than they have been given.

Our focus has been on organizational change and we have examined the sequence from the environment and sentiment base to goals and structure rather than from goals *to* structure. But the organizational leadership's commitment to a set of goals may also influence the structure. In some cases, goal commitment can act as a deterrent to the process of bureaucratization. To implement the more radical goals, an appropriate structure can be imposed on the organization: Members must invest more time and effort, sometimes to the point of professionalization; members are recruited from groups that have low commitment to a family or a career; workers are paid little and are frequently transferred to prevent attachment to the material rewards of office, and to prevent the creation of local support or empire building; the MO has a localized branch or even a cell structure with frequent meetings. In short, the militant MO is given a quasi-exclusive structure not only to implement goals, but also to maintain them in the face of pressures to become more conservative. The organization of CORE and SNCC illustrate some of these structural devices against goal displacement.

In focusing on change of organization we may have introduced our own metaphysical pathos; we have not looked at the other side of the coin, organizational stability, although the conditions are often the obverse of those discussed for change. However, some differences would enter in. For instance, Gusfield (1957) has discussed the problem of generations in the WCTU. There, the circulation of elites in an organization is related to the rate of growth and the organization's relation to the larger social movement as well as to internal structural and constitutional conditions. As a general problem, the problem of stability can be encompassed within our framework.

We have proposed some general hypotheses specifying conditions of membership, goal type, success and failure, environmental conditions, and leadership that determine the extent and nature of the change of organizational goals. We have illustrated our propositions, but illustration is not proof. What is now needed is a systematic testing of the propositions, using large numbers of historical and contemporary case studies—in short, a comparative analysis of social movement organizations.

Notes

This chapter is a revised version of a paper originally read at the annual meeting of the Institute for Social Research, Chicago, May 1964. It grew out of courses taught jointly by the senior author with David Street and, at an earlier time, Arthur Stinchcombe. It also grew out of a study of change in the Young Men's Christian Association of Metropolitan Chicago supported by the National Institutes of Health (GM-10777) USPHS. We have benefited greatly from critical readings by Mike Muench, Norman Miller, Joseph Gusfield, Eugene Weinstein, and Thomas Smith.

1. Although Michels' iron law of oligarchy was originally applied to political parties of the Left, while Weber's routinization of charisma referred to a more general process, both deal with the adaptation and subsequent accommodation of social movements to the society. We treat them as one general line of analysis. Weber stresses the process of rationalization of organizational structure to a greater extent than does Michels. For any single organization, Weber is more concerned with internal processes than is Michels, who focuses more on goals.

2. In academic courses, the study of social movements for a long time has been the province of collective behavior courses. The sociological approach to organizations utilized here helps to bridge the gap between organizational analysis and collective behavior. Essentially, this chapter deals with a particular type of complex organization, the social movement organization. Although many textbooks on collective behavior deal with the organization of social movements none that we know of use organizational analysis to systematically account for the transformation of movement organizations. See Neil Smelser (1963) and Kurt Lang and Gladys Lang (1961). C. Wendell King (1956) uses a combination of a natural history approach and organizational analysis in accounting for the transformation of movement organization.

3. The notions of incentive structure used in this work are based on those of Peter B. Clark and James Q. Wilson. Briefly, three major types of incentives can be offered by organizations to harness individuals to organizational tasks: material (money and goods) incentives; solidary incentives (prestige, respect, friendship); and purposive incentives (value fulfillment). Although any organization may be able to offer all three, different types of organizations have more of one than the other to offer.

4. Of course, if members devalue material incentives or have independent access to them and if organizational goals represent central life interests of members, gaining and maintaining membership commitment represents less of an organizational problem. In a very different context, V. I. Lenin (1929) recognized that the central problem of movement organization is gaining and maintaining commitment. Where most people think of organizational structure as pyramidal, Lenin described structure in terms of concentric circles of lessening commitment and participation. Arthur Stinchcombe first drew our attention to this point.

5. The effect of attitudes of the larger society towards social movements on members' ideology, self-perception, and on organizational tactics and structure has been discussed by Ralph K. Turner (1964).

6. Our distinction follows that of Lang and Lang (1961, p. 488) who, following Sighele, distinguished between "inward and outward" movement organizations.

7. In the case of the temperance movement both the movement and its MOs had both goals at different points in time. See Joseph Gusfield (1963).

8. Success or failure in goal attainment effects the ebb and flow of sentiment toward the social movement and its organizations. We treat the topic separately

because (1) it represents a determinant of the ebb and flow of sentiment, not just a dependent consequence; (2) success or failure may be the result of organizational activity, whereas we have been treating the ebb and flow of sentiment as to a great extent being a resultant of the conditions in the larger society; (3) success or failure may question the validity of a given organization regardless of the sentiment for the social movement; and (4) because we have a lot to say about it.

9. By and large, mergers and coalitions require ideological compatibility. Although extremist parties from both sides may work for the overthrow of the government (as in the Weimar Republic, for instance), they usually do not engage in planned coordinated attack. They do not support the center against the other extreme, and they independently work against the established government. For the role of ideological compatibility in coalitions, see William Gamson (1962).

10. Following Osgood and Tannenbaum (1955) one might even argue that the merged movement will be perceived as more extreme than it really is. They hypothesize that if an associative bond is perceived between two objects of evaluation, the object that was originally more neutrally viewed will gain a more extreme evaluation while the extremely viewed object will lose very little of its polarized evaluation.

11. These problems have arisen in the recent attempt to merge two MOs oriented to military disarmament, SANE, and United World Federalists. These two organizations have differed in that the UWF has had historic attachments to the upper class, to Quakers, and to proper institutional types. It has been more educative and persuasive in technique, SANE has had a nervous, more alienated, liberal base, and has used heavier handed propaganda techniques. The proposed merger has been sharply questioned by members.

12. But see Norman Miller (1963). See also a most neglected minor classic by Walter Firey (1948). For a history of the American Socialist experience that focuses on its proneness to factions and splits, see Daniel Bell, (1952).

13. It may be that the relation of splitting and developing factions to chances of attaining goals is curvilinear rather than linear. As movement organizations approach gaining power, latent conflicts over means, ends, and the future distribution of power, which have been suppressed in the general battle, rise to the fore.

14. Analogously, such processes may take place in student and other highly age-graded movements. The graduation of the founding generation parallels the death of the charismatic leader (Goldsmith, 1965).

15. A current example of oligarchization attended by radicalization is the growth of the Berkeley Free Speech Movement, which appears to have begun as a representative coalition of campus groups but developed into a mass movement coordinated by an oligarchical executive committee. The committee was composed of leaders with the strongest commitment to "radical" mass tactics (and also apparently, the most concerned with the ultimate issues of alienation rather than the immediate issue of free speech).

6

From Evangelism to General Services: The Transformation of the YMCA

Mayer N. Zald and *Patricia Denton*

As the environments of organizations change, as the needs or demands of clientele change, organizations must, if they are to persist, be able to adapt goals, structure, and services. Even if they manage to persist despite environmental changes, organizations differ in their direction of change. In the process of organizational operation, some seem to displace original goals, becoming more rigid in operation and detached from their potential membership base—as, for example, in the Townsend movement and the Women's Christian Temperance Union (Messinger, 1955, pp. 3-10; Gusfield, 1955, pp. 221-32; Gusfield, 1957, pp. 323-30). On the other hand, other organizations are able to transform goals without narrowing them, to maintain a high degree of organizational flexibility, and to develop an enlarged membership base, as in the case of the Young Men's Christian Association, one of the most pervasive service organizations in the United States. Starting as an evangelical association for young men, the YMCA has become a general leisure-time and character-development organization found in almost every city (96 percent of cities with a population over 50,000 [Carey, 1959]).

The YMCA has shown a remarkable ability to adapt itself to differing community needs and to expand its membership base to groups previously outside of its purview. Where originally it served only young men, it now serves both sexes and all age groups. And its rate of growth, from about one million members in 1930 to over two and one-half million in 1957, has been faster than that of the population at large (Carey, 1959). At the same time that it has been growing, it has discontinued programs that either did not seem to meet membership needs or were taken over by other agencies. As an organization, then, the YMCA has been growing and adapting; it is a successful organization. Like all organizations, however, the YMCA fills a particular niche in the organizational life of communities. It has tended to have a stronger base in lower-middle-class and middle-class areas than in working-class areas, and it has tended to recruit board members from Protestant elites rather than from other elites. Furthermore, unlike many service organizations that focus on control of deviants or on rehabilitation, the YMCA is largely concerned with developing the skills and character of its members. Here we are interested in examining the features that account for the YMCA's particular niche in American society, as well as the components of organization that contribute to organizational flexibility and growth. This chapter is essentially a study of the transformation and molding of organizational character; it attempts to delineate those characteristics that give the YMCA its distinctive features and shape its mode of response to environmental pressures and change.

After the discussion of the transformation of the YMCA from an evangelistic social movement to a general-service organization, our analysis of organizational operation will be primarily cross-sectional and structural, focusing on four central factors: (1) the dependence of the YMCA on a paying clientele, (2) its federated structure, (3) the YMCA secretary's lack of a highly developed ideology and his dependence on the local board of director, and (4) the legitimation of a wide range of programs and services by broad character-development goals.

History

The key to the successful transformation of the YMCA is the shift from its emphasis on religious proselytization to its emphasis on goals of character development—physical, intellectual, and social, as well as spiritual. Once this change occurred, new programs could be instituted within the framework of these goals and legitimated by them to meet the shifting demands of clientele.

Early History and Expansion

The YMCA was founded in London in 1844 as an evangelical lay organization to convert single young men, who, during the burgeoning period of industrialization and urbanization, were migrating to the city in large numbers.[1] The movement grew rapidly. Within several years, YMCAs were started in Boston and other American cities. Initially, only young men converted to evangelical churches could become members. Soon, however, applicants were allowed to join even if not converted, although the management of the association was reserved to members of evangelical churches.

A few months after the YMCA started, many of its lasting characteristics were already in practice: members paid dues; wealthy businessmen contributed to its support; it was interdenominational; and, at least in England and America, control was reserved to the laity, although ministers might be included on the boards of directors.

Although the causes of the association's expansion are not clear, certain factors stand out. First, the definite Christian orientation of the movement tied it into the religious revivals, as well as the sponsoring of prayer meetings, Bible readings, and lecture series. Thus, the YMCA movement had definite goals and programs that focused its members' energies.

Second, the movement spread by a diffusion process based on local enthusiasm rather than by a process of centralized direction and allocation of personnel. Visitors to the London YMCA or to the early YMCA in Boston became enthusiastic about the idea and took it back to their own communities. This method of expansion depended on strong local support, ensuring a continuing base in each community.

Finally, each local YMCA usually had a reading room, a list of job openings, a coffee shop, and a list of wholesome boarding homes. These sorts of things gave the association a material base in the community and also allowed it to minister to some of the basic needs of the young, single male.

Transformation of the Organization

The question of the transformation of the organization, however, is distinct from that of initial growth and success. The factors facilitating growth may be precisely those that hinder later change. Specifically, the narrowing evangelistic goals of the YMCA that were important to its early success might have, in the increasingly secularized society of the late nineteenth and early twentieth centuries, led to an organizational impasse, cutting the organization off from the mainstream of American life.

Three interrelated trends characterize the successful adaptation of the YMCA to a changing society and consequent new demands by clientele. As we have noted, the basic goal of the organization changed from evangelism to the broader and more secularized one of developing the "whole man";[2] membership criteria were successively broadened to include all religions, ages, and both sexes; and control was extended to followers of any religion.

Within the framework of the new goal, program emphasis shifted away from the overtly religious to the development of the mental, physical, and social capacities of members. The inclusion of activities for physical training created more conflict than programs for mental or intellectual development did, because it challenged conservative religious views of the proper forms of recreation.[3] Their addition, however, is an important indicator of the ability of the YMCA to identify changing clientele needs correctly and to meet them. With increasing leisure time and the decline of physical work in the late nineteenth century, Americans rapidly developed an interest in sports and physical exercise.[4]

From 1860 to about 1900 the emphases on physical development and on general evangelism were both debated issues in many YMCAs, and emphasis on overt or formal religious programs was declining. By 1900 local YMCAs—in America, at least[5]—had begun to reduce their religious services because of the low public response to these programs.[6] In the depression of the thirties, staffing of religious programs was largely eliminated in order to reduce expenses.

The other great transformation of the YMCA—the greater inclusiveness of membership and the extension of participation in control to those who were not members of evangelical churches—also broadened the base of the organization. Inclusion of women in the program dates from the beginning of public lectures, although formal membership was not granted until 1934. In general, the YMCA experienced less difficulty in extending services to other age groups and to women (although competition with the Young Women's Christian Association, a completely separate organization, was a subject for negotiation) than in extending control to others than members of evangelical churches. YMCAs in predominantly Roman Catholic countries began to define evangelical churches as including the Roman Catholic Church; however, in the United States it was not until after 1930 that active membership (that is, voting membership) was extended to Catholics and Jews. Under current interpretations, anyone who believes in the general purpose of the YMCA may participate in policymaking, and a limited number of Jews as well as Catholics serve on the boards of directors of various YMCAs.[7]

How can we account for this general broadening of goals and greater inclusiveness of membership and control groups? The transformation of membership criteria is easily understood. Originally restricted to young men in order to meet the common interests of the large number of single men living in the cities at the time of its inception, the YMCA, unlike some other men's social groups, was not created as a refuge from women; nor were its evangelistic activities limited to men. Extension of service to women and to other age groups allowed the organization to broaden its scope of operation. Greater inclusiveness of membership was clearly in the interest of the controlling groups of the YMCA who wished to see its growth. Less clear, however, are those elements of organizational structure that permitted and fostered change in control and, most important, in the scope of programs.

The basic organizational conditions that allowed the organization to transform its evangelical goals seems to have been its interdenominational character and its control by laymen rather than clergy. Neither church organization nor clerical ideology constrained the direction of organizational change. If the YMCA had been dominated by a single denomination, it probably would have been absorbed into it.[8] Also, since both its staff and directors were not members of the clergy, considerations of church policy and theology were less important than if the organization had been controlled by clergymen. Laymen committed to the organization and to its general Christian goals were free to assess the societal changes and concomitant practical needs that could be met by the organization.

Constant Elements in Organizational Operation

Although the YMCA has experienced radical transformation during its 100-year history, there are several constant elements in its operation: it has avoided political embroilments, and its services have been preventive rather than rehabilitative. Ever since controversy arose over the appearance of proabolition speakers on the YMCA podium, the YMCA, especially at the local level, has supported a policy of avoiding controversial problems not directly defined as relevant to its character-building goals. Whereas the YMCA has always defined its mission as more contingent on social reform, actively pursuing the solution of such problems as race relations, the YMCA has generally implemented its goals by serving clientele rather than by attempting to change the environment. In part, this approach is historically based on its origin as a membership association rather than as a charitable institution. Hopkins (1950, p. 6) asserts that both in its inception and continuing practice, the YMCA has been guided by people of the white-collar classes to help members of their own class. Although this assertion is partly true, many members of the YMCA have subscribed to social gospel and noblesse oblige notions of reform. The YMCA has actively contributed to relief for the needy, through the distribution of food and clothing, and to the incorporation of immigrant masses through its Americanization and language classes. Ideas of social gospel and social reform springing from the organization's basic Christian identification are ever-present, but subordinated, forces for charitable and rehabilitative work.

The policy of political noninvolvement and of a preventive program is related, as will be shown, to elements of organizational structure, specifically to the federated relationship among associations, to control of the organization by a lay elite, and to an "enrollment economy." The discussion of organizational structure and operation that follows draws heavily on elements suggested in our historical review.

Organizational Structure and Operation

Effect of Transformation on Program and Clientele

The transformation of organization goals and criteria for membership has had important consequences for the program and the clientele of the organization. The YMCA's explicit purpose of character development limits the organization in only two ways—it must attempt to help people develop, rather than merely to sell them services, and it must help them develop along socially approved lines. Broadly stated goals permit wide diversification and are conducive to organizational flexibility. These goals encourage the use of varied means. Any program is encouraged that "helps people to develop." Programs have ranged from athletic activities to bridge and dancing classes, club programs for adolescents, and residence rooms for single men and women. To support typical programs, the YMCA must provide only supervisory staff and such rather general facilities as meeting rooms or gymnasiums, which can be used for other programs.

The breadth of YMCA programs can be further understood in the light of the organization's dependence on a paying clientele. Because of its enrollment economy,[9] programs are instituted and discontinued according to membership demands. In meeting clientele needs the YMCA has included, in its definition of character development, courses that help people advance in their jobs, such as courses in typing, supervision, and human relations. The statement of goals in Christian terms, however, has lent continuity to the organization as it changed programs, and justified to staffs and boards an expenditure of time and energy even when such expenditure was financially unrewarding. Moreover, Christian purposes give the organization a basic legitimacy, which purely secular organizations often cannot claim.

The transformation of membership criteria is another factor in the YMCA's flexibility. The broad goals of character development do not specify a market with respect to age or sex, permitting the organization to adapt its programs to the composition of the population and the competing services of the local community. For example, if other agencies serve youth, or if there are few youths in the community, the YMCA can serve older people. Since 1940, the number of women in the organization has quintupled (see Table 1). Moreover, the number of young men between eighteen and thirty years of age who are members has been decreasing, both relatively and absolutely, for over three decades. Much soul searching among YMCA staffs has accompanied this decline, which signifies the loss of a goal-defining target population. The decline may be attributed to the fact that young men are no longer as isolated in large cities, or to a decrease in their interest in religion. Whatever the explanation, the important point is that the YMCA has been able to expand its membership without this group.

We have already noted that its goals and enrollment economy tend to make the YMCA a general-service organization for the middle class, or at least the more integrated members of the society. This tendency is reinforced by an organizational structure that ties the local YMCA closely to the wishes of the local governing body and the local clientele. Both the flexibility and the limitation of YMCA organizations are based on its federated structure, the relationship of local elites to professional staff, and its financial base. When these factors, contributing to strong control from the local community, are related to the problem of managing membership sentiment, we can see the constraints tying the organization to an essentially middle-class and preventive orientation.

Federated Structure

Spreading from community to community by a diffusion process, local YMCAs have been outgrowths of community action rather than imposed or created from outside. Structurally, the stress has been on local autonomy.

Five levels of organization exist: the local association, the metropolitan association, the area council, the National Council, and the World Council. In smaller communities the YMCA is locally controlled and operated. In a metropolitan area, even though buildings are likely to be owned by the metropolitan association rather than by the local department or branch, strong emphasis is placed on the autonomy of the individual branch (department) and staff. Furthermore, the National Association and its staff are supported by dues paid by the local associations, and members of the National Council are elected, not appointed. Executive staff members of the local YMCA are appointed by the local board of directors. Thus, though uniform professional standards have been established (a national records system is operated, personnel files are circulated, and national aims are formulated), the local community sharply constrains organizational policy.

The federated system with its emphasis on local autonomy has ideological support. Around the turn of the century, there was intense conflict between the local associations and the International Committee (the then-dominant national organization) (Dedmon, 1957, pp. 147-56). In a series of meetings, the faction pressing for local autonomy and control prevailed. Related to its Protestant origins, the YMCA ideology stresses the importance of maintaining a self-governing association.

TABLE 6.1
Membership of Men and Women in the YMCA, 1930-60, by Age (in Percent).*

Year	Total member- ship	Under 12 yrs.	12–17 yrs.	18–29 yrs.	30 yrs. and up
Men					
1930	1,034,109	8.0	22.4	46.3	23.3
1940	1,224,410	12.7	28.4	34.5	24.4
1950	1,840,273	19.1	26.0	28.0	26.9
1957	1,939,977	25.8	23.8	16.6	33.7
1960**	2,069,327	30.0	22.8	14.5	32.7
Women					
1941***	98,666	13.5	32.7	29.7	24.1
1950	248,088	18.0	43.9	19.1	18.9
1957	487,833	22.1	40.9	15.8	21.2
1960**	590,583	23.5	39.7	14.6	22.2

*Clifford M. Carey, "Perspectives for YMCA Growth in the 1960s," in 1959 YMCA Year Book (New York, 1959).

**Estimates

***No previous official records.

Elite Control and the Professional Secretary

If a federated structure were coupled with local, professional control, the constraints of the local community might be lessened. However, the YMCA is unusual among private service organizations in its commitment to lay control, and board members are largely drawn from local elites. The pressures in most large-scale organizations toward increased managerial and professional control, although present, are strenuously resisted in the YMCA. For instance, at least two-thirds of the delegates to national conventions must be lay members; board participation and involvement is sought; a committee structure that ensures a broad base of consultation and involvement on program as well as financial decisions is maintained.

Lay control of the local YMCA is important because of the attitudes and values of the controlling boards and because of the relationship of the YMCA professional to his board members. Although originally composed of young men, today the controlling boards of the YMCA are primarily recruited, as are most boards of private agencies, from the upper ranks of local business circles. A small number of lawyers and doctors is included. YMCA board members are also often active churchmen.

The secretary contributes to maintaining lay dominance and broad character-development goals for the YMCA in two ways. First, his own social background and attitudes predispose him to accept the dominant modes of YMCA operation. Second, his relationship to the board and his own professional image lead him to accept and even encourage board dominance; he does not assert a professional ideology or skill pose.

Although many different types of people are recruited to the secretaryship, a dominant type can be described. The "ideal" secretary is a Protestant from a medium-size town, of a lower-middle-class background. He has attended a small, often denominational, college and may have considered becoming a teacher or minister. It is likely that he was a member of the YMCA during his adolescence, and he may have gone either to a YMCA or to some other religiously oriented camp, an experience of meaning for him. He is a good churchman, but not especially articulate in theological discussion. He prefers physically active programs to more passive and verbal programs and, both by personal preference and professional necessity, he is likely to be a Rotarian or a Kiwanis member.[10] Although he is more liberal in social outlook than his board, he accepts their authority and respects their point of view.

He does so for several reasons. Inasmuch as the executive secretary of the YMCA in a small town is employed by the lay board, he is more dependent on them than many professionals. Even in a metropolitan association, getting along with the board is a prerequisite of successful operation. Although he is recommended for the position by staff higher up in the hierarchy of the association, his success or failure depends greatly on his ability to work with the local board and satisfy it. Although the same is true of any executive of a welfare agency, the dependence of the local YMCA secretary is intensified by his lack of ideological insulation from the board.[11]

A branch may have only a few professionals on its staff and, more important, the secretary possesses neither a set of skills nor a specialized knowledge base that could legitimate his claim to greater wisdom in association affairs; doctors, engineers, lawyers, or even social case workers are not similarly lacking. To be certified as a secretary, an applicant needs a bachelor's degree, with a few courses relevant to YMCA history and religious philosophy, and YMCA work experience; no specific academic discipline is required or preferred. Since he does not have a sharply defined professional ideology, the secretary is not likely to initiate radical changes in a program or to uphold professional standards that cannot be met by his board. Although, like other professionals, the YMCA secretary manipulates the composition of the board to achieve his ends, his own attitudes and values are not likely to lead him into sharp conflict with them. YMCA secretaries are rarely fired because of theological or ideological conflicts with the board.

The control that the secretary does have, based on full-time involvement and his greater knowledge of alternatives and programs, is offset by his having grown up in a movement whose organizational ideology specifies lay dominance and emphasizes that the secretary's job is not to define goals but rather to help others to implement theirs.[12] The secretary is therefore not likely to define his own role as that of leader; he sees himself as an educator.

Lay control and the absence of professionals with a strongly developed ideology and professional code support the YMCA's broad goals. The lack of ideological attachment to programs helps account for the flexibility of means,[13] while lay, interdenominational control minimizes ideological attachments to goals. These factors, however, do not explain the middle-class orientation of the YMCA. Although the recruitment base of the staff and their ideology do not immediately lend themselves to the society,[14] the financial bases of the local YMCA and the problem of managing membership sentiments make possible a better understanding of this orientation of the organization.

Financial Base and the Problem of Managing Membership Sentiments

Like voluntary health and welfare organizations, such as the American Cancer Society, Family Service Agency, and settlement houses, the YMCA is dependent on the Community Chest or direct contributions to meet its needs. Unlike these, however, membership fees and returns for business services, such as cafeterias and hotel rooms, are a major source of funds.[15] Almost all programs are expected to "pull part of their own weight."

This dependence on membership fees and business features limits its clientele base and, at the same time, fosters organizational flexibility. Since its conception of organizational goals is diffuse, the YMCA has the flexibility to initiate and abandon programs in accordance with clientele demand. Although dependent on membership fees for financial solvency, the YMCA has continued to support programs that do not pay their own way. Both its club and youth programs, as well as its international work, require considerable financial support. Even though a local YMCA strives for financial solvency, its programs are not all equally self-sufficient. It would be possible for it to support social service programs while having fee-supported programs in other areas. That it does not is largely a function of the problem of managing membership sentiment.[16]

To state it concisely, it is easier to do missionary work at a distance than at home. Since the lay membership that controls and participates in the YMCA often uses the facilities that it supports financially, the use of these same facilities by social deviants, such as delinquents, or other social "undesirables" constitutes an organizational risk. Unless both board and membership are especially prepared and educated, moves to incorporate the socially unintegrated are likely to have adverse effects on commitment, participation, and financial support.

There are three types of relationship that the YMCA can have with groups that are not incorporated into the middle class. First, it may provide charitable services. For example, the YMCA has participated in the distribution of clothes for the needy, the epitome of missionary work at a distance. Second, as the unincorporated groups become more socially acceptable, as they take on attributes and behavior patterns of the middle class, the YMCA may assimilate them. As working-class affluence has increased, and as the leisure patterns of sports and recreation typifying the middle classes have spread, there have been no barriers other than economic ones to working-class participation in the YMCA. Third, the YMCA can develop outreaching programs specifically aimed at incorporating and involving the "undesirables." Such programs would involve the YMCA in attempts to solve social problems and, if the "undesirables" were brought into contact with other members, might lead to the alienation of members.

On the other hand, initiation of these "social-problem" programs would reaffirm the Christian identity of the organization for both professionals and lay leaders. To the extent that such programs are financed by a foundation or a Community Chest rather than by members, financial dependency on an uncommitted clientele would be eliminated, and professional reference groups would become salient. Programs to incorporate the socially deviant have been rare, however.

Missionary work at a distance helps to maintain a sense of Christian commitment while it avoids involvement in controversial domestic social problems. Since the YMCA is not ideologically committed to solving social problems, it typically avoids local social-service work, and the secretary avoids alienating both board and membership. Although his Christian commitment might lead him to confront his board on race-relations problems, the secretary finds it easiest to maintain support in the local community if he avoids controversy and social reform. Officers and staff of the national and area organization, on the other hand, are in a position to suggest programs that are not closely dependent on conservative elements in the community. Lay as well as staff leadership on the national level are also bound to be more committed to the abstract purposes of the organization than those using the YMCA on the local level and are likely to see it as an international fellowship of Christians rather than as a general-service organization. Moreover, professional staffs at the national or metropolitan level are less dependent on lay personnel and interact more with other professionals. Their ideological position is therefore freer.

Factors like the low level of professionalization, the dependence on local elites, and the role of membership participation may impose limits on the ability of the organization to pursue its basic goals. The consequent limitations of organizational pursuits can be seen as a set of organizational dilemmas. The very factors that have contributed to growth may create problems of effectiveness.

Organizational Dilemmas and Role Problems

Two major role problems may arise from the character of YMCA goals and operation, the dilemma of membership dependency, and the dilemma of program formulation. The two are interrelated and contribute to the role problems of the YMCA secretary.

Dilemma of Dependence on Membership

Any organization must meet the needs of clientele if it is to succeed. Many organizations, however, and especially "people-changing" organizations, assume that the goals and special knowledge of staff give them a clearer picture of client needs than the clients themselves have. Social workers, doctors, and clergymen share the belief that the professional has tools and knowledge that make his wisdom and knowledge of client needs superior to that of the client. The YMCA secretary, too, believes that he best knows how to promote the greater personal development of members.

Since client payment for services is essential to the maintenance of the YMCA, however, the staff members are constrained by an enrollment economy; they find that they must sell such products as recreation facilities, hotel rooms, swimming classes, bridge and dancing classes, and so on, which may only tangentially relate to their goal of character building, to leading members away from egocentrism, and to building membership involvement. In fact, in the past, programs that personnel felt were directly related to their goals, for example, Bible classes and discussion of current affairs, were discontinued for want of support. In recent years, the club program for adolescents has also shrunk.[17]

The flexibility of means in relation to goals permits the organization to meet its needs by offering programs of interest to clientele, but its dependence on clientele willingness to pay limits its program and impact to items that clients recognize as useful to themselves. Given low professional identity and the emphasis on fiscal solvency, it is easy for the staff to replace poorly paying programs with financially rewarding ones. And since clients may not be committed to the Christian aspects of YMCA goals, the secretary finds himself working for a clientele with limited commitments to basic goals.[18]

Dilemma of Program Formulation

The dilemma of dependence on clientele is related to the dilemma of program formulation. We refer to more than just the limitation to clientele-financed programs; we refer to the general structure of character building and preventive approaches. Both the middle-class and Christian bases of the organization lead it to a conception of organization programs that restrict its clientele to those who seem to be adapting successfully to the society. The problem for organization staff members is twofold: how do you know you are being effective, and how do you maintain your belief in the importance of your work? The first problem is solved by recourse to counts of program participation: how many people used the swimming pool or attended classes? The second is solved by the secretary's largely unquestioning belief that the actions he engages in are of value. This belief is supported by the people who surround the secretary, especially his board—a salient and authoritative reference group. However, both staff members and relevant publics sometimes question the ultimate value of the purely recreational facilities.

The dilemmas of client dependence and program formulation may contribute to role problems for the secretary. Can he see the results of his efforts—the development of character? Does he have an ideology that permits him to justify his own self-conception and role? Does he have a set of professional relationships that develop and encourage his active pursuit of his aims?

To some extent we are posing a set of false problems. For many secretaries, the YMCA is a totally satisfying experience. The kinds of activities offered are consonant with his personal values. Since he does not have either high intellectual or financial aspirations, and since he likes physical activity and working with people, but is not especially introspective, the YMCA provides a good fit for his personality.[19] What follows probably applies to a minority of the YMCA secretaries, more to the program and youth club secretaries than to those who direct physical education activities, and more to the service-oriented secretary than the activity-oriented secretary.

The problems of the service-oriented secretary tend to make him disenchanted. In private conversation, the secretary refers to the fact that "many people think they can buy the Y" or "they think they are getting a commodity; they don't have a sense of the Y as a movement—a movement of Christians working for a better world." The secretary can see the Christian element of the organization most in work that he himself does not do, in the YMCA's international work, for instance. Disenchantment stems from the clientele-based nature of the program. The immediacy of the satisfactions of, say, an adoption worker or a volunteer working for the Infantile Paralysis Foundation is frequently absent. The YMCA secretary often has to be satisfied with activities rather than perceived changes in people as measures of achievement.

Not only is the secretary involved with programs that often lack immediacy, but he is also in direct and continuous contact with clients and boards and in minimum contact with fellow professionals. Since his own professional identity is not clearly related to a set of skills or ideology, he is unable to impose his definitions of goals or activities on either the board or the clientele. Both the problem of disenchantment and the problem of professional identity are rooted in the very structure of the organization.

Conclusion

The historical transformation of the YMCA led it to become a general, all-purpose, service organization. In analyzing its basic elements, we have stressed the breadth of the YMCA's goals and means, the wide range of clientele served, the dependency on elite control, the low professionalization of staff, and the preventive and character-developing nature of its programs. We have also pointed to the relation of the YMCA's financial dependency to its success. For any individual YMCA, the factors discussed are variables, not constants.

Our analysis has stressed that the organization has been largely tied to a relatively well-integrated base, but there are pressures for change within the organization. The mere fact that older buildings are located in rapidly changing neighborhoods creates pressures for new programs and financial arrangements. Furthermore, the shifting currents of the educational system lead to different staff perspectives. These changes, if they come, may require changes in the financial structure of the organization and in the recruitment of staff. As the community becomes unable to support the YMCA, external funds may have to be tapped, causing problems for local autonomy and providing a new set of standards for goal definitions. These changes may require that the staff learn a new argot and new techniques in order to deal with deviant groups. The changes may also affect the basic identity of at least part of the organization and are likely to be resisted by staff and boards alike.

Our analysis has purposely focused on the YMCA alone, but the aspects of organizational structure discussed should be useful in analyzing the process of change in other organizations. We offer four propositions about organizational change implied by our discussion.

First, *federated structure.* To the extent that organizations have decentralized and relatively autonomous decision centers, they can adapt to environmental changes quickly, in accordance with local needs and pressures. Parts of the organization may experiment with new programs even before other parts recognize the need for change. On the other hand, with centralized organizations, once they do recognize that environmental pressures require changes, the rate of change may be much faster.

Second, *broadly defined organizational goals and rules.* To the extent that organizational goals commit the actor to narrowly defined objects or to only one program, organizations will probably have difficulty in adapting to environmental changes that seriously affect the appeal of those programs. On the other hand, broadly defined goals and means permit an organization to encompass many types of programs and thus permit flexibility.[20]

Third, *low development of professional ideology.* Our analysis suggests that low professionalization facilitates change. The more ideologically committed the professional is to the means he uses, the more difficult it will be to change the organization in which he operates.

Fourth, *enrollment economy.* An enrollment economy is immediately sensitive to the changed demands of the marketplace. Organizations that are dependent on some form of enrollment economy (a form of competitive marketplace) are forced to recognize quickly the environmental changes affecting the demand for services. On the other hand, organizations protected from the marketplace, such as religious organizations, welfare organizations, or social movements, may soon find themselves poorly adapted to the changing order.

Notes

1. Historical detail can be found in Luther L. Dodgett (1896) and in C. Howard Hopkins (1950).
2. We do not mean to imply that the change from evangelistic to broad, character-development goals occurred all at once or before any changes in program. Quite the opposite: YMCAs in local communities slowly added programs that met with public response; in this process, original goals were transformed.
3. For a discussion of this conflict in the Chicago YMCA, see Emmett Dedmon (1957, p. 100).
4. For a discussion of the spread of sports and the church's reaction to them, see Foster Rhea Dulles (1940, pp. 201-10).
5. YMCAs in Europe, especially in Germany, have always been more religiously zealous and pietistic than those in England and the United States, and those in England retained a closer connection to religion than those in America. Dodgett (op. cit., pp. 171-72) asserts this for 1855, and YMCA staff members today still claim that the differences exist. But these national differences are beyond the scope of this essay.
6. The YMCA had provided more than just Bible classes; it acted as a coordinating agency for interdenominational interests. Some YMCA leaders thought of it as the new Universal Church, and the YMCA has always worked for church cooperation. As the churches developed their own coordinating mechanisms, such as local and federal councils of churches, and as they developed their own Sunday schools and auxiliaries, the demand for YMCA services in these areas diminished. On the other hand, the YMCA's relationships with the denominations, especially the more conservative ones, had always been somewhat strained, for the clergy of various denominations were bound to find the YMCA's religious teaching at variance with their own doctrine. For a discussion of these relationships, see S. Wirt Wiley (1944). In a sense, the YMCA was "pulled" into general services by the transformation of society and "pushed" by the increasing capabilities of the institutions of the churches.
7. See Clifford M. Carey, *YMCA Boards and Committee of Management* (n.d., p. 11). Whereas some 27 percent of the YMCA's membership is Catholic, only about 5 percent of the members of the YMCA's boards of directors are Catholic.
8. Some sects are begun by lay evangelists who begin spreading word of the Lord, hoping to get members to join already established denominations. On the history of the Elim Four Square Gospel, see B. Wilson (1961). What would have happened to the YMCA if George Williams had become a full-time evangelist, requiring financial support, rather than a merchant prince of London? This may have been a crucial organization choice point. Dwight Moody, the famous American evangelist, was the secretary of the Chicago YMCA. He left the organization to become a full-time evangelist after 1860; the organization's character was already established.
9. An "enrollment economy" exists when the meeting of financial needs is depen-

dent on the enrollment of members in activities or classes. The term is Burton Clark's (1956, p. 332).

10. A recent study by Roy Grinker (1962), with the collaboration of Roy Grinker, Jr., and John Timberlake, suggests that at least one of the major sources of professional YMCA personnel, George Williams College, has a student body that largely conforms to this picture. The students have average intelligence (110 median), very little psychopathology, and low mobility aspirations. They are active churchmen, relatively unintrospective, and accept authority and tradition. See also Emil F. Faubert (mimeo., 1961).

11. On the necessity of insulation for the maintenance of ideological organization, see James D. Thompson (1960, pp. 389-409).

12. In "Politics as an Ecology of Games," Norton Long (1960) argues that professionals in welfare and service agencies must build and maintain a community elite if they are to be successful. This state of affairs is especially true of the YMCA secretary. Since the program he is running does not have the immediacy of appeal of such an agency as the cancer foundation, the secretary must build a continuing relationship between his organization and local elites if he is to be successful.

13. The lack of a specific professional skill requirement also contributes to organizational flexibility in the use of personnel. The number of accredited YMCA secretaries in the United States has remained around 4,000 since 1930, although membership has tripled. Since the organization does not assert that only professionals are competent to deal with clients, the YMCA has greatly increased its use of part-time and volunteer personnel. As Clark (1956, p. 334) points out, the very nature of the enrollment economy also leads to using a large number of part-time employees, since specialties are required to staff varied activities.

14. There is no reason why the YMCA should work with the socially deviant and less integrated, but historically there have been both internal and external pressures for the YMCA to work with socially deviant groups. The question at stake here is why the YMCA has not generally responded to this pressure. Some programs of the YMCA of Chicago have aimed at the socially deviant. The special conditions necessary for maintaining this type of program will be analyzed in a later study.

15. On the average, 32 percent of YMCA income came from dues and program fees in 1961, 34 percent from business features such as residences, 25 percent from contributions and endowments, and 8 percent from miscellaneous sources. Cf. Clifford M. Carey and Sanford M. Reece (1962, p. 34).

16. Hans W. Mattick suggested the phrase "managing membership sentiments." See also Arthur Vidich and Joseph Bensman's (1960, p. 257) discussion of the lack of mission work among the unchurched by the ministers of Springdale.

17. Clark (1956) argues that the worker in adult education is buffeted by pressures of a paying clientele to lower his professional standards. He is put in conflict by his allegiance to the strong external peer group of educators to uphold his standards. This source of cross-pressure with clientele or board demands is largely lacking in the YMCA. The peer professional group of the YMCA secretary (Association of Organization Secretaries) exists largely within the organization. Some secretaries identify strongly with welfare-service groups, which give them an independent basis for standards; others identify strongly with the churches. But for many YMCA secretaries, professional standards are largely based on organizational practices.

18. A management consultant firm which did a survey of the membership of one YMCA in 1940 concluded: "It is evident from the findings of this investigation that, in the minds of the majority of the members and former members, and, to a slightly smaller extent among non-members, the Department of the YMCA is primarily a place in which to swim, to play handball, to play billiards and pool, and to lift weights, and to make acquaintances among congenial young men of like tastes. In other words, the Department appears to coordinate, in the thinking of most of the men interviewed, with the gymnasiums and swimming pools provided by the parks, schools and other public and semi-public institutions. A membership in the YMCA seems to them to represent the purchase of the privilege of using the Department's pool, gymnasium and recreational facilities. There is very little evidence that the majority of the men interviewed have any real conception of the function of the YMCA other than a place for athletic activities, recreation and an opportunity to meet other young men.

    "Certainly, there is little evidence that the men take a real or sincere interest in the Department as an institution. Their attitudes toward it and toward the acceptance of responsibility through work on committees and councils is extremely superficial."
19. Personal conversation with Roy Grinker, M.D.
20. Of course, broadly defined goals with little specificity may permit too much flexibility, in that they may result in a weak commitment.

7

Social Movement Industries: Competition and Conflict Among SMOs

Mayer N. Zald and *John D. McCarthy*

Although the literature on social movements is vast, there has been surprisingly little systematic analysis of the interaction of social movement organizations (but see James Q. Wilson, 1973; Zald and Ash, 1966; Gusfield, 1966; Nelson, 1974). Of course, practitioners and the practical theorists have developed strategies for interorganizational relations. Lenin, for instance, knew how to freeze the Mensheviks out in the cold, and his able disciple, Willi Muenzenberger, knew how to create a popular front. Naturally enough, practical theorists have not analyzed the range of possible forms of social movement organization interaction, concentrating instead upon problems of the moment.

If social movements were unified affairs, with one charismatic leader or SMO dominating and holding together the movement, then we could ignore movement organizations—the formal organizations that pursue movement goals—and industries—the congeries of organizations that pursue the goals; at best, such a focus would be marginal, perhaps devoted to understanding factionalism. But it is apparent that social movements are rarely unified affairs. Whether we study revolutionary movements, broad or narrow social reform movements, or religious movements, we find a variety of SMOs or groups, linked to various segments of supporting constituencies (both institutional and individual), competing among themselves for resources and symbolic leadership, sharing facilities and resources at other times, developing stable and many times differentiated functions, occasionally merging into unified ad hoc coalitions, and occasionally engaging in all-out war against each other. Organizations associated with a social movement and with its countermovement may also interact. By definition pursuing antithetical goals, such organizations compete for legitimacy and resources but under some circumstances may also cooperate with one another.

The fundamental task of this chapter is to gain analytic purchase on the variety of SMO interorganizational relationships and to begin to specify the conditions under which these various forms of interaction are most likely to occur. In the past, social movement analysts and analysts of complex organizations spoke rather different languages. In our attempt to merge these two approaches, we will utilize the concerns and conceptualizations of both. Our earlier work has been informed by the assumption that analysis of SMOs can be informed by perspectives of organizational theory and research in general. Recent organizational theory and research has focused upon the interrelationships between society, organizational environment, and organizational behavior. Here, we focus primarily upon competition between organizations within the social movement sector, paying attention primarily to intra-industry relations.

Gerlach and Hine (1970) argue that a number of social movements can be characterized exclusively as a web-like structure of informal, unorganized relations of cooperation and communication among local cells. Nevertheless, many SMOs have more coherent organization structures and combine several local units. Our discussion focuses upon organizations that are bureaucratic, as Gamson utilizes that term (1975); that is, organizations that have several levels of membership, lists of members (however faulty), and some kind of written document describing the structure of the organization. Also, we focus upon organizations that pursue goals in more than a local environment; they pursue goals aimed at changing society in general rather than just local conditions.

Even though scholars writing about social movements have paid little attention to interorganizational relations, it has been a lively topic in the study of complex organizations. Whereas such study dates, possibly, from Levine and White's important article on exchange relationships among organizations (1961) and Litwak and Hylton's early article (1962) but includes also the emphasis upon organization-environment relations found in the writings of Selznick (1949) and James D. Thompson (1967). In the last decade students of organizations have mapped the forms of determinants of interorganizational relationships (for summaries, see Evans, 1978; and Negandi, 1978). They have explored exchange relations among social welfare agencies, the emergence of federated relations (temporary and permanent), conflict emerging from low domain consensus, the emergence of joint programs, mechanisms used to mediate between clients and organizations, and those used to reduce environmental uncertainties. We draw upon a number of strands of research in this tradition. In particular, we discuss perfect and imperfect competition, ideology and conflict, cooperative relations, and factionalism.

Perfect and Imperfect Competition

Although organizational analysts have tended, until rather recently (cf. Pfeffer, 1978), to focus upon cooperation instead of competition between organizations, those who have addressed competition have normally utilized the imagery of the market mechanism while at the same time recognizing the social constraints that alter and shape such mechanisms. Let us briefly describe the current consensus about interorganizational competition.

Businesses offering similar products to a large number of potential buyers need not directly interact, but they are able to view the consequences and behavior of others, and are aware of pricing and product decisions through market mechanisms. Pure, or perfect, competitive markets involve homogeneous goods, many sellers (offerers), and many buyers (users). Imperfect competition occurs when there is product differentiation or barriers to entry, or both, somewhat restricting market access. Where product differentiation is possible, sellers may attempt to divide the market into segments that they "capture," to reduce competition, and to establish more dependable and organizationally favorable relations. As the number of sellers becomes smaller, we can speak of a movement towards an oligopolistic industry; buyers have limited choices and the number of sellers is small enough so that one or a few may dominate and constrain the choices of others by their influence on buyers, or the sellers may directly interact and concert behavior (establish a cartel).

Organizations (firms) offering relatively similar products may, in some cases, have to deal with a single buyer or supplier (monopsony and monopoly). Such situations create great pressures upon the organizations to concert their behavior. What does such a perspective suggest about SMO competition?

Competition for Resources and Legitimacy

To survive in modern society, SMOs need financial resources if they are to pursue goals in more than a local context. Money is needed for personnel, transportation, office supplies, and the like. Organizations can survive without money when personnel donate their time and when money is transferred to them for non–social movement purposes (unemployment insurance payments are widely used for subsistence by SMO organizers). Thus, students can live off their parents, or other organizations may "lend" their personnel and facilities to SMOs for full-time or part-time activity. The Southern Christian Leadership Conference, for instance, depended heavily upon the resources of black church groups in its early days

(Oberschall, 1973), and many universities tacitly loaned faculty, chaplains, and students to the anti-Vietnam war movement. But where SMOs employ or wish to employ full-time cadres, even at starvation wages, they will need to regularize or institutionalize the flow of money into the organization. Sometimes, of course, SMOs have windfall resources. Ralph Nader sued General Motors, which had spied on him and attempted to entrap him in illegal and immoral behavior, his action leading to a $500,000 settlement, which he used for his enterprises (McCarry, 1972). Lenin orchestrated the courting of two sisters, heiresses to a large fortune, who provided an infusion of funds (Wolfe, 1955).

Unless individuals or organizations can be coerced to participate in SMOs (as occurs in armed conflicts, where SMOs use coercive techniques to raise manpower and money), SMOs must appeal for support. Consequently, at the most general level, SMOs must compete not only with all other SMOs, but with voluntary organizations of other kinds as well as for the time, effort, loyalty, and money that citizens can give or withhold. Here, however, we focus upon the competition between SMOs within SMIs and, peripherally, upon the competition between SMIs. Competition is for symbolic dominance: Which SMO has the best programs, tactics, and leaders for accomplishing goals? SMOs attempt to convince sympathizers to follow their lead.

Competition for Resources Controlled by Individuals

Organizations within an SMI "ought" to cooperate in goal accomplishment; after all, they seek similar goals. However, because they share to a greater or lesser extent the same adherent pools, both individual and institutional, they are in basic competition for resources from adherents. The intensity of this competition is related importantly to resource availability; to the extensity of the demands SMOs place upon constituents or those who provide the varied resources to the organization; to the social heterogeneity of potential supporters; and to the interaction of these three factors.

Hypothesis 1: Under conditions of the declining availability of marginal resources, direct competition and conflict between SMOs with similar goals can be expected to increase.

Although money is not the only type of resource, it is the most flexible. Obtaining funds from individual constituents (conscience or beneficiary) depends partially upon the availability of marginal dollars. The amount of discretionary resources available is linked to the state of the business cycle, the number of sympathizers, and the ability of organizations to penetrate the pool of sympathizers.

A recent case provides a useful illustration. This is what has been called an "acrimonious dispute" between the National Association for the Advancement of Colored People and the NAACP Legal Defense and Educational Fund (LDF). The Fund, as the latter is called, separated from the NAACP in 1957, under pressure from the Internal Revenue Service, in order to preserve the tax deductible feature of its financial support. As Brown says, "Few people, however, were aware of that separation. As a result, for the past 22 years the NAACP and the fund (LDF) often were thought of as the same group. Donations intended for one often went to the other, and that was the essence of the dispute" (1979, p. A5). The NAACP has decided to attempt to bar the Fund from using its initials in attempts to raise funds in the future. While there has been some tension between the two organizations over the years, it is noteworthy that the conflict has become increasingly strident at a time when resources for civil rights organizations have been declining.

Hypothesis 2: Among more inclusive organizations (which demand relatively little from the majority of members), the competition for resources between similar organizations should be less intense than that between more exclusive organizations (which demand heavy commitments from members).

We would expect that multiple memberships would be common in industries with many inclusive organizations, while multiple memberships are frowned upon by exclusive organizations. Exclusive SMOs treat membership as a zero-sum resource. (However, exclusive organizations may use multiple membership as a way of infiltrating other organizations. In this case, multiple memberships results from concerted policy.)

To repeat, SMOs must pursue resources, and, all other things being equal, such competition should be more intense under conditions of resource scarcity. But for some SMOs, even during times when resources are not scarce, it is possible to view constituents of related inclusive organizations as potentially recruitable even while they maintain commitments to other SMOs. Given the extensive literature on voluntary associations generally and social movements in particular, we know that few people affiliate very extensively, but a small portion of people are rather widely affiliated. Indeed, a number of studies (Von Eschen et al., 1971; McFarland, 1977) have shown extensive multiple memberships in the social movement sector. Thus, even though SMOs in the same industry may be competing for the same resources (i.e., the labor and loyalty of the same people), since no organization commands the total loyalty of most of its constituents, this competition is not zero-sum and, consequently, should not be especially rancorous. Once a person gives funds, future solicitations from other SMOs become more likely.

Competition between inclusive organizations in an industry takes the form of slight product differentiation (offering marginally different goals) and, especially, tactical differentiation. Different SMOs may specialize principally in litigation strategies, or lobbying strategies, or protest strategies, or particular targets. Such differentiation provides a rationale for committed constituents to become affiliated with a number of SMOs pursuing goals in a number of different ways. This is, we believe, the major form of competition between inclusive SMOs within SMIs in modern America.

Since organizations pursuing similar goals compete for resources, SMOs will form that are based upon differential perceptions and tastes of adherent pools in order to capitalize on such preexisting differences. As well, when resource availability is expanding, existing organizations can be expected to expand their range of targets and tactics when possible.

Hypothesis 3: The range of appeals and the variety of organizations that develop are partly related to the preexisting heterogeneity of potential supporters. Differentiation of appeal is more important for inclusive than exclusive SMOs.

SMO goals and programs are, of course, importantly determined by the shape of the task, the range of the institutional targets, and the means to change targets, which stem from a more-or-less well-articulated ideology. But a heterogeneous potential support base calls forth and permits a range of definitions of the situation.

Though product differentiation may appear sharp to the nonmembers of more exclusive SMOs, that differentiation is probably less important to growth and resource accumulation than it is for more inclusive organizations. Since ideological transformation is typical of more exclusive SMOs and some evidence exists to suggest that members and nonmembers are quite similar prior to ideological transformation (Heirich, 1977; Gerlach and Hine, 1970), what preexisting value heterogeneity there is among potential supporters is probably of less importance for growth than the appropriateness and sophistication of recruitment mechanisms (McCarthy and Hoge, 1978). Consequently, the apparent range and variety of offerings of more exclusive organizations is more related to internal processes than to the preexisting preferences of potential supporters.

Product differentiation is more important for recruitment among inclusive organizations and especially so among inclusive organizations that do not depend upon face-to-face interaction. For these organizations, product differentiation functions much as it does in the marketplace. If marginal dollars are in plentiful supply, the possibility of offering slight changes in products in order to capture some of the increased potential market is more likely. These changes may take the form of new organizations, spinoff organizations expanding their range of related issues, targets, and tactics. In the first two cases, additional organizations are added to the field, thus creating the potential for increased competition for resources on the part of existing organizations. When organizations expand their offerings, they enter into competition for resources with other existing organizations with whom they have not competed in the past. The recent history of the American Civil Liberties Union (ACLU) provides a case in point. Originally an organization devoted exclusively to supporting litigation on First Amendment issues, the ACLU expanded its goals during the early 1970s to include ending the war in Vietnam, fighting against the Nixon administration, and fighting for women's rights and abortion. In the process, it gained tens of thousands of new members through its mass-mail solicitation and became an organization competing for resources with other existing organizations such as the National Organization of Women (NOW), the National Abortion Rights Action League (NARAL), and many antiwar organizations. But these were times of expanding marginal dollars, and little outward conflict occurred between these organizations. Presumably, the expanded appeals brought additional funds into the coffers of the organization. We might expect that the adding of new product lines for an organization such as this one with widespread name recognition would put it, as with firms, in a better competitive position in the social movement sector. Unfortunately, such a diversification strategy proved costly to the ACLU when it took an unpopular First Amendment stand to defend the Nazi marchers in Skokie, Illinois. As Mann (1978) persuasively argues, the heterogeneity of the membership, which was built by expanding the goals of the organization, meant that many new members brought in by these recent appeals could not be expected to support the Skokie decision. The result was a drastic decline in membership renewals for the organization.

Competition for Resources Controlled by Organizations

So far, we have focused upon the competition for support from individual sympathizers—how to transform sympathizers into constituents. But funds are also raised from institutional sources. These funds may be more or less restricted in purposes. Thus, money given to an SMO by a governmental agency for a foundation, for instance, may provide money for a voter registration drive, but in fact not control expenditures tightly. However, since foundations are observed by Congress and their operations controlled by federal statute, they tend to be quite politically sensitive. The least-restricted money from institutional sources may well be from church organizations, especially the many "social concern" departments in the Protestant denominations. These groups aggregate a proportion of a total givings from the membership and disburse it over a range of organizations and projects. (Such funds are probably more restricted than money provided by individual constituents, since these bodies also operate under accountability procedures.) Elsewhere (McCarthy and Zald, 1977) we have argued that in the United States, the more resources provided to SMOs by individuals are insulated from political control and from membership pressure, the more an institution is free to distribute resources as it wants.

However, remember that competition for funds from individual constituents requires a process very different from attempting to obtain funds from institutional sources; the former requires more public relations skills and styles, and the latter requires more program developmental skills. Lawson (1978) reports that the increase in funds available from institutional sources to the various organizations of the tenants' rights movement in New York City has created both a wider diversity of SMOs and increased levels of competition for the available funds. Where there are limited numbers of institutional funders, competition appears to be zero-sum. Competition becomes conflict as those who cannot gain access to such funds attack the legitimacy of those who can. Most of the SMOs Lawson describes appear to be inclusive.

Hypothesis 4: Institutional funding, when publicly known, will increase conflict between more inclusive SMOs.

Whether this hypothesis holds for more exclusive SMOs is not clear to us, since it is difficult to untangle the effects of organizational structure, goals, and institutional funding for such organizations.

Ideology and Conflict

The conflict that occurs between SMOs over legitimacy is normally discussed by analysts under the rubric of the "functions of radical fringe." As the SMOs of an SMI pursue related goals, some organizations offer a more comprehensive version of the problem and more drastic change as a solution. These organizations are normally called *radical*. Naturally enough, authorities are likely to prefer to deal with organizations that state less comprehensive versions of change. By virtue of the authorities' recognition of some SMOs as legitimate spokespersons and others as not legitimate, conflict is almost guaranteed between SMOs over those who have been accepted, however marginally, by authorities. The rich rhetoric describing fine degrees of cooptation and "selling out" grows out of this process. The legitimated SMOs may gain even more legitimacy from authorities and bystanders counter-attacking the unlegitimated SMOs, but with a resultant increase in the level of the inter-SMI conflict. The longstanding conflicts between communist and noncommunist trade unions in the United States during the 1940s and 1950s illustrates this process. Under other conditions, no response by the legitimated SMOs reaps the reward of increased legitimacy. The process is described in detail by Killian for the recent civil rights movement (1972).

Hypothesis 5: Assuming that SMOs are competing for similar audiences, as SMOs within an industry become further apart in their conception of the amount of change and the tactics required, rancorous conflict increases.

So far, we have discussed competition and conflict in which SMOs present verbal claims about themselves and their opponents and competitors. Most often, the appearance of shared goals mutes the direct and more violent attack of one SMO on another, but rancorous and deadly conflict is not unknown between SMOs in the same SMI. In modern America, rancorous conflict occurs in such settings primarily over the legitimacy of representation of constituency or over exclusive membership.

In the United States, there are two settings in which SMI conflict has occurred: between sect-like SMOs with comprehensive visions of change, and between labor organizations that must, by virtue of the legal and political circumstances under which they operate, require membership exclusivity with regard to other organizations.

It is widely observed that small, sect-like SMOs tend to devote extensive energies toward bitter conflicts with other SMOs that seem to noncombatants only marginally different. For instance, in the late 1960s the Black Muslims and Malcolm X's Organization for Afro-American Unity engaged in murderous conflict. A major reason for the intensity of such conflict appeared to relate to the great sacrifice and commitment required of their members: members are a scarce and valuable resource and as such have normally required a major SMO investment in socialization.

Hypothesis 6: The more SMOs with exclusive membership requirements compete for a limited pool of potential members, the greater the potential conflict.

Another situation producing rancorous and deadly conflict occurs, at least in the local context, when organizational survival is at stake. The recent conflict between the United Farm Workers Organization and the Teamsters Union in the fields of California illustrates the intensity that such conflict can reach. Conflict between the American Federation of Teachers and the National Education Association in many school districts and colleges demonstrates the same process in milder form.[1] In these cases, organizations depend upon membership enrollment in order to win recognition from authorities. The loser in these battles is not accredited as a bargaining agent and must leave the scene.

Utilizing our resource mobilization logic, then, and viewing the social world from the point of view of a particular SMO highlights the possibilities of conflict between it and other SMOs offering similar products. But the relative lack of conflict and the extent of cooperation among related SMOs then calls for some explanation. How can we account for cooperation between SMOs that, all other things being equal, our theoretical perspective leads us to believe should be vigorously competing?

Cooperation: Exchange, the Division of Labor, and Domain Consensus

In the production of a product or the carrying out of social functions, a set of organizations may develop differentiated but interlinked roles. They then establish exchange relations. Here is where the emphasis upon exchange, domain consensus, and conflict over domain has become relevant to analysts of complex organizations. These relationships vary in their importance to the parties, their stability, and the amount of coordination and mutual adjustment that takes place. To review:

1. Ad-hoc, small-item exchanges may take place in which lower-level personnel of an organization find it advantageous to utilize the services, products, or facilities of another organization.
2. Policy coordination and rules governing interchanges are likely to emerge when two or more organizations are dependent upon each other for an important part of their input or output. These policies and rules are likely to be reviewed by upper-level personnel in organizations. Where the interchange is regular but over changing conditions or issues, interagency committees or liaison groups may emerge to monitor the relations.
3. Cooperative relations occur to the extent that the skills, competencies, tasks, and prices of the partners to the exchange are agreed upon by all parties (this is what is meant by "domain consensus").
4. Where stable relationships have emerged with highly differentiated but interlinked domains, the organizational partners may exchange information and monitor their environments for mutual enhancement.
5. In some cases, cooperating organizations may set up joint organizations or projects. As opposed to coordination, the joint program involves

some autonomy of action for the personnel of the joint program; in essence, a new organization is created.

These cooperative relations occur in both the profit-making and non-profit sectors. A number of researchers have pursued a description of the role of interlocking boards of directorates in the business sectors, showing their widespread occurrence and patterned nature and speculating upon their probable role in coordinating the interorganizational sector.[2] There have also been studies of joint ventures in the for-profit and nonprofit sectors.

Other researchers, such as Domhoff (1976), have explored social relations between the leaders of private sector organizations, again showing widespread contact and extensive communication allowing the development of interorganizational undertakings about cooperative ventures. Finally, several analysts have argued that private sector organizations have cooperated in the development of certain federal regulatory agencies as a means of reducing competition and of stabilizing industry operation.

With such leads to follow, we can isolate a number of factors that serve to facilitate and shape cooperation among SMOs. We shall discuss several of these: task specialization, social control, interlocking boards of directors, overlapping membership constituencies, and inducements from authorities and elites. Each of these factors may produce either formal or informal cooperation.

Task Specialization

Where an SMI is fairly well established, comprising several different SMOs, informal domain agreements and exchanges emerge. They emerge usually between those organizations sharing relatively similar conceptions of goals and allowable tactics. First, SMOs may agree upon geographic and functional turf. Basic to domain consensus are economies of expertise and closeness of constituent relationships.[3] On the one hand, legal organizations, lobbying and information groups, and other technical services develop within specific SMIs and consequently have available an expertise that other SMOs in the SMI would find difficult and expensive to duplicate. On the other hand, the highly technical groups rarely develop strong links to constituents.

Hypothesis 7: Domain agreements are more likely to be reached allowing extended cooperation among SMOs with different but not contradictory task specializations than among those SMOs that pursue goals with similar tactical formulas.

Although the SCLC employed lawyers, they largely protected the organization and its leaders from arrest. We know that clear domain agreements existed between the Congress of Racial Equality and the NAACP during the "freedom rides" in the South, where the NAACP strained its resources to provide legal defense for CORE members arrested in local areas (Meier and Rudwick, 1973). We suspect that a similar exchange relationship developed at the height of the civil rights movement between the SCLC and both the American Civil Liberties Union and the NAACP Legal Defense Fund. The NAACP was the major legal arm of the movement.

External Social Control

Hypothesis 8: Social control produces increased cooperation among SMOs when the social control efforts threaten the very existence of a number of SMOs.

Violence, legal restriction upon operating procedures, and arrests not only commit SMO constituents to their own SMOs (Gerlach and Hine, 1970), but also commit SMOs within the same SMI to one another. This pattern appears in even broader contexts, sometimes even including SMOs from diverse SMIs in momentary cooperative ventures—for instance, the Japanese invasion during World War II. The Berkeley Free Speech movement (FSM) at the University of California is another example of a coalition that formed as a response to an outside threat. The FSM grew out of an attempt by authorities to restrict off-campus political organizing by on-campus organizations. A wide variety of organizations with sometimes related and sometimes disparate goals coalesced when their base of operations was threatened. Originally, the United Front was formed, eventually becoming the FSM. The United Front included all three campus Republican groups along with a right-wing conservative society and a wide array of left-wing groups (Draper, 1964).

Social control engenders the same kind of cooperation between SMOs within the same SMI. Political trials regularly have such an effect. The notorious trials of Industrial Workers of the World leaders during the 1920s served to develop cooperative relations between organizations that normally worked at arm's length from one another (Dubofsky, 1969). The cooperative defense funds that normally arise in such circumstances serve to link SMOs informally to one another. An unintended effect of such trials when they are badly managed (as in the United States during the 1960s and in pre-revolutionary Russia) is to develop bonds between leaders of diverse SMOs, thereby setting the stage for future cooperative ventures.

Overlapping Constituents: Boards

Much like modern corporations, many inclusive SMOs in modern society develop boards of directors or advisory councils. These boards serve various purposes, including providing legitimation, with various constituencies, technical and political advice to SMO leaders, and links to various elite and institutional funding sources. We are not aware of a systematic evaluation of boards of this type, but a quick look at boards within any SMI shows extensive overlapping membership—or, in recent parlance, interlocks. For instance, the leaders of one SMO may be found on the board of directors of similar SMOs. Dignitaries such as Ramsey Clark or Benjamin Spock can be found on a wide variety of boards. It may be possible to describe inter-SMI and SMO relations by inspecting the amount of interlock, much as has been attempted by analysts of the corporate world in modern America. Of course, such interlocks can also be used to infer integration into the larger society by attending to the other positions held by members.[4]

Hypothesis 9: The more the interlocks, the greater the cooperation among SMOs.

The perspective of the board member who sits on the boards of two similar SMOs ought to incline that individual toward counseling cooperation in the pursuit of goals. Though board members are normally in a formal position of approving the behavior of the SMO, we suspect that these boards, like corporate boards, are often rather less than vigorous. However, the circulation of information in these settings ought to keep each SMO so linked informed of the activities of the closest competitors for resources. Following what we know of similar processes in the corporate sector (Domhoff, 1974), we would not be surprised to find the existence of "watering holes" (such as Stewart Mott's townhouse across from the Supreme Court in Washington, D.C.), where those who occupy extensive interlocking positions gather socially. It is known, for instance, that leaders of the civil rights movement in the South convened at the Highlander Folk Center in Tennessee, and later in Kentucky. These informal groupings should serve to further coordinate the activities of SMOs within an SMI and relations between ideologically linked SMIs[5].

Memberships

As we noted above, many citizens belong to a number of voluntary associations, a subset of them belonging to a number of SMOs. Consequently, any SMO should have some set of its constituents belonging to other related and other apparently unrelated SMOs. We could characterize SMOs by their degree of overlapping constituencies; the inclusive/exclusive dimension includes the end of this continuum as one of its elements.

Hypothesis 10: The more SMOs have overlapping constituencies, the more they should be constrained toward cooperation.

We should immediately add, however, that where we normally refer to the inclusive SMO as a "front group," the cooperation is induced through infiltration. Overlapping memberships ought to provide communication between affected SMOs, though not as directly as interlocking boards of directors.

Overlapping memberships have different sources and consequences at local and national levels. In local organizations, or chapters of national organizations, clusters of people may belong to a number of similar organizations that pursue similar but discrete goals. The clustering is created through interpersonal networks. Meier and Rudwick (1973) describe the operation of CORE and the NAACP in the South during the height of the civil rights movement of the 1960s as one commonly marked by overlapping membership at the local level. In some circumstances, there was almost complete overlapping membership—hence, tactical cooperation was guaranteed.

National organizations with inclusive and nonfederated or only partly federated constituents may find themselves in a situation in which many of their constituents hold memberships in similar SMOs created through interchanged membership lists. McFarland (1976) shows, for instance, that approximately 30 percent of the members of Common Cause are also members of the League of Women Voters. There is extensive overlap between the membership of the National Abortion Rights Action League (NARAL), Planned Parenthood, and the National Organization of Women (NOW) (personal communication). Some of this overlap appears to occur when the same or similar mailing lists are used in solicitations for membership in parallel SMOs. SMOs lend or rent their lists to one another. SMOs may also contract with a single firm to handle solicitations, and the same pool of lists may be used by more than one SMO. We would expect, for instance, that Richard Viguerie's centrality as a mailing firm for organizations on the right would serve to increase the likelihood of overlapping memberships between similar conservative organizations. The extensity of the overlaps should constrain potential conflict between such organizations. Membership surveys are not at all uncommon among such organizations, so it is reasonable to assume that many leaders are aware of such overlaps. Since such membership is quite unstable (many organizations with a mail order membership experience less than 50 percent renewals each year), one would expect leaders to be rather careful to show appropriate cooperation, while at the same time retaining images of product differentiation.

Elite and Third-Party Constraints

Finally, cooperation between SMOs may be encouraged by authorities and elite institutions. During the days of the Johnson administration, the president held many meetings with "civil-rights leaders." Though there was extensive conflict between some of these groups at times, some element of cooperation was encouraged as the leaders of SNCC and the more moderate civil rights groups maintained ties through the efforts of the president. Churches and foundations that support the social movement sector regularly call for cooperation between SMOs pursuing similar goals. Since such funding institutions tend to place great importance on the role of efficiency in goal accomplishment, from their vantage point conflict is counterproductive. When in the business of providing resources, such institutions can back up encouragement with threats and actual sanctions. Dealing with a small number of funding institutions or authorities puts contradictory pressures on SMOs; it heightens conflict because zero-sum situations are created, but it also creates a demand for cooperation.

Hypothesis 11: If the funding institution is selecting one among many proposals from different SMOs, conflict is encouraged; if coalition grants are being made, cooperation is encouraged.

SMOs in modern society are linked to one another and to other organizations in a wide variety of ways. These linkages serve to mute the conflict that might be expected from a conception of SMOs as just organizations seeking survival and growth. It is those organizations that are isolated from widespread linkages where we would expect to find more rancorous inter-SMO conflict.

Alliances, Cartels, Federations, and Mergers

Not only do organizations cooperate and exchange; they sometimes form supraorganizations—cartels, federations, alliances, and mergers. These forms of organizational behavior have been extensively discussed by organizational analysts. In the merger, two or more formally separate organizations combine into one new organization; the merger can occur by mutual consent or through a hostile takeover. In the federation, units retain their identity but give up certain discretionary rights to the new organization, or, in the dominated alliance, to one of the component units. Federations and alliances differ in their depth and purposes. Indeed, the relatively permanent coordination of policies discussed above can be considered one form of alliance. The formation of alliances, however, is also likely to result from the necessity of dealing with a powerful (monopolistic) resource provider or buyer. Public and private organizations offering similar services and products may need "trade associations" to represent them to the outside world.

Finally, a wide variety of private sector organizations may cooperate in ad hoc alliances when an outside threat or a potential outside advantage is perceived. Examples are alliances formed to counter federal taxation and labor politics.

Managerial technocrats might see in the plethora of SMOs in an industry a magnificent opportunity for rationalization by merger. After all, economies of scale would result from the merger of these small, inefficient organizations. And just think how much simpler it would be if the movement spoke with one voice! But an organizational realist, such as James Q. Wilson (1973), would surely point out that the managerial technocrats are both unwise and naive. Naive, because the technocrats assume that efficiency is a prime concern of SMO leaders when it is not, and because they miss the strong drive to organizational maintenance of leaders and their key constituents. Unwise, because they assume that speaking with one voice increases the effectiveness of the movement when, in fact, the effectiveness of a movement, both in mobilizing support and attaining change, may be aided by having many organizations. Moreover, as Gerlach and Hine (1970) demonstrate, there are major advantages to having diversity within an SMI: diversity allows for innovation in tactics and makes it difficult for authorities to target social control efforts. But ideologically compatible SMOs do form alliances and mergers under special sets of circumstances. SMOs will join together for special events. Marches and mass demonstrations are often run in consortium fashion with several different organizations mobilizing constituencies and interlinked networks. Joint planning and ad hoc liaison committees are used for these occasions. Our conception of ideological leadership and Olson's theory (1965) of the contributions of organizations to the provision of collective goods lead us to believe the following hypothesis.

Hypothesis 12: The leading or dominant organization in a movement will make contributions greater than its proportional share of resources to carrying out large events for special purposes.

Although coalitions, both formal and informal, are common, mergers between SMOs seem relatively rare. One condition that seems to spur mergers is the same one that can also spur bitter conflict, and that is between competing labor SMOs. The United Farm Workers Organization identified with Cesar Chavez, for instance, was formed out of two ethnically distinct SMOs, and the merger of the AFL and the CIO is well known. The condition of labor representation seems to offer an incentive for both conflict and merger that does not normally exist to the same extent in other SMIs.

As we noted above, monopoly funders may require, as part of their commitment to fund, united action or programs on the part of SMOs, or at least the working out of domain agreements. In this sense, funders may have a technocratic bias that may or may not correspond with organizational effectiveness. Monopoly funders also create formal alliances as did the Ford Foundation in its funding of the Southwest Council of La Raza (Goulden, 1971, p. 270ff.). This council was designed to fund and direct local boards drawn from existing Mexican-American organizations in a number of states in order to create united action. Similarly, holders of political power may impose an alliance because they want to know to whom they can speak—who represents the movement. On the SMO side, unification comes about because an SMO's leaders realize the elite will pick up on divisions and magnify them, or will not know to whom to listen. A related environmental press toward the formulation of alliances is the need to present a unified front in lobbying activities. Lawson's (1978) description of the development of federations of tenant organizations in New York City in recent years seems to represent such a process. The state legislature provided not only the potential for statutes affecting common goals but also resource flows to various organizations engaging in tenant actions of a diverse nature.

Alliances may often come about as the SMO scents victory; then coordinated action to achieve goals has a higher priority than organizational maintenance. Besides, at such times organizational maintenance is not under threat, and money and resources tend to be easily mobilized. But at such times no one worries about actual mergers. On the other hand, mergers are often suggested in declining movements; then, mergers may represent the only mechanisms for maintaining a viable organization. One other form of alliance, the popular front, represents a coalition of like-minded SMOs against a clear-cut countermovement group.

Hypothesis 13: The more clear-cut and vigorous the countermovement, the easier it is to mobilize an alliance.

The need for a unified defense transcends ideological differences. The Southern Conference for Human Welfare represents just such an alliance. Formed in 1938, The Southern Conference, Krueger (1967) says,

> was not a Communist Front (as many had charged), but a popular front, a conglomeration of individuals from organizations as diverse as the Baptist Church and the Communist party united about a minimum program on which all of the constituent factions could agree. That minimum program

aimed at repairing the defects of American Capitalism, bring the South up to the economic and social standards of the rest of the country, and finally obtaining elementary justice for American Negroes. (p. 181)

Of course, alliances may stem from common ideological prescription of targets as well.

Factionalism

Both economists and sociologists have a bloodless conception of inter-organizational relations, and the sociologists, oddly enough, tend to ignore power imbalances in these relations. The language of domain consensus tends to assume that the partners have shared or at least nonconflicting goals. But organizations may wish death on one another; they may want to absorb the other, take over its domain, squash the competition. As we have noted, the greater the commitment to a zealot's view of the proper state of the world, and the less effective the control of competition, the more one can expect illegitimate, violent, and deadly interorganizational relations. Finally, one other aspect of interorganizational relations deserves mention. *Inter*organizational relations may emerge from *intra*organizational fac-tionalism. Especially in social movements (see Zald and Ash, 1966; and Gamson, 1975), factionalism may lead to splits and the formation of new organizations. A similar process occurs in other organizations when prin-cipals (partners, senior executives) split, taking resources and reputations with them.

Factionalism is probably the form of intra-SMO relations that has re-ceived the most note historically. Probably as a result of the extensive factionalism within left-wing, sect-like organization during the 1930s in the United States, the impression was left that exclusive SMOs are more likely to develop factions, leading to the amoeba-like growth of new SMOs. Gamson's (1975) evidence on fifty-three SMOs suggests that exclusive or-ganizations are no more likely to develop factions than inclusive organiza-tions are. The impression that they do may derive from the fact that bitter conflict tends to occur between newly formed, exclusive SMO spinoff fac-tions. The impression comes, then, from the after-split behavior of the SMO. Some subset of the constituents of an SMO may split off to form a new SMO relating to similar goals for a number of reasons and under a number of different conditions.

The Organization of Afro-American Unity, Malcom X's organization, represented an offshoot from the Black Muslims of Elijah Muhammad. The new organization included several members of the Muslims and was clearly viewed by the Muslims as a competitor for their exclusive members.

The bitter conflict that occurred between these two organizations fits older impressions of the process of factionalism.

The Students for a Democratic Society represent a somewhat different case (Sale, 1973). Originally a youth arm of the League for Industrial Democracy, they split off from the parent body when the price of a stable resource flow was nondeviation from the operating tactics and, especially, membership criteria of the LID. Neither organization was exclusive in structure, and, though pursuing somewhat similar goals, the two organizations did not compete for the same constituency or engage in open conflict.

Another case, again quite different, is that of the splitting off of the Friends of the Earth (FOE) from the Sierra Club. FOE was created after a faction of the leadership of the Sierra Club lost several debates about tactics. The forming of the new organization was not an occasion for acrimony, however, and the parent organization lent the new organization its mailing list, as FOE attempted to recruit a constituency that backed up its more aggressive lobbying tactics (Wagner, 1972). FOE seems to have drawn its constituency largely from the constituency of the parent organization, and the two SMOs have cooperated in a number of joint activities since. Here, two inclusive organizations, the second a result of factionalism within the parent body, have not engaged in bitter conflict and, in fact, have cooperated rather extensively. FOE has received grants from institutional funders for operational expenses, especially during its early phases.[6]

Hypothesis 14: When factionalism and the spinning off of new SMOs occurs, the extent of exclusivity of membership and the extent of integration into a wider array of non-SMO organizations are both related to the extent of after-split conflict.

Conclusion

Inter-SMO relations are a central dynamic of any social movement. Whether one reads the history of the making of the Russian Revolution or the spread of evangelical Christianity, the pattern of conflict and cooperation leaps to the eye. The resource mobilization perspective's focus upon SMIs led us to ask how interaction within industries parallels the forms and dynamics of organizational interaction found in the literature of economics and the sociology of complex organizations. The parallels are striking.

Only the naive assumption that SMOs all share a common goal and therefore have little interest in conflict and competition has kept scholars from examining such central processes. In addition, since scholars often do case studies of single SMOs (the usual style is to move from a concern with a movement to a study of that movement's dominant organization)[7] industry-wide phenomena are usually treated only in passing.

We have offered a number of hypotheses about the pressures toward cooperation and conflict in an industry and the forms and permanence of these interactions. Obviously, analysis of these processes is dependent upon a prior description of the structure of an industry. Thus another theoretical task remains: accounting for the differences in industry structure—the number, size, and market locations of SMOs in an industry.

Even with such an analysis, our job would not be finished. Although we think the parallel with economic processes is striking, we should remember that there are differences. In particular, competition for dominance among SMOs is often for symbolic dominance, for defining the terms of social movement action. Social movement leaders are seeking symbolic hegemony. At some point, social movement analysis must join with cultural and linguistic analysis if it is to understand fully cooperation and conflict in its socially specific forms.

Notes

1. Systematic violent conflict between competing SMOs in such contexts, of course, demands special organizational structures. The Teamsters organization, the Black Muslims, and Synanon, for instance, possess squads who specialize in such tactics. Most SMOs do not.
2. See, for instance, Pfeffer (1972) and Allen (1974).
3. Mitchell and Davies (1978), in discussing environment coalitions, argue that newer members of preexisting coalitions implicitly accept the existing division of labor in joining them. Stallings (1977) argues that the preexisting structured relations in local communities affect the likelihood and shape of emergent coalitions.
4. See Aveni (1978) on the NAACP and Curtis and Zurcher (1973) on local antipornography campaigns for examples of the importance to SMOs of linkages to individuals and organizations both within and beyond particular SMIs.
5. Mitchell and Davies (1978) point to the importance of common headquarters locations in Washington, DC, as well as sporadic conferences of professional staffs for the cooperative efforts of many national environmental organizations.
6. Later, in fact, FOE split again when some staff members left to form the Environmental Policy Center, designed as a lobbying group without members (Wagner, 1972).
7. Even in Gamson's (1975) otherwise notable study of fifty-three SMOs, sampling procedures were used that led to ignoring the position of SMOs in an industry— as if we could study the Russian Revolution by studying the Mensheviks alone.

PART IV
MOVEMENTS WITHIN ORGANIZATIONS

Introduction

In an organizational society much social change takes place within organizations and voluntary associations. And, just as in the larger society, much social change takes place through well institutionalized processes. Managers are appointed with a mandate to change organizations, or as stress and crisis confront the organization legitimate authorities respond and change it. Those normal processes parallel the institutional processes of change in the larger society. But some organizational change is accomplished through social movement-like processes. Subgroups in the organization may become discontented with the status quo. Authorities may ignore the perspectives of the subgroup, exert social control, or be replaced.

The two chapters that comprise this section examine social movement processes in organizations. The first essay, published in 1978, is an exercise in analogical theorizing. Borrowing from the analysis of social movements in society, it asks what might be the analogous social movement forms and processes that take place within organizations. Social movement forms can be classified in terms of their scope and location in the social system. Mass movements involve many participants, usually from the lower rungs of society; insurgencies, or insurrections, are more restricted; coups d'état involve a few participants who control vital resources for the top authorities who move with stealth. The same variety is found within large-scale organizations.

The second essay, originally published in 1966, is an attempt to examine social movement phenomena in the Methodist Church. Protestant denominations vary in their structure. As a general rule, the more hierarchical the church and the greater the church discipline, the more likely it is that dissidents withdraw or are limited to small pockets of criticism. On the other hand, many Protestant denominations have congregational and decentralized structures. Individuals and congregations can resist the policies chosen by central denominational authorities. James R. Wood and Mayer Zald here document the resistances of congregations in the South to the attempts of denominational authorities to integrate the Methodist Church to promote civil-rights policy.

The two essays in this section reverse the analytic flow that characterizes the essays in the rest of the volume. Generally, an organizational approach is used to explain social movement phenomena. Here, a social movement approach is employed in order to explain organizational phenomena.

8

Social Movements in Organizations: Coup d'Etat, Bureaucratic Insurgency, and Mass Movement

Mayer N. Zald and *Michael A. Berger*

Power structures and political processes of organizations are important components of organizational analysis. Theoretical perspectives as disparate as those of Cyert and March (1963) and Zald (1970a, 1970b) contain notions of political processes or political structure as central components. And a large number of empirical studies examine the role of politics and power in the allocation of resources (Pfeffer and Salancik, 1974) as determinants of organizational satisfaction (Tannenbaum, 1962); as factors in the evolution of procedural rights, due process, and quasi-judicial processes (Evan, 1965; Pondy, 1964); and as influencing decisions on major capital investments or acquisitions such as computers (Pettigrew, 1973). Moreover, a number of papers treat power distribution as the outcomes of organizational tasks, contingencies, or dependencies (Crozier, 1964; Thompson, 1967; Perrow, 1970; Zald, 1962; Hickson et al. 1971).

Although this literature is rich and growing, it has two noticeable shortcomings. First, because so many of the organizational studies are synchronic, the study of things political is only rarely linked (either as independent or as dependent variables) to the study of organizational change. Second, studies or theories of organizational politics rarely take note of their kinship with investigation of political processes in nations and communities (but see Zald, 1965). Thus, they ignore a massive amount of thinking and research that might be relevant to work on organizations.

The fundamental assumption of this essay is that social movements or phenomena resembling them occur in organizations. That is to say, just as political sociologists study social movements in nation-states because they represent the cause and effect of societal change occurring outside institutionalized channels, so, we believe, the student of organizations needs to examine social movement phenomena in organizations because they too may be the cause and effect of emerging organizational change.

Implied by our assumption is the use of social movements in the larger society as models of or analogies to activities within organizations. For example, in the fall of 1975 Robert Sarnoff, president of RCA and son of the founder of the company, took a trip around the world to visit RCA's foreign plants. He had recently announced the reassignments of some of the senior executives; also, the company had suffered alarming financial reverses from the 1973-75 recession and Sarnoff's strategic decision to enter the computer industry. In his absence, senior executives convinced RCA's board that Sarnoff's reorganization was inappropriate and that he should be replaced. It is reported that when he returned he was handed a letter of resignation for his signature ("His Master's New Voice," 1975). The phrase that might characterize this bloodless change in leadership is "organizational coup d'état."

In a similar vein, in the late 1950s Brigadier General Hutton (faced with official opposition based on written agreements among the Department of Defense, the Army, and the Air Force) developed the armed helicopter. Starting with baling wire and lashing machine guns to the frame, a group of midrank officers evolved the quick-strike, mobile air cavalry. The army's air force is now the third largest in the world, behind the United States Air Force, and that of the Soviet Union (Bergerson, 1976). The term that best describes the action of the Hutton group is "bureaucratic insurgency."

Finally, there have been many protest movements and rebellions within organizations. Fights between local and national unions with management and the national union on one side and the local on the other (Berg, 1962; Serrin, 1973), the cleavage in 1976 within the Board of the New York Stock Exchange leading to the ouster of the president ("The Big Board's New Mr. Big," 1976), and organizational schisms within the Southern Methodist groups (Wood and Zald, 1966, chapter 9 in this volume) can all be characterized as mass movements in organizations.

These phenomena are important for sociological analysis because they affect the major priorities of organizations, the control of organizational resources, organizational survival, and growth. Moreover, they not only occur within organizations but also reflect the larger trends and politics of society. That is, struggles for executive office, clandestine product development, student revolts, seizure of plants, the admiral's revolt, and the fight for control of unions can be viewed as autonomous events, but such analysis misses an important point: social movements in organizations are often the situs for the working out of political issues and trends of social change. Organizations exist not only in environments (the "in" thing to study these days), they exist in society.

The central argument of this chapter is that much conflict in organizations occurs outside normal channels. It is "unconventional opposition." Just as in nation-states, when conflict occurs outside institutionalized channels, the tools of social movement analysis are brought into play, so too in organizations: much unconventional opposition and conflict can be subjected to social movement analysis. To support this argument, we consider the three types of social movement phenomena distinguished briefly above: organizational coup, bureaucratic insurgency, and mass movements. These types are analogous to major types discussed in the literature of social movements. Different kinds of organizational conditions facilitate the occurrence of one type or another. Moreover, these forms of opposition occur at different locations in the social structure; they use different tactics; and they have varying effects upon the organization. A resource-mobilization perspective is used here to analyze the determinants that may affect the occurrence of each form, the processes of interaction between authorities and partisans, and the factors that determine outcomes. We discuss the possible implications of the social movement for the organization, and we also evaluate the utility of our analogical model.

Analytical Perspective

Analogical theorizing proceeds by demonstrating that concepts and images used for describing and understanding one set of phenomena are counterparts of aspects of some other phenomena. Analogies have only weak theoretical utility if the phenomena have very different components; that is, if the analogy resembles the phenomena in question only in surface ways, we can speak of it as a metaphor or simile. Metaphors and similes are weak analogies. On the other hand, to the extent that the process and structures are isomorphic, that the things being compared resemble each other in great detail and in the interconnection of their parts, analogies become increasingly appropriate, and we can speak of them as strong analogies (see Willer, 1967; Nagel, 1961). We argue that there are many similarities between organizations and nation-states and that in fact our comparison of social movements in organizations with those in nation-states represents a strong analogy. (The differences between nation-states and organizations and the limits to the analogy are discussed in the Conclusion.) In this section we show first that a body of literature has been developing that implicitly or explicitly treats social movements in organizations in terms similar to those used in analyzing nation-states. Then we comment on the approach to social movements used here. Finally, we articulate the main dimensions of organizational politics and polities relevant to our analysis.

Previous Literature

Although they have not conceptualized them in social movement terms, a number of writers have described events in organizations that parallel descriptions of social movements in nation-states. There have been many studies of social movements within a particular organizational setting. In educational organizations, Heirich (1971) examined processes of polarization and the spiral of conflict at Berkeley; Kelman (1970) focused on events at Harvard; Daniels and Kahn-Hut (1970) reported on social movements and faculty involvement at San Francisco State; and Lipset and Altbach (1969) looked at the university student in politics and in university politics in different nations. In industrial settings, Britt and Galle (1972) extended Kerr and Siegel's (1954) classic study of strike proneness to show how the volume of conflict varies with proneness to conflict, extensity, and intensity of conflict. In other contexts, Martin (1954) and Wicker (1975) described riots in prisons that can be seen as protest movements; and Adams (1970) examined ideology, conflict, and heresy trials in Protestant seminaries. Finally, there is an increasing literature on change, ideology, and forms of protest and insurgency in the professions (Needleman and Needleman, 1974; Ross, 1975; Epstein, 1970; Gerstl and Jacobs, 1976). This literature will eventually provide a rich base for secondary analysis. But from our point of view it is limited by its failure to set the problem of unconventional opposition and conflict in a comparative and more middle-range theoretical perspective.

In contrast, we have identified six articles that begin to grapple with the problems of conceptualizing social movement phenomena in organizational settings. These articles use terms and modes of analysis very similar to those employed by analysts of political process, conflict, and social movements in the larger society.

In a prescient and almost forgotten article, Selznick (1943) examined the battles for control of voluntary organizations such as political parties and trade unions. Although most of the article deals with the general theory of bureaucracy, the final section examines the relationship of the rank and file to leaders, the growth of factions, and the ideologies of centralization and autonomy.

In two articles that parallel Selznick's concern, Burns (1955, 1961) discusses the ways in which formal and informal groups may encompass political goals and develop strategies and rhetoric to support their ends. In the earlier article (1955), Burns distinguishes cliques and cabals in organizations. While both types of informal groups were vehicles for handling uncertainty about status and role function, cliques were made up of older employees with no status differences, oriented toward protection, reassurance, and withdrawal from the realities of failure. Cabals, on the other hand, were made up of younger workers, had a distinct leadership hierarchy, and were oriented toward improving their own position in the allocation of power and resources by means of the cabal itself.

In his later article (1961), Burns shows how two aspects of organizational politics intertwine: the pursuit of self-interest and the mechanisms by which external and internal conditions of organizations are translated into institutional change and changing allocations of resource and status. Burns draws his illustrations from studies of universities and businesses.

Bucher and Strauss (1961) argue quite explicitly that the process of professional segmentation can be described in social movement terms. They suggest that professionals are loose amalgamations of "segments," pursuing different objectives, using different means, held together more or less delicately under a common name at a particular period in history. Citing differences within the medical profession between general surgery and urology, for example, the authors argue that differences in sense of mission, work activities, methodology, clients, interests, and associations lead to the formation of "segments" similar to social movements and that since professions occur within institutional arrangements, the dimensions of social movement analysis (i.e., ideology, goals, participants, leadership, and tactics) can be used to evaluate the struggle over possession of resources.

Whereas Bucher and Strauss examine segments of professions, Leeds (1964) examines the development of nonconforming enclaves within hierarchical organizations with commitments to normative goals (e.g., military units, religious organizations). She explores how dissident charismatic leaders and their followers deviate from organizational priorities and form partially autonomous enclaves with specialized missions. One of the advantages of Leeds' analysis is that it begins explicitly to discuss authority responses and their influence on outcomes.

Leeds describes the protest-absorption process as a structural weapon in the hands of authorities for converting the nonconforming enclave into a legitimate unit by giving it autonomy, in exchange for an agreement that it will abide by the regulations of the organization. She contends that the primary consequence of the protest-absorption process is the introduction of change.

Finally, Lammers (1969) employs quantitative techniques to study twenty mutinies and twenty strikes. He distinguishes three types of protest movements in organizations—promotions of interests, seizure of power, and secession—and argues that the form of the movements varied with the compliance structures of the organizations (Etzioni, 1961). Lammers's article discusses the determinants of the incidence, duration, and outcomes of protest movements in military and industrial organizations. Although we believe his emphasis on the relationship of compliance structure to the type of movement is too simple (see Zald and Jacobs, 1978), his article is important not only because it is an early example of the use of quantitative comparative techniques in the study of organizational social movements but also because it shows how a deep analysis of the structure of these organizations enriches our understanding of social movement processes within them.

These six articles are important to us for several reasons. First, they are explicitly framed in terms of concepts parallel to those used in the description of politics, unconventional opposition, and social movements. Thus, they confirm us in our belief that it is useful to make the analogy more explicit. Second, all of the articles provide rich illustrations of a number of the processes that must be accounted for. Yet from our point of view they are limited, because they do not carry the analogy far enough. That is, they either limit themselves to a narrow range of organizations (e.g., voluntary organizations in Selznick [1943], hierarchic organizations in Leeds [1964]), or they limit themselves to a narrow range of social movement phenomena (e.g., mass movements in Lammers [1969], bureaucratic insurgencies in Leeds). Our task is more encompassing: it is to set the determinants of the occurrence and outcomes of the broad range of types of social movements in the full range of organizational settings.

Perspectives of Social Movements

Since our approach draws consciously on analogical techniques, the description of social movements in organizations employs the descriptive dimensions of social movements in society. A social movement is the expression of a preference for change among the members of a society. Social movements differ in the *breadth of support* within the society (people who believe in the goals of the movement, contributors of time and money, activists and/or cadre); in their *goals* (the extent of change required and the level of concrete specification of goals); in the *strategy* and *tactics* of their carrier organizations; and in the *location* of their supporters in the social structure (these dimensions are elaborated below).

The resource mobilization approach to social movement analysis has two components that make it especially useful here. First, it examines the cost of participation in social movement action as well as the distribution of grievances. That is, it examines what Oberschall calls the risk-reward ratio. Second, it treats mobilization of resources from whatever source as a central topic. This is especially important in the study of social movements in organizations because such key resources as votes of stock, police intervention, legal support, board member votes, and strike funds may come from outside the group of immediate protagonists. Amount and sources of resources and risk-reward ratios are then combined with dimensions of organizational structure and process to explain the forms and rates of social movements in different organizations.

The resource mobilization approach is closer to a political sociology than to a collective-behavior tradition. First, it treats many of the issues that social movements deal with as rooted in the enduring cleavages, status relationships, collective definitions, and traditions of the social system. Second, it examines the infrastructure of society that supports or hinders the development of collective action. Infrastructure supports include means of communication, work schedules, and discretionary resources. Thus, the preexisting networks, associations, and organizations of involved groups may facilitate or hinder collective action. Finally, the resource mobilization perspective is concerned with the responses of authorities and the multiple linkages among authorities, partisans, and reference elites (Gamson, 1968; Lipsky, 1968).

This last point is especially important in understanding both the choice of tactics and the outcomes of social movements. Tactical choices are dependent upon prior relationships between partisans and authorities, the degree of consensus on goals between partisans and authorities, the amount of trust, and the relevant resources that partisans control. Authorities, for their part, must respond to partisans. They attempt to control or facilitate social movements depending upon their resources and capabilities for control and the extent to which social movement goals are consonant with their own goals. Since one purpose of our analysis is to account for social movement outcomes, analysis must concentrate upon the situation, the response of authorities, and the social movement itself.

Organizational Polities and Politics

Societies vary in their forms of government. The terms "tyranny," "democracy," "federation," and "republic" are crude descriptions of forms of government. So, too, do organizations vary in their forms of government. Many of our words describing them parallel those for societies. "Bureaucracy," "corporation," "federation," "cooperative," "voluntary association"—all have an element descriptive of the form of rule of an organization. Just as the political process of society can be characterized in terms of the rights, duties, and privileges of differently situated individuals and groups in relation to each other and to the formal institutions of government, so, too, do the organizational constitutions define rights and duties of members and officers in relation to decisions and behavior (see Swanson, 1971; Zald, 1970a, 1970b).

The organization constitution defines legitimate mechanisms for attempts to reach decisions and allocate resources. Behavior within these legitimate channels, processes, and positions is termed "conventional politics." Unconventional politics are attempts to reach decisions or effect the allocation of resources outside these legitimated channels, processes, and positions. Unconventional politics include both proscribed or "illegal" behavior and behavior toward which the constitution of the organization is largely neutral. Social movements in organizations are forms of unconventional politics.

Elsewhere the major components of polities and of political analysis of organizations have been treated in some detail (see Zald, 1970a, 1970b). Here we comment on three aspects of organizations that are critical to our later analysis: the dispersal of power and authority, the relation of organizations to the larger society, and the choice of action options for members situated in different positions in the organizations.

The living constitutions of organizations differ in their dispersal of power and authority. Our crude nominal labels such as "corporate hierarchical," "federation," and "voluntary membership association" often relate to the constitution of authority and the claims of organizations over their members. Thus, a corporate organization is one in which the corporate officers, no matter how selected, have rights of discretion and disposal over the resources of the organization. "Hierarchy" refers to clear strata in the organization, to superordinates' statuses. On the other hand, a federated organization restricts the rights of officers: in contrast to corporate hierarchical forms, federated organizations retain rights for the units and rights for the selection of officers that are not gainsaid in the corporate form. *Within* federated or corporate forms there may be wide variations in the internal distribution of rights. Both universities and businesses may be examples of corporate hierarchical organizations, but traditions and norms of tenure in the former and requirements of corporate loyalty in the latter may lead to much more open politics in the university than in the business. Similarly, many labor unions and the New York Stock Exchange can be characterized as federations, yet the extent to which central officers can intervene in operations of the peripheral units may vary widely.

Obviously, the corporate-federated distinction does not exhaust the analysis of organizational constitutions. Other components are the inducement-incentive contracts of the organization that set the terms of what members expect of the organization and vice versa, and the goals and means of the organization that set the boundaries of legitimacy and use of resources.

Organizations are webbed by the larger society. Rights of tenure, conditions for dismissal, use of punitive sanctions, and so on may be determined or limited by the larger society. At a very general level, the conditions for organizational discretion in relationship to goals, products, and personnel are all conditioned by societal norms. More particularly, since the society may prohibit authorities within organization from punitive actions and require the organizations to permit or even encourage group formation, the constraints imposed by the larger society may provide a powerful stimulus for social movement formation. Similarly, laws surrounding stockholder rights, the financing of proxy fights, and the like affect the cost of mobilization and the ability of organizational authorities to control and respond to internal social movements.

Finally, the formation of social movements in organizations is closely related to the microecology of aggrieved groups in the organization, their chances of remedies within the organization, their options for exit, and the costs and benefits of switching versus fighting (Hirschman, 1970).[1] Organizations vary in the extent to which they control important incentives or sanctions desired or hated by members, and the extent to which the members can easily exit and obtain the same incentives elsewhere. Sailors at sea must mutiny; soldiers can more easily desert. Because of differences in ownership of property and in organization, members of Protestant congregations can secede; members of Catholic churches face much greater difficulty in commanding the resources to create a new church (fellow members are more committed to the particular structure, and the central organization owns the physical facilities). Younger officers have too much invested in the military to resign; an officer with 20 years of service can retire at half pay. All these are examples of situational determinants that affect the choice of organizational members to engage in social movement action or to leave the organization. They are situational determinants of the forms in which discontent is expressed.

Given the range of polity forms, the extent to which society may or may not impose constraints upon particular types of organizations that facilitate or hinder internal social movements and the microecology of groups and individuals, it is beyond the scope of this essay to offer a general theory of social movements in organizations. The variety of social movements and the range of polity situations are just too great to be fully analyzed in a single essay. Instead, we devote most of our comments to social movements in corporate hierarchical organizations. We discuss movements in federated and other organizations only briefly, to indicate the direction a fuller analysis would take.

Social Movements in Corporate Hierarchical Organizations

Corporate organizations are those in which the units and facilities are "owned" by the group legitimated as the corporate office. That is, legitimate authority resides in the center (e.g., with the board of directors or chief executive officers). Among themselves corporate organizations may vary in the extent of decentralization-centralization of this legitimate authority. Federated organizations, on the other hand, are those types in which the units (locals, departments, chapters, or partners) have clear property rights and discretion which is established in the constitution of the focal organization (and possibly backed up by force of law). Moreover, they may have legitimate rights in the selection of executives and the establishment of policy. Voluntary membership associations, in contrast, can be either corporate or federated, but their distinguishing characteristic is that the members contribute resources upon which the central authorities depend. Thus authorities of voluntary associations have less discretion vis-à-vis organizational policy and are often in a precarious position vis-à-vis members (Clark and Wilson, 1961). Federated and voluntary organizations might therefore be called "upside down" organizations, for the flow of dependence is inverted from our conception of hierarchically arranged organizations.

All of these organizations may experience social movements. Hierarchical organizations differ from others in two major regards that have consequences for their political life. First, concentration of authority and power in a hierarchic structure means that there are higher costs of dissent and departures from organizational policy. Second, in such organizations subordinates have less normal access to the choices of major policy and of successors to executive offices. Conversely, in federated and voluntary organizations, units and members control both the resources that can be devoted to combating policies and legitimate access to organizational choice. This leads to two general and interrelated propositions: (1) federated and voluntary organizations are likely to have more open politics than corporate hierarchical organizations; (2) when unconventional politics take place in corporate hierarchical organizations, conspirational forms are likely to be more prominent.

The argument is not that conspiracies are absent from federated organizations or voluntary associations. Where the stakes are high, a minority may reject the well-institutionalized channels of a federated organization in attempting change. Nor are we arguing that corporate organizations are likely to have more phenomena resembling social movements. By raising the probability of success or lowering the cost of participation, open political systems may encourage unconventional political behavior. The major thrust of our argument is that there is a push to conspiracy in corporate hierarchical forms. Let us discuss three types of social movements in corporate organizations: coups, insurgencies, and mass movements. For each type we define the phenomena, specify determinants, discuss process, and describe likely outcomes. Illustrative hypotheses are given.

Organizational Coup d'Etat[2]

In his book *Coup d'Etat*, Luttwak (1969) argues that a coup is not an assault from the outside; it is a seizure of power from within. Second, he points out that a coup is usually politically neutral, with no immediate goal other than succession. Whatever policy emerges is a matter for the postcoup regime. Finally, he asserts that the technique used in a coup is not to confront, overwhelm, or smash down the adversary through sheer weight of power. On the contrary, it is a technique of judo in which the opponent's own advantages of weight and balance are turned into weapons against him. Luttwak therefore defines a coup in a nation-state as "the infiltration of a small but critical segment of the state's apparatus which is used to displace the government from the control of the remainder" (p. 12). Many coups involve subalterns, but a coup may involve one segment of a ruling junta ousting the current head of state.

By analogy, an organizational coup can be defined as the infiltration of a small but critical group from within the organization's structure to effect an unexpected succession. The term "infiltration" is used to denote the secrecy with which the plan is carried out. The small but critical group includes the palace guard of the chief executive officer (CEO) or some combination of inside and outside directors. The primary goal is succession, though less proximal goals of policy and change are implied in the political action.

Organizational coups can be contrasted with expected replacements (such as limited terms in office or retirement) and sudden successions that result from death. In the former, the succession is expected and conducted with a high degree of public awareness. In the latter, the succession is unexpected, yet once the initial shock of death wears off, replacement activities follow the regular institutionalized procedures. Organizational coups, on the other hand, are unexpected and deviate substantially from routinized procedures. That is to say, they are planned and executed without the CEO's knowledge or public awareness; otherwise the CEO would be able to retaliate. In addition, they involve the quick appointment of a new successor, which is at variance with the more usual procedure of search, trial, interviews, and selection. Five examples of organizational coups have been uncovered; here are brief illustrations of the climactic events in three of them.

[Interpublic] For Marion Harper, Jr., the sky fell shortly after 10:00 A.M. on Thursday, November 9, 1967. The setting was the windowless boardroom of the Interpublic Group, the world's largest advertising business, on the forty-fourth floor of Manhattan's Time-Life building. The occasion was a special meeting of Interpublic's board of directors with Harper presiding as chairman and chief executive officer.

For nineteen years Harper, now fifty-one, had been in charge of the burgeoning organization. His energy, his ideas, his ambitions had pushed, dragged, bullied Interpublic into a $700 million business.

A twelve-page agenda had been prepared and distributed in advance. When Harper brought the first item before the board, one of the directors interrupted and requested permission to question Taggart, the chief financial officer, on the group's current financial situation . . . Harper, suspecting nothing, allowed the question. . . . Another director spoke. Taking note of the gravity of the situation he moved that the first order of business be the replacement of the chief executive officer. The motion was immediately seconded. The vote: six ayes, one abstention. (Wise 1968, p. 136)

[Ford Motor Company] It was a press conference compounded of equal parts of vinegar and butter. The scene was a Detroit gathering called by auto mogul Henry Ford II last week to announce that the Ford Motor Company board of directors had voted to relieve President Simon E. Knudsen of his duties.

The bitter taste stemmed from Knudsen's calling of his own press conference an hour and a half earlier to say he was "puzzled by this sudden and unexpected action." Beaten to the punch, Chairman Ford was maneuvered out of the standard references in such situations to "a mutual understanding" and was forced to fall back on . . . "Sometimes these things just don't work out."

The butter, on the other hand, was what wouldn't melt in the mouth of Knudsen's arch-rival, ambitious Lido A. Iacocca, whose satisfied smile was in sharp contrast to the sober expressions on the other Ford executives present. ("Behind the Palace Revolt at Ford," 1969, p. 138)

[RCA] Robert W. Sarnoff always had a tough act to follow. His father, David, a one-time wireless operator who rose to brigadier general, had taken a relatively small company in the fledgling electronics business and, over four decades, built it into the giant RCA Corporation. Bobby—he was never able to shake either the nickname or the label of "the general's boy"—had ideas of his own, and after his father left the top spot at RCA, he pursued them vigorously. But two recessions and one gross miscalculation took their toll— last week, in a move that shocked Wall Street and company officials, RCA's board of directors ousted Bobby Sarnoff, 57, as chairman and chief executive officer. ("His Master's New Voice," 1975, p. 79)

In the Ford Motor case and the RCA case, the stories relate how senior executives organized and presented a bill of particulars to outside board members and key stockholders and pushed for the coup. In the most recent case we have found, that of the firing of Franklin Jarman of Genesco, a similar conspiracy from below is reported (Mullaney, 1977).

Determinants

What are some of the conditions that make coups more likely in one kind of hierarchic corporate structure than in another? First, the subalterns must be quite dependent on the executives for their positions. The ethos of business corporations is to stress executive loyalty at the same time senior executives serve on the sufferance of the CEOs (Kanter, 1977). If they did not serve on the sufferance of the CEO, they could criticize him. On the other hand, in universities deans and professors have tenure and can call for the resignation of the president. While there might be some negative consequences, they cannot be fired. We have not found any cases of coups in universities. We have found several cases in which deans and/or professors have openly called for the resignation of the president or the circumscription of his role.

Second, a coup in which subordinates want one of their own to be the CEO, cannot work in organizations in which the CEO is often or usually brought in from the outside. One could conspire to have a university president forced out, but the conspirators would not have a guarantee that the successor would come from inside. The same argument applies to metropolitan school systems. In contrast, in business corporations, especially large ones, the CEO is rarely brought in from the outside. Third, the conspirators need access to those board members who control the key resources—votes. And some board members may be more important than others. They may control large blocks of shares or major lines of credit or contracts. Fourth, corporations often have officer-directors. Unlike almost any other corporate form, there is often continuing interaction between the CEO's subalterns and his employers (indeed, some subalterns may even serve as "employers" if they are internal directors).

Finally, when are coups d'état most likely to occur? Chief executive officers with recent records of bad decisions and poor performance are more likely to be faced with coup attempts than others. Yet even CEOs who have decent records of profit performance are not immune if they have created enemies. We have found several cases in which interpersonal hostilities and power battles led to the coup. For instance, if the CEO has recently taken steps leading to the demotion or lowered power of subalterns, it is likely that he has incurred their enmity. Until the demotion is fixed and they are isolated from power, the potential for a coup attempt is very high.

Processes of Interaction

Regardless of the sources of their grievances, once a conspiratorial group has agreed to attempt to force out an executive, it must gain access to key board members or stockholders to carry the battle. Two authority processes must be considered. First, the CEO must be neutralized. Otherwise he can counterattack either by mounting a persuasive argument or by isolating and dismissing the conspirators. Second, board members and stockholders must be convinced. They must see their high cost of maintaining the current CEO arrangement. In two of the cases we have examined, board members had been contacted at earlier times but took no action then. The second time around, a more persuasive case was made. Moreover, it is clear that the CEOs were always surprised by the action and were often out of touch with their offices. In the RCA case described above, Sarnoff was visiting plants in Australia when the conspiracy took place. In the Genesco case, Franklin Jarman was on his honeymoon in Jamaica.

In other cases a coup attempt may occur when the CEO is sick, and a sick CEO may recognize that a force out is coming. For instance, recently Donald Kircher was replaced as head of the Singer Manufacturing Company (Hough, 1975). He had warned subalterns and the board a year or two earlier that any attempt to use an interim management arrangement to replace him while he was sick would be fought. But when he became sick again and realized that he would not be able to resume the mantle, he easily gave up the office.[3]

Outcomes

What are the outcomes of a coup? At least two types must be distinguished: the consequences or results for the participants and the consequences for the structural operation of the organization. The coup attempt may fail, as when conspirators marshal support but board members dismiss the attempt as self-serving for the conspirators, and the CEO isolates or dismisses them. If successful, the coup may lead to a change in personnel, a change in the system, but have few other consequences, little change of the system. Students of coups in nation-states have remarked that coups often have little impact upon the larger society because they are not related to any underlying structural change. Coups in organizations may have relatively few consequences below the elite level. The coup leads to a change in the chief executive and possibly to a few shifts down to the assistant vice-president level. Beyond that there is no necessary change. Product lines and company policy may be only tangentially at stake. Whether a coup leads to change other than personnel shifts depends upon the connection of the coup to any underlying trends in the organization and its environment. The coup is very important to the organization and its environment. The coup is very important to the immediate participants, but the irony is that a company's long-range profitability is heavily dependent upon industry profitability and the position of the company in that industry. Within the normal range of company performance, who becomes CEO is unlikely to have great impact upon the company (see Lieberson and O'Connor, 1972).

In the cases we have examined, organizational coups do not relate to political issues in the larger society, but they do relate to societal or industrial change. First, the CEO's stance on major strategies may have been found to be in error (e.g., the RCA case). Second, a coup may relate to hostile merger or takeover bids. Takeover and merger bids may lead to conversations between the company that expects to take over and factions in the executive office. Thus, forcing out a CEO may be partially related to political factions within the organization more or less favorable to the company buying it out. The parallel at the nation-state level occurs when the coup anticipates loss of a war. The coup puts in office a CEO and ruling group more favorable to the potential occupying power or prepares for continuation of the war.

The main themes of our analysis of coups can be expressed as a set of hypotheses (one each for occurrence, process, and outcome).

Hypothesis 1: In corporate hierarchical organizations that (a) do not protect the positions of senior executives and (b) do promote within, (c) provide senior officers access to board members, and (d) experience poor performance or other undesired situations attributable to the CEO, coup d'état attempts are more likely to occur than in other types of corporate organizations.

Hypothesis 2: Successful coups are facilitated by surprise CEO neutralization and by the support of the more powerful board members and shareholders.

Hypothesis 3: The first-order effects of a coup are the reshuffling of executive positions; larger changes in the organizational system are rare.

Bureaucratic Insurgency

Bureaucratic insurgency differs from a coup in its target: its aim is not to replace the chief executive but to change some aspect of organizational function. It differs from a mass movement in extent of support and number of adherents. It resembles a coup in that for much of its duration it may be conspiratorial. It resembles some mass movements in that its goals are limited to change in specific aspects of the organization. In nation-states insurgency, as we are defining it, is analogous to the action of a pressure group or professional movement (McCarthy and Zald, 1973). It typically involves a limited mobilization of personnel. At the organizational level, bureaucratic insurgency in corporate organizations is an attempt by members to implement goals, programs, or policy choices that have been explicitly denied (or considered but not acted upon) by the legitimate authority of the focal organization. The activity of the insurgents therefore takes place outside the conventional channels of politics of the organization.

Determinants

Bureaucratic insurgency is most likely to be found in organizations or organizational units that have strong normative elements or organizations that are dependent upon staff who have strong professional-ideological and moral commitments. These normative commitments provide personnel with reference bases to evaluate organizational products, priorities, and procedures. (On normative, coercive, and utilitarian compliance bases, see Etzioni [1961]; see also Clark and Wilson [1961] and Zald and Jacobs, 1978.) The participants in bureaucratic insurgency may also include the subalterns of executives, but usually they range deeply into the organization, throughout middle management, and, in organizations using professionals on the line, down to the line staff.

When the desired activity or change has been explicitly denied, bureaucratic insurgency may take the form of conspiracy. Here the insurgents know they are pursuing disapproved lines of action (i.e., using organizational time and resources in ways that have been countermanded by authority). If the insurgency is reformist or narrow, discovery of the conspiracy may lead to repression, not necessarily expulsion.

Often, however, insurgency operates in gray areas where organizational behavior has not been explicitly prescribed. Thus, insurgents attempt to establish their own definition of the situation or shift the weighting of priorities. Bureaucratic insurgency is also aided by factionalism or sympathetic support from the organization elite. For example, members of the control apparatus may overlook information which would suggest that a conspiratorial insurgency is actually taking place. The well-known phrase "You can do it, but I don't want to know about it" is a case in point.

A conspiratorial bureaucratic insurgency is thus facilitated by a low capacity for surveillance on the part of the central authorities. The effect of limited surveillance is compounded by organizational complexity; the larger the organization, the more diverse its structure, the more autonomous the units, and the more imprecise the reporting system, the more likely it is that an insurgency can continue for long periods of time.

We can delineate three major subtypes of insurgency: program or product development, whistle blowing, and policy choice. In program- or product-development insurgency, the insurgents accept the overall structure of authority in goal setting but attempt to introduce new techniques for accomplishing goals or refinements of organizational programs. Middle-level officials or line professionals with discretion in allocating organizational resources, the insurgents pursue their own concept of organizational programs or product development while watching over their shoulder for the elite interference. Social workers running group programs or allocating welfare funds, army officers developing the armed helicopter, engineers, developing the air-cooled engine at General Motors, or HUD bureaucrats attempting to push cities to have more racially integrated housing may all operate and be involved in this first type of bureaucratic insurgency.

Whistle blowing is a form of insurgency in which an insurgent deviates from loyalty norms to describe the disjunction between organizational functioning and public expectations. Whistle blowing may require only one insurgent. For instance, A. Ernest Fitzgerald, a systems analyst for the Defense Department, testified to the Senate on the massive cost overruns in building the Lockheed C-5A cargo plane ("Defense: Ernest Fitzgerald RIF," 1969). Fitzgerald acted by himself, but more organized whistle blowing is feasible. Underground newspapers can serve as outlets for private information that will discredit the elites.

A third type of bureaucratic insurgency focuses upon the main goals and policy choice of the organization. In 1949 the "admirals' revolt" questioned policies of the Defense Department that seemed to lead to a diminished role for the Navy ("Revolt of the Admirals," 1949). Once the insurgency came out in the open, it began to resemble a mass movement. The difference between mass movement and insurgency lies in the greater openness of the former, the number of people involved, and the extent to which multiple organizations or units are involved. The admirals' revolt was an insurgency at the top that was taken to higher authorities, Congress, and the public. (The route was to Congress because the Defense Department is controlled by the executive.) One suspects that this form of large-scale and open insurgency at the top occurs only in corporate situations in which the insurgents have some degree of protection (e.g., good retirement plans or high job mobility) or in which the issue, the reward, the prize, is vital to the interests of the contesting elite.

External Support and Authority Response

Whereas the organizational coup d'état requires the involvement of key board members, a wider range of external supports is necessary in insurgency. For instance, whistle blowing is fully dependent upon external support, for by definition organizational authorities have been unresponsive and typically have attempted to quash complaints. The insurgency may also be aided by explicit material support. Army officers developing the armed helicopter cooperated with small machine-tool companies that helped the officers machine and construct weapon supports and modify the helicopters. Bureaucratic insurgents may also arrange for client groups to request procedures or programs that ultimately serve the insurgent's *and* the client's end.

If monetary or technical resources are not required, the major support is likely to come through professional and movement perspectives. That is, the insurgency is fueled by societal social movements and a professional ideology that has been previously learned or is currently fashionable. The social and ideological support of a radical caucus or an association of radical urban planners provides such reference support (see Ross, 1975).

The response of authorities to insurgency depends at least in part upon their perceptions of the opportunity costs of compliance and the extent to which the insurgency is defined as compatible or incompatible with elite preferences and priorities. Thus, some insurgents may be aided by some members of the elite; others may be seen as so removed from elite operative goals that the elite's aim is to quash the insurgency.

Outcomes

Outcomes of insurgency include failure and repression, continued segmental operation, enclave support, and total incorporation.

Failure and Repression. When authorities discover insurgency and find it opposed to their definition of organizational priorities, they may suppress or disband the insurgency. Members may be expelled from the organization or punished. Officers and priests can be sent to undesirable posts; they can be forbidden to pursue their line of action. However, authorities must calculate not only the degree of threat presented by the insurgents but also the consequences for relevant others, both in and out of the organization, of taking a given line of punishment against the insurgents. To the extent that the insurgents are in fact moral exemplars in the organization, overaction leads to the possibility that the authorities themselves will be discredited.

Even if the insurgent group is disbanded, however, it can still bring about changes in an organization. If the authorities or other members of the organization take over the decision premises and orientations of the insurgents, over time the organization may change. (Such a paradox parallels the impact of social movements in society: for instance, the Populist movement in the United States gained many of its goals even though many of its leaders never attained power.)

Segmental operation is the maintenance of the insurgency over long periods of time with no formal recognition from the center and without change in organizational products or goals. It occurs most often in organizations with multiple goals where there are continuing ambiguities and dilemmas in elite control.

Enclave support is likely when external pressures lead the executives to recognize and tolerate the insurgency. This outcome (as in demonstration projects or the setting up of separate departments or units) is likely if organizational goals are multiple and units are only partially interdependent with each other. The formal recognition of an insurgency is similar to Leeds's (1964) process of "protest absorption," but she addressed a much narrower range of phenomena.

Total incorporation of the insurgency depends upon the ability of the insurgents to get executive compliance or agreement. If over time the developed program or product can be shown to be consonant with the executive goals, the organization may fully incorporate insurgents' perspectives, and the insurgents may be promoted. Such total incorporation eliminates the raison d'etre of the insurgency. The adoption of the armed helicopter and related strategies of mobile infantry as a major component of warfare is an example of a totally incorporated insurgency.

Three hypotheses summarize our argument about insurgency:

Hypothesis 4: Insurgencies are most likely to occur where professional and normative commitments provide an independent base for perspectives on goals, products, and polities.

Hypothesis 5: The more complex the organization and the more difficult the surveillance, the longer the duration of insurgency.

Hypothesis 6: The outcome of insurgency depends upon the extent to which the insurgents threaten authority and the costs to authorities of suppression.

Mass Movements: From Protest to Rebellion

As noted earlier, bureaucratic insurgencies may span many levels in an organization. They range from small cabals at the top to the concrete and concerted efforts of middle-level managers and professionals. When small, they may have a conspiratorial cast. On the other hand, as they become more organized, they may develop coordinating committees or caucuses that begin to resemble mass-action movements. As their numbers grow and their tactics move toward withdrawal of labor, petitions, and boycotts, they begin to resemble mass movements.

Mass movements at the nation-state level range from movements of protest to rebellion. They are defined as collective attempts to express grievances and discontent and/or to promote or resist change. They vary in goals from those aimed at melioristic change of specific practices or rights to those aimed at redefining the distribution of power, constitution of rules, and norms of society. By analogy, mass movements in organizations range from the expression of minor grievances (not previously acted upon by authorities) to major attempts to seize control of the organization.

Mass movements differ from insurgencies and coups in number of participants and the visibility of their actions. Coups and insurgencies may be restricted to face-to-face groups and become visible only toward the end of their histories. Mass movements, on the other hand, may be initiated by a small group, but larger numbers must be mobilized if the initiators are to gain their ends. Examples of mass movements are work slowdowns, wildcat strikes, mutinies and secessions, mass desertions, and prison riots.

It is important to note that, while the proximal goal of the movement is to change the behavior and goals of organizational authorities and the structure of organizations, the real goal may be changes in the larger society. Thus, the student movement disrupted the University of California at Berkeley, Columbia, Harvard, Michigan, and Wisconsin and had as proximal targets changes in administrative behavior. But the real goals were to change the behavior of Lyndon Johnson and Richard Nixon or, in more radical form, the structure of American society. Similarly, a plant seizure or strike may occur to achieve concrete gains, but it also may be a weapon for changing governmental policies or the government itself.

A paradox confronts us in thinking about mass movements in organizations. In discussing coups and insurgency, we drew on sparse evidence; on the other hand, when one turns to the study of mass movements, the literature appears rich, systematic, and quantitative. After all, economists and sociologists have been studying the factors related to strikes, industrial conflict, and unionization for two generations. And more recently quite sophisticated quantitative analyses have decomposed the determinants of the numbers, breadth, and duration of strike activity (Britt and Galle, 1972). Yet the first glance is deceiving. For strikes need not represent the social movement-like phenomenon of unconventional politics. They may represent a fully institutionalized political system of organizations.

Winning union recognition and the legitimation of strikes is part of a social movement process in society and in specific organizations. Yet the union has now become one of the political mechanisms for aggregating preferences and resolving conflicts in the organization. Snyder (1975) has shown that one can predict aggregate strike behavior from aggregate economic variables *after* a collective bargaining system has been institutionalized. From our point of view, institutionalized unions that engage in strike action are part of normal politics.

Of course there are some parallels between industrial strikes and mass movements in organizations. Both involve mobilization of workers and the calculation of costs and benefits. Yet the mechanisms for mobilization, the costs of organizing for collective action, and the extent of organization and societal support are different enough so that we cannot incorporate wholesale the literature on industrial conflict in our explanation of organizational mass movements.[4]

Determinants of Mass Movements in Organizations

Olson (1965) has taught us that mass movements aim to provide collective goods. The provision of collective goods entails free-rider effects; since the goods will be provided to all, individuals have little incentive to work for their provision. Free-rider problems are overcome in coups and insurgencies: in both forms the benefits accrue to a small group of participants, and in insurgency social control and solidarity incentives, coupled with career incentives and normative commitments, suffice to sustain the insurgents.

The question becomes, what organizational conditions facilitate mass action? Our perspective on resource mobilization and the interplay between organizations and their societal environment leads us to five hypotheses about the relations of size, homogeneity, vertical segmentation, exit options, and associational density. All of these hypotheses assume grievances or a gap between the current situation and desired alternatives. (Since our analysis here is more detailed than our earlier discussion, we couple hypothesis and analysis rather than presenting the hypotheses in summary form.)

Hypothesis 7: The larger the size of the subordinate group, the greater the probability of organizational mass movements.

Classical theory and recent studies of riots in cities lead us to expect that larger subordinate groups in organizations are more likely than smaller groups to develop into social movements. There are several reasons for this. Larger groups are more likely to include some members who develop grievances. Larger groups are more likely to be cut off from superordinates (see below). Larger groups are more likely to generate associations within them. In a study of prison riots and confrontations in the largest prisons, Wilsnack (1976) finds that the very largest (over 1,000 inmates) were more likely than the smaller ones in his sample to have experienced nonriot resistance (confrontation, refusal to work). Similarly, Peterson (1968) finds that large campuses were more likely than small ones to have been involved in antiwar protests. For most industries we would expect that large establishments are more easily organized than smaller ones.

Hypothesis 8: The greater the homogeneity within the subordinate group, the more likely that subordinates will challenge superordinates.

On the one hand, group consciousness is facilitated by homogeneity and shared values. On the other hand, heterogeneity may facilitate conflict within a subordinate group and the possibility of alliances between subclasses of subordinates and superordinates. This hypothesis follows Kerr and Siegel (1954). Thus we would expect that organizations with little occupational differentiation would be more likely to have superordinate-subordinate conflicts.

Hypothesis 9: The greater the vertical segmentation, the more likely that grievance channels, mobility channels, and communication channels in general are blocked.

This hypothesis has been proposed in the social movement literature (see Oberschall, 1973) and offered as an explanation for strike proneness (see Kerr and Siegel, 1954). Of course it dates back at least to Pareto. In organizations in which occupational status and ethnic class status are overlaid, we would expect segmentation to be especially strong and both within-group solidarity and the chances for resentment to be high.

Hypothesis 10: The more difficult or costly it is to exit and the greater the commitment to the incentives of the organization, the more likely social movements are to form.

In some ways this hypothesis, which just restates Hirschman's (1970) exit-voice thesis, parallels Thibaut and Kelley's (1959) analysis of "comparison-level alternatives." Thibaut and Kelley, of course, were interested in whether people continued their line of action within a social interchange or moved outside that interchange. It is apparent that different personnel in organizations and positions are confronted with differences in comparison-level alternatives. The value of the comparison-level alternatives can be broken into two components: the cost of exit and the value, negative or positive, of the perceived option once attained. Comparison level is the net value of the current situation or line of action minus the cost of exit and the value of the goal, once obtained. Some organizations have extremely costly exits. Military institutions raise the costs of exit very high. Nevertheless, it is apparent that exit is less costly in an army than in a navy at sea. Under relatively similar levels of dissatisfaction and grievance, we would expect soldiers to mix use of desertion and protest, whereas sailors at sea use only mutiny. Blake's (1976) study of military resistance to the Vietnam War reports cases of mutinies in military prisons and among troops on the line (refusals to move into combat), but it is our impression that the number of actual mutinies on the line is much lower than in the more contained prison situation. All of the mutinies that Lammers (1969) studied were naval ones. There are, of course, cases of whole units of armies deserting; these should probably be seen as secessions. They are not protests of the bottom against the top; instead, they are led by dissident officers who disagree with either the treatment of their units by the authorities or the policies of authorities in prosecuting the war and in relation to subject populations (see Solzhenitsyn, 1973).

Earlier we noted that strike rates do not necessarily reflect social movements in organizations; they do, however, reflect disagreements with management offers or existing conditions. With regard to the hypothesis under consideration, Stern (n.d.) finds a negative correlation, over communities, between quit rates and strike rates.

A final derivation from the exit-voice hypothesis can be suggested. The classical situation for exits is free markets with low costs for information and transportation. There, buyers or sellers easily compare options, and consumers switch from seller to seller with no protest. However, our hypothesis suggests that consumer protests increase as monopoly increases—a relationship amply confirmed by American history—and monopoly can be defined as the opposite of exit choice. Monopoly exists when a single seller controls the sale of a good and there are no close substitutes for it.

The exit-voice hypothesis has a strategic role in accounting for the structural conditions of mass movements in organizations. First, it allows us to account for variation within an industry (defined as a set of organizations offering somewhat similar products) of two forms of expressing dissatisfaction—exit and voice. Second, it helps to provide an answer to Olson's question: Why collective action, when collective action is accompanied by free riders? The implication of Hirschman's argument is that, if one option for individuals, exit, is removed, an individual must weigh taking no action against taking some action that will promise a surplus of benefits. Stated differently, the removal of the exit option raises the comparative discounted benefits of the voice option. But Olson's challenge still remains. Our next hypothesis treats it more directly.

Hypothesis 11: The greater the associational density and the higher the proportion of organizational participants who are members of associations, the easier it is to mobilize.

A major part of the critique of the mass-society theory of social movement has been that people who are most involved in voluntary associations and political organizations are also more likely to be involved in social movement actions (see Oberschall, 1973). There is supporting evidence in organizations. Although not dealing with social movement participation, Lipset, Trow, and Coleman's (1956) study of the International Typographical Union makes it clear that the associationally dense culture of the ITU facilitated political involvement. Similarly, studies of the student protests find that antiwar protest was correlated with the proportion of students in leftist organizations (Peterson, 1968). And Von Eschen, Kirk, and Pinard (1971) found that early participants in the civil rights movement sit-ins were likely to be part of established, politically oriented organizations, often student based. But if the hypothesis said only that members of ideologically committed associations were more likely to take action than members of uncommitted associations or ideologically committed individuals, it would not say much. Its real thrust is to argue that belonging to associations and networks eases the cost of information flow and mobilization. In relation to Olson's question, it suggests that, even if the associations are not formed to pursue the specific target of collective action, a dense associational field within a hierarchical organization facilitates internal social movements.

Our last hypothesis in this series relates to organizational recruitment of participants.

Hypothesis 12: The more an organization recruits members critical of existing conditions, the more likely it is to generate an internal mass movement.

Although obvious, Hypothesis 12 reminds us that issues and grievances within organizations are developed in the larger society. Since organizations may draw upon different segments of society for subordinates, "exactly similar" internal conditions may be responded to and redefined by recruitment of members from varying backgrounds. The issues of the multiversity and the war in Vietnam could have been defined as grievances in South Dakota and Alabama as well as at Wisconsin and Berkeley. That they were responded to differently in academic communities is probably as much a result of self-selection as the internal organization of universities. A similar argument about differential recruitment applies to the locus of social movements in prisons and in manufacturing industries.

The hypotheses about mass movements presented above deal with the factors facilitating mobilization within organizations,[5] but they do not deal with the goals of mass movements. Nor do they deal with the support and control of movements from both within and without the organizations.

Goals, Facilitation, and Control

Mass movements in organizations range from narrow protests against specific organizational practices (e.g., the quality of food in the cafeteria) to shopping lists of practices, calls for the restructuring of authority or changes in the relationship of the organization to other elements of the society, and, at the broadest level, the restructuring of society itself. Let us examine the interaction among the goals of the movement, indirect and direct support, and the response of authorities.

When goals are narrow, the movement and the response of authorities are usually only weakly linked to external factors, either ideologically or materially. (To be sure, the standards for judging conditions internal to the organization may relate to the conception of adequate conditions in the society; e.g., what is adequate food in a prison in Turkey will not be seen as adequate in an American prison.) Indirectly, however, even narrow issues implicate the relationship of the organization to society. For example, the quality of food is related to the budget of the organization, and addressing specific grievances may be constrained by organizational resources and resource dependencies.

When the goals of the movements are broader, encompassing change in the authority structure of the organization in the larger society, we find the movement deeply dependent upon the larger society for the ideological acceptability of the goals; such dependency reshapes the response to the movement of external actors. In recent years, for instance, workers in England and France have seized plants which were about to be closed or have massive layoffs. Given the much more extensive nationalization of industry in these countries than in the United States and given ideologies of worker participation in management and socialism, such attempts at worker control have received both financial and political support. Similar moves to close plants in the United States are met with stoicism, some union bargaining, some community protest, but little governmental intervention or attempts to shift the criterion of authority or ownership.

External material and coercive resources may be mobilized by either the movement or authorities. Strikers are dependent upon several kinds of external resources—in particular, money for food and the honoring of the strike by other potential employees. Indirectly, the society supports or constrains the movement by its general provision of resources. For instance, Thieblot and Cowin (1972) have shown that the length of strikes in American communities is affected by ease of access to welfare payments. The easier the access, the longer the strikes. More directly, strikers may be funded by individuals and organizational contributions to maintain them. Coercive resources are provided or withdrawn by the police, military, and courts, who facilitate or inhibit authorities' and protesters' tactics of reprisal, boycotts, lockouts, etc. The provisional withholding of these coercive resources is based upon the general laws and attitudes governing their development and on the specific behavior and linkages between the movement, authorities, and external groups.

The response of authorities to mass movements is affected by the goals and tactics of the movement, the autonomy of organizational authorities, and their own ideological predisposition.

Note first that authorities may have little discretion to respond. For instance, prison administrators are not autonomous; they can rarely respond positively to the demands of rioters or protesters. Indeed, if the list of demands is long, the protesters recognize this dependency, and their first moves are to ask for the involvement of political authorities. Similarly, in many countries (most Latin American countries, France, etc.) the universities are not autonomous of the ministry of education. A mass movement in the university, especially if it moves into the streets, is responded to by political administrators, not university officials. Where officials do have discretion, several strategic policies may be adapted. Lammers (1977), in a comparative study of the response of university authorities to student movements, lists four general combinations of strategies, tactics, and goals:

CHART 1

Strategies	Tactics	Goals
Repressive	Fight off	Elimination
Concessive	Buy off	Appeasement
Preventive	Stand off	Nonemergence and dissolution
Experimental	Join in	Copartnership

In the first, the authorities attempt to eliminate the movement and its leaders. They suspend students and use heavy sanctions. In the fourth, the authorities appear to buy in to the goals of the movement and move to align the organization with the goals of the movement. Lammers goes on to assess how different types of tactics will work in different types of universities. For instance, he is skeptical about the viability of the experimental strategy and the tactics of joining in in large universities, and he believes that preventive strategy allows universities to continue to carry out their educational and research missions with less disruption than the use of either concessive or repressive strategies. (He does not consider in detail the interaction of opposition and authority strategies.)

Outcomes

In mass movements, immediate outcomes depend upon the ability of partisans and authorities to sustain conflict and the extent to which there are viable options for bargaining. If situations are defined in zero-sum terms, a sheer power calculus can be used. But in open-conflict situations, a variety of symbolic and partial solutions may permit both parties to win. Mass movements with specific and narrow goals may accomplish a change in the system of a specific organization, with little impact upon society. On the other hand, movements with broad goals are likely to fail unless they are part of a broader movement in the society at large.

The ability of partisans and authorities to maintain a conflict depends on their ability to mobilize resources and on the continuous availability of resources. This is especially important in understanding the difference between mass movements in such organizations as universities, with high turnovers of personnel, and those occurring in such organizations as factories, with greater continuity of personnel and organization. Thus, although in a university the movement may be at high tide in the spring, the lack of continuity of student generations and the departure of student leaders at the end of their senior year lead to a high cost of remobilizing resources. On the other hand, workers in continuous organizations with a longer career span of leaders have fewer problems in maintaining continuity. In universities with off-campus student enclaves, however, developing a culture of activism that lasts longer than a student generation might lead to more movement continuity. Similarly, when student politics is more entwined in national politics, professional staff members from national political organizations (e.g., SDS, NAACP, CORE) may supply needed continuity.

As the continuation of the mass movement raises the costs to both members and authorities, search for settlement options takes place, much as in protracted conflict in society at large. Authorities may grant concessions, symbolic or material, or they may legitimate the movement and incorporate it in the decision structure. These would be considered successful outcomes.

The outcome of organizational rebellions may be failure. The reasons are straightforward: organizations are encapsulated in society, and an attempt to change an organization radically may strike at the heart of the authority relations of the larger society as well as in the organization. Such broad-ranging movements can succeed only where they are joined with existing conflict and rebellion throughout the society. However, the visibility of mass rebellions in organizations give them a life beyond their immediate outcome. For instance, the Soledad Brothers and the events at Kent State University live in the symbolic history of American social movements. They recall an ideology and conflict that reminds all adherents of the defined inequities and injustices in society. Therefore, to the extent that mass movements occur and have some continuity, they can lead to the enshrinement and reliving of dramatic events in the future.

Three hypotheses summarize our discussion of mass movements in hierarchical organizations:

Hypothesis 13: Exit-voice options, subordinate homogeneity, vertical segmentation, selective recruitment, size, and associational density affect the costs and extent of solidarity, cleavage, and mobilization.

Hypothesis 14: The goals and duration of mass movements depend upon ideological and material supports in the larger society.

Hypothesis 15: Outcomes of the movements are dependent upon authority responses, continuity of movement participants, and relationship of the movement to movements in the larger society.

Comparative Summary

Earlier we mentioned several dimensions of social movements: breadth of support, goals, tactics, location in the social structure, relation to external support, and duration. Let us compare coups, insurgencies, and mass movements in corporate organizations along these dimensions (Table 1 presents the comparison in brief form).

Breadth of Support

Social movements may vary in number of adherents (believers) and number of constituents (individuals or organizations who act in support). As the previous analysis suggests, an organizational coup d'état involves a small group (the palace guard). Bureaucratic insurgency and mass movement, on the other hand, may include a department in the case of the former and/or significant segments of the organizational population in case of the latter. Breadth is important, for it implies the amount of mobilization costs. In a coup, mobilization is restricted to a small cabal; therefore organization costs may be low. In contrast, insurgency may require the cooperation of a larger group of organizational participants, some of whom might not evaluate benefits to be worth potential risks. In mass movements, increasing breadth heightens the mobilization problem considerably, thereby leading to increased costs in organizing for collective action.

Goals

Goals can be evaluated in terms of the amount of change desired, the extent to which it is a change in the system of authority and relationship to the society. In a coup d'état, personnel changes are usually the only goal. Structural or policy changes may follow the unexpected succession, but these are not the primary aim of the movement. Furthermore, the goal of personnel replacement is concrete. Bureaucratic insurgency and mass movements, on the other hand, may involve objects aimed at transforming the basic structure, policy, and resource distribution of the organization itself. As insurgency or a mass movement becomes more involved in the structure and policy of the organization, goals tend to reflect larger abstract values such as mission, justice, and equitable treatment.

Choice of Tactics

Choice of tactics (e.g., violence or nonviolence) depends on a calculus that includes legitimate resources, degree of access to or exclusion from

TABLE 8.1
Dimensions of Social Movements in Organizations

Dimensions	Movement Type		
	Organization Coups	Bureaucratic Insurgency	Mass Movement
Breadth	Small conspirational group	Medium-sized enclave or one whistle blower	Large group
Goal	Succession which may or may not lead to future change	Challenging the efficacy of existing norms to effect moderate organizational change	Expressing discontent and promoting or resisting narrow or broad goals
Main tactics	Infiltration and persuasion (e.g., using CEO's own record against him	Violating rules and procedures without violence	Direct confrontation and possible violence
Activists' location in the organizations's social structure	Organization elite	Middle managers and professionals	Lower-level participants
Linkage with external elements	A few key supporters, ususally banking interests or key board members	Several important supporters beyond financial interests alone	Elaborate linkages of ideological and material support from society
Duration of overt conflict	Conspiracy may brew over a long period; very brief actual coup	Varies; can last several years, depending on how long the organization can stand the nonconformity	Varies, from a day to several months depending on how the organization can stand the disruption and on the extent to which movements' members can mobilize for the conflict

legitimate channels, the cost of using violent tactics, and the perceived utility of tactics in accomplishing strategic goals. In coups, the palace guard is likely to have considerable legitimate resources available in terms of their knowledge of internal affairs and their authority to direct large segments of the organization. In addition, their access to board members, years of experience, and cohesion lead one to hypothesize a relatively peaceful choice of tactics, though they may include the threat of resignations.

Bureaucratic insurgents possess fewer legitimate resources, are more excluded from authority, and experience greater risks (e.g., being fired) in the use of violent tactics. In this case, tactics are also likely to be secret and nonviolent. Mass rebellions, on the other hand, represent the farthest extreme. With few legitimate resources for bargaining and limited or no access to authority, tactics may include the use of violence and disruption of the normal functioning of the organization.

Location in the Social Structure

Social movements differ in their location along vertical, horizontal, and sociodemographic dimensions. The vertical dimension refers to the location of adherents in the hierarchical system of the organization. The horizontal dimension includes both the spatial and functional differentiation of the organization. These differentiations provide the basis for the development of within-group solidarity and differentiated concepts of organizational mission, problems, and priorities. The sociodemographic dimension refers to the age-sex-social background of groups that combine to shape orientations and perspectives within the organization.

In an organizational coup, the palace guard is located close to the authorities. That is, the guard actually will be the elite in the status hierarchy and therefore experience very little spatial or functional differentiation. This lack of differentiation should lead to high within-group solidarity and congruence with the board concerning organization mission, problems, and priorities. Such congruence is bolstered by similar social backgrounds, age, and sex. In contrast, the orientation of the insurgent department is likely to diverge from that of the authorities and be predicated on the distance from them on spatial and functional differentiation vis-à-vis other parts of the system, and on wider variations in age, sex, and social background. Finally, rebels will probably be most detached in their orientation from authorities due to high vertical separation, extreme spatial and functional differentiation, and wide variations in age, sex, and social background.

Linkage with External Elements

Coups require linkages with key stockholders, outside board members, or key financial supporters. Insurgencies, on the other hand, are fueled by ideological and professional support. Mass movements with broad goals are heavily dependent upon support from outside the organization. These include the cooperation of agents of control (police), material resources, and political and ideological support.

Duration

Finally, the duration of conflicts varies considerably. The coup, though possibly brewing for a long period, is over in a few short hours; mass movement and insurgency, on the other hand, can continue for long periods of time.

In every case we have been considering in this section, there is a central legitimate authority and a relatively clear hierarchic distribution of power. We now describe social movements in organizations in which the central authority is usually weaker vis-à-vis the units or members.

Social Movements in Federated and Other Organizations

A complete analysis of social movements in organizations will include descriptions of the variety in social movements across the wide range of organizations that diverge on major constitutional dimensions, such as voluntary associations of different types (e.g., organizations with purposive goals such as political parties, social movement organizations, special-purpose interest groups, professional associations, associations conveying solitary incentives). These organizations differ from corporate hierarchical organizations in several regards relevant to social movement and political processes. First, members and units typically stand in a different relation to the organization and to the center, the titular authorities.

The vertical stratification system does not dominate the system of rule. Most voluntary associations do not control major stocks of incentives of the members; thus exit is easier. Time commitments of members are low, and the authorities are less in a position to impose strong sanctions. Second, the constitution of authority in these organizations restricts the rights of the center vis-à-vis members or units. In federations, ranging from business partnerships to labor unions to Protestant churches, the units are basic elements of the organization, retain rights of operation in their own domains, and share in decisions about the direction of the total organization. These organizations possess political systems which, if not democratic, at least establish a flow of authority and legitimation from the members and units to the central organization. They establish procedures for succession to major office that involve the unit or members; they establish procedures for the members or units to affect major policies and directions for the organization. What effect do these differences in polities have on the kinds of social movements that emerge?

As noted earlier, professional associations, voluntary associations, and federated organizations have more open politics than do hierarchical organizations. At least dissent, factionalism, and conflict are less likely to be repressed. In many ways, then, one can move the whole apparatus of political sociology analysis into these polities with even less modification. Moreover, theoretical and empirical works have examined phenomena resembling social movements in these organizations before, though often under different guises. Thus, the literature on factionalism and democracy in unions (see Edelstein and Warner, 1975), on the conflict in the Methodist Church (Wood and Zald, 1966, chapter 9 in this volume), on factionalism in political parties (Wilson, 1966), and on change in professions (Ross, 1975; Epstein, 1970) begins to describe the phenomenon in question.

In general we expect that coups and insurgencies are less likely to occur in these organizations, and factional fights and secessions are more probable.

Federations

A federated organization is defined constitutionally by the rights reserved to the units. Both constitutionally and in practice, there is variation in the relationship of federated units to their centers and to each other (Sills, 1957). For instance, a federated union may have weak and apathetic units, so that the central organization essentially dictates policy and makes it extraordinarily difficult for any local initiative to materialize. In contrast, other units may command resources, loyalty, and a spirit of independence that make them a perennial thorn in the side of both management and central union offices (Kuhn, 1962). Similarly, church organizations may range from episcopal structures in which the living constitution gives great power and command to the bishop, to congregational structures in which the local congregation controls and appoints the minister, owns the church, and does not need to accept any policy directives from the center.

Social movements in federated organizations usually take the form of rebellions of single units or coalitions of units against the center. Conspiracies may occur if the dissident faction's composition or goals are abhorrent to the dominant coalition in the organization. For example, the establishment of front organizations by the communist party is not such ancient history, nor is the conspiratorial takeover of the Social Democratic party by Lenin-led Bolsheviks.

The greater the degree to which local units control (own) the resources of the units (the physical facilities and/or the loyalties and identification of the members), the more likely it is that schisms and secession will occur. Thus, as compared with hierarchic corporate organizations, social movements in federated organizations may lead to a breakup or splintering off of various segments of the organization. The history of American Protestantism is rife with such schisms and secessions. Schisms also occur in political party systems where proportional representation rules exist. In contrast, when voting rules lead to winner take all, political parties retain their factions.

There are essentially two types of schisms. In one, whole units secede; in the other, groups of members within units find the program or policy of the organization unacceptable and secede with the intent of setting up a new organization. The former is probably more easily accomplished, since the whole unit secedes with an organization and facilities already in place.[6]

Less dramatic than schism or secessions, members or units may lead the battle for changes in policy. For instance, the Episcopal Church, which combines hierarchical and federated features, has had a long, drawn-out battle over the adoption of a new translation of its book of prayer. This movement has been led by college English professors and has brought about a reversal in church policy. By the same token, trade-union locals may hold out against the settlement negotiated by the international union. This is not to suggest the center is without power in federated organizations. For instance, a recalcitrant local can be put in trusteeship and its officers, stewards, and business agents suspended. Since putting a local into trusteeship also leads to cutting off funds and abrogating votes, it is a potent weapon for the center. In Protestant denominations, the center's power over the dissident congregation ranges from censure to lockouts and even to heresy trials.

Voluntary Associations

Social movement organizations, professional associations, social clubs, and local community-betterment groups are characterized by heavy dependence upon their membership and membership commitment for their maintenance. As noted above, because the organization is not a purveyor of major stocks of incentives, the center must curry favor; and executives are heavily dependent upon persuasion, symbolic rewards, and providing services and friendship to maintain commitment.

In some voluntary associations, open conflict and politics are muted precisely because the conflict would lower the commitment of members and lead to high rates of exit. Organizations that depend upon solitary incentives attempt to avoid conflict; they develop a politics of accommodation. If conflicts do emerge, they may lead quickly to individual or group secession. Even voluntary associations with purposive goals must avoid conflict, for the losing factions are likely to secede.

Professional Segments

One more type of social movement in organizations deserves mention: a movement in a profession that infiltrates both corporate hierarchical and professional associations. Bucher and Strauss (1961) describe the growth of segments in social movement terms. The members develop a sense of group identity and difference from the rest of the profession; they develop a program of action. In professional associations, such segments operate loosely either through caucuses or through attempts to change the policies and structure of the association. In hierarchic organizations, they can be described as bureaucratic insurgents.

Conclusion: The Utility of the Model and Research Prospects

This analysis has suggested that the similarities of nations to organizations permit us to utilize concepts of social movements drawn from the former to examine similar processes in the latter. Much more than a metaphor is intended. Organizations and societies are similar enough so that a strong analogical model can be and has been employed. There are indeed strong similarities. Both organizations and nation-states, for example, are composed of groups located in a stratified system of statuses and with differential access to resources. They are both webbed by ideologies that often cause conflict in terms of which perspective will lead more efficiently to goal accomplishment and whose perspectives on goals ought to be adhered to. They both have group cleavages. They both have systems of rules and of social control, and they both have group and individual resistance to their rules and control.

On the other hand, there are differences that weaken the analogy. A state has a legitimate monopoly over coercion, whereas an organization does not. Moreover, a state has a pluralistic set of goals. It is not even clear how one can conceive of the goals of a state; whereas the goals of an organization seem at least more concrete. Nation-states are relatively large in territory, whereas organizations are more concentrated geographically. Nation-states can present great obstacles to mobility (i.e., entry and exit), whereas in most organizations, except for coercive types, entry and exit are comparatively easy. Finally, the cleavages and structure of nation-states endure for generations and are transmitted through families and the class system, while the cleavages of organizations have a less enduring base.

The question then becomes, what are the consequences of these differences for the strength of the analogical model? First, the claim that the state has legal powers of coercion, whereas the organization does not, suggests that organizations will not have a full range of strategies with which to deal with conflict groups. Yet it can be argued that the organization's ability to expel, isolate, or apply sanctions to its members represents similarities to legitimate coercion and that both nation-state and organization use coercion that is circumscribed by legitimate norms.

Second, the claim that goals in a nation-state are more abstract and organizational goals more concrete implies that movements may be easier to mobilize in an organization. Yet it can be argued that in both cases there is duality of goals. That is, there is a distinction between official and operative goals. Official goals are the entities' general purposes, as set forth in its charter, whereas operative goals are the actual goals sought which are determined by group interests (Perrow, 1961). Furthermore, it can be asserted that the recent civil-rights, end-the-war, women's, and environmental-protection movements have all had very precise goals.

Third, the argument that states are larger and organizations smaller implies that mobilization costs may vary as a function of size. In some sense this may be true, yet it can also be argued that the processes are the same and only the scale is different. If both entities were standardized to control for size, the results might be very similar.

Fourth, the assertion that the two entities differ in mobility potential implies that the exit option may be readily available in organizations, hence leading to fewer movements, whereas exit from one's nation-state is more difficult, suggesting a greater reliance on voice (i.e., movements). Yet this reasoning ignores the facts that (1) changing one's job represents a serious disruption; that is, while job mobility may be theoretically possible, on a practical level it is not always desirable; and (2) apathy and passivity are just as prevalent at the nation-state level as at the organization level, suggesting that the formation and execution of movements in both are equally problematic.

Finally, even generational turnover in organizations is variable: although class ideology may have to be transmitted more rapidly in organizations, people are not so transient that ideology and alternative accounts may not be transmitted within organizational generations (see McNeil and Thompson, 1971).

The differences between nations and organizations do imply differences in the social movements that will be generated. In organizations they are likely to be smaller, less likely to use violence, less likely to have well-developed ideological systems, less likely to have long-range continuity. These, however, are matters of degree, not quality differences. These "little" social movements are similar in enough regards that parallel processes and dynamics can be seen, and sometimes they are not so little.

A more serious difficulty with the approach has to do with its utility for research. How can we gather data on these processes? How can we study these events? For example, the propositions imply a sample of organizations to evaluate structural and dimensional determinants of the occurrence and form of a movement. Often, however, published accounts of occurrence and form are sketchy or nonexistent. Further, it is very difficult to learn about movements that were aborted or suppressed. For nations, some enterprising historian will describe such movements. Who will describe them for organizations? While research in this area is difficult, it is by no means impossible. Compared with research on some aspects of social movements in nations, it is actually easier. The difficulties come largely in the quantitative study of coups and insurgency. We typically learn of them after the fact and only if they hit the "news." Yet both can be examined by ethnographic case studies. Even a systematic sampling of informants in organizations can provide us with a sense of the range of insurgencies and coups in organizations. For instance, using a sample of organizations, an investigator could gather a record of all successions to top positions over a number of years. He then could use informants and organizational histories to examine the processes of succession. Or, following Wilsnack's (1976) lead, a survey could be designed tapping the range of social movement phenomena in an organization, from protest to petitions to riots, over a defined period.

The advantages of studying social movements in organizations are obvious: there are only 100 or so nations, there are thousands of organizations, and there is probably more variation in the polity of organizations than in nations. Even the study of outcomes of social movements is easier within organizations than within nations. Analyses of social movements in nations have been notorious for the looseness with which outcomes—success, failure, goal displacement, movement becalmed—are discussed. Given the range of process in society, attributing change to a social movement is like looking for a needle in a haystack. (See the critique and programmatic statement on this problem by Snyder and Kelly, 1979.) At least in organizations the boundaries of effects have clearer space-time limitations. Specific policies, authority relations, and changes in rights and prerogatives can be pinpointed.

This essay has identified a new agenda for organizational analysis. Instead of following the traditional approach to conflict, power, and exchange, the essay conceives of many such processes as unconventional politics that give rise to movement-like phenomena. More specifically, the essay distinguishes organizational coups, bureaucratic insurgencies, and mass movements to argue that a combined approach of analogical theorizing and resource mobilization may explain the form, occurrence, and outcomes of such phenomena. After offering a number of propositions relating to a resource mobilization perspective, we evaluated the strength of the analogy and implications for research.

The model we have presented here has, we believe, several uses. First, it brings together under one conceptual structure partial analyses of social movement phenomena employed by others. That is, we are able to link a number of analyses of insurgency, strikes, enclave formation, and other phenomena that have been conducted without reference to each other. Second, our approach suggests a number of possible research strategies to illuminate a phase of organizational life that has been hidden in darkness. Third, it suggests a new paradigm in the study of organizations: the study of mobilization processes (see Benson, 1977). Finally, and most provocatively, it opens up once more a host of questions that have seemed settled. Can we, for example, look at the Protestant Reformation not as an issue in theology, nor as an issue in the relationship of societal constitution to collective ideation (Swanson, 1967), nor as an issue in state formation, but as an organizational rebellion? Seen from Rome, the Protestant reformers must have looked like bureaucratic insurgents, and the insurgents had to mobilize internal and external support.

Notes

We are indebted to Ivar Berg, Anthony Oberschall, David Snyder, and anonymous reviewers of the *American Journal of Sociology,* where this article first appeared, for their critical comments, for illustrations, and for continuing encouragement.

1. Albert Hirschman's *Exit, Loyalty and Voice* aims at predicting when individuals within organizations protest and when they leave. Its subtitle, *Responses to Decline in Firms, Organizations and States,* indicates the generality of the choice between exit and voice. Moreover, several students of national politics have found this book, though concerned primarily with organizations, to be equally applicable to the expression of choice in nation-states. The strength of Hirschman's analysis is that it forces us to think of two modes of expressing discontent (exit and voice) together, whereas most of us have treated these separately. Economists have focused on the exit option; political scientists have focused on the voice option. For several papers on exit and voice, see *Social Science Information* (1974, 1975).

2. This section is drawn from a paper by Berger (1975).

3. CEOs who are forced out often receive remunerative contracts ("golden parachutes" to erase their sorrow): appointment as consultants with no duties and pay close to what they received in office are common.

4. The problem here parallels an analytic gap in the study of social movements and politics in society. Party politics and the aggregation of preferences through the institutionalized political process are treated separately from social movement emergence, growth, and change. Yet social movements with political goals influence the institutionalized system and may become part of it. Similarly, the

institutionalized political process uses many of the same forms of mobilization as social movements (see Garner and Zald, chapter 12).

5. It should be apparent that many of these hypotheses might also be used to predict the determinants of coups and insurgency (e.g., exit options for senior and middle managers may relate to participation in coups and insurgency). We have elaborated upon them in connection with mass movements because we had more evidence and illustrations with which to support them. A general theory of social movements in organizations might well start with them.

6. In episcopal structures the church building is often owned by the central church, even though possibly paid for by local donations. And in court battles over expulsion, the building may revert to the overall association. On the other hand, in congregational structures the local denomination may own the building.

9

Aspects of Racial Integration in the Methodist Church: Sources of Resistance to Organizational Policy

James R. Wood and *Mayer N. Zald*

Certainly, one of the most difficult developments in American society during the last ten years has been the growth of a civil-rights movement aimed at the destruction of racial segregation and discrimination. Scholarly and journalistic attention has focused on the growth of the movement and its effects in the political arena, in education, and on community life. But little attention has been given to the impact of the movement on the internal life of large-scale organizations, to the attempts of organizations to implement policies and perspectives stemming from the political ideologies and perspectives of the larger society. In this chapter we focus on the consequences for its southern subgroups of an organization's (the Methodist Church) attempt to implement policies aimed at racial integration.

Our analysis has been guided by Selznick's concept of unanticipated consequences. Selznick (1953, p. 258) has alerted us to the fact that "observable unanticipated consequences" of purposive action are evidence of the breakdown of organizational control. Where such consequences are present, there are likely to be sociologically identifiable forces at work—forces tangential to the rationally ordered structures and stated goals of the organization. The adaptation of leadership to these forces results in "'character defining' commitments, which affect the organization's capacity to control its own future behavior" (Selznick, 1957, p. 35).

It seems plausible to expect, however, that the unanticipated consequences and character defining commitments will vary with the organizational context in which they occur. In particular the extent of unanticipated consequences, their open subversion of organizational policy and the extent to which leadership will have to accommodate to organizational subgroups depends on the relative balance of sanctions (positive

223

and negative) controlled by the organization vis-à-vis its subgroups. In general, the more the balance favors administrative leaders, as in the military or in bureaucratic structures with weak employees, the less likely it is that unanticipated consequences will seriously threaten organizational policy. The present study deals with a Protestant denomination, a voluntary organization that has an especially weak balance of incentives and sanctions over its members.

National Policies of the Methodist Church

The Methodist Church was formed in 1939 by the unification of the Methodist Episcopal Church; the Methodist Episcopal Church, South (which had left the unified church in 1844); and the Methodist Protestant Church (out of the main body since 1828). The basis of the union was the jurisdictional plan which while placing white conferences in geographical jurisdictions, placed all the Negro conferences in one nongeographical jurisdiction. It appears that many churchmen in the South expected this arrangement to be permanent. Methodists from other areas were, at the least, aware of the expectations of these churchmen.[1] But the events surrounding World War II soon made such an arrangement untenable to Methodism outside the South. Thus, because of the race question, almost from its beginning united Methodism has been a troubled union. The South has been on the defensive from the first, and has successfully stalled off drastic measures to integrate the church. Nevertheless, in 1958 (less than 20 years after union) Amendment IX to the constitution set up machinery for and at least implies the purpose of abolishing the Central (Negro) jurisdiction.

> The Central Jurisdiction shall be abolished when all of the Annual Conferences now comprising it have been transferred to other jurisdictions in accordance with the voluntary procedure of Article V of this section. (Methodist Church, Doctrines and Discipline, 1964, p. 34)

By 1964 it was evident that the various boards, seminaries, publications, etc., of the national church were determined that the church should be integrated in local churches as well as in jurisdictions and conferences. One of the many indications of this purpose is the revision of certain statements about church membership in the *Discipline* for 1964:

> Therefore all persons, without regard to race, color, national origin, or economic condition, shall be eligible to attend its worship services, to participate in its programs, and, when they take the appropriate vows, to be admitted into its membership in any local church in the connection . . . . A member of

a local Methodist church is a member of The Methodist Church anywhere in the connection. (p. 49)

Also, beginning with 1964 each candidate for the Methodist ministry is asked the question:

> Are you willing to relate yourself in ministry to all persons without regard to race, color, or national origin, including receiving them into the membership and fellowship of the Church? (p. 150)

The events taking place in the context of these policies may be fruitfully viewed from Selznick's theoretical perspective. First, we will present empirical evidence from one of the southern conferences of "observable unanticipated consequences" of the Methodist Church's integration policy. Secondly, we will attempt to delineate the accommodation made by conference leaders to the forces that lie behind these consequences. Finally, in the face of resistance from such an important source of the denomination's strength, we will analyze the character defining commitments of the national church leading to the persistence and increase of its efforts at integration.

Unanticipated Consequences: Resistance to Integration

While organs of the church at the national level have been mainly responsible for formulating policies aimed at integration, the annual conference has operating responsibility and most immediate interaction with the local churches. Evidence of unanticipated consequences presented is based on data from one of the southern conferences to which we give the fictitious name of Southern State Conference of the Methodist Church. Geographically this unit of the Methodist Church covers roughly half of a southern state. It is divided into twelve districts, each under the supervision of a district superintendent. Collectively, these men make up the cabinet of the bishop. The bishop and his cabinet promote the various causes of the Methodist Church and, each year, make the appointments of pastors to churches. There is a yearly meeting of the conference attended by the ministers and delegates from each local church. The *Journal of the Southern State Conference* records the proceedings and reports of these annual meetings. In 1964 the conference was composed of 531 pastoral charges (some with more than one church), 200,881 full members, and 10,843 preparatory members. Properties and other assets amounted to $70,846,362.

The first two evidences presented (giving to race relations and use of

FIGURE 9.1
The Number of Churches* Giving to Race Relations and the Number Using Only
Methodist Literature is Decreasing, While the Number Giving to Methodist
Student Day Increases

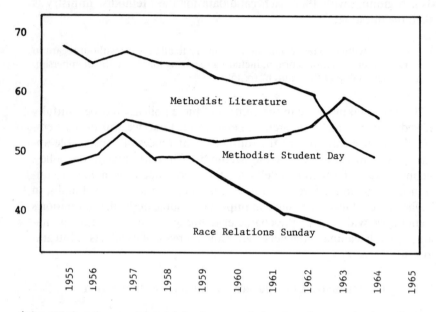

*The 69 churches ranking highest on an index based on pastor's salary, number of members, and giving to World Service.

1961 is not included for the two-budget items because the conference had a nine-month year due to a change in the month of the annual meeting.

Methodist literature) are based solely on statistical reports in the conference *Journal* over a ten-year period. The third evidence (the refusal to assign "liberal"[2] pastors to the key southern Metropolis churches) is based on *Journal* reports of pastoral appointments, and the rating of pastors as conservative, moderate, or liberal by three ministerial informants. The final evidence (concerning the Methodist Layman's Union) has its source in certain documents of the union and in information gathered during interviews with twenty pastors of the conference.

Number of Churches Giving to "Race Relations"

Although "Race Relations Sunday" is set aside for a special offering, most churches simply place this item (and other "Special Day" items) in their budget. This money goes to Negro educational institutions in the

South. Although it is possible to perceive this item as irrelevant to integration (and, in fact, some otherwise vigorously protesting churches do give), there is no plausible explanation for these churches[3] failing to give other than that they are protesting integration efforts. We, therefore, expected a decrease in the number of churches giving to "race relations" during the ten-year period under study. Figure 1 compares the downward trend in the number of churches giving to race relations with the stable-to-upward trend in giving to another voluntary offering, Methodist Student Day (a scholarship fund). This comparison allows us to emphasize that the drop in the number of churches giving to race relations is contrary to the general trend in benevolence giving.

Number of Churches Using Only Methodist Church School Literature

The denomination stresses exclusive use of its own literature. The pastor reports to the annual conference whether the church uses only Methodist literature. Since this literature has become increasingly specific in its support of integration, we expected a decrease in churches using only Methodist literature. This finding is also presented in Figure 1.

The Number of Liberal Ministers in the Key Southern Metropolis Churches

It is recognized generally that Southern Metropolis is the center of power of the conference. Thirteen of the top thirty churches are there; the bishop resides there; principal church-owned institutions are there; the annual meeting of the conference as well as most of the committee and board meetings are held there. There are, therefore, advantages to ministers in being located in Southern Metropolis. Any appointment takes on extra prestige for being in Southern Metropolis.

Some of the liberal interviewees suggested to us that there has been an exodus of liberal ministers from the key churches in Southern Metropolis. To investigate this claim three conference informants were asked to rate the conservatism or liberalism of a long list of ministers. The list included pastors (over a ten-year period) of the thirteen churches in Southern Metropolis which are in the top thirty churches of the conference (the most prestigeful appointments). The data presented in Table 1 indicate that at the beginning of the decade the pulpits were almost evenly held by liberals and conservatives, but by the end of the decade the liberals had been forced out.

Three facts gathered in the interviews make the table even more impressive. (1) The lone liberal voice in these churches in 1961 and in 1962 was the target of increasing pressure to move. In 1961 the bishop told him to tell his pastoral relations committee that he was moving. He was so sure

TABLE 9.1

The Number of Liberal Ministers in the Key* Southern Metropolis Churches

Rating Year:	1955	1956	1957	1958	1959	1960	1961	1962	1963	1964
Conservative	5	5	5	7	8	10	9	9	11	10
Moderate	2	3	3	3	1	1	2	2	1	1
Liberal	5	4	4	3	4	2	1	1	0	0
Not able to assign	1	1	1	0	0	0	1	1	1	2

*Those 13 Southern Metropolis Churches which are in the top stratum of the conference.

of moving that he burned his calling cards and began to pack his books. At the last minute he was permitted to stay. He insists that it is because no other available church would take him. (2) One of the four liberals in Southern Metropolis in 1959 was forced to move at the end of his first year. For a man of this stature to leave at the end of one year (especially to a far less prestigious church) is highly unusual.[4] (3) At the 1958 annual meeting the then most outspoken "liberal voice" left the Southern State Conference for a church in New England. He had stayed more than ten years in a church which would be considered a stepping stone to the top stratum of churches. Close friends report that he was repeatedly told he would have to stay there as the only top openings were in Southern Metropolis and none of them would have him.

The Methodist Layman's Union

In early 1959, the Methodist Layman's Union was organized with the one purpose "to oppose, actively and intelligently the integration of the two races in our churches and church activities." Such an unofficial organization was deemed necessary because the "last three General Conferences of the Methodist Church" have made it very clear that "no official body of the Methodist Church (with exception of such local bodies as Boards of Stewards) is free to oppose actively the Methodist Church on this issue."[5] The first mailing of the organization, announcing the first general meeting for March 1959, began:

> Few laymen are aware that the united Methodist Church in the South is in grave danger of being torn asunder. A Commission was appointed at the last General Conference to study plans designed to bring about integration in our Church. We are informed that the Commission will recommend vital changes in the jurisdictional system which, if put into effect, will jeopardize existence of the united Church in the South. Is your Church willing to stand up and fight this destructive movement? (printed letter, n.d.)

The Layman's Union came into being as a direct response to the announced purpose of the national organization to integrate the church. Once in existence this organization itself became a center of power, solidifying and focusing hitherto sporadic efforts at resistance. This point will be discussed further.

Some Causes of Resistance

What sociological forces create this resistance to national policy? We first observe the relationship between the evidences presented above and the concentration of Negroes (percent non-white population) in the twelve districts of the conference. We then discuss more fully the meaning of this relationship for our understanding of how and when the church becomes committed to the sociological forces in its environment.

We reasoned that areas with a larger percentage of Negroes would be more committed to a segregated way of life both because there would be more actual benefit from the exploitation of the Negro and because there would be a more drastic change in social relationships should integration become a reality. It seemed plausible, therefore, that the indices of resistance to integration tactics of the national church would be sharpest in those areas where a high percentage of the population was non-white. Because the areas are themselves more committed to segregation, they are more concerned to enforce the commitment upon the church.

"Race Relations" Giving

To test the above hypothesis we (1) calculated the percent non-white of each of the twelve districts (1960 census), and then (2) devised an index of giving to race relations. This index was the result of dividing the number of charges[6] in the district apportioned $500 or more for World Service into the number of such churches *not* giving to race relations in 1964. A high score indicated low giving. The product moment correlation of the percent non-white of the district with the index of giving to race relations was .84 (see Table 2). Returning to our analysis of the top performance churches, we examined the relationship between a church's being in a high percentage non-white district and that church's not having always given to race relations during the period 1954-64. Tables 3, 4, and 5 show that this relationship exists but that it is far stronger among the top stratum churches than among those of the second stratum.

Methodist Literature

There is a negative relationship between a church's being in a high percent non-white district and that of a church's using all Methodist literature in 1964. Table 6 shows this relationship in the top sixty-nine churches.

Ministerial Appointments

Table 7 shows that in the top stratum a slight relationship is indicated between a church's being in a high percentage non-white district and its having a conservative or moderate minister in 1964. (However, one would not normally reject the null hypothesis in this case.) There is no such relationship in the second stratum and, therefore, in the top sixty-nine churches as a group. This finding is consistent with the view held by all the ministers interviewed that the laymen in the top stratum churches have

TABLE 9.2
The Relation of the Percent Non-White of the District to Race Relations Giving,
1964

District	Percent Nonwhite	Index of Race Relations Giving*
Ninth	8	.00
Fifth	13	.25
Seventh	13	.18
Sixth	13	.36
Eighth	16	.12
Second	21	.62
First	26	.62
Eleventh	27	.73
Tenth	30	.50
Twelfth	30	.50
Fourth	35	.60
Third	35	.71

r = .84   *high score = low giving

TABLE 9.3
Churches in High Percent Non-White Districts are Less Likely to Give
Consistently to Race Relations: The Top Sixty-Nine Churches, 1954-1964

	Not always giving	Always giving
High percent nonwhite	31	18
Low percent nonwhite	6	14

ϕ = .30 one-tail test P < .02

TABLE 9.4
Churches in High Percent Non-White Districts are Less Likely to Give Consistently to Race Relations: The Top Thirty Churches, 1954-1964

	Not always giving	Always giving
High percent nonwhite	13	3
Low percent nonwhite	4	10

$\emptyset$ = .53 one-tail test P < .01

TABLE 9.5
Churches in High Percent Non-White Districts are Less Likely to Give Consistently to Race Relations: The Thirty-Nine Second Stratum Churches, 1954-1964

	Not always giving	Always giving
High percent nonwhite	18	15
Low percent nonwhite	2	4

$\emptyset$ = .15 Fisher Exact P = .3053

greater influence in the appointive process than do those in churches of less importance.

The Methodist Layman's Union

The only handy indication which we have of the relationship of percent non-white to the Methodist Layman's Union is the fact that of the South-

TABLE 9.6
Churches in High Percent Non-White Districts are Less Likely to Use All
Methodist Literature: The Top Sixty-Nine Churches, 1964

	Using all Methodist Literature	Not using all Methodist Literature
High percent nonwhite	35	14
Low percent nonwhite	19	1

∅ = .26 one-tail test P < .05

TABLE 9.7
Churches in High Percent Non-White Districts are More Likely to Have
Conservative or Moderate Ministers: The Top Thirty Churches, 1964

	Conservative or Moderate Ministers	Liberal Ministers
High percent nonwhite	13	1
Low percent nonwhite	8	3

∅ = .27 Fisher Exact P = .21

ern State Conference signers of the organization's *Pronouncement* and the additional men whose names appear on a later letterhead, thirty men are from high percent non-white districts while only three are from districts with a low percentage of non-whites. If churches represented, rather than men, are used as an index (some of the signers belonged to the same churches) the figures are twenty-two to three. In all, ten of the districts are represented by the signers. The two districts not represented have a low concentration of Negroes. It is known that the Layman's Union had no effect in one of the three low percent non-white districts which did have a *Pronouncement* signer. That district had a general meeting of laymen to discuss the issues and head off any attempts to organize the Layman's Union. The union was never able to secure a church in which to hold a meeting in that district. (The extent of union activities in the other two low non-white districts is not known to us at this time.)

Before we more fully develop our argument, let us recapitulate the material presented above. We have cited instances in which attempts to make gains for integration have resulted in losses to other basic values of the organization. Since some more liberal churches are increasing their giving to Negro education (Race Relations Sunday), it may be that this value is not seriously threatened by the protest documented here. The reduction in the use of Methodist literature, however, appears to be a more serious threat to the cohesion of Methodism. The dangers of a center of power outside of and opposed to the official structure of the church are also evident. The silencing of the prophetic voice in the Methodist pulpits of Southern Metropolis not only illustrates the precarious status of the value of freedom of the pulpit, it is also a dramatic instance of a consequence of integration policy that is opposite to its intention. We next turned to the search for the "centers of power and interest in the social environment" responsible for these unintended and unwanted consequences that are symptomatic of the breakdown of organizational control. We observed that the evidences we presented were related to the concentration of Negroes.

To relate the unanticipated consequences to the presence of a large percentage of Negroes in the population is not in itself to explain the resistance to integration. But the percentage of the population that is non-white may act as a signpost directing us toward the forces we seek. In the southern environment a symbiotic process has resulted, on the one hand, in greater dependence upon the Negro and, on the other, in stronger societal mechanisms for keeping him "in his place," i.e., powerless and, therefore, exploitable[7] or, at least, harmless. Where there is a large proportion of Negroes the dominant group is not only more dependent on the Negro but also more worried about the danger of losing its dominance. These people are committed economically, politically, and emotionally to a way of life which they not only do not want to change, they are afraid for it to change.

In a generally threatening atmosphere the attempts of the national organization to integrate their local churches is an especially severe threat for at least two reasons. First, the integration of the church would be a severe breakdown of the kinds of mechanisms which preserve dominance. Voluntary association on an equal basis would eventually lead to the type of personal relationships which would undermine dominance.[8] Second, the church has long provided theological, philosophical, and moral justification for the "Southern way of life." The Methodist resistors are good and loyal churchmen, reflecting what they and their fathers before them have heard from their ministers, who say in a *Pronouncement*:

SEGREGATION IS IN HARMONY WITH THE PURPOSE AND WILL OF GOD

It is trite to say that God made the various races of human kind and placed them in separate areas on this planet. Perhaps that was just a happen so; but many of us are inclined to believe that God does not work by happen-stance. We are constrained to believe that his works are by design.

Few will gainsay that Divine Providence, in His wisdom, designed the linguistic differences and genetic characteristics which have served to keep the peoples of the earth segregated into tribal, national or racial groups from prehistoric times down to our day. (Methodist Layman's Union, 1959, p. 9)

No wonder they can say in response to a statement of the national church's integration intentions:

What we didn't know is that the life of the Church is out of harmony with the Gospel in refusing to mix white and colored races in all church circles. But this causes us to wonder why the so-called "out of harmony" status of the Church was discovered only recently. (printed letter, Methodist Layman's Union, May 5, 1961)

To accept the integration of the church as a mandate of the Gospel is to surrender any honorable defense of their way of life. There is little wonder that they have chosen to resist the integration of their churches.

Given the plausibility of this resistance and its greater strength where there is a greater concentration of Negroes, what organizational needs of the Southern State Conference have constrained its leadership toward accommodation to this resistance? In particular let us consider the matter of the influence upon pastoral appointments.[9] This required that the laymen influence the bishop and/or one or more of the district superintendents. Why did these men listen to the laymen's demands?

This could be interpreted as simply a marketplace situation in which the customer, taking advantage of a buyer's market, is able to lay down the conditions under which he will do business. The leadership has an organization to run, money to raise, buildings to build. Yet they have no monopoly when it comes to the church. Laymen have threatened and made good their threats to stop going to and supporting the church and its institutions, to go to another church, or even to start another church.[10] Furthermore, it appears from our data (Tables 4 and 7) that it is precisely the more powerful and prestigious congregations that have most openly resisted national policy. The leaders of the Southern State Conference are competing in an open market for members, and also for financial support from members of the community who are not Methodist. They need the national denomination; but even more they need to pay their mortgages, fill their churches, meet their benevolence quotas, etc. In this kind of situation, it could have happened that threats from individual laymen and individual local boards determined the actions of the cabinet. Cabinet members would be especially sensitive to pressures from the prestigeful congregations. It is more plausible, however, that the coordinated efforts of the Layman's Union are an important key to understanding the capture of appointive power by the laymen.

Data in Figure 1 and Table 1 indicate that the first year of the Layman's Union's existence (1959-60) was a pivotal year in the trends we have shown.[11] However, it is interesting to note that these trends continue in spite of the fact that our interviewees generally agreed that the Layman's Union is now defunct. We suggest the following interpretation: The Layman's Union may reflect that until recently (perhaps until the early 1950s), but no longer, the conservative layman could trust the clergy to protect his point of view. Increasingly in the 1950s, it became evident that the more liberal view would prevail among the clergy. Just preceding the organization of the Layman's Union this may have been symbolized by the liberal voices in some of the key Metropolis pulpits. Perhaps this organization reflected the layman's recognition that he could no longer depend entirely upon conservative clegymen to defend him against integration.

How has the situation now changed so that less need is felt for this kind of organization? What has taken place appears to be the kind of bargaining Selznick (1948, p. 35) calls informal cooptation that has to do with "the sharing of power as a response to specific pressures." In this kind of arrangement the power-yielding interest group is "interested in the substance of power and not its forms."[12] Having won for the laymen the "ear" of the cabinet and of other official centers of power, the laymen may now be willing to work through the official channels. If they have gotten what they sought in the bargain, the official leaders have also gained (or recovered) something—their security as holders of authority. One may think that the commitments to lay interests are a high price to pay for keeping authority and decision-making in official channels; the leaders may have reasoned, however, that, even with the limitations imposed by their commitment to the laymen, as long as they made the decisions there was at least some possibility of control over them. On the other hand, if an unofficial organization were permitted to make its demands from a position of extra-organizational strength, there would be little possibility of control.[13]

If by further investigation we confirm this interpretation of the forces and accommodations underlying the rise and decline of the Methodist Layman's Union, then we will have "explained," according to Selznick's criterion, the organizational behavior under study. Selznick's statement of the relation of organizational behavior to organizational needs serves both as a summary of our theoretical argument and as a fitting conclusion to this section:

Observable organizational behavior is deemed explained within this frame of reference when it may be interpreted (and the interpretation confirmed) as a response to specified needs . . . . The needs in question are organizational, not individual, and include: the security of the organization as a whole in relation to social forces in its environment; the stability of informal relations within the organization; the continuity of policy and of the sources of its determination; a homogeneity of outlook with respect to the meaning and role of the organization. (Selznick, 1953, p. 252)

However, we must not forget that there was a third party—the national organization—which, with respect to its stated integration policy, on the surface stood only to lose in this local bargain. In the final section of this essay we briefly discuss the reasons that the national organization did not alter its policy in order to reestablish the lines of its authority over its troublesome southern subgroups. This organization had other commitments.

The Sources of the National Organization's Commitments to Integration

The Southern Conferences, in toto, contain 38 percent of the members of the Methodist Church and account for 34 percent of the giving to benevolences. It is certainly not an insignificant minority that the national organization crosses with its integration policies. Why do integration efforts increase in spite of southern protests?

Selznick describes how an organization becomes committed to certain goals by the actions of its subgroups and allied groups. This has been the case in the present situation at three points.

First, the Methodist Church has long been active in the movement toward greater cooperation between denominations (the ecumenical movement). But many of these denominations do not have the southern commitments which the Methodist Church has.[14] (It is, perhaps, significant that the Southern Baptist Church does not belong to the National Council of Churches.) Consequently, as the civil-rights movement has gained momentum a great deal of the discussions, statements, and actions of the ecumenical movement to which the Methodist Church is so deeply committed have centered around integration. We see at work here the processes which Selznick (1957, p. 59) describes:

Cooperation with other organizations is another field of administrative action fraught with policy implications. Cooperation threatens a loss of control, since commitments in action tend to spill over the limits of verbal agreement . . . . Proposals for cooperation in a particular area must be examined to see

whether in action they will generate unwanted consequences for other parts
of a program or for the organization as a whole.

Second, subgroups press for the implementation of their points of view.
As Selznick (1953, p. 256) states: "In order to preserve a special interpretation the subgroup presses for the extension of that interpretation to the
entire organization so that the special content may be institutionalized.
This has happened as, under the pressure of the civil-rights movement, the
non-southern church has given to the Christian concept of brotherhood the
content of full and immediate integration.

Third, the Methodist Church formulates national policy in boards, committees, and special conferences. There is a tendency for persons participating in these groups to be (and to become) more liberal than the
membership in general. Thus, these groups are susceptible to the pressures
of elements of the church which do not wish to understand the practical
problems of the southern church. In the present militant climate this lack
of understanding has become acute. These committees and boards take
action in the name of the organization as a whole; the latter then becoming
committed to a policy or course of action that was not anticipated by its
formal program. From the national boards and committees spring the
pronouncements and programs most objectionable to many in the southern church.

There are other more general sources of the Methodist Church's commitment to integration.[15] Along with clergymen in general, many Methodist
ministers have gone through an agonizing reappraisal of the meaning of
racial brotherhood. Furthermore, in the face of the increased activity of the
civil-rights movement, many involved laymen and clergy have had to make
decisions about an *action now* (from marching to board policy) that could
easily have been bypassed at an earlier time. But these general processes
influence policy through the specific sources cited above. Thus, the national church has become so committed to integration that in making
policy the Methodist Church has not faced up to the full implications of the
pluralistic organizational character it took on at the reunion in 1939. If it
had done so, perhaps it would not so soon have ignored the commitments
inherent in that pluralism, and thus have designed a better strategy for
altering that particular pluralistic arrangement. The strategy employed has
had the effect of solidifying the forces underlying segregation. A similar
type of strategy employed by a more hierarchical organization might be
more effective because of the relation of the executive to lower levels in the
organization.[16]

Of course, we cannot say what other unanticipated consequences might
have occurred if the Methodist Church had *not* adopted these policies

aimed at desegregation. Forces of resistance to the church might then have emerged among the large Negro constituency, among some of its northern supporters, and among its professional personnel, the ministers.

Notes

1. The debates preceding unification are conveniently summarized in Dwight D. Culver (1953, pp. 60-78).
2. In this essay "liberal" always refers to a man's attitudes and actions on the racial question as the informants suppose these to be perceived by laymen.
3. It will be noted that we deal mainly with the two top strata of churches. These strata are determined on the basis of three criteria: number of members, amount of pastor's salary, and amount given to World Service. We deal with these churches not just because they represent the bulk of members, finances, and power of the conference, but also because we expected that at these levels there would be fewer extraneous variables influencing the indices we have selected. For example, of some of the smaller churches the question could be raised whether they fail to give to race relations simply because they cannot afford to do so. There is no doubt that the top sixty-nine churches we consider can afford to give.
4. It is seldom that we hear of a Methodist minister "losing" his church because of his position on race. In the Methodist system it is never more than a year until conference time when he may be smoothly "promoted" to another church. In a call system the people are more likely to demand the pastor's immediate departure.
5. This statement was written after the 1960 General Conference.
6. In this case a charge is usually the same as a church. A pastoral charge can, however, have more than one church.
7. Robert Ezra Park (1952, p. 161) wrote that Dominance "determines the orderly distribution upon the soil and in the occupational pyramid of all the individuals which society, as organized, can support, and disposes of those for which it has no place." Dollard's (1957) discussions of economic gains and of prestige gains are still relevant. "Relatively, middle-class people get much higher returns for their work than do the lower-class groups who perform the more laborious tasks. In practice this second advantge means that the middle group has a larger share of the goods and services which flow from the common operation of the socio-industrial machine in Southern town and county" (p. 99). About prestige, he says, "The novelty in the South is that one has prestige solely because one is white. The gain here is very simple. It consists in the fact that a member of the white caste has an automatic right to demand forms of behavior from Negroes which serve to increase his own self-esteem" (p. 174). A social scientist recently returned from Mississippi observed that one of the hardest things for the privileged classes to take is the change now going on with regard to the deference a white man can expect from the Negro.
8. Thompson (1960, p. 408) points out that homogeneity is also a necessary defense for the voluntary church as distinguished from the giant enterprise. He sees the implications of this fact for racial integration.
9. The matters of race relations giving and use of Methodist literature are local church decisions. The only person (representing the conference) likely to pro-

test here is the pastor. In many cases he does not protest even though he would like to. One of our interviewees reported: "In race relations, few ministers feel free to preach convictions. It is not hard for laymen to move him if he does. Recent history in a Southern state shows that what the laymen want is what the laymen get." Asked about himself, he said, "I don't know that my people know my convictions fully. I have been discreet. I have tried to encourage open minds and freedom for the pulpit and for teachers. I've never been forthright and direct in considering the ultimate conclusions of my convictions." Another minister told us that the race issue had always plagued him. "It is used as a device for undercutting the people's confidence in their minister. It has been a constant dread hanging over me." Our informants rated this last man as conservative in the eyes of his laymen. It is easy to see that a minister's race convictions are "precarious values" in the South. See Clark (1956) for a discussion of precarious values.

10. The withdrawing of a local church or churches from the Methodist Church or the withdrawal of members in large groups to start other churches is not uncommon in the Deep South today. This is another observable unanticipated consequence of the church's integration policy. We hope to explore further this aspect of southern resistance at a later time.

11. A Layman's Union letter in 1961 notified the people that they should keep careful watch over the literature and that, should they decide to change, the union would be glad to furnish them with a list of acceptable publishers. One of the interviewees told us that the union also had a list of acceptable and unacceptable ministers in the conference.

12. An example of this type of cooperation involving other conference leaders involves the World Service giving. World Service is the basic benevolence of the church. It is a major source of prestige for conferences as well as for local churches. Until recently this conference included, as a part of the World Service, asking a small percentage to go to the National Council of Churches. This organization is in ill repute in the South because of its racial stands and involvement. At least one church cut out World Service entirely, others reduced their giving, still others threatened. As a result, the conference leadership removed the objectionable item from the World Service asking. Churches which want to give to the National Council of Churches now must do so separately and voluntarily.

13. Of course, one can also imagine that the leaders were much influenced by the desire to hold their positions of leadership with their prestige and other perquisites. If gains secured from cooperation have allowed the Layman's Union to fade away, it will be interesting to see whether that organization will be revived in the future. The conference has just been assigned a new bishop, who some of our liberal informants insist will not let the laymen have as much say as in the past.

14. And the Methodist Church contains 62 percent of all Negroes belonging to predominantly white denominations (1955 estimate)!

15. Of course, these three factors are at work in a social environment quite different from that we discussed as characterizing areas with high concentrations of Negroes. There is an extensive literature centered around the question of the effect of society upon the values and policies of churches. Yinger (1957) sum-

marizes and/or cites much of this literature in his discussion of social change. See also Charles Glock and Benjamin B. Ringer (1956).

16. Wood (1967) has completed a larger study that examines the considerations which underlie policy alternatives (including attempts to overcome resistance to integration) given the particular political economy of the Methodist Church.

PART V
MOVEMENTS AND
COUNTERMOVEMENTS

Introduction

Resource mobilization theory, we have argued, is an advance over earlier approaches to understanding social movement action. But resource mobilization theory, too, has missed an important aspect of social movement dynamics: social movement mobilization creates and encourages countermovement mobilization. In the course of analyzing social movements, in dissecting the internal structure of movements, their tactics, their relations to authority (which are often the countermovement), we have tended to ignore the processes of countermobilization, the tango of movement and countermovement as SMOs and adherents on both sides attempt to defeat each other, convert third parties into adherents, and draw authorities to one side or the other.

Both of the essays in this section were written by Bert Useem and Mayer Zald. In the first essay we have wrestled with the difficult problem of conceptualizing the interaction of movement and countermovement. There are no special problems in conceptualizing countermovement. The same form of analysis used for thinking about movements will do. There *is* a problem in conceptualizing movement-countermovement *interaction*. This is a loosely coupled form of conflict. The CM *needs* the movement. No movement, no countermovement. The loosely coupled nature of the interaction and the temporal interaction creates difficult analytic problems. Until recently, sociological studies of process over time have lacked rigor and precision. Here we compare forms of interaction to fights, games, and debates. The interaction of movements and countermovements that are sometimes tightly coupled and sometimes loosely coupled means that a movement and countermovement may be at different stages of mobilization and organizational development at any single point in time.

The second essay in the section examines the pro-nuclear power movement as a countermovement to the antinuclear power movement. It notes that the distinction between a pressure (or interest) group and a social movement is sometimes unclear. In this instance, the pro-nuclear movement was in part created by the nuclear power industry, and thus might be called a pressure group. But whatever success it had (and its success was fairly limited), depended upon the ability of the SMO to free itself from its appearance as an industry front. It had to become, and did become, more like a social movement than it was in its earliest phases. The fact that the countermovement was closely tied to established institutions raised questions about its legitimacy and placed restrictions on the tactics that did not hinder the elements of the antinuclear movement.

10

Movement and Countermovement Interaction: Mobilization, Tactics, and State Involvement

Mayer N. Zald and *Bert Useem*

The growth of the antiabortion movement, the pro-family movement, the antibusing movement, the rise of Moral Majority, Phyllis Schlafley's Eagle Forum, and the presidential victory of Ronald Reagan has spawned a small industry of scholarly and popular writing about conservative and reactionary social movements. Quite reasonably, sociologists have joined these efforts and we are having a small boomlet in studies of conservative countermovements. (See, e.g., Useem [1984], Luker [1984], Conover and Gray [1983], and Useem and Zald [chapter 11] for case studies; and Lo [1982] and Mottl [1981] for more general treatments.)

These writings join earlier work on right-wing movements; for instance, Lipset and Raab (1970), Aaron (1981), and Bell (1964). This essay, too, is motivated by and gains momentum from our awareness of the growth of right-wing movements. But its thrust, its angle of vision, is somewhat different. Most students of conservative movements search for their social bases, leading organizations, and actors. They do for countermovements what others have done for movements. But our interests are more interactional. We are interested in how movements generate countermovements, and how they then engage in a sometimes loosely coupled tango of mobilization and demobilization. And we are interested in how, in the language of McCarthy and Zald (1977, 1981), the structure of the social movement industry (SMI) shapes the tactics and structure of the countermovement industry (CMI). Finally, we explore the relationships among movement, countermovement, and authorities.

Our central argument is that movements of any visibility and impact create the conditions for the mobilization of countermovements. By advocating change, by attacking the established interests, by mobilizing sym-

247

bols and raising costs to others, they create grievances and provide opportunities for organizational entrepreneurs to define countermovement goals and issues. Movements also may have a "demonstration effect" for potential countermovements—showing that collective action can effect (or resist) change in particular aspects of society. In the last two decades social movement researchers have expanded their analytic and empirical frame of reference. We now have a rich set of tools and concepts to study social movements—the social psychology of attitudes and ideology, the dimensions and conditions of solidarity, the nature of SMO change, the processes of resource mobilization, and the analysis of competition and conflict among MOs are part of the kit bag of sociology. And recently we have begun to examine the interaction of authorities and movements (Gale, 1982; Marx, 1979), an important and much neglected topic. What is surprising, however, is the neglect of the dynamic interplay of movement and countermovement. Much of a movement's activity is aimed at neutralizing, confronting, or discrediting its corresponding countermovement. Similarly, the countermovement gains its impetus and grows from showing the harmful effects of the movement. It attacks the movement leaders, bombs its sites of program action, and associates the movement with evil. It chooses its tactics in response to the structure and tactics of the movement.[1]

An examination of movement-countermovement interaction overlaps imperfectly with the issue of class antagonisms and opposition. Over the long haul, class opposition only sporadically spills over into M/CM action. Class opposition often takes place through the routine operation of social institutions—at the workplace, in the courts, and in the established workings of the political system. Although class opposition may generate social movements (Schwartz, 1976), it also may not. Garner and Zald (chapter 12) show how class opposition shapes the orientation of the social movement sector.

Further, a class conflict model predicts too *little* social movement activity. Many contemporary and historical M/CMs are generated by ethnic, religious, ideological-cultural, and status antagonisms. Although economic and class antagonisms may be intertwined with these other sources of movements and countermovements, it would be an act of theoretical dogmatism to assume that class oppositions preponderate.

This essay sketches out the components for the analysis of movement-countermovement (M/CM) interaction. In the first section we situate this analysis in the study of social conflict. The key question there is how does M/CM analysis differ from the study of any social conflict whatsoever? To use Rapoport's (1960) classification, how does it compare with the study of fights, games and debates, and of wars? The second section presents a recipe book for describing M/CM location in the social structure and problems of CM mobilization. The third section discusses the battle joined, forms of conflict, and interaction. The fourth section is devoted to the analysis of the interplay of M/CM and authorities. Ms and CMs are locked in a struggle to convince and convert authorities. In a complex polity there are a wide variety of M/CM authority relations. Finally, the conclusion addresses the place of M/CM interaction in the larger historical and cultural setting.

Conflict Theory and M/CM Analysis

Zald and McCarthy (chapter 7) define a social movement as the mobilization of sentiments in which people take actions to achieve change in the social structure and the allocation of value. A countermovement is the mobilization of sentiments initiated to some degree in *opposition* to a movement. It follows in time a mobilization to change society. Actors identifying with the countermovement orient themselves to the actions of the movement. That is, they see themselves as either directly countering the movement or undoing its effects. If, however, the original movement's supporters or SMOs have vanished, then the new mobilization effort must be considered a movement, not a countermovement. We should also note that a countermovement may in turn generate a counter-countermovement that is different from the original movement. Thus, for instance, the antiabortion movement developed in response to the success of the pro-choice movement. A "counter-counter" movement then emerged motivated by the fear that the antiabortion movement had theocratic and antipluralist goals. The counter-countermovement should be considered a new movement since it has promoted goals broader than those of the original pro-choice movement and has mobilized a somewhat different constituency.

The key word in the definition of countermovement is *opposition*. For a framework to analyze opposition and processes we turn to conflict theory and its various forms. M/CM interaction is a kind of intergroup or inter-collectivity conflict. It shares certain attributes with fights, debates, games, and wars. What does it share with and how is it different from other forms of conflict?

At first glance, M/CM interaction has several properties that have been well analyzed in the conflict literature (see, for instance, Kriesberg, 1982). Mobilization of one side leads the other side to mobilize as well. Community conflict within established communities is well described by writers such as Coleman (1955), Heirich (1971), and Coser (1956). They show that, given an initial conflict, the ties between the contending community groups break down, permitting other preexisting issues to surface; each side in the conflict has an incentive to raise new issues that can recruit uncommitted bystanders; the struggle increases solidarity within each conflict group and the misperception and primitivization of the other group's behavior; polarization and mobilization increase in a reciprocal dynamic.

As we tried to apply this form of conflict theory, we found it somewhat limiting. First, while the explanatory power of the community conflict model has been demonstrated with regard to the mobilization of geographic communities, it fits less well when mobilization cuts across traditional community lines. When a movement's and countermovement's constituencies are not based on preexisting geographical, ethnic, or institutional community divisions, the concept of community polarization has little relevance. In those circumstances, the emergence of the movement and countermovement and their dynamic interaction arise only as a product of the movements' organizing effort itself, rather than from the disintegration of preexisting ties. For example, it would make little sense to describe the breakdown of the preexisting ties between the pro- and antinuclear forces, because the movements' constituencies did not exist as groups before the conflict began.

Second, the most general formulations of conflict theory (not Marxist class conflict approaches) pay little attention to the historical context and process by which interests in conflict get defined. Conflict theory tends to start from defined opposition. But how interests and counterinterests get defined is an important problem for us. Historical process is important in another sense: conflict theory starts from the parties in view, when the latent sentiments on both sides are activated. There is a tendency to see the parties as kind of matched pairs, mobilizing at the same time. But as we thought about cases, it was clear that we needed a looser conceptualization. Countermovements vary in how quickly they mobilize. For example, both the antiabortion and the pro-nuclear power movements mobilized relatively quickly in the face of victories and mobilization on the other side. In contrast, the antiprohibition forces took more than a decade to get up a head of steam (see Kyvig, 1979).

There is a larger problem. Because conflict theory is very general—it must theorize about (for example) martial and marital conflict—it ignores the specific terrain over which M/CMs struggle: Movement and countermovement use specific means to promote or retard social change gains. To treat tactics at all, conflict theory must disembody them into abstracted "moves" played in a series of games. But we think it necessary to stay closer to concrete tactics.

In searching for a frame of reference we turned to a specific kind of conflict. Possibly the analysis of wars would provide a template for analyzing M/CM interaction. SMs and CSMs command pools of resources to be used in a variety of battlefields. Just as one nation may be stronger at sea and weaker on land, so an SM may be stronger on the streets and weaker in the courts. Moreover, a victory or defeat in one arena or battlefield shifts the locus of attack, the nodal point for the next major battlefield. For instance, once the pro-abortion forces won the Supreme Court to its side, antiabortion forces shifted to the issue of federal funds for abortion. We presume that antiabortionists would like to gain Supreme Court support. Yet until new constitutional grounds are found, or a different reading of the biology of "life" is convincingly presented, or a new Court is appointed, this battlefield is foreclosed.

The course of the war also affects a state's ability to mobilize resources. In the course of the war, a state may use up all of its resources, or through alliances gain added resources. SM and CM may undergo a similar process.

Certainly, the analogy to war suggests the importance of the historical context, and that the buildup of grievances is not necessarily reciprocal. Moreover, analysts of war also pay a great deal of attention to strategy and tactics. The mobilization of resources, the problems of logistical support, attention to the nature of the battle, and the relevance of technology to different battlefields are the core of military analysis.

The analogy to war has additional power if we do not restrict the comparison to wars between nation-states in the modern state system. Conventional warfare has a certain clarity of beginning and ending that might lead us astray. Wars are declared, peace treaties signed. On the other hand, movements and countermovements start up and stop without formal announcement. In this respect they are more like guerrilla wars and ethnic insurgencies. One side may think the battle is over, while the other side has only gone underground.

Another limit to the analogy is that the role of third parties is different. In modern warfare, third parties may play significant roles either as allies or neutral arbiters between the contending states. The United States, for example, has assumed both roles in the Middle East. Still, victory in war turns on the destruction of the opponent's military forces. An analogous process does not exist in the conflict between movement and countermovement. Rather, the key issue for movement-countermovement conflict is the capturing or convincing of authorities.

In addition, conventional wars are waged between well-defined actors, and who speaks for the parties is clear. This is not true of movement-countermovement conflict, where the representation of the aggrieved constituency is often contested. Moreover, the goals of conventional warfare, the destruction of the opposing army, is less ambiguous than those of movements and countermovements. M/CM only partially orient their behavior to the actions of the other.

Finally, in Rapoport's (1960) terms, wars are more like fights or games, while social M/CM interactions are more like debates. Fights are attempts to vanquish or conquer opponents with little or no attention to costs; in games opponents use strategies and compare costs of alternatives to outwit opponents. Debates rely on persuasion to convince and convert opponents and authorities. Of course, wars may have elements of debates, and social movements in conflict may have elements of games and fights, but social movements and countermovements generally involve symbolic agitation. Indeed, even when they use violence they may be signifying. The violence is not, literally, to win a decisive coercive victory, but is to signify the strength of forces and the cost of continuing battles. Moreover, except in the case where the social movement has very limited and specific goals, it is involved in an ideological battle; the long-run victory is a matter of changing values, symbols, and frames for action (see Gusfield, 1981).

Let us draw some guidelines from this too-rambling perusal of conflict-related literature. Social M/CM interaction can be treated as a form of conflict behavior. Thus, the literature on polarization, spirals of conflict, and heightened mobilization is directly relevant. But four qualifications, or limits, must be observed. First, M/CM relations must be seen as loosely coupled conflict. The parties to the conflict change over time. In addition, there may be discontinuity between the mobilization of the M and CM, so that CM sentiments may not be quickly mobilized. The definition of the conflict issues is part of the agenda. Finally, the CM and SM may fight on different battlefields so that how the issues are joined, where adherents perform, is problematic.

Second, movement-countermovement is often a kind of a debate. Like parties to a debate, movement and countermovement try to persuade each other and third parties with rhetoric, moral arguments, and appeals to reason. The persuasion component is absent, or less prevalent, in fights and games.

Third, the tactical repertoires of movement and countermovement are shaped by the existing theology and social structure. In this respect, movement and countermovement are like wars, but unlike games and debates, where tactics are defined by accepted rules of the game.

Finally, movement and countermovement confront each other within the context of a larger society. They attempt to coerce, to change perceptions of, to seek support from publics, reference elites, authorities, and other external groups.

Getting Started: Components for M/CM Analysis

It is difficult enough to get relatively complete descriptions of a movement, let alone of a movement-countermovement and their interaction. Nevertheless, analysis of M/CM interaction must start from a well-grounded description of both sides. In this section we suggest the central elements of an M/CM analysis.

Comparative-Historical Description of Movement and Countermovement

We now have a relatively well-developed set of categories for describing social movements. These include (1) the distribution of sentiments in socio-demographic space; (2) the major SMOs and their interrelations in the SMI; (3) the funding-labor resource supports; and (4) the repertoire of tactics as these relate to social base (1-3) and to targets (e.g., courts, elites, administrative agencies, media, and legislatures).

It should be apparent that a cross-sectional comparative analysis will reveal the differential social location and organization of the movement and countermovement. In the process the different resource dependencies and tactical dilemmas are described. Useem and Zald (chapter 11), for instance, show that the pro-nuclear energy groups faced problems of credibility and legitimacy because many of them emerged from and had the support of industrial firms in the nuclear power industry.

Sociologists, unfortunately, tend to deal with short time periods. As soon as we introduce a longer time frame into our comparative analysis, shifts in both the support base, coalitions, tactics, SMI organization, and relation to authorities become apparent. Events from one period limit the choices and responses of the next.

Two issues from the civil rights movement and its countermovement illustrate the point. First, note that initially it was not at all clear that the federal government would use force to back up the Supreme Court's 1955 ruling in *Brown*, the decision requiring the desegregation of public schools. President Dwight D. Eisenhower did, however, call out the national guard when Arkansas Governor Orville Faubus blocked the integration of Little Rock's schools. This changed the balance of terror and violence in the remaining years of the southern civil rights movement. Blacks and whites in the movement were still terrorized, but the federal government's demonstrated willingness to intervene limited the tactics of the countermovement (see Ashmore, 1982).

Second, on the organizational side, *Brown* triggered a tremendous growth for the countermovement. Throughout the post–World War II era there had been attempts by the pro–civil rights groups to break the back of racism in the South—challenges to the primary system, fights over voting rights, contests over participation in the Democratic party. None of these prompted a large antimovement because they seemed impotent. The *Brown* decision signaled that a central institution, the segregated school system, could be challenged effectively. In response, large segments of the middle class and elite mobilized in the nonviolent Citizens Councils (see

Carter, III, 1959; McMillen, 1971; Bartley, 1969). What is most interesting from our perspective is that the councils disappeared as the federal courts reaffirmed the Supreme Court's decisions and federal marshals implemented court orders. By the early 1960s the councils had largely vanished, and the schools were, at least in a token fashion, integrated. Further, no large scale *organizational* mobilization occurred in the boycott and sit-in phase of the civil rights movement in the late 1950s and early 1960s, even though southern authorities, individuals, and businessmen continued to resist desegregation quite vehemently. The key point is that the mobilization and interaction of M/CM must be nested in a historical context. Cross-sectional description must be carried forward and back.

Mobilization Problems of the Countermovement

As implied above, special attention must be paid to the timing of the CM mobilization. Here the war metaphor distracts, for an attack of a nation requires it to mobilize, unless it is to supinely accept defeat, while movements may win major battles before CM sentiments are mobilized. What effects the timing and form of the countermovement mobilization?

Movement Success. First, a countermovement is likely to emerge if the movement appears to be accomplishing its goals. A movement's success demonstrates to a countermovement's constituency the benefits of collective action. For example, movement victories in cases before the U.S. Supreme Court crystallized the antiabortion and southern anti–civil rights movement. The antiabortion movement emerged following the Supreme Court decision to decriminalize abortion in 1973 and the White Citizens' Councils date from the 1954 decision outlawing racially segregated schools.

A countermovement is unlikely to mobilize, however, if the movement wins a huge, crushing victory. Under these circumstances, the countermovement will become paralyzed as supporters see little chance of success. For example, by the mid-1960s the southern white resistance had dissipated, even though the civil rights movement continued its struggle. Between 1954 and the early 1960s the civil rights movement gained the moral support of a broad sector of the American public and the legal and coercive backing of the federal government. We suspect that the segregationists' failure to keep schools segregated contributed to the inability of white southerners to systematically mobilize in the next phase of the civil rights movement.

Similar reasoning explains why the antiprohibition forces delayed the mobilization of the repeal movement until ten years after the passage of the constitutional amendment prohibiting alcohol. Repeal of a constitutional amendment, especially immediately after it is enacted, is a difficult task and the antiprohibitionists had become discredited and disorganized.

Thus, the antiprohibition forces needed additional time before they could launch a movement.

Appropriate Ideology. A second factor affecting the timing of CM mobilization is the development of an ideology that arouses enthusiasm and creates commitment (Bottomore, 1979, p. 47). Countermovements often lack such an ideology at the outset, but may develop it as the struggle proceeds. For example, the Catholic Church's doctrine concerning the "sacredness" of life provided the antiabortion movement with an ideology in its nascent stage. This relatively narrow doctrine, however, was not capable of mobilizing individuals and groups outside the church. Only with the development of an ideology about the relationship of abortion to family life and the role of women in society was the antiabortion movement able to draw on a broader constituency. Similarly, the pro-nuclear movement was initially mobilized around the industry's claim that nuclear power is a safe and efficient energy source.[2] However, the mobilization of a constituency outside the industry required a doctrine relating nuclear power to the promotion of the standard of living, achievement of independence from foreign oil, and establishing the altruism of its own constituency in comparison to the purportedly self-serving goals of the antinuclear activists.

Availability of Resources. Countermovements may be delayed if there are no groups with discretionary resources available to invest in collective action. A countermovement's location in the social structure will largely determine the availability of such resources. Often, movements are launched by groups from "below" and attack established interests. Since they respond to these attacks, countermovements will often (not always) be linked to established interests and organizations. Countermovements' ties to the established order tend to both help and hinder the provision of the requisite resources. On the one hand, countermovements will be launched by corporate groups rich in fungible resources such as money, office space, and clerical help. On the other hand, the countermovement's ties to the established order may preclude the use of these resources for noninstitutionalized action. The nuclear power industry, for example, controlled many of the resources needed by the pro-nuclear movement, but was reluctant to provide them. The industry was accountable to stockholders, the Nuclear Regulatory Commission, and other federal, state, and local government agencies. These ties prevented the use of industry resources for any but the most mild type of protest.

These difficulties, however, are not necessarily insuperable. One strategy used by countermovements is to maintain a decentralized structure. This allows established groups within the movement to provide the necessary resources to the movement, and yet allow it to disassociate itself from actions taken by groups it has helped bring into existence. For example,

Boston's political establishment was heavily involved in the antibusing movement launched in that city in the fall of 1974 (Useem, 1984). City officials held key posts in the antibusing movement organization and the facilities of city hall were used for antibusing activities. City officials, however, could not easily advocate violence or other illegal forms of resistance, since the federal court and U.S. Justice Department were monitoring their actions. Several of them were lawyers, and feared disbarment and the loss of their livelihood should they openly resist the federal court. Militant and occasionally illegal actions, however, were taken by other adherents. For example, during the first two years of desegregation, antibusing protestors congregated in front of the schools in their neighborhood. The demonstrators taunted black students as they entered and left the school, and on several occasions hurled rocks at buses carrying blacks. After one such protest, a crowd of several hundred attacked and beat a black man who had happened to stop his car at a red light near the demonstration. The antibusing leaders did not participate in these "spontaneous" actions. Although the established leadership did not actually participate in these actions, they often provided their tacit support for them. Elvira "Pixie" Palladino, a top leader in the antibusing organization ROAR and elected member of the School Committee, commented on the beating of a black man: "My first reaction from the pit of my stomach, was that he got exactly what he deserved. He had no business of being over there [South Boston] in the first place" (*Boston Globe*, May 25, 1975).

Constraints and Opportunities. Finally, a factor much overlooked in the study of movements as well as countermovements, the public agenda may or may not "permit" the emergence of movement or countermovement. Ms and CMs cannot advance if they are seen as unpatriotic or frivolous, or otherwise discredited. Wars, depressions, the existence of other movements, and the focus on other events crowd the space for M/CM action (see Downs, 1957, 1972; Walker, 1983). It can be argued that the growth of the movement promoting new-right economics is really an effort to overturn Franklin D. Roosevelt's New Deal economic policies, which was postponed by World War II, and the cooptive election of Eisenhower. Similarly, World War I effectively blocked the antiprohibition forces. The war discredited the leadership of the antiprohibitionists because many were brewers of German origin (Kyvig, 1979).

In addition, political structures vary in the opportunities they provide to movements. Schwartz (1981), for example, argues that the American governmental system provides more points of entry to social movements than the one in Canada. This encourages attempts to change the social structure in the United States. Similarly, Lipset's (1968) analysis of why a mass socialist movement arose in Saskatchewan, but not in neighboring North

Dakota or Alberta, emphasizes the impact of differing electoral systems on social movements. Lipset argues that since the social and economic structures of all three regions were nearly identical, structural or psychological factors cannot account for the movements' differing success in the three regions. Rather, the variations are explained primarily by differences in the electoral mechanisms in the regions.

By paying attention to the special mobilization problems of the CM, we do not imply that they have more problems in mobilization than the movement. Indeed, since CMs are often linked to the elite and established order, they may have more resources (e.g., money and established organizations) available than movements, even while their repertoire of tactics is constrained by their class origins and commitment to order. Focusing upon the timing of CM mobilization comes out of our awareness of the loosely coupled nature of M/CM interaction. It helps explain the nature of that coupling. But the character of M/CM interaction is also defined by the targets and battles of the parties engaged.

Spirals of Mobilization? The Battle Joined

With a historical view of both movement and countermovement before one, it becomes possible to lay out the phases of mobilization and demobilization. Sociological analyses of conflict tend to assume a close connection between the mobilization of one party in a conflict and the mobilization of the other. They assume a "fight," and tight and reciprocal action is expected. They also tend to focus more on the mobilization phase than on the demobilization phase (for an exception, see Kriesberg, 1982). A spiral of conflict and demobilization is most likely to occur where there is a singular target of conflict (e.g., an attempt to integrate a specific bathing beach, or close a specific nuclear power plant), or, where there are unified parties to the conflict, so that one party calls forth resources as the other party calls forth resources. Unitary targets, single decision points, or meet-ing places of conflicting groups lead to tightly connected spirals of mobilization. It is apparent to actors of both sides that a battle is taking place and that one side is missing, or threatening to win; failure to mobilize, to respond, will permit a victory to the other side. Fights over school board policy, or conflicts about holding of parades, all have a focal point for conflict.

However, sometimes the loosely coupled nature of M/CM interaction means that there may be wide departures from tight spirals. First, many sympathizers and adherents are not tightly tied to SMOs and the solidary bonds that integrate them into movement-oriented action. Second, because the CM and SM face different environments, their cognitive maps of potential risk-reward (see Oberschall, 1973, for micro risk-reward maps) may lead one party to be demobilizing because, for instance, they have recently won a victory, while the other party mobilizes because the victory for the other side presents the hard grievance around which they can mobilize.

Finally, as noted earlier, movement and countermovement differ in the length of time they have been fighting and in the internal social organization. Rather than a spiral of conflict, one may sometimes see opposing paths of mobilization and demobilization. If, for instance, the movement has appeared to be successful, its supporters may believe that they can rest. The emergence of a CM may create despair and hopelessness: The movement may rekindle the flame only as new generations of adherents are brought into the debate, or after the older generation has retreated and rejuvenated its commitment.

So far, we have described the spirals of conflict, or their absence, largely in terms of individual actors and their motivation. The mobilization of organizations may have a different trajectory from the mobilization of adherents. The SMI grows as the pool of adherents and resources enlarges and is exploited by movement entrepreneurs. SMOs are staffed by cadre with deeper commitment than sympathizers or adherents. There very well may be time lags and disjunctions between the cycles and peaks of sentiments and the level of SMO activity. SMOs develop protected niches, sources of funding and support from institutions (e.g., churches, foundations, and government grants), and from individual contributors to the SMO per se (organizational loyalty). Thus, SMOs may exist and engage in battles long after sentiment base support has cooled. We take it that much of the battle over school busing after 1970 was based upon movement organizations disconnected from the presumed underlying population. (In Atlanta, Georgia, the local black population was largely opposed to the attempt of NAACP, Inc. Fund lawyers to press the case for county-wide desegregation.) The disjunction between the mobilization level of SMOs and the sentiments for action of sympathizers is very important for understanding the interregnum periods of social movement conflict. SMOs, operating out of protected niches, continue their programs and wait for another wave of social movement support to emerge so that they can once again mount the crest. Thus, the amount and character of M/CM conflict is a product of SM resources and tactics, not just the level of individual mobilization.

The Battle Joined

The strategic and tactical character of the battle changes over time. McAdams (1983) describes a "cascade" of tactics as the movement's early successes with one tactic are countered by learned responses by authorities and countermovement actions, followed by a new cycle of tactical innovation and response. After early successes, which may lead to an increased flow of resources to the movement, to media coverage, and to concessions from authorities, the opposition groups learn to defang the tactic. If the movement has been successful in court cases, the lawyers for the opposition learn new defenses, appeal strategies; they learn to rewrite laws and policies that are less easily overturned by the movement. Or, if the movement is successful in organizing boycotts and in eliciting media coverage, the opposition learns how not to overrespond and provoke pictures of violence. As the opposition is successful, hope declines for movement adherents, media attention shifts elsewhere, etc. McAdams treats the movement as the innovator, the CM and authorities as responders. Equally, however, the CM may be the innovator, as in the pro-life movement, and the movement may be the responder. But McAdams establishes a crucial point. Movement and countermovement each adjust their tactics as they gain responses from key constituencies, win or lose battles, appear to be achieving support, or gaining objectives.

A wide range of forms of battle exist, from direct confrontation, to lobbying authorities, to speaking to disparate audiences, to debating the shadows of previous generation. M/CM may meet head-on in an "encounter," a face-to-face interaction with a single focus of attention (Gamson, Fireman, and Rytina, 1982). In an encounter, members of each group have a heightened awareness of the other group, and respond accordingly. The most dramatic encounters often take place "on the streets" or other public locations loosely regulated by authorities. For example, during the height of Boston's school desegregation controversy, local antibusing movement advocates became deeply involved in a racial confrontation between blacks and whites at Carson beach, a strip of public beach between all-white South Boston and a black housing project. The conflict began when a white crowd attacked six black salesmen visiting the city who were strolling on the beach. The NAACP then organized a "picnic" demonstration several days later to assert blacks' rights to use the beach. The antibusing leaders organized a counter-demonstration. A massive fight broke out between the two demonstrating groups.

Other types of encounters are more structured and less likely to involve violent conflict. For example, the representatives of the pro- and antinuclear movements have frequently debated on university campuses and television public affairs shows. The most highly structured type of an encounter setting is probably the court. Many of the cases described in Joel Handler's *Social Movements and the Legal System* (1978) involve movement and countermovement representation in legal battle (see also Barkin, 1979).

Second, movement and countermovement can be joined in the sense that they attempt to influence the same third parties. For example, the movement to legalize marijuana and the countermovement to oppose its legalization both attempt to influence the public, national and state legislators, and the medical establishment. Rarely, however, do they meet in a face-to-face encounter.

Finally, movement and countermovement may be joined only in the sense that they attempt to undo the effects of the other. It is a countermovement, not a new movement, to the extent that it is engaged with organizations and actors representing the original movement, or it debates the position of the movement. The antiprohibition groups that eventually forced the repeal of prohibition came close to being a new movement. They were led by different groups than had lost the original battle. The groups that fought the enactment of prohibition consisted of brewers and distillers. The repeal effort was led by prominent businessmen from elite families (some of whom were Dupont connected). They were not so much pro-alcohol as they were antigovernment interference. They converted some supporters of prohibition by arguing that prohibition was not eliminating alcohol drinking at the same time that it was contributing to lawlessness and "lack of respect for law." The Association Against the Prohibition Amendment (AAPA) was originally bipartisan, but saw the Democrats and Roosevelt as more likely supporters of repeal. Raskob, a key leader of AAPA (and a senior Dupont and General Motors executive), became the chairman of the Democratic party. The leaders of AAPA split from the Democrats when they believed that Roosevelt was taking a statist tack. Many of them went on to found the Liberty League, an organization dedicated to restricting the role of government. We consider AAPA a countermovement because it did have to confront some of the same groups that had supported prohibition and because the debate was framed in terms of the value of the legislation which the movement had promoted.

Strategy and Tactics

Movement and countermovement interactions may vary in the environmental context in which they meet. They may also vary in the extent to which the groups locked in conflict seek to exclude the other group from the political arena. Movement and countermovement may attempt to damage or destroy the other group, preempt or dissuade the other group from mobilizing, or recruit the other group's members.

Damaging Actions. One strategy used by movements and countermovements is to try to raise the cost of mobilization for the other group. Let us examine in some detail the efforts of the pro-nuclear movement to raise these costs for the antinuclear movement.

Before proceeding, two caveats are necessary. First, it is often difficult to distinguish "industry activities" from "movement activities." For example, when a utility company presses charges against antinuclear "trespassers," is this a pro-nuclear movement activity or simply a business effort to protect its property? We consider activities directed against the antinuclear forces "movement" activities when those who initiate or engage in them view them as part of a political struggle. This "rule" is problematic in that it relies on often difficult to measure state-of-mind factors.

A second caveat is that our focus in this section is on specific actions against SMOs and individuals affiliated with these groups. Of less concern are the broader strategies used by one movement to defeat another (see our comments on preemptive strategies, below). For example, the attempt of antiabortion movement groups to amend the constitution would be treated as part of overall strategy, not an action directed against the pro-abortion movement. Bombings of abortion clinics or disruption of pro-abortion rallies would be treated as direct acts against the movement.

The pro-nuclear movement took a number of actions against the antinuclear movement. Using the categories developed by Gary Marx (1979) to describe government action against the protest movements of the 1960s, we discuss attempts to gather information, limit the flow of resources, and portray the antinuclear movement in a negative light.

A central aspect of government efforts to damage the protest movements in the 1960s was the collection of information on dissidents. As Marx notes, "knowing that agents are gathering information on it may make a social movement less open and democratic, require that limited resources be devoted to security, and may deter participation" (1979,p. 99). Some pro-nuclear groups have initiated surveillance activities of antinuclear activists and organizations. Utility companies took pictures of antinuclear demonstrators, copied license plate numbers near antinuclear rallies, and maintained files of individual antinuclear activists *(Wall Street Journal,* January 1, 1979). Whether these information-gathering activities were intended to damage the antinuclear movement is open to question. Industry spokespeople claimed that they were part of legitimate security measures. Nuclear power critics, however, charge that the surveillance programs are designed to discourage support for their movement. For example, in a hearing before a state regulatory commission, an antinuclear group charged that a utility's surveillance program had served to "suppress and chill opponents of nuclear power and anyone else who differs from [the company's] policies" *(Wall Street Journal,* January 11, 1979).

In addition to collecting their own information, several utility companies hired security firms to collect information on antinuclear protestors. A West Coast utility publicly acknowledged that it retained two security firms, Research West and Information Digest, for that purpose.

Similar information was revealed in files obtained in the litigation that followed the 1977 and 1978 Seabrook nuclear powerplant construction site. There the utility also hired two private security firms, Operational Systems, Inc. and Information Digest, to obtain information on the Clamshell Alliance (Peterzell, 1981, p. 69).

At least one "citizens" group, the U.S. Labor party, collected information on the antinuclear movement for the explicit purpose of damaging the movement. The Seabrook files (mentioned above) revealed that the Labor party had provided the New Hampshire State Police and the FBI with details of the Clamshell's tactical plans to occupy the powerplant. When asked about these and other efforts to collect information on the antinuclear movement, a Labor Committee spokesman stated: "This is political warfare. We're running a political intelligence operation to expose them (antinuclear activists). We will cooperate with any organization willing to root out this evil" (Guardian, December 5, 1979). The Labor Committee also claims to have infiltrated the Clamshell Alliance, including its top leadership, for the purposes of information gathering (Guardian, December 5, 1979).

Finally, the industry's two main trade associations, Atomic Industrial Forum and Edison Electric Institute, maintained files on antinuclear opponents. In at least one instance, the trade associations requested utility companies in a number of cities to attend and report back on meetings of a particular antinuclear group (Washington Post, November 21, 1977). In addition, the AIF allegedly disseminated information on antinuclear leaders to its members, including utility companies (Campaign for Political Rights, 1979, p. 3).

Another tactic used by the government to damage protest movements in the 1960s was to restrict the flow of resources to them, physical facilities, and employment opportunities (Marx, 1979, pp. 99-100). The pro-nuclear movement also attempted to reduce the antinuclear forces' access to resources. Pro-nuclear activists tried to eliminate the federal funding of citizen intervenors in regulatory proceedings. The Federal Trade Commission, ACTION, the Department of Energy, and other governmental agencies and programs traditionally provided such funds (Metzger, 1980, p. 40). Several pro-nuclear movement organizations, such as Americans for Nuclear Energy and the Nuclear Legislative Advisory Services, led efforts to prevent further disbursement of government funds to antinuclear intervenor groups (Nuclear Legislative Advisory Service, June 21, 1981; Nuclear Advocate, June 1980). In another effort, several campus chapters of pro-nuclear movement groups organized efforts to eliminate the use of student fees to fund campus antinuclear organizations (personal interview by B. Useem with participants, 1981).

As a last example, two pro-nuclear groups have used civil litigation to financially damage an antinuclear organization. The New Hampshire Voice of Energy (NHVOE) and Americans for More Power Sources (AMPS) have sued the Coalition for Direct Action at Seabrook, a faction within the Clamshell Alliance. The suit's stated purpose is to "recover the cost to the taxpayer for the added protection necessary to protect life, limb, and property" during demonstrations at the Seabrook nuclear powerplant construction site *(INFO,* no. 143, 1980, p.4). According to Tina Coruth, president of NHVOE, "Our suit is a way for the Seabrook demonstrators to pay their own way. It's not right for the New Hampshire taxpayer to pick up the tab for the added police protection during those antinuclear demonstrations" *(INFO,* no. 143, 1980, p. 4).

Finally, CMs and authorities may attempt to create an unfavorable public image of the movement (Marx, 1979, pp. 96-98). The pro-nuclear movement also used this strategy. Several utility companies have collected and disseminated derogatory information on antinuclear groups. Between 1973 and 1977, Georgia Power Company, for example, operated a sophisticated surveillance program on company critics, including the antinuclear Georgia Power Project. A former company investigator described the surveillance program as "dirt-gathering" efforts to label its opponents as "commies and queers" (Center for National Security Studies, 1981, pp. 67-68). Similarly, in 1978, Philadelphia Electric Company photographed antinuclear demonstrators and kept files on their activities. The company gave copies of the photographs to a local television station which used them in a story that ridiculed the demonstrators. An antinuclear group filed an administrative complaint with the State Public Service Commission, charging that rate payers' money was being illegally used on a campaign to spy on and "suppress and smear" critics of nuclear power (Center for National Security Studies, 1981, p. 75).

The U.S. Labor party also attempted to discredit the antinuclear movement. In 1977, the Labor party told New Hampshire state authorities that a planned demonstration at the Seabrook construction site was "nothing but a cover for terrorist activity" (Center for National Security Studies, 1981, p. 7). Governor Meldren Thompson and the *Manchester Union-Leader* accepted and widely publicized the allegation. The Labor party has made similar charges against antinuclear activists in Maryland and New York (Center for National Security Studies, 1981, p. 7).

The pro-nuclear movement was initiated to directly counter the anti's dramatic success in mobilizing public support, undercutting the economic viability of the industry (see Useem and Zald, chapter 11). In other cases, the battle may be more indirect. Movement and countermovement may attempt to rally different segments of the public and/or reference clients to bring pressure on authorities. Or the movement may be fighting a legal battle in court, while some countermovement organization leads a legislative battle.

Preemptive Strategies. Alternatively, a movement may design its strategy and tactics in ways that undercut the moral and political basis of a mobilization or counter mobilization. Gandhi's *satyagraha* campaigns in India and South Africa, for example, were designed to undercut the moral position of their opponents. And the pro-life movement's dramatization of fetal pain and response puts pro-choice adherents on the defensive.

Oberschall (1973, chapter 6) argues that Martin Luther King, Jr. succeeded in part because he delayed a major counterattack by southern whites. White control of jobs and credit, the court systems, and the political apparatus gave the white power structure sufficient leverages to crush a black insurgency. King's tactic of nonviolent resistance made direct retaliation more difficult:

> King must be seen as a man who solved a technical problem that had stumped Negro leaders for generations. As a powerless group living in the middle of a powerful majority that hated and feared them, Negroes could not stage an open revolt. To go unto the streets under those conditions with open demands for change was suicidal. . . . King and the sit-in students solved the technical problems by clothing a national resistance movement in the comforting garb of love, forgiveness, and nonviolence, a transformation that enabled Negroes to stage an open revolt without calling it an open revolt. (Lerone Bennett, quoted in Oberschall, 1973, p. 22)

Choice of strategy involves much beyond merely the nature of the opposition—the repertoires of action available, the acceptability of tactics to constituency, resources available, and relations to authorities. But one component affecting strategic and tactical choice is M/CM relations.

Persuasion and Recruitment. Lastly, movements and countermovements may develop a strategy of attempts to persuade the members of the opposition group to join their side of the controversy.

In general, however, movements and countermovements are unlikely to take this strategy as part of short-term strategy. First, it requires an individual to disengage from one movement and then engage one in opposition to it. The individual must both reverse his or her ideological position, and oppose a group of people, organizations, and causes with which he or she was recently associated. Second, the pool of neutral bystanders is usually much larger than the number of potentially recruitable individuals in the opposition group. Thus, recruitment drives aimed at bystanders is likely to net more recruits than one directed at the opposition.

Nevertheless, there are circumstances in which movements can recruit from the opposition group. For instance, the Mensheviks and Bolsheviks assumed an oppositional relationship in the period between the February and October revolutions. The Bolsheviks triumphed in part because they recruited large numbers of disaffected Mensheviks. (Of course, for most participants the oppositional relations of Mensheviks and Bolsheviks was of lower permanence than their mutual opposition to the old regime.) Factors that made the transfer of allegiance possible included Menshevik support of an increasingly unpopular war, an emerging belief that only the Bolsheviks could defend the government against counterrevolutionary forces, and Bolshevik support of workers taking over factories and peasants seizing land (Thomas, 1981). In our own time we have seen "neoconservatives" emerge from among the intellectual leaders of the moderate Left. We suspect that conversion occurs in loosely coupled conflict over long time periods more than in tightly coupled conflict.

The battle joined includes conflict in the courts, in the streets, and in the hearts and minds of persons. Often it involves the attempt of movement or countermovement to gain the cooperation of authorities. Yet there are a wide number of authority-M/CM relations possible.

Movement, Countermovement, and Authorities[3]

The traditional model of social movement analysis begins from a stable position—a government in place, facing groups with routine access (members) and groups with no access. As groups with limited access develop grievances they attempt to enlarge access and may mobilize in social movements. Similarly, groups with routine access may find their ability to gain authoritative allocations undermined. They, too, may resort to social movement mobilization. State officials, authorities, and their differentiated agents (civil servants, military officers), may have their own interests. They may "represent" groups in civil society, but they may also embody ideologies and interests that lead them to press for changes in other parts of the state apparatus. Yet it is also possible for groups to conflict in society with but minimal state intervention; movement and countermovement proceed with marginal use of the police and authorities.

Here we wish to examine the forms of interaction of movements and countermovements with authorities. It should be clear that we are largely discussing authority-M/CM interactions in societies where a separate civil society exists: where the state and its administrative apparatus does not deeply interpenetrate the fabric of family and associations and does not monopolize public discourse. Where these conditions are not met, where forms of total rule occur, movement sentiments are driven underground or take the form of personal and small-group dissidence.

FIGURE 10.1
Models of SM-CM-Authority Relations

A

Movement ◄────► Countermovement

Conflict Model Minimal
State Involvement

B

Authority ◄────►Movement

Authority is the
Countermovement

C

Authority

Movement   Countermovement

Competitive Model
Minimal Direct Conflict

D

Authority

Movement ◄────► Countermovement

Conflict Model
State Involvement

E

Authority in   Authority in
Region   Region

Movement   Countermovement

Dual Sovereignty Model
Rebellion and Revolution

F

National Authorities

Movement   Local Authorities

Countermovement

Pluralistic
Government Model

"_____" = attempts to pursuade, influence, or destroy

"-.-.-.-.-." = alliance or sponsorship

Figure 1 presents some of the possible models of authority-M/CM relations in an open society. It would be possible to present a more graphically
elegant and complicated set of models. Negative and positive lines could be
added, identities between state and SM made, intensities shaded. But for
our crude and preliminary purposes, these models suffice. Model A (conflict with minimal state intervention) occurs where the movement and
countermovement battle for members or for control with little attempt to
change laws or to gain state support. Bromley and Shupe (1981) and Shupe,
Bromley, and Busching (1981) have examined the relationship between the
Unification Church (Moonies) and anti-Moonies in these terms. The anti-
Moonies consisted of the parents of Moonies and deprogrammers. The
state could have become involved if the police had been willing to intervene when the church claimed their members were being kidnapped. The
deprogrammers and parents used the rhetoric of "family matters" to insu-
late themselves from police action.

A striking feature of this model is how few cases it describes. Movement
and countermovement usually appeal to authorities. First, movements do
not control the resources and are not sufficiently stable to implement major changes in society. Rather, they attempt to shift the cost of achieving
change from themselves to the government and polity at large. The civil
rights movement, for example, could to some extent desegregate public
facilities through their own actions. The lunch-counter sit-ins were in part
an attempt to directly effect change. Still, the change they sought was so
massive that it could only be achieved when the government was engaged
to apply its resources to the problem. Similarly, antinuclear demonstrators
occupied plant construction sites with the purported goal of physically
blocking further construction. But the overall success of the movement
depended much more on the position taken by the government and on the
response of capital markets than specific effects of antinuclear demonstrators on the industry.

Second, one side or the other is likely to perceive that it is in its interest
to seek the involvement of authorities. Usually this is the weaker of the two
parties, since the stronger will prevail as long as the dispute remains private
(Schattschneider, 1960). The movement to desegregate public schools in
Boston, for example, sought the intervention of both the state government
and the federal government in its battle with the locally more powerful
white countermovement. If, however, the stronger party can reasonably
count on the government to back up its claims, it may be the party that
seeks government intervention. An example of this is the 1978 dispute
between an insurgency movement in the U.S. Steelworkers Union and the
union's established leadership. The insurgency movement, led by Ed
Sadlowski, had expanded the scope of the conflict by obtaining the finan-

cial support of liberal and radical groups outside of the union. The union leadership asked the federal government, under existing legislation, to enjoin the insurgents from accepting outside contributions. Although the insurgents sued in federal courts to overturn the legislation and were initially successful, the Supreme Court upheld the legislation (*New York Times*, June 15, 1982). The blow was fatal to the insurgency movement.

Model B (authority is the countermovement) occurs where the movement directly attacks the state and the state *is* the countermovement. Arno Mayer's (1971) analysis of conservative authorities' response to working-class upheavals from the middle of the nineteenth century starts from an identity of interest between conservative groups and state authority. Authorities and conservative interests are at one. Or, to return to the issue of the anticult movement, Shupe, Hardin, and Bromley (1983) demonstrate that the West German government, which plays a large role in religion education, has played an important role in anticult activity, while the United States government has not.

Model C places the state at the center of the conflict between movement and countermovement. Both movement and countermovement attempt to convince authorities of their position and demonstrate their strength. The triangle is left "open," however, since movement and countermovement do not directly attack each other. The struggle over repeal of prohibition looks something like this. Model C is a model of competitive debate.

The "closed" triangle of Model D suggests that movement and countermovement seek to both make demands on the government and damage the other movement. The model describes the conflict between the pro- and antinuclear movements, as described above.

Model E represents a revolutionary situation, where movement and countermovement have established that to a significant part of the population they are the government. The movements control territory, raise taxes, conscript soldiers, and perform other governmental functions (Tilly, 1978, pp. 190-92).

Model F indicates that the local government can be aligned with countermovements in a struggle against central authorities. The model describes the antibusing movement in Boston and the anti–civil-rights movement in the South. In both cases, local officials helped sponsor and mobilize a countermovement. National officials became aligned with the movement.

It would be possible to make this analysis more complex. Not only do local and national authorities vary in their movement alignments, but so do authorities in different agencies at the same level. Richard Gale (1982) has described the complex growth and interaction of the environmental movement and countermovement with federal and state agencies. He uses a stage and institutionalization model to describe the ebb and flow of the relation to specific agencies. Movement and countermovement attempt to make alliances, to seize opportunities for gaining power. The institutional differentiation and ideology of authorities provides the ground for political opportunity.

For politically oriented movements and countermovements, state authorities and agents are the target in view; their actions are oriented to either changing authoritative allocations, to gaining support (or limiting authoritative intervention), or to becoming the authorities themselves. Whether through revolution, marginal accommodation, or conversion, the immediate target is state action.

Conclusions: History, Social Change, and Social Movements

In this chapter we have explored how movements and countermovements interact. Beyond static description, we have attempted to describe the dynamics or processes of countermovement mobilization. One aspect of the problem is to account for the speed of mobilization of the countermovement. We presented several hypotheses about the availability of an appropriate ideology, the existence of infrastructure supports, and the extent of the movement's success to account for the countermovement mobilization. We also examined the interaction, the battle joined, of M/CM. Also suggested is that there is a cascade of tactical change as movement and countermovement learn from each other, develop new tactics, and meet with success or failure. Finally, we examined the interaction of M/CM and authorities. A variety of models were schematically presented. It is important not to reify the state. It is complex and contradictory, sometimes representing class interests, sometimes a mediator, sometimes pitted against itself.

Our discussion has been framed in terms of winning specific battles or authoritative allocations. However, it would be possible for movements to be quite successful in winning specific battles or policies, yet to lose in the long run. Conversely, many of the short-run battles may be lost, but in the long run the grounds of decision-making are radically changed. It is beyond the scope of this essay to enter the vital discussion of the nature of culture and symbolic change that has been so invigorated in recent decades. Although we have no easy template for the study of symbolic change, large progress has been made. From the historical studies of Raymond Williams (1960) and John Dunn (1979) to the systematic study of political cognition of Modigliani and Gamson (1979), we are learning how to examine the transformation of symbol systems. Here we make some brief comments on the relation of ideology and symbolic attachments to movements and countermovements.

First, movements and countermovements are nested in long waves of ideology and counterideology. These ideas, in turn, are rooted in long-term views about right action and the relations among groups, citizens, and the state. The ground for mobilization must be prepared. Some of the ground of social movement ideology may be quite remote. For instance, many modern social movements assume that social relations are manipulable. Many countermovements, on the other hand, rest on the opposite assumptions: The manipulation of social relations is *not* feasible, and the social change sought by movements invites social chaos. Most movements emphasize what can be changed; countermovements emphasize what cannot.

Movement and countermovement must develop ideologies that convince bystanders and authorities of the rightness of their views. Social movements have the problem in their nascent stage of getting on the agenda and of making their priorities and view of the world acceptable to those who think the ideas are strange and wrong. There are a wide variety of techniques for doing so. Principles of rhetoric and the social psychology of belief systems tell us something about how this occurs, whether or not SM cadre and leaders consciously use the principles. Sewell (1985) and Skocpol (1985) have recently debated how culture and ideology enter the analysis of revolutions. Sewell emphasized the broader cultural forms and beliefs; Skocpol argues for the group and organizational shaping of the specific ideological repertoire. Their example needs to be extended to movements of less total scope.

Countermovements have a special problem. They must "remember the answers." Often their leaders and cadre are in the position of defending policies whose justifications have receded into the routine grounds. They seem to be going backward, their policies justify the status quo and established routines. The problem for many countermovements is how to make older symbols relevant to newer situations. They must both discredit the ideas of the movement and show how older ideologies have relevance to new situations. Sometimes they must reframe older symbols or ideas in new terms—antiabortion becomes pro-life, pro-nuclear power becomes pro-energy.

The long waves of ideology and counterideology are treated by historians of ideas. One point of entry for the sociologist of social movements is to map the nexus between idea "entrepreneurs" and specific SMOs and industry modes.

An awareness of the long wave of movement ideology also points up another issue, the maintenance of social movement and countermovement sentiment under repression. It is striking how major ideologies and political values resurge when state repression is lifted. One would have thought that the Franco regime, with its thirty-five years of dominance, could have wiped out commitment to democracy, to socialism, and communism. But the end of the regime was followed in short order by full-blown parties and ideological apparatuses. How many generations does it take? How deeply into primary group structure must the state intrude in order to eliminate civilizational ideologies, major systems of thought and belief about the social structure and possibilities?

Finally, but related to the last, attention to the long waves of sentiments and symbols raises the issue of how movements resurface over the decades. Feminism was strong in the early part of the century, died in the Great Depression, and was resurrected in the early 1960s (Scharf, 1980). To some extent, new leaders resurrect old exemplars and issues, recreate, selectively, our past to fit present needs. The debate between movement and counter-movement draws upon the cultural stock, but transforms it.

Notes

We are indebted to Emilie Schmeidler and Linda Kaboolian for discussion of many of the ideas in this essay. We are also grateful to Brian Ewart, Peter Kimball, Mildred Schwartz, and Charles Tilly for comments. This essay was developed while we studied the pro- and antinuclear power movements with grants from the Society for the Psychological Study of Social Issues, the Phoenix Memorial Project of the University of Michigan, and from a Department of Energy grant to the university. During the course of this research, Useem held a postdoctoral fellowship under an NIMH Training Grant on Sociology and Social Policy.

1. We suspect that the neglect of movement-countermovement interaction is related to the difficulties of diachronic, processual, and interactional analysis, especially when it is applied to such diffuse and changing entities as social movements.

2. Useem and Zald (chapter 11) document the process by which supporters of nuclear power transformed their ideology and organization to appeal to and gain support from groups without direct attachment to the utilities and reactor construction firms.

3. There is a bothersome analytic-conceptual issue in this section: Is any action of an authority that bears on M/CM interaction part of the M or CM? Stated differently, how does one differentiate political and authoritative action from M/CM action? A definitive answer cannot be given, but a range of answers can. At one extreme, action by authorities that is well institutionalized and legitimated in the social system may have impact on social movements but is not in itself considered social movement activity. Through fully institutionalized means, Margaret Thatcher has impact on the fate of conservatism and socialism in Great Britain. On the other hand, Costa-Graves' "Z" and the CIA's intervention against Allende in Chile are examples of countermovement activity. This view of M/CM activity as it relates to the action of authorities is based upon a Western, legal-rational model of state activity. It posits a separate institutionalized politi-

cal sphere, with Ms and CMs operating outside of, or at the margin of, the institutionalized sphere. At the other extreme, if one takes an ideational view of social movements, ignoring or downplaying the mobilization of movement activity in the definition of social movement, the distinction between state action and social movement action becomes meaningless. Margaret Thatcher is clearly part of the conservative countermovement, indeed a leader of it. But *then* one loses the ability to make distinctions between social movement activity and political activity in general (or one shifts it down a level, to the distinction between institutionalized and uninstitutionalized). We maintain the distinction between authoritative action and social movement (or countermovement) action. However, to the extent that state action is largely directed to carrying out pro- or antisocial movement actions, we have a conceptual difference with little empirical relevance.

11

From Pressure Group to Social Movement: Efforts to Promote Use of Nuclear Power

Bert Useem and *Mayer N. Zald*

In the division of labor within the social sciences, sociologists deal more with social movements and political scientists deal more with pressure groups. Yet both would agree that pressure groups and social movements seek to influence government policy. The difference between social movements and pressure groups is not often explicitly discussed, but there are at least three key differences. First, pressure groups are ordinarily part of the *polity*, the set of groups that can routinely influence government decisions and can insure that their interests are normally recognized in the decision-making process. In contrast, social movements are launched by groups without access to government power, and whose interests are generally not recognized in government policymaking. Second, when pressure groups take actions to influence the government, they rely on previously mobilized constituencies. Social movements attempt to mobilize constituencies for the first time. Third, social movements tend to use noninstitutionalized tactics, channels of influence, and organizational forms. Pressure groups, on the other hand, employ a political system's conventional form of collective action.[1]

A social movement organization becomes a pressure group when it gains routine representation in, and access to, the government. The new member of the polity may still use the rhetoric of a social movement, but in actual behavior and tactical form the movement resembles other groups in the polity. It moves from outside to inside the legislative and administrative arenas. Much of the sociological interpretation of the transformation of social movements emphasizes the routinization, institutionalization, and growing conservatism of organizations that once led vital social movements (Zald and Ash, chapter 5 in this volume). Thus, the National Association for the Advancement of Colored People, the American Federation of Labor–Congress of Industrial Organizations, and the Farm Bureau be-

273

came accepted members of the polity with varying residual attachment to social movement rhetoric and movement forms.

Much less attention has been given to the opposite process, in which polity members begin to lose their standing. As we conceptualize this process, authorities begin to distance themselves from the members of the polity. Authorities are no longer routinely accessible, and the interests of the polity members are increasingly disregarded. One option for the pressure group in this situation is to transform itself into a social movement.

Pressure groups lose their position through two different, though related, processes. In the first, changes in technology, economic organizations, and values lead to a general loss of status for a pressure group and the interests it represents. Thus, a decline in public support for prohibition and temperance led to a decline in the power of groups that favored prohibition. In the second process, a pressure group is attacked by other groups that challenge the legitimacy of the current status and operation of the pressure groups and the interests it represents. Where a pressure group has public standing and a claim to represent legitimate social interests, the attack by another group forces the pressure group to defend itself. The two processes are related because the evolution of the first process facilitates the development of direct challenges.

This essay examines the development of the pro-nuclear movement in the United States as an example of the partial transformation from pressure group to social movement. The term *pro-nuclear movement* is used here to refer to the collective effort to promote nuclear power as an energy source. The data for this analysis are drawn from semi-structured interviews with 58 pro-nuclear activists. We conducted interviews in the fall of 1979 and the winter of 1980, using a snowball-sampling technique to generate the final sample. Most of the interviews took place in New England, Michigan, and Washington, D.C. We also attended several pro-nuclear workshops and conferences. This gave us the opportunity to informally talk with pro-nuclear activists from across the United States and to monitor discussions among activists. In addition, we collected and analyzed materials issued by the pro-nuclear movement, as well as relevant newspaper and magazine articles. Finally, we conducted interviews with a small sample of antinuclear activists, also in New England, Michigan, and Washington, D.C.

This essay is divided into two major sections. In the first we examine the transformation of the pro-nuclear forces from a pressure group to a social movement. This transformation occurred in part because of a challenge posed by the antinuclear movement. The pro-nuclear movement developed two wings, one based in industry, the other in the community. In the second section, we show that the two wings have substantially different problems of tactics and legitimacy. We argue that the problems of a protest group vary with the group's base of mobilization and its positions in the social structure.

From Pressure Group to Social Movement

In this section, we examine the transformation of the pro-nuclear forces from a pressure group to a social movement. The pro-nuclear movement developed as a countermovement to the antinuclear movement. The pro-nuclear forces qualify as a social movement insofar as they have mobilized an uncommitted constituency, lost much of their ability to routinely influence government policy, and emphasized a new repertoire of social movement tactics. At the same time, the pro-nuclear movement has retained some of the characteristics of a pressure group; at issue is the question of degree (Gamson, 1975, p. 16).

The transformation of the pro-nuclear forces from a pressure group to a social movement was a response to a threat to its polity status. Specifically, the antinuclear movement challenged the right of the pro-nuclear lobby to determine policy on nuclear energy. We use the term *antinuclear movement* to refer to the organized, collective effort that tried to stop the use of nuclear fission to generate electricity, by closing down existing plants, halting the construction of new plants, and implementing strict safety standards for the disposal of radioactive waste and the operation of nuclear reactors.

The antinuclear movement first emerged as a serious protest movement in the United States in the late 1960s. During the 1970s it grew dramatically in size and intensity. Local citizen groups, at first confined to a few isolated organizations, were numerous by the mid-1970s. National and regional protest rallies drew hundreds of demonstrators, notably in Seabrook, New Hampshire; Rocky Flats, Colorado; and the area around Three Mile Island, Pennsylvania. Civil disobedience was used against nuclear plants under construction (Berger, 1977; Gyorgy, 1979; Mazur, 1981; Stever, 1980; Walsh, 1981; Wasserman, 1979).

Since the late 1970s, the antinuclear movement has been winning the struggle against nuclear power in the United States[2]. The best evidence for this is the erosion of government support for the nuclear industry and the near-collapse of several sectors of the nuclear industry. During the 1950s and 1960s, the federal government strongly supported nuclear development through direct subsidies and other promotional measures (Bupp and Derian, 1978; Montgomery and Quirk, 1978). In the mid-1950s, utility companies were unwilling to invest large sums of money in reactors and generating equipment, mainly because they were concerned about their financial liability in the event of an accident. In response, Congress in 1957 placed a ceiling of $560 million on a firm's liability for any one nuclear accident. Reactor orders soon followed (Del Sesto, 1979, p. 57; Weingast, 1980, p. 232).

By the early 1970s, however, federal, state, and local governments began to implement a series of measures that seriously undercut the industry's economic viability. The various levels of government enforced stricter safety regulations, delayed the licensing of new plants, failed to implement a nuclear waste disposal system, refused to allow utilities the rate increases they deemed necessary to finance nuclear construction, restricted sales of nuclear generators to foreign countries, and tightened environmental restraints (Stobaugh and Yergin, 1979; Stroops et al., 1979; Temples, 1980; Weingast, 1980). Faltermayer (1979, p. 117) estimated that two-thirds of the cost of a nuclear powerplant finished in 1978 was a result of stricter design criteria imposed since 1969 by the Nuclear Regulatory Commission (NRC) and its predecessor, the Atomic Energy Commission (AEC).

The precarious state of the U.S. nuclear industry is highlighted by three factors. First, since 1977, there has been a de facto moratorium on orders for new nuclear plants in the United States (Stobaugh and Yergin, 1979, p. 125). Stroops et al. (1979, p. 17) estimate that the long-term viability of the plant construction industry requires that utilities order at least four to six new plants a year. Second, the U.S. share of the nuclear export market has dropped from 100 percent in 1972 to 20 percent in 1978 (Stockton and Janke, 1978, p. 4). Finally, the industry is finding it difficult to attract and retain well-trained personnel, which may "lead to a fatal debilitation of research and management capability" (Stroops et al., 1979, p. 18).[3]

In sum, during the 1950s and 1960s, the nuclear industry was a "member of the polity" in the sense that its interests were promoted by the government and its views were taken into account. During the 1970s, the industry's status was threatened by the antinuclear movement and state and federal policies inimical to the industry's interests. In response, both the industry and its sympathizers began to mobilize.

At the beginning of the 1970s, hearings on the licensing of nuclear powerplants were usually uncontested and routine. The industry's four major trade associations, including the Atomic Industrial Forum and the American Nuclear Energy Council, maintained active lobbying offices in Washington. In addition, various firms specializing in nuclear architecture and engineering, reactor manufacturing, and uranium mining lobbied for nuclear power. Many of the industry's lobbyists were former members of Congress or of government agencies that regulated nuclear power. For example, Craig Hosmer, who was director of the American Nuclear Energy Council from 1975 to 1977, was formerly chairman of the Congressional

Joint Atomic Energy Committee (Berger, 1977, p. 168; Temples, 1980, p. 244). The industry made little attempt to influence public opinion, except through occasional "public service" advertisements. Professional engineers and scientists might belong to professional associations, but their focus was largely on technical issues, oriented to member education and technical research. Popular support was not mobilized to defend nuclear power against the antinuclear forces. As antinuclear sentiment grew, however, and as authorities adopted policies harmful to the nuclear industry, standard pressure-group tactics were maintained; in addition, a pro-nuclear movement emerged. In the process of evolving from pressure group to social movement, two wings of the popular movement emerged—one based in industry, the other in the community.

The Industry Wing.

Organizations emerged from the firms that build, purchase, or supply nuclear plants and their components, and these firms' trade associations. The industry developed these organizations to undertake noninstitutionalized action, and committed personnel to them. These organizations are discussed next.

The Committee for Energy Awareness (CEA) was formed shortly after the 1979 accident at Three Mile Island. The CEA was originally launched and funded by the industry's two major trade associations, the Atomic Industrial Forum (AIF) and the Edison Electric Institute (EEI). Established in 1953, the AIF in the late 1970s had over 800 members from all sectors of the nuclear industry (Atomic Industrial Forum, 1979). The EEI is an association of the 200 largest investor-owned utilities, most of which operate nuclear powerplants (Berger, 1977, p. 144). Organized under a steering committee of eight senior industry executives, the CEA was staffed by public relations experts on temporary loan from the trade associations and nuclear firms. The committee's activities included sponsoring a "Truth Squad" of two nuclear engineers that followed and publicly responded to antinuclear activists Jane Fonda and Tom Hayden on their 1979 nationwide tour; organizing a pro-nuclear advertising campaign; publishing a national newsletter, *Energy Upbeat*, for pro-nuclear advocacy groups; organizing round-table meetings with major newspaper and magazine editors to discuss nuclear issues; sponsoring a retreat in April 1980 for selected pro-nuclear leaders from across the United States; and creating a communications plan to assure the flow of "accurate" information from a nuclear plant in the event of an accident.

Nuclear Energy Women (NEW), an organization composed primarily of women employed in the industry, was created in late 1975 by fourteen professional women in the nuclear industry. NEW's staff director worked for the AIF, and her office was in the association's Washington, D.C. head-quarters. The AIF required NEW to regularly report and justify its activities to AIF management. On October 18, 1979, NEW organized a "Nuclear Energy Education Day," during which more than 4,000 "energy coffees" were held in private homes across the country. The coffees involved discussion of energy issues and featured presentations by experts on nuclear power (Cook, 1979). The organization has also established a speakers' bureau of women willing to give public lectures in favor of nuclear power and has tried, so far unsuccessfully, to persuade women's organizations such as the National Organization of Women and the League of Women Voters to reverse their antinuclear positions.

Several nuclear industry firms also became involved in the pro-nuclear movement. Westinghouse Corporation, a major supplier of nuclear equipment, was particularly active. In 1975 it established a "Nuclear Information Program" to help promote public and government support of nuclear power (Cook, 1980, p. 16). One of the groups' activities, the "Campus America" program, sent highly trained and well-rehearsed Westinghouse employees to debate antinuclear activists on college campuses; it even payed the expenses of antinuclear debators (Nickel, 1980). Westinghouse also commissioned a research firm, Cambridge Reports, Inc., to conduct longitudinal national surveys on attitudes toward nuclear power. The surveys were designed to help pro-nuclear forces more effectively communicate their message to the public. For example, the Cambridge surveys revealed that support for nuclear power was lowest among women, blacks, and young people. Drawing on the survey findings, Cambridge Associates specified the arguments and channels of influence that are most effective in reaching these three groups. Finally, Westinghouse encouraged its 140,000 employees to become involved in the pro-nuclear movement, especially the 13,000 to 15,000 who worked in Westinghouse's nuclear division. Employees received a monthly news magazine publicizing the types of pro-nuclear activities their colleagues were involved in and listing upcoming events. Employees were urged to participate in town meetings and other forums that provide an opportunity to promote nuclear power. T-shirts with the slogan "Nuclear Power, Safer Than Sex" were available to employees at a nominal cost.

Energy Research Group (ERG), a Boston-based engineering-consulting firm, was organized in 1973 by five graduates of the Massachusetts Institute of Technology. It was active in the pro-nuclear movement at both the regional and national levels. ERG served as a consultant to many of New England's pro-nuclear organizations, providing advice on how to deal with the media, organize public forums, and influence decision-makers. At the national level, ERG conducted the retreat sponsored by the CEA in 1980, and helped organize the pro-nuclear movement's Second National Conference on Energy Advocacy, held in June of the same year. In addition, ERG has drafted several important pro-nuclear documents. One, commissioned by the CEA, detailed how industry has and can be involved in the pro-nuclear movement. Another, distributed by the AIF, outlined strategies available to utility companies in the event of a plant-site occupation by antinuclear demonstrators (Goldsmith and Shants, 1978).

The Community Wing

Groups based in local communities were a major force in the pro-nuclear movement:

The New Hampshire Voice of Energy (NHVOE) had a working-class and nonprofessional middle-class membership and leadership. The organization began in 1975 when a group of women from Manchester, New Hampshire, complained to the local utility about a proposed rate increase. A utility executive told the group that the construction of a controversial nuclear plant in the area would help stabilize the cost of electricity. After researching the issue, the women established a pro-nuclear organization. The group then grew through friendship and kinship networks, though the initial group of women were the most active. The group's headquarters was the home of one of its members. The NHVOE gained national prominence in 1977, when it sponsored the country's first pro-nuclear demonstration in Manchester, New Hampshire, on March 17, 1977, attended by over 4,000 people (Committee for Energy Awareness, 1980, p. 1).

The Massachusetts Voice of Energy (MVOE), formed in 1978, was comprised of nuclear engineers in a single architect-engineering firm and nuclear engineering graduate students at a university near Boston. We considered it community-based, rather than industry-based, for two reasons. First, neither the firm nor the university sponsored the group or encouraged participation in it. Top management in the firm, in fact, attempted to dissuade employees from participating. Since only a small fraction of the firm's business was nuclear-related, management feared that the political controversy arising from employee participation might jeopardize its other business. One member of the MVOE we interviewed felt that a promotion he had been expecting had been delayed because of his pro-nuclear activities; another resigned from the firm because of management "harassment" for MVOE activities. The university provided no support to the campus branch of the group. Second, mobilization took place primarily through friendship networks. The students were a closely knit group, who all worked together in the same study office area. Most of the engineers were friends before joining the MVOE. Among its activities, the MVOE testified in state legislative and regulatory hearings, established a pro-nuclear speakers' bureau, and sponsored such events as dumping of empty barrels into Boston Harbor to dramatize U.S. dependence on foreign oil. In sum, both the nuclear power industry and community groups provided an infrastructure on which the pro-nuclear movement developed. The existence of these two bases of mobilization gave rise to two distinct wings. One, the industry-based wing, emerged from the nuclear industry. It was a more or less conscious attempt by industry leaders and groups to counter the antinuclear movement. The second, the community-based wing, was initiated by individuals integrated into community-based groups and resembles a "classical" social movement. These two bases of mobilization have in turn shaped the movement's mobilization dilemmas and tactical choices.

Mobilization Dilemmas, Tactical Choices, and Legitimacy

The pro-nuclear forces have organizational dilemmas and problems directly related to their identification as industry representatives. That is, in the process of becoming a social movement, with its larger claim of ideological and collective goals, they have been tainted by their history as a pressure group. Moreover, links to industry and the social position of the pro-nuclear groups shaped tactical choices. Our discussion is organized around four analytic themes. First, we explore the problems associated with the achievement of movement legitimacy. Second, we analyze the availability of infrastructure support to a movement. Third, we examine tactical constraints. Finally, we consider the strategic advantages of a centralized versus decentralized structure.

Movement Legitimacy

A movement achieves legitimacy in two ways. *Legitimacy of numbers* is achieved by mobilizing a significant number of internally disciplined people committed to seeking an alternative distribution of power (Tilly, 1978, p. 125; 1979, p. 25). The polity allows into its ranks only those groups that are able to mobilize large numbers of people. Thus, legitimacy is achieved by demonstrating that a committed and mobilized citizenry supports political change. A movement achieves *legitimacy of means* by convincing the public that it is an appropriate vehicle to achieve its constituents' goals. A movement not only must justify its goals, but also justify its *modus operandi* as a social movement. Legitimacy of means helps a movement recruit new members and gain access to the media, and makes government repression less likely and less effective (Rimlinger, 1970; Zald and Ash, 1966). The pro-nuclear groups faced disparate problems in securing both types of legitimacy.

Achieving *legitimacy of numbers* entails two different types of problems for the two wings of the pro-nuclear movement. The community groups' most pressing problem was a shortage of resources, such as money, time, and organizing skills. Some groups could not afford to rent an office and were forced to use a member's house as headquarters. Other community activists we interviewed said they lacked important skills, such as the ability to deal with the media. Most complained that the demands of family and work restricted the time they could devote to the group tasks. Activists complained bitterly about the resources allegedly controlled by the antinuclear movement. They claimed that antinuclear groups had ample money, donated by musicians and foundations; time, since members did not hold jobs or worked for the movement at subsistence wages; and organizing skills, since many members participated in other movements in the 1960s and 1970s. Pro-nuclear activists saw themselves as far less fortunate. Their lack of resources seriously inhibited their mobilization efforts, which in turn has undercut the community groups' claim to legitimacy, since they could not muster the appearance of a well-organized and widely supported effort.

The industry-based wing of the pro-nuclear movement, on the other hand, had more than adequate organizational and monetary resources. The Committee For Energy Awareness, for example, had an operating budget of $1.6 million in 1979 (Burnham, 1979). And the Energy Research Group had a well-equipped professionally administered office, and a politically experienced and sophisticated professional staff. The major problem faced by the industrial groups was the need to demonstrate that the movement was neither merely a paper organization, nor an industry group protecting its own economic interests. A CEA organizing manual states: "[Government] officials rationalize that people who support energy development do so primarily to protect corporate investments or employment opportunities and therefore discount their opinions" (Committee for Energy Awareness, 1980, p.1). The industry-based wing tried to create the image that a sincere, committed citizenry supports its efforts.

The nature of the respective legitimacy problems of the two wings of the movement suggests a basis for cooperation between them. The industrial groups were rich in resources, but lacked members; the reverse was true for the community groups. The CEA organizers' manual describes industry's efforts to assist the community groups:

> Citizens can provide credible, non-industry spokespersons able to reach decision-makers, educate the public, and challenge the opposition more effectively than industry. Their pro-energy messages are better received and often their actions can be more attention-getting than corporate activities. . . . Industry can play a significant role in supporting citizen activities. In fact, a

number of very successful activities have been conducted with industry support. . . . At a minimum, the commitment by the company wanting to effectively support pro-energy activities must contain the following: staff support time and secretarial time, printing and Xeroxing, and money for direct contributions. (Committee for Energy Awareness, 1980, p. 3)

In this vein, an East-coast utility company reimbursed local activists for expenses incurred in attending the Second Annual Pro-nuclear Conference in Chicago in 1979; the CEA hired a New York consulting firm to train community activists in media techniques; Westinghouse and many other corporations supplied pro-nuclear groups with literature, speakers, and technical advice at a nominal cost or for free; and the AFNE donated funds to the Maine Voice of Energy to help that group defeat an antinuclear state referendum in 1979 (Stevens, 1980).

Industry support, however, threatened to undercut one basis for the legitimacy of the community groups—their claim to sincerity. If an industrial group's support was too overwhelming, the recipient community may have been publicly viewed as an extension of the professional sector.

The pro-nuclear movement devised several strategies to deal with this problem. One was to conceal industry involvement in the movement. For example, during a workshop at the national pro-nuclear conference in Chicago, discussion leaders advised participants not to use utility postage machines when sending out mass mailings. On one occasion when a postage machine had been used, antinuclear activists had traced the meter to the utility, providing further ammunition to discredit the pro-nuclear group. Similarly, a NEW member, employed in the public relations department of a utility company, initiated a petition calling for "legislation to keep our seven regional nuclear plants operating and to finish those planned for the 1980s." The petition failed to mention the sponsor. Another technique was to exclude industry employees from membership in community organizations. A pro-nuclear group formed in the Three Mile Island area, for example, prohibited utility employees from formally joining the group, although they were allowed to attend meetings and participate in group activities. Finally, some community groups refused to accept money from industry, though they normally welcomed free services such as secretarial help, expert advice, and printing assistance less likely to taint their image.

The industrial groups faced a different set of risks when they supported community groups. The CEA manual urged "industry [to] have faith that the [community] group's overall thrusts will be positive" (Committee on Energy Awareness, 1980, p. 2). This faith, however, was sometimes difficult to generate. For example, a high-ranking public relations employee of a New Hampshire utility company told us that top management initially resisted a suggestion that the company support a community group. Management feared that the group would act irresponsibly and reflect poorly on the firm. Similarly, a utility executive explained to an annual meeting of the Atomic Industrial Forum the potential problems associated with utility funding of community groups. State utility regulators require such funds to be drawn from stockholders, rather than ratepayers. Stockholders may object to the use of their money for this purpose.

Achieving *legitimacy of means* involves demonstrating that a social movement is an appropriate vehicle to achieve its constituents' goals. This is especially difficult for movements based on establishment mobilization. Industry's mobilization of the pro-nuclear movement appears to have violated a norm that protest movements are a vehicle reserved for otherwise powerless groups. The logic behind the norm seems to be that, since privileged and represented groups are able to use institutionalized means of influence, it is unfair for them to use noninstitutionalized means as well—a defining characteristic of a social movement.

The industry-based wing of the pro-nuclear movement used a number of techniques to help establish legitimacy of means. The most important of these was its attempt to recruit blacks and women, a high priority. Movement leaders we interviewed felt that blacks and women were especially effective spokespeople, since their presence gave the movement a grass-roots image. This was borne out by the experience of a woman activist, employed in the public relations department of a utility company. She reported that when she spoke as a utility employee, her "credibility was next to zero"—audiences were hostile and media coverage was inadequate and critical. However, when she spoke as a representative of Nuclear Energy Women, she usually received sympathetic press coverage and her audiences were more open to her pro-nuclear arguments.

Another strategy used by industry was to expand the scope of the movement's goals. Beginning in 1975, the pro-nuclear movement evolved from a single issue to a multi-issue movement. The movement's original focus on nuclear power was widened to include promotion of other forms of energy (e.g., coal), attainment of economic growth, defense of "the American way of life," support for a free-enterprise economy, and independence from foreign oil. This expansion of the number of goals helped establish legitimacy of means in two ways. First, goals expansion helped to recruit more blacks and women. The leadership of the National Association for the Advancement of Colored People, for example, endorsed nuclear power in part because they believed it would promote economic growth and social mobility (Wilson, 1980). Second, it seemed more reasonable to launch a movement when basic values were under attack than when the issue was the promotion of a particular technology. An employee of the General

Electric corporation, for example, advised an Atomic Industrial Forum conference: "If you're about to enter the nuclear debate—don't. It's a loser! The issue of the energy debate is not energy; the issue is, rather, life-styles and the structure of society" (Wolfe, 1978, p. 3).

In sum, a group undergoing a transformation from pressure group to social movement must demonstrate that its claims receive the active support of a citizenry not financially dependent upon the industry, and that, even though it may have ties to the polity, a social movement is an appropriate vehicle to achieve its goals.

Movement Infrastructure

Freeman (1979) argues that the existence of one movement may generate resources for subsequent movements. The antiwar and student movements of the 1960s, for example, furnished the antinuclear movement with a personal communications network, established underground newspapers, office facilities, and trained activists. The pro-nuclear movement was less fortunate. Although several right-wing groups supported the pro-nuclear movement, including the John Birch Society, the Ku Klux Klan, and the National Caucus of Labor Committees,[4] they largely remained on the fringe. The one mobilized constituency the pro-nuclear forces have most assiduously attempted to draw into their movement, women's and feminist organizations such as the National Organization of Women and the League of Women Voters, adopted antinuclear stands. Many established feminist and women's magazines, ranging from *Ms.* to *Redbook*, have supported the antinuclear position. Thus, the pro-nuclear movement was forced to mobilize without the benefit of trained activists and an already mobilized constituency.

Five grass-roots activists told us that their lack of experience in movement organizing substantially slowed down their mobilization efforts. They had to acquire new skills and establish a network to share ideas. Yet the availability of an existing infrastructure may be less important if other resources are available. The pro-nuclear movement's greater monetary resources reduced its relative disadvantage. It was able to hire sophisticated public relations firms to train and advise pro-nuclear groups, run national and regional conferences, and print literature and training manuals.

Constraints and Choices

Movements, by definition, use noninstitutionalized means to achieve their goals (Wilson, 1973). They vary considerably, however, in the extent to which they employ violent or disorderly tactics. While the antinuclear movement occasionally used civil disobedience and tactics such as occupying plant sites, the pro-nuclear movement used only nondisruptive tactics such as letter writing, petitions, and legal demonstrations. Two factors, both related to the pro-nuclear forces' partial transformation from pressure group to social movement, explain this difference. First, while governments often lack an effective intervention technique to control more spontaneous, locally organized, and diffuse forms of protest, this is less true with established movements, which provide the government with a concrete social target (Marx, 1979). In the case of the pro-nuclear movement, the government's social control agents could use regulatory, legal, and tax mechanisms to suppress illegal actions by the corporate sector. Second, when a group has a high or moderate degree of access to the government, it has something to lose by taking militant actions against the government. Antinuclear activists felt relatively free to use disruptive tactics since they had (or believed they had) little or no influence over the government's energy policy. The pro-nuclear forces, however, wielded considerable— although declining—influence over government policy. Disruptive tactics would have jeopardized this channel of influence.

Movement Centralization

Social movement researchers disagree about whether the centralization of power within a movement promotes success (Barkan, 1979; Gamson, 1975; Gerlach and Hine, 1970; Piven and Cloward, 1977). Most groups in the pro-nuclear movement had only loose ties to one another and no single organization either spoke for the movement or had authority over other organizations. Nor was there any single organization that defined the issues or was the center of public attention. This decentralization benefited the movement in two ways. First, licensing and operating a nuclear plant requires approval from many federal, state, and local regulatory and legislative bodies. Community groups could often play a crucial role when these bodies deliberate. One of the pro-nuclear movement's main activities was to represent pro-nuclear "citizens" in these decision-making processes. Often, however, to obtain formal intervenor status, a group must establish that they represent a constituency directly affected by the contested proposal. Centralization of a movement could undercut any such argument, since it would suggest that the organization represents a non-local constituency. More importantly, the proliferation of independent citizen groups increased the overall impact of the pro-nuclear forces. The reasons for this are explained by a Westinghouse Corporation document:

> It's not really necessary that every activity of all the groups in a particular region be coordinated with other groups or with industry activities. In fact, it is more important that policy makers hear a number of different views all pointing to a similar direction from a number of different directions. (Kearns, n.d., p. 10)

Indeed, one pro-nuclear activist told a training workshop that he had split his one group of forty into two groups of twenty, since this allowed the same number of people to have twice the representation during a regulatory proceeding. He urged other groups to do the same.

Second, decentralization allowed the community groups within the movement to engage in activities that would not have been open to them if in a tightly directed organization dominated by industry. The Committee for Energy Awareness manual states:

> Specific activities that citizens' activities can do that often industry cannot are: litigate in court on certain issues; provide many pro-energy voices in hearings before utility commissions, regulatory agencies, and the legislative branch; volunteer for election campaigns; run for office; [conduct] pro-energy initiative campaigns . . .; ensure that policy makers understand and represent attitudes of the *public*. (Committee for Energy Awareness, 1980, p. 2, italics added)

A centralized movement structure would inhibit these activities for two reasons. First, federal and local election laws restrict corporate involvement in the electoral process. Second, these activities gain credibility and lose some of their self-serving appearance when "citizen" rather than corporate groups initiate them.

Our analysis supports those who argue that a decentralized structure promotes a movement's goals. We believe, however, that the particular advantages of decentralization enjoyed by the pro-nuclear movement are peculiar to movements with ties to established institutions. For other types of movements—for example, when factionalism is a problem or when coordination is important—a centralized structure may be more advantageous.

Impact of the Pro-nuclear Movement

There are two other issues related to this discussion: the nature of movement/countermovement interaction and the question of impact. The pro-nuclear movement emerged as a countermovement to the antinuclear movement. As such, much of its energies were spent directly attacking the activities of antinuclear organizations: it collected information on the antinuclear groups and used it to disrupt antinuclear activities, cut off the flow of resources to antinuclear groups, and gave the antinuclear movement a negative image in the media (see chapter 10).

It is difficult to assess the extent of the damage inflicted on the antinuclear movement by pro-nuclear groups. It is likely, for example, that the pro-nuclear movement's surveillance of antinuclear activity inhibited some citizens from participating in the antinuclear effort. It is nearly impossible, however, to estimate the number of those dissuaded from participation. Similarly, the Clamshell Alliance, a New England-based antinuclear organization, disbanded in 1979 in part to avoid the legal suit against them brought by two pro-nuclear organizations (Atomic Industrial Forum, 1980). It is difficult to determine the independent effect of the suit, however, since many other problems plagued the alliance, such as factionalism. The suit may have only acted as a catalyst in an ongoing process of disintegration. Thus, in many cases, it is not possible to distinguish the effects of the pro-nuclear movement's efforts to damage the antinuclear movement from mobilization problems encountered within the antinuclear movement itself.

Ironically, the positive effects of pro-nuclear actions on the antinuclear movement are easiest to detect. First, the pro-nuclear movement's efforts bolstered the argument that nuclear power brings with it a curtailment of civil liberties. Second, the pro-nuclear movement's actions provided antinuclear activists with an additional issue around which to organize. One national organization, Campaign for Political Rights, and several local organizations developed committees or projects to combat the pro-nuclear movement's efforts to damage the antinuclear movement. Third, the presence of a common enemy produced alliances among antinuclear activists and other groups, especially political rights groups. A manual for antinuclear activists explains how this process occurred: "Groups concerned about civil liberties will become involved in supporting the political rights of antinuclear groups—and at the same time they will become informed on issues related to nuclear power" (Campaign for Political Rights, 1979, p. 6).

Ultimately the pro-nuclear movement has been unable to reverse the decline of the nuclear industry. By 1982, construction costs had escalated, safety problems were unresolved, bond rating services downgraded the credit ratings of utilities having nuclear plants, and design and construction flaws in plants have brought heavy fines from the NRC and construction delays. Particularly alarming to the industry is that utilities have cancelled or delayed indefinitely nineteen plants currently under construction, despite outlays of hundreds of millions of dollars (Bernstein, 1982; Sheets, 1982). The industry that spawned the pressure groups was itself becoming increasingly demoralized; many individual firms were reconsidering their commitment to the industry.

Summary and Conclusion

A pressure group may become transformed into a social movement when challenged by another social movement. The pro-nuclear movement grew out of a struggle with the antinuclear movement over government policy toward nuclear power. The pro-nuclear movement's initial organization as a pressure group shaped the character of its mobilization problems. The movement had to demonstrate that large numbers of committed citizens backed it, and that the movement was not merely a front for the nuclear industry. The movements' two wings provided a basis for this demonstration, but they also produced a tension within the movement. The movement's location in the social structure also affected its choice of tactics: its origins as a pressure group precluded the use of highly disruptive tactics and a centralized organizational structure. Finally, industry involvement in the pro-nuclear movement illustrates the significant role that established groups and institutions may play in the mobilization of social movements. Movements are usually, but not always, launched by groups from "below." This raises an important question: How is the position of an established polity member undermined, and how does it respond?

Notes

This essay was written, and the data for it collected, while Useem was a postdoctoral fellow under a grant from the National Institute of Mental Health (MH-14,698-04-5). Research support was provided by the Society for the Psychological Study of Social Issues, the University of Michigan Phoenix Memorial Project, and the Department of Energy.

1. See Tilly (1978) for a definition of polity membership; Gamson (1975) for a distinction between mobilizing and non-mobilizing groups; and Wilson (1973) and Smelser (1962) for distinctions between institutionalized and noninstitutionalized forms of collective action.
2. Of course, factors other than the actions of the antinuclear movement have contributed to the industry's problems. For example, since the early 1970s, the growth in the demand for electricity has abated, construction costs of new nuclear powerplants have risen steeply, and the market for utility stocks has faltered, making it more difficult to raise the capital needed to build a new plant (Bernstein, 1982; Bupp and Derian, 1978; Montgomery and Quirk, 1978).
3. Bernard Cohen (1979, p. 14), a prominent nuclear physicist, emphasized the impending crisis in the industry: "Up to 1973 [the industry] got lots of orders which they're still working on. But they've had very few new orders for plants sinced 1973. As I see it, the critical time will be about 1981. If there's not a substantial influx of new orders by then, there will be massive layoffs in the nuclear industry, and all the experts in various aspects of the nuclear system will find work in other areas. And once that happens, it would take a very long time to reassemble them."
4. Leftist groups and others have charged that the National Caucus of Labor Committees is actually a police front, not a citizens group, but this charge has never been verified.

PART VI
SOCIAL MOVEMENT SECTORS
AND THE FUTURE

Introduction

The first essay in this volume conceptualizes the social movement sector as the totality of organized activity for social change in the society. But how do we analyze the social movement sector? What are the differences between nations that lead some to have large SM sectors and others, at similar levels of industrial-economic development, to have much smaller sectors? Here, Roberta Ash Garner and Mayer Zald attempt to develop some provisional answers to this difficult question. They attempt to show how the political and economic structures of a society and the traditions of associationalism and centralization shape the size and orientation of the social movement sector. The analysis is both cross-national and historical. They attempt to show how the structure of politics and of political parties influence the structure of social movement activity. For instance, the more political parties are closely tied to a Right-Left alignment, the more social movement activity is assimilated to the ongoing dynamics of the political system. They also attempt to show how the orientation of the social movement sector may be more or less dominated by one large and coherent set of issues, such as the franchise and rights of the working class, but may be characterized by multiple issues in another period. For instance, in contrast to some of our Italian examples, and, in spite of the encapsulating terminology, the progressive era in the United States consisted of several movements, including those for civic reform, others aimed at control of industry, and still others aimed at alleviating poverty and protecting women and children.

While Garner and Zald attempt to examine the development of social movement sectors on a comparative and historical basis, Mayer Zald concludes the volume with a discussion of the future of social movements in the United States. He combines resource mobilization theory with the political and economic analysis of the SM sector developed by Garner and Zald in an attempt to forecast the future of SM organizational forms and sectoral orientations.

Forecasting the future is always a risky business. It is difficult enough to try to understand what has gone before. We believe that the conceptual tools we have developed in these essays are some modest help in both efforts. But we have no doubt that new developments in social change activity will force yet again the development of new conceptual tools.

12

The Political Economy of Social Movement Sectors

Roberta Ash Garner and *Mayer N. Zald*

Cross-national comparisons indicate that nations differ in the overall amount of social movement activity that is generated. It is often suggested that the United States provides more fertile soil for the growth of social movements than do other nations. Moreover, over time societies differ in the amount of social movement activity that they support. Cycles of mobilization for quite disparate causes seems to occur. This total amount of social movement activity is the social movement sector.

Our basic assumption is that to understand the course of social movements we have to understand them as a *configuration* and within a *determining environment*. Thus, we must examine the totality of movements in a society, rather than isolated movements, and identify the elements of social structure that shape this totality of movements (the movement sector). What we are proposing is, first, a set of terms or conceptual tools for extending the analysis of social movements to the SM *sector* and, second, a set of propositions for explaining variations in the sector.

In the first section we define the social movement sector. The second section identifies major components, and in the third section we discuss determinants. Major determinants include the economic base, conjunctions of the business cycle and structural change, and the political and ideological system. Since the object of analysis is sectors within societies our methods must be comparative and historical.

Social Movements and the Movement Sector Defined

A most inclusive definition of a social movement is any sentiment and activity shared by two or more people oriented toward changes in social relations or the social system. This most inclusive definition would analytically encompass social movements at any level of social organization

293

(small group, formal organization, community, nation). It would also include movements aimed at changing social relations through changing individuals, such as Alcoholics Anonymous or proselytizing religious movements. It would treat as marginally related or as presocial movements, sentiments and activities that express discontent with the social order but not oriented towards relatively specific or articulated change. Phenomena such as the "beats," the "Teddy boys," may express discontent with the social order and may be the ground out of which social movements grow, but they are peripheral to our analysis.

In this essay we are primarily interested in a subset of all social movement activity. Our focus is upon social movement activity largely oriented towards change that is achieved in the differentiated political arena—changes in the system of political rule or in the specific policies, symbols, and distributional allocations of territorially based authorities. Social movements in groups or organizations that are not articulated with pressures on formal authorities are outside of our ken. Similarly, social movements largely aimed at change through recruiting and changing individuals are ignored, unless they articulate with politically oriented activity. Our concern is with political social movements.

Some definitions of social movements assume that they operate outside of institutionalized channels. For us, here, such an assumption is too limiting. Ronald Reagan and Margaret Thatcher are connected to conservative social movements. Some social movement sentiments and activities exist whenever authorities and their policies are sources of contention. Only if a regime is very widely accepted (through either the elimination of dissent or through positive socialization, ideological hegemony, and widespread policy success) would a society with a differentiated policy have little or no social movement activity. While we are largely concerned with social movement activity outside of well institutionalized channels and forms, how it articulates with more institutionalized political action is part of our problem.

Given this inclusive approach to social movements, what is the social movement sector? The social movement sector is the *configuration* of social movements, the structure of antagonistic, competing and/or cooperating movements that in turn is part of a larger structure of action (political action, in a very broad sense) that may include parties, state bureaucracies, the media, pressure groups, churches, and a variety of other organizational factors in a society. Configuration refers both to the *amount* and *structural relations* of social movement activity and the orientation, or goals, of action.[1]

In which societies can we identify a social movement sector? An SMS only appears in societies that have a distinct political system. Primitive societies rarely have social movements unless they have been integrated into the political or economic system of more developed societies; once such contact takes place, rebellions, millenarian cults, and so on occur frequently. Traditional societies with distinct political systems have sporadic movements—the rise of Islam is one such example. But often such movements remain unstable eruptions—a permanent sector does not emerge. Movements are especially weak in societies in which class relations are highly personalized. A social movement sector is most likely to become a permanent feature of the social system in capitalist societies. Distinctively, they have a separation of the state from civil society, they have a rational legal bureaucratic authority, and they maintain a large sphere of private voluntary associations. The more societies are pervaded by rational legal forms, the more life focuses on formal organizations; the more people think in terms of state and economy, and the more they believe that human action constructs the social system, the more a movement sector becomes a permanent subsystem of the society.

Dimensions of Social Movement Sectors

A brief comparison of the social movement sectors of Italy and the United States may provide some illustrations that we can use to identify key dimensions of social movement sectors, dimensions that describe the structure of these sectors in most capitalist democracies. In Italy, the entire sector is highly politicized and tightly tied to the party system and the state. Politicization has several dimensions: action takes place to alter, influence, and/or react to the Italian state; the state is defined as the element of the status quo and the main instrument of change; the movements of the sector and of parties (Barnes, 1977) are defined on a left/right basis; there are few—essentially no—religious movements or cults and only a limited number of lifestyle/personal identity movements.

Banfield (1958) and Almond and Verba (1963) give quite a different picture of Italian society. They stress the passive and alienated features of Italian political culture. Ours is an alternative view: Italy is a society so highly mobilized by parties, unions, corporatist groups, and the church that there is relatively little space left for a differentiated movement sector. Of course, the two images are not really contradictory (corporatist mobilization may in fact be a cause of passivity). Moveover, Italy (particularly northern Italy) is no longer the same society that it was when the earlier studies were done. In short, the nonpolitical social movement sector appears relatively small and political social movements separate from well-established institutions are few; sector activity is encapsulated in party-related political forms; the number of unorganized currents is also relatively small; much of the sector overlaps the institutions of cultural life, universities, and the media, probably because these are the institutions in which people are most weakly integrated into the organs of party and corporate life. The range of issues addressed by the SMS is largely secular and political.

In comparison to Italy, the U.S. SMS includes a large nonpolitical sector, and the political sector is differentiated from the party system. There are a large number of groups that are organized around religious and lifestyle issues, mobilized around issues that have little to do with the state; the vast majority of the 400 to 500 cults (comprising a couple million adults) are largely outside the political system in the usual sense of the term (Wuthnow, 1983). Even groups that have to deal with political organizations seem to do so only in a transitory or tactical way. The political component as a whole seems to correlate poorly with a right/left political dimension. The range of goals do not reflect an easy left/right dimension, and action is aimed at many different levels in the system. Many of the movements are localistic and spontaneous, whether they are cults, lifestyle currents, or neighborhood movements.

So in one country there is a relatively structured, highly politicized SMS that is tightly bound to the institutionalized political subsystem; in the other country, a sprawling and diverse SMS with a low degree of political action and often only the most tenuous ties to the state or to other political institutions. Our intent is to sharpen understanding of the determinants of these differences without elaborating many obvious dimensions (e.g., Italy is a more politicized society, while the U.S. is localistic and decentralized; in the U.S. civil society is generally more important than the state, etc.), although we think these statements are probably true.

These two short sketches help us identify important dimensions of the SMS. Remember, we are trying to characterize features of social movement action as a *whole* in a society. Some of these features are derivable from individual social movements, but others are global features, not reducible to characteristics of individual movements. The dimensions are (1) size, (2) degree of organization, (3) social location of support and of locus of action, (4) alignment with the left-right orientation (singular ideological polarization), (5) autonomy from other institutions, and finally (6) the character of change over time.

Size is measured in terms of the number of organizations and the number of participants in social movement activities of any kind. We are interested in size relative to other sectors of activity, the more institutionalized one (political parties, churches, etc.) and in the size of the sector compared to its size in other countries and over time.

Degree of organization is roughly speaking the ratio of membership in formal organizations to all types of participation. In some societies, and at some points in time social movements generate a great deal of participation in formal organizations, in other cases they do not. Individual movements and the sector as a whole vary in their organization and the relation of organizations to protest and individual spontaneous behavior. This dimension is also important for understanding the difference between dissent and currents of opposition in the socialist states. What *type* of organizational form is taken on by those movements that do coalesce into organizations is also a characteristic of the movement sector as a whole, and not merely a characteristic of individual movements. The sector as a whole varies in whether it is dominated by professional movement organizations or other forms.

The *social location* of the sector refers to its social geography. There are obvious structural variables—class, region, ethnicity—that locate the groups that are most easily mobilized. Another way of charting social location is by the locus of action, institutions, and settings in and around which social movements emerge. The SMS may focus on "weak link" institutions—institutions in which basic societal tensions or contradictions appear. A weak link institution is characterized by a destabilized or destabilizable system of social control, a mobilizable population, and a set of focal grievances at the center of contention between authorities and the relevant population. In the last few decades the universities and high schools have been a major institutional site. Burawoy (1976) has identified the contradictions that precipitate movement action in the university of a developing nation (Zambia) in an article that contributes to the concept of "weak link" institutions; Piven (1976), has identified the welfare system as a weak link institution; and Hirsch (1979) has commented on the shift from the workplace to the community as a "weak link" in advanced capitalism.

Social movement sectors also vary in their alignment with a left-right political spectrum (Barnes, 1977). This alignment is historically based on the amount of class conflict and the extent to which politics is heavily polarized along class lines. Such alignment is also related to the extent to which the movement sector is politicized at all. Note that one could have a highly politicized, strongly left-right aligned movement sector that did not "adhere" to the political institutions but to some other set of institutions (like the educational ones).

This last comment implies another dimension, the degree of SMS *autonomy from other organizations and sectors* (especially the political system), not only in terms of member overlap but also in terms of strategies and structural linkages. The SMS may heavily overlap institutions such as those of religion or education.

It is clear that some of these dimensions have more to do with the amount and organization of the sector (size, organization, autonomy), and others have more to do with the orientation of the sector, social location of support, and left-right orientation. The sector may change over time in these characteristics in one country, but be more or less impervious to change in another society.

This suggests a final concern. An important aspect of the SMS is the *character* of its *change over time.* In some societies the SM sector's size, organizational structure, and content (its issues and ideological foci) vary markedly over time and seem sensitive to economic changes and social control pressures. In others, even though action and movement organization may fluctuate, the sector maintains its integrity. This can most clearly be seen by comparing Italy and the United States in the Cold War period of the 1950s. It was a period of relatively low activity in both countries, but in Italy the traditions and sentiments underlying the SMS were not disrupted (although perhaps decreasing organizational activity) while in the United States they were. In other words, the Cold War and accompanying social control produced a deactivation of social movements in the U.S. but not in Italy. In large measure, these differences were the result of the role of mass left-wing parties in Italy that were and are absent in the United States.

These several dimensions of the social movement sector are themselves quite complex phenomena, not easily adumbrated. Nevertheless, they give us purchase on seeing the sector whole. Now the question becomes what shapes or determines the range of sector performance on each of these dimensions.

Systemic Constraints

By systemic constraints we mean those characteristics of the environment of social movements that shape and limit the possibilities for social movements. At the most general level of analysis the politically oriented social movement sector is determined by the number and size of social categories with infrastructures of social relations, interpersonal networks, community structure, and formal organization with mobilizable resources that develop actionable issues (Tilly, 1978). Actionable issues develop as authorities take action, as ideologies, values, and interests change, and as the political structures shape options.

The number of categories that are mobilizable into the bases of social movements are quite large and vary from society to society. But it is clear that the major categories which are turned into competing cleavages across modern societies are those related to economic structure, race and ethnicity, religion, regional cleavages, and, to a lesser extent, sex and age. In a more complete treatment of the determinants of the orientation of the social movement sector we would take each cleavage-category and ask how and when it turns into a major determinant of social movement sector orientation. For instance, it is apparent that class, and even ethnic, issues are submerged when groups unite to overthrow colonial domination. Nagel and Olzak (1982) have begun to synthesize a large number of historical cases to show how ethnicity emerges, reemerges, and reconstitutes itself as a social movement-political issue. Drawing on Barth (1969) and Hannan (1979), they argue that increased interdependence leads to increased competition for jobs and resources among previously segregated groups. Nagel and Olzak go beyond Barth and Hannan by considering how the changing structure of and policies of national and international governments provide political opportunities for mobilization and for resource support and advantages to be gained. It would be possible, then, to begin by asking how is the social movement sector shaped by ethnicity and ethnic change, treating economic and class relations in less detail. Instead, we begin by examining how the economic and class systems shape the social movement sector, treating ethnicity in passing.

Our discussion of economic systemic constraints is in two parts: (1) the patterning of productive activities and associated class relationships and processes that we refer to as the structure or base, and (2) cyclical phenomena that overlap structural changes and produce a patterning we call conjunctural factors. The shape of the sector is also heavily influenced by political structure and opportunity; thus after discussing economic constraints on the sector, we turn to political constraints.

The Structure of the Economy and Class Relations

A major determinant of the SMS is the base of productive activities and its corresponding social relationships. By this we mean the structure of the economy—patterns of ownership, size and type of productive enterprises, relations between a public and a private sector, nature of work relations and management within enterprises, forms of the labor market, types of employment and occupation, wage scales and income distribution, and the political associations concerned with production. National economies exist within the global political economy, which cannot be ignored. We will also consider parts of the system of "reproduction of the relations of production," that is to say, the articulation of the family, community, and socialization process with the mode of production (Althusser, 1971).

Class Structure, Class Conflict, and Contradictory Positions

A classic method of movement analysis is to identify the social base of a particular movement. More than that the system of class relations in a society shapes the configuration of social movements. The configuration of social movements changes as new classes appear and other classes decline or lose their positions of dominance.

There are many studies of the social base of single movements or related types of movements: for example, the working class has supported a variety of left-wing movements (Hobsbawm, 1964; Abendroth, 1972); the declining traditional petty-bourgeoisie has given rise to a status group politics (Gusfield, 1969) and has supported fascist and authoritarian movements; smallholders (in certain respects, a special kind of petty-bourgeoisie) have been extensively involved in movements (Heberle, 1945; Stinchcombe, 1967; Hofstadter, 1963; Woodward, 1963); the new stratum of employed technical and professional workers was associated with the New Left of the 1960s (Mallet, 1975; Gorz, 1967).

A change in the productive system is associated not just with one class and its accompanying movement but with a new set of classes and their interrelated movements. For example, the emergency of capitalist agriculture in the twentieth century in the Po Valley generated *both* left-wing movements of agricultural laborers and the fascist movement supported by the *agro-capitalists*; the origins of Italian fascism were in paramilitary groups that attacked the organizations of the laborers in that region. A new organization of production generated a set of movements—more precisely, movements and countermovements (Cardoza, 1975). Moreover, there is no simple relationship of a single class to a single political position; the political action of any given class is contingent on the class structure as a whole and the political action of other classes.

Aside from recognizing the system of class relations as a determinant of the SMS, it is important to recognize that class position is not unambiguous and that some positions may be particularly ambiguous and contradictory (Wright, E. O., Wright, E. O. et al.). Middle strata are especially likely to be in contradictory positions and thus it is not surprising that these strata have shown a high level of volatility, movement action, and often variable or even unpredictable political behavior. At the level of the individual, a contradictory class position (as defined by Wright) may mean high levels of cross-pressure, or role strain. At the level of the class, movement action may be volatile. Ironically, it is precisely these stressed, volatile positions that contribute to the stability of the society as a whole, reducing its tendency to polarize into class blocs (Lipset, 1959, pp. 77-78).

Contradictory class positions can be seen as a structural feature of a whole system. A society with a large number of contradictory class positions may be prone to movement volatility. Since advanced capitalism seems to generate large blocks of contradictory positions (like the employed petty-bourgeoisie mentioned earlier), its patterns of movement activity may be more unstable and spasmodic than the movement activity of the late nineteenth century (which was characterized by what now seem the relatively predictable actions of the expanding proletariat and the declining traditional petty-bourgeoisie).

The Dual Economy and the SMS

The structure of class relations is of course shaped by the organization of the economy. One can just as easily begin analysis of the determinants of the social movement sector by examining the group structure and interests generated by the organization of the economy. How did the structure of the economy in the 1950s and 1960s relate to SMS configuration?

Schematically, the economy had two private sectors: a monopoly sector of very large enterprises (some of which were actually monopolies, while others were oligopolies) and a competitive sector of small capital. In a number of West European countries (England, France, Italy) the monopoly sector also depended on large amounts of state investment; in the United States it has been more substantially private. The monopoly, or concentrated, sector had strong unionization (although not all monopoly enterprises were unionized); the competitive sector had low wages and drew on the reserve army of the unemployed.[2]

This particular configuration of the economy in turn generated a particular configuration of social movements. The working class was divided into a stably employed unionized part and an un- and/or marginally employed part, with objectively different interests. The privileged sector of the working class opted for continued corporatist union action at the workplace. As citizens and taxpayers, privileged workers took a somewhat dim view of the demands of the underprivileged sector for welfare, although they did support measures like the minimum wage. Adhering to the union corporatism, the stable working class was relatively unlikely to engage in social movement activity. When it did support social movements, union leadership could use social movements as part of interunion turf building, as in the conflict of unions in support of Cesar Chavez's Union Farmworkers, or they could transcend their members' commitments and interests (Wood, 1981).

The unprivileged sector of the working class behaved in a diametrically opposite way. It was prone to localistic, violent, and weakly organized actions, such as the ghetto riots of the 1960s or the clashes between groups of unemployed men in Naples in the spring of 1978. Since the marginal working class had weak links with the workplace, many of its actions took place at other social sites, such as the neighborhoods or the high schools. The pattern is precisely the one described by Piven and Cloward—spasmodic action, volatility, little stable organization, little national organization, often high levels of violence. (Unlike Piven and Cloward [1977, 1978], we do not see these characteristics as virtues but as acts of desperation.)

These actions (when they are not purely destructive lashing out, little distinguishable from crime) frequently function like those of the preindustrial urban mob; that is, they signal to the state that it must carry out some type of short-term remedial program (Hobsbawm, 1965). Thus, they raise the costs of the state and the taxpayers and may give rise to reactionary sentiments and movements.

There is considerable national variation within this overall pattern. One source of variation is the overlap of the dual economy with major lines of cleavage, such as race, ethnicity, age, and sex. In many Northern European countries the lower half of the working class is substantially composed of foreign workers; thus, unemployed can be "exported" to the home countries of these workers—as John Berger remarks, unemployment is one of Switzerland's most valuable exports. There is correspondingly little social movement activity within the country. When guest workers are absorbed into the monopoly sector, in West German auto plants, they have been relatively well integrated into the union structure and have not constituted an independent movement base.

The dual economy may overlap regional disparities, so that one geographical area has a disproportionate share of the lower working class: in Italy, the South; within Yugoslavia, Serbia and Macedonia. The overlap of race/ethnicity and the dual economy creates a split labor market. The split labor market leads to a variety of ethnic movements—exclusionary movements by the dominant group, separatist and inclusion movements of the dominated (Bonacich).

The Embedding of National Structures in the Global Political Economy

The orientation of the sector is also shaped by the global political economy. In many cases, military and paramilitary intervention supplement economic pressures. In the vicissitudes of national liberation movements in Africa or the problems of the Left in Latin America, we do not need to look for an invisible hand of structural constraint; the hands of the large powers are all too visible. Or, to take another example, the strategy of the PCI in Italy was largely set by the decisions made at Tehran and Yalta and on the battlefields: Once Italy was clearly in the Western sphere of influence, the PCI was under great pressure to take the *Via Italiana* to socialism, the "Italian Way" of participation within the framework of bourgeois democracy.

Social movement analysis by sociologists has usually focused upon mobilization within a single nation-state. But it is important to emphasize that the leading issues of the sector may be defined across national borders, and that resources may flow across national borders. Social movement activity in one nation provides a template, a possibility for change to relevant groups in other nations. Not only the idea or model of change, but a flow of personnel, weapons, and resources may flow across national borders. It was true in the American Revolution, in Allende's Chile, in the rash of movements of 1968, and in the "Green" movement of the 1980s.

Reproduction of the Relations of Production

A system for reproducing and perpetuating the relations of production accompanies the economic system. In part, this system consists of a political and ideological superstructure (which we will examine later) but in part also of institutions such as the community, the family, consumption, behavior, and the school. The system of reproduction of the relations of production (RRP) interpenetrates the social movement sector through its effects on lifestyle choices, community structure, and "weak-link" institutions.

Lifestyle Choice and Community Networks. The RRP can be very closely linked to the system of production. For example, in the company town or in the cities of early industrial capitalism (like Manchester or the New England mill towns) the conditions of community and family life were set directly by the conditions of production. Housing, schooling, consumption, even procreation and recreation, were tailored, shaped to industrialists' need for a labor force.

An important feature of advanced capitalism is the relatively high degree of autonomy of production from RRP. It reaches its greatest degree of autonomy in the consumer society in which "the customer is king"; the possibility of a free play of taste, whim, impulse, and choice has become a major legitimating formula for advanced capitalism. The ideology of "everyone can be a small businessman"—i.e., realize himself in the sphere of production—no longer holds; it has been replaced by the promise of choice of richly varied lifestyles.

This large gap between production and the RRP is manifested in the large number of available consumer goods, relatively large amounts of leisure time, physical separation of the workplace and other spheres of life, high rates of migration, and a high degree of free choice in lifestyles (including patterns of family life). Thus, lifestyle, consumption, family life (in a broad sense of "family"), and community life not only take up a large part of each individual's time, but also become psychologically weighty areas of choice.

This gap between production and RRP means that there is a large space for movements that deal with community problems, with lifestyle choices, and with self-definition. This gap has been particularly characteristic of

American capitalism and has permitted the florid development of identity, lifestyle, moralistic and community movements. These movements (from theosophy to Gay Liberation) are movements that appear to lack an economic base, but are in fact made possible by the loose articulation between production and RRP. In this sense, they are a product of the structure of advanced capitalism.

"Weak-Link" Institutions. As noted earlier, "weak-link" institutions are those where conflicts or contradictions appear. Stable systems of social control break down, a mobilizable population with grievances is at hand. A third element of the articulation of production with RRP is that conflicts in the productive system may be shifted to institutions of the RRP.

In the late nineteenth century, the system of production itself was still clearly a socially weak link in capitalism. The workplace was often the site of disorder—strikes, riots, etc. Class conflict could be clearly seen as class conflict because it took place at the point of production. By World War II, a series of social inventions (e.g., scientific management, assembly lines and other technological innovations, corporatist unions), had reduced or veiled conflict at the point of production. Even if disputes over working conditions and wages evidence themselves in recurring strikes, the conflict is contained as part of a legitimated bargaining negotiation. System stress shifted to other points, particularly to the state and to certain institutions in the RRP—especially the schools, as the sites of selection or labeling for class position (Coleman, 1961; Stinchcombe, 1964; Cicourel and Kitsuse, 1963; Bowles and Gintis, 1977; etc.). The schools have had to bear the burden of multiple contradictory functions: selection as a process must go on while at the same time the school has to perpetuate an ideology of upward mobility for many, if not for all; the school also has to cope with the problems of adolescence and in recent years has become more and more of a "parking lot" in which people are kept out of the overcrowded labor market. Under conditions of mass youth unemployment (especially in Italy and England) even the selection function has broken down. Thus, the school is typically a weak link institution and many social movements start there or are acted out there: the lunch-counter sit-ins, the antiwar movement, May '68 in France, the destructively antiauthoritarian actions of the Italian *autonomi*, etc.

Summary: The Structure of the Economy and Class Relations

A large number of propositions are embedded in the discussion. Let us summarize some of the main points:

1. The more the economic base takes the form of a dual economy, the more: (a) poor people's movements become distinct phenomena, (b) the

harder it is to build unified movements of all the subordinate classes and strata, (c) many movements take on the form of corporatist interest groups with the upper working class organized into defensive trade unions and the lower working class organized into ethnic pressure groups and/or "poor people's" uprisings.

2. The more relative autonomy there is in the RRP from the relations of production (via suburbanization, marketing, and a consumer ideology): (a) the more identity and lifestyle movements will emerge (e.g., gay liberation, "pro-choice" and "Right to Life," feminism, and the Moral Majority, etc.), (b) the more movements will be residence or lifestyle based, rather than workplace based, a development that coincides with those discussed in no. 1 above (Hirsch, 1979), (c) the weaker reinforcing overlapping social networks will become, coinciding with the disintegration of traditional working-class culture (Hirsch, 1979; Linenwebber, 1980), (d) the more the "weak-link" institutions, the points at which conflict occurs, shift from the working place to the institutions of the RRP. The educational system bears special stress because it is increasingly a selection site in which assignment to different strata occurs, including assignment to one or another part of the dual labor market.

3. The more contradictory class positions there are in the society the larger the number of movements, the less clear their class bases, and the more volatile the sector as a whole.

4. The structure of the social movement sector is not a product of class support bases that are independent of each other, but of a structure of interrelated classes. For example, a polarized social movement sector emerges when there is open class conflict and few intermediate strata or contradictory class positions. Under these circumstances, the two antagonistic classes draw such strata into major class blocs. Late nineteenth-century Europe, Russia in 1917, and some of the Central American nations today represent such polarized cases.

Phases of Capitalism and the Business Cycle

In the previous section we linked the shape of the social movement sector to the structure of the economic system. However, attention to change in the orientation and structure of the sector as a function of change in the economic system was treated but in passing. Moreover, in the broad view, the transformation of the sector is simultaneously responsive to the transformation of polities, the growth and spread of national political systems, the elaboration of government, and the incorporation of groups into the polity (see Tilly et al., 1975; Gamson, 1975). Thus, the task is herculean. Let us suggest how phases of capitalism and swings in the business cycle relate to the transformation of the social movement sector.

In the phase of early industrial capitalism (1780-1830), only the beginnings of working-class movements can be discerned among the British working class. The concerns of the bourgeoisie are still conflicts with landed interests. Petty-bourgeois radicalism in its Jacobinist and Jeffersonian manifestations is strong. Working-class movements shift from the antimechanization movements of artisans and agriculture workers to more political and nationally organized forms like Chartism.

Industrial capitalism is consolidated by a series of upheavals from 1848 to 1870. The emancipation of slaves and serfs, the formation of modern nation-states in Central and Southern Europe, and the extension of voting rights are among the accomplishments of these "last bourgeois revolutions" in a phase of economic expansion.

The triumph of the bourgeoisie sets the stage for severe conflicts and a high level of movement activity between 1870 and 1914. This is the period of "labor wars" in the emerging monopoly industries in developed nations (such as railroads, steel, and mining). It is the period of movements of farmers against railroads and other monopoly industries. Coalitions of workers and petty-bourgeois succeed in further extending voting rights and other elements of democracy (Therborn, 1977). The mass-based socialist parties of Europe are organized and grow rapidly. In the periphery, millenarian movements take place in response to colonial expansion.

During the interwar period working-class movements grow but take on more institutionalized forms: labor unions, mass socialist parties, and the communist parties associated with the Comintern appear. As a response to both capitalist crisis and working-class political power, fascist movements with a petty-bourgeois base appear to try to deal with both the long-term decline of the petty-bourgeoisie, its short-term crisis, and the threat of proletarian organization. The movements in the periphery shift from millenarian visions to more political forms, usually nationalist and sometimes socialist. In the most prosperous of the advanced industrial countries, like the United States, lifestyle movements appear on a mass scale, spurred by affluence and the rising media industries.

In the phase of postwar developed capitalism (1945-1980), working-class movements are contained, both repressed in the Cold War atmosphere and coopted in a long wave of economic prosperity, but excluded groups, blacks and women, mount campaigns for greater inclusion. Lifestyle movements expand in consumer societies. In the periphery many, though not all, nationalist groups gain de jure control of territory and resources (if not always de facto), setting the stage for a new focus of conflicts on a global scale. Vietnam, Angola, Cuba, Iran, and so on represent the transformation of nationalist movements into international conflict.

We have read from the historical record the relation of phases of capitalism to the size and shape of the social movement sector. Major movement forms appear linked to the transformation of the political economy. And crises of the political economy are tied to *major* swings in the business cycle, to rampant inflation, to large depressions that feed the demands for change. Is it possible to argue that the business cycle has systematic linkages to the leftward or rightward shift of the social movement sector? Is there a short-term as well as long-term relation of the sector to the economy?

For the early part of this century, we would probably have argued that upswings in the United States were associated with conservative revivals, and downswings with increased unemployment, with Left-oriented movements. Yet the issue is more complex than this. Some of the relevant items that need to be considered can be drawn from studies of strike behavior and industrial conflict and from the relation of political choice and election results to the state of economy.

Recent research shows that for Western countries the volume of strike behavior increases as employment rises. With slightly less certainty we know that as real wages decline (in the face of inflation), strike rates increase (Hibbs, 1976, 1978; Cronin, 1980; Edwards, 1981). Since World War II strike rates have systematically declined, but only in those countries where labor is well incorporated in a stable and dominant political coalition (Hibbs). However, strike rates do not necessarily relate to social movement activities. Yes, unions feel they can demand less, and actually win less in recessions. Yes, corporations can drive harder bargains. But that does not necessarily drive political and social movement surges Left or Right.

Tufte (1978) has shown how negative events in the economy affect voting in the United States. The "ins" lose, as the economy sours and parallel illustrations can be found in other countries. For example, the Portuguese economy acted as a limit for the leftward shift and the upsurge of Left movements following the revolution of 1974. The economic limit was the high rate of inflation that followed the successes of Left movements; it translated into political action on the one hand by the voting behavior of middle strata and the northern small-peasant proprietors, and on the other hand by International Monetary Fund pressures for austerity.

What the limiting effect of the economy means for movements is that the realistic alternatives that they can propose and pursue (if they come to power) may not correspond to the position of their larger support base and/ or their own militants. The more general proposition is that the short-run oscillation of the economy will affect the Left-Right dynamics of the social movement sector, depending upon who is in power and who is blamed for the current state of the economy. Moreover, business-cycle related oscillation in movements and in political behavior is likely to be especially sharp in societies that are not politically polarized into two class blocs, i.e., societies with intermediate strata (the "vacillating petit-bourgeois elements" of orthodox rhetoric).

Several other relations of the SMS to business-cycle action should be noted. First, we suspect that large downswings in the business-cycle crowd out noneconomic-oriented social movements. Conversely, prolonged upswings may encourage a proliferation of other kinds of social movements both because more discretionary resources become available for social movement usage, and because noneconomic issues—matters of lifestyle, personal taste, general ideology—can occupy the public arena. Second, the major phases of capitalism and the smaller phases of business cycle can join together and their resolution and polity choices lead to structural change that sets the ground for the next phase and shape of the social movement sector. Finally, although crises of capitalism and extreme problems created by business cycles fuel social movement mobilization, the direction and breadth of movement goals depends upon ideological and organizational factors and regime response as much as upon economic conditions per se.

The Political and Ideological System

In the long haul of the transformation of modern society, social movement mobilization has been reactive to the attempts of authorities and the state to intrude upon local and traditional arrangements, and, at later stages, proactive in making demands upon the state and seizing opportunities provided by the state. Thus, understanding how the political system determines and constrains the social movement sector is a fundamental problem (Tilly et al.).

The term "political system" is used in a more or less common-sensical way. In advanced capitalism the political system has some degree of autonomy from the economy (a relative autonomy, compared to feudalism, for example). There is no sharp boundary between "social movements" and other political action; political systems differ in the extent to which political action is organized into social movements, into parties, and into oganizations of the state apparatus. One of the contributions of resource mobilization theory has been to strike down the distinction between social movements ("bizzare, irrational, marginal, and separate") and other forms of political organization, like parties, government agencies, or pressure groups ("rational, institutionalized"); RM theory has shown us that the patterns of strategy and organization action are quite similar and that in fact movements are only one type of organizational action. Here, however, we treat some parts of the political system as external constraints on social movements. The nature of the political system viewed as an external constraint can be used to explain the amount of mobilization, the degree of formal organization of social movements and the predominant forms of such organization (Prezeworski, 1980). The political system also presents constraints on movement strategy and tactics. Beyond the issue of strategy and form lies the fact that the state is the major instrument of coercion in the society. Insofar as many social movements seek to impose a vision on a whole society, on a population that cannot always be persuaded as individuals, social movements must use the state.

Centralization and Decentralization

The extent to which a political system is centralized or decentralized shapes social movements by presenting different targets for social movement activities. Centralization has a spatial dimension (i.e., local to national) and a functional dimension (i.e., relative autonomy and role of executive, legislative, and judicial institutions).

In a highly centralized system local movements can win few victories. As long as budgets are set nationally, prefects are centrally appointed, laws are applied nationally, and parties operate as disciplined national organizations rather than as collections of local notables—there is little point in purely local movements. France is a case in point. On the other hand, in the federal system of the United States, laws and regulations are set at the state and local level, local units have rather large fiscal and regulatory power, and party policy is made by negotiation between local powerholders; thus, local movements can win victories. "Grass-rooting the system" is a possibility in the United States but would make little sense in France.

Italy represents an interesting intermediate case, although closer to the French than the American situation. The abortion movement in Italy illustrates the complexity of the situation. The decision to allow abortion was made nationally, in Parliament, along party lines; unlike the United States no local or regional laws were made, nor was there a breach of party stands by individual legislators. Thus, the movement to liberalize abortion had to be a national one. However, the new legislation has to be implemented locally, in hospitals; there is already evidence that there will be considerable variation within Italy, with poor women in conservative regions virtually denied while the better-off and those in more modernized areas will be able to obtain them. Thus, we can expect more local movement activity around this issue in the future.

The ideological apparatus may also be centralized. For example, television, radio, and educational institutions may be directly controlled by the regime. Where they are centralized they are a possible target for national movements—especially movements constituted as parties. For instance, in Italy the Left (especially the PCI and PSI) won a victory when it gained control of Channel 2, a "Left" government channel distinct from the more Right DC-oriented Channel 1. Similarly, movements or parties may attempt to capture or influence the ministry of education in societies in which the educational apparatus is centralized. These national targets are not available to movements in the United States.

Centralization and decentralization may also be understood *functionally* in terms of the powers of particular political institutions. For example, specific acts of legislation may make courts more or less available as avenues for social movement action (Handler, 1978). Nelkin and Pollak (1980) show that the antinuclear power movement was much more successful in West Germany than in France because the relevant legislation allowed the courts in West Germany, but not in France, to intervene in substantive matters.

Legal Constraints on Social Movements: Civil Liberties and Social Control

Obviously, a constraining feature of the political system is the extent to which the state permits the existence of social movements and limits their actions, their right to recruit and organize publicly, their right to organize as parties or factions within parties, their right to launch media of opinion, and their right to use a variety of tactics.

It is more useful to think of a range or spectrum of civil liberties than of a simple dichotomy: liberal-totalitarian. For example, within the clearly repressive end of the range, Fascist Italy was nevertheless much "looser" than Nazi Germany. In the latter, every type of opposition party or movement was crushed, while in the former, some opposition organization continued to exist. For instance, in the spring of 1943, widespread strikes against piecework rates were organized by the PCI and the spontaneous efforts of workers throughout northern Italy—unthinkable in Germany.

Not only does the nature of efficacy of political sanctions vary but also their target, thus shifting the weight of social movements to the Left or the Right. For example, German's *berufsverbot* (the denial of government jobs to people of vaguely subversive learnings) is in practice applied far more vigorously against the Left (Communist party members but also pacifists and even left-wing socialists) than against the Right. On the other hand, in Italy, the reconstitution of a fascist party is specifically illegal, although in practice these laws have not been very vigorously applied. Still, the Scelba law and its more recent variants dampen fascist movements and shrink the "space" available to the Far Right.

In the absence of all or most civil liberties, movements may take the form of currents of opinion that are hardly movements except in a very abstract or intellectual sense. Such has been the case with "dissent" in Eastern Europe and the beginnings of the women's movement in pre-1974 Portugal, exemplified by the "three Marias." Such movements of dissent then tend to be confined to a small cultural elite and have little ability to communicate with the large mass. Of course, authoritarian regimes cannot always maintain their iron hand, party controls may become ineffective, and semiautonomous institutions such as the church may shelter nascent movements.

Private and Public Sectors and the SMS: Cooptation, Clientelism, and "Manageable Movements"

Movements are strongly constrained by the extensiveness of the public and private sectors, although there are no simple formulae to spell out the effects. On the one hand, in societies in which there is an extensive public sector, there is also more legitimacy for subjecting institutions to political scrutiny and action (Gundelach, 1982a, 1982b). Society tends to be more politicized. Italy is a good example of such a situation. The major television and radio stations are government-run (although private stations have increased in recent years) and thus are assumed to represent particular political positions. There is a large amount of state investment (about 60%) and thus investment policies are a matter of political discussion.

On the other hand, in a society with a smaller public sector, such as the United States, matters like media policy or investment patterns are difficult to make part of public discussion. Desires to alter them have difficulty operating directly through the political system. Instead, groups have to act as private pressure groups directed at the networks or corporations, or they have to engage in a prior action of legitimating government intervention in the private sector. For example, in Italy, television programming for the government channels is a possible topic of public political debate; in the United States it is a matter either of purely private voluntary group action or it can be politically influenced only after an extension or more stringent application of government regulatory powers. Thus, the tactics and the legitimating formula for action in the two systems have to be different.

The extensiveness of the state sector is also expressed in the state's propensity to launch quasi-movements and countermovements. Some capitalist states (like the Nazi and Fascist states) were highly activist, creating a large structure of youth groups and corporatist groups. Even when independent movements, parties, or unions are not restricted or banned, these state-sponsored structures may drain resources from them.

The state may make the decision to support particular movements, entering into relations of clientelism or cooptation with them. For example, in the 1960s the U.S. government was ready to aid a variety of poor people's movements and groups (Jenkins and Perrow, 1977) and even to create its own cooptive quasi-movements (Helfgott, 1974). The result is frequently to create movements with relatively narrow ends.

Moreover, state action may reshape group boundaries. Nagel (1982) finds that coalition among native American tribes is largely a response to changes in federal policy, who can make claims, and how the government will entertain proposals.

Italian politics involves a very elaborate structure of such clientelistic groups, many of them created or nurtured by the Christian Democracy (DC). When the Christian Democrats are in power, this corporatist structure is largely passive and clientelistic, receiving favors. When the DC is out of power locally, this structure is activated like a dead-man switch to fight for its old handouts, undermining efforts at reforms for a more universalistic and progressive system of services that the Left (PCI or coalitions of Communists, Socialists, and smaller leftist groups) tries to launch. The PCI has responded by building up its own structure of groups, with a support base in the stable working class—and in its Red Belt strongholds, also among petty-bourgeois. It has been less eager and able to organize among the *emarginati* (the poor).

Left movements tend to press for extension of the public sector (more regulation of industry, more public services, etc.), but such expansion within the framework of capitalism often does not result in the transitional reforms sought by the Left (Garner and Garner, 1981). Rather, the result is either a streamlining of the operations of capital (Garner, 1977; Kolko, 1963) and/or an extension of a structure of corporatist clientelism, including the generation of manageable quasi-movements, which become an important element in the social movement sector.

Party Structure

Party structure is probably the single most important variable for understanding the pattern of social movements. Movements can only be understood as one part of a range of options that also includes political parties. Movements compete with parties. Movements infiltrate parties. Parties spin off movements, either deliberately or in the process of factionalizing. Movements appear within parties. Movements become parties. Both are organizational forms for pursuing political ends, so it is not surprising that they are so closely intertwined.

The difference lies in the use of "party" to mean an organization that has a routinized method of gaining some degree of power over the state apparatus, while "movements" seem more oriented toward civil society. (But even this distinction is problematical—the Armed Forces Movement of Portugal in 1974 appeared in the heart of the state coercive apparatus itself [see Bandiera, 1976].) We generally will use "party" to mean an organiztion that competes in elections, realizing that there are organizations called parties that are solely revolutionary and parties that control a state apparatus. We might almost say, "party: movement: church: sect." The former (party, church) are more institutionalized. There are many ways in which party structure affects movements.

Ease of Starting Parties

Where launching a new party is relatively difficult for constitutional reasons (e.g., the number of signatures required to get on a ballot, the single-member districts that effectively rule out minority parties, illegality, etc.), movements are less likely to become parties (Duverger, 1963). A good illustrative contrast is provided by the United States where movements rarely become parties and 4th Republic France with a proliferation of parties, many of which were movement-like. Even where legal constraints on minority parties do not exist, tradition and/or patronage may close off "space" for parties outside of the major established ones.

Rephrased into resource mobilization terms—there is no point in pursuing an electoral strategy if the payoffs are not worth the difficulties of becoming a party and mounting a campaign.

When movements become parties their structure often changes. For example, as the PCI became increasingly oriented to electoral politics in the late 1950s, it shifted from a cell structure to the typical structure of Italian electoral parties.

Organization of Parties

The nature of the existing parties impinges on movements. Where, as in the United States, the parties are largely congeries of interest groups with little national discipline or a party line, it makes good sense for a movement to expend effort on becoming an interest group within a party. This strategy may allow it to have some influence on party stands and ultimately on the national policy in "its area of specialization" without making too many compromises. This situation tends to induce many movements organized to act as intraparty interest groups each with limited specialized (and thus usually corporatist) goals. Movements may even become lobbylike with staffs of movement-professionals and large peripheries of mailing-list supporters who are occasionally mobilized.

On the other hand, where parties are strongly centralized, national organizations with party discipline and ᵕ party line (like the PCI and the PCF), movements are less likely to enter the party as interest groups. The movements find the parties impermeable. In these situations the relationship even becomes reversed: instead of the parties being composed of movements and interest groups, the parties deliberately create quasi-movements to attract particular constituencies. Instead of the constituencies creating movements to exert pressure on the parties, the parties create interest groups to woo constituencies—for instance the youth groups of the PCI and PCF.

Particular mechanisms of party organization shape the relationship of parties to movements. For example, the existence of primaries tends to weaken party discipline. A strong hold on patronage jobs, even in the absence of ideological discipline, strengthens party unity and makes a party less open to movements (J. Q. Wilson, 1966, 1973).

The undisciplined nature of American parties makes them hospitable to social movements. Lacking a decisive and comprehensive ideological vision of the world (such as is approximated even by the more pragmatic of the Euro-communist parties or by Mrs. Thatcher's Conservatives), they can absorb and lend support to single-issue movements, and promote these goals once the party is in power. A good example is the success that the Right-to-Life movement has achieved in getting Republicans to support its cause.

The more disciplined parties may however spin off movements, factions that rebel against the party line (chapter 5); again the analogy to the church/sect is suggestive. Parts of the French and Italian Left are in fact spinoffs from the Communist parties.

The thrust of our argument here needs reiteration. The politically oriented social movement sector is a continuation of politics by other means. Both its size and shape are affected by sanctions and rewards used by the state to channel political behavior. The number of movements, their organizational form, and their tactics are responsive to state structure and action.

Epilogue: The American and Italian Social Movement Sectors Reappraised

We return to the comparative material to illustrate our discussion of systemic constraints: A comparison of the Italian and American social movement sectors will show how the determining factors produce different outcomes.[3]

The United States is characterized by a dual economy in which there is a strong superimposition of ethnicity and labor market position. The reproduction of the relations of production is rather "distant" from the system of production, with a high degree of suburbanization, a long period of emphasis on consumption, a geographical dispersion of working-class communities, and a general weakness of working-class cultural institutions. The political system is decentralized and focused on two major parties neither of which is unambiguously class-based.

Italy is likewise characterized by a dual economy but one organized along regional (and to some degree age lines) rather than ethnic lines. The economic and cultural trends that distance the system of reproduction of the relations of production from production itself have been underway for a shorter time period than in the United States; at the same time, the industrial working class has not only been ethnically homogeneous but also has a long-standing cultural tradition. The political system is still centralized and characterized by nearly thirty-five years of national domination by a single center-right party (the DC), an equally long period of governmental exclusion of the other major party (the PCI), and a fairly large number of smaller parties that can only exercise leverage as "swing parties" and coalition partners.

What are the outcomes for social movements? In the United States we find a multiplicity of movements, many of them concerned with "lifestyle" (i.e., RRP) issues, operating either outside of the political system or acting as pressure groups within the major parties. Movements do not strongly define themselves with respect to class base and are only haphazardly Left-Right aligned.

In Italy, on the other hand, we find a smaller number of movements (partly because movements can more easily turn into parties, partly because the diversity of lifestyle concerns has emerged later). They are more clearly aligned along a Left-Right axis and are more integrally tied to definable class bases. The political system is far more clearly the tactical focus of the movements and they are more likely to be nationally organized than American movements.

This type of analysis suggests some predictions for the future. The most likely outcome is convergence of the characteristics of the U.S. and Italian social movement sectors. Why?

First, the current crisis—the shared conjunctural economic situation—creates similar pressures in both. More specifically, we can expect more movements in the United States to define the situation as one of the economic problems (i.e., to move at least slightly toward a class model of problems), to identify Washington as the source of problems (i.e., to take a more secularized, political, and national view of problems), and to develop more politically oriented tactics. The strong right-wing political thrust of the Moral Majority is an example of this potential shift. "Social-issue" movements (i.e., movements generated by cultural dislocations and conflicts) have had to focus on public policy. In this respect, we can expect a "Europeanization" of American social movement behavior, but with more popularly based right-wing movements and a continued interest in lifestyle issues.

On the other hand, short of a complete economic collapse, we can expect the distancing of the RRP from the system of production to continue in Italy as changing consumer and media habits generate a degree of Americanization. Shifts in concern from clearly class issues to lifestyle issues are most strongly heralded by the Radical party with its emphasis not only on civil liberties but also on demands for decriminalization of all abortions (defeated in a referendum in May 1981), abolition of hunting, and similar "American-style" questions; these demands have been accompanied by "American-style" tactics like mass petition drives and the attempts to hold referenda.

The emergence in recent years of a small but intense Catholic revitalization movement, located in the northern urban middle strata in Italy, also supports the hypothesis of trends toward American-style movements, centered on issues of the inner life and religious communalism. At the same time this phenomenon reinforces our view of the middle strata as volatile in the contents and direction of their movements.

Another pressure towards "Americanization" is the growing overlap of youth and a weak labor market position—this feature of the Italian economy has helped to create volatile and violent youth movements, increasingly detached from a working-class base (that had still been connected to them in the "hot autumn" of 1969).

Our remarks about the directions of the SMS in Italy and the United States should not obscure the larger message of this essay. The social movement sector differs between nations in both its size, organization, and orientation. As the mode of production changes, as the global political economy refocuses, so too does the orientation and composition of the social movement sector. In every society the mode of production is a major determinant of the nature of political action and of the social movement sector; the special features of the advanced capitalist mode of production (the loose articulation of production and RRP, the diffusion of welfare state policies into civil society, the existence of many contradictory and intermediate positions, the internationalization of the political economy, and the high-tech potential of the forces of production) themselves create a new form of the social movement sector: internationalized, concerned with the impact of technology, targeted on the state, and only indirectly connected to class relationships at the workplace. In this vein, in recent years two "new" movements have surfaced, the antinuclear movement and the environmental movement. In some countries and at some points in time they are separate, in other cases they are joined. The linkage of resource mobilization theory and political economy analysis (as attempted here) helps explain the pattern in cross-national variation, as social movement action is channeled by the prevailing national political opportunities.

Notes

Prepared for a Conference and Festschrift in Honor of Morris Janowitz, May 14 and 15, 1982, Chicago. We are indebted to John McCarthy, Aldon Morris, Gerald Suttles, Charles Tilly, and Bert Useem for comments on an earlier draft.

1. McCarthy and Zald (1977) provide an alternative definition. They define the sector as the *sum* of all social movement *industries* in the society. A social movement industry is the set of movement organizations oriented toward a similar social change goal. Our definition of the sector is more inclusive and less "economistic" than McCarthy and Zald's, since it includes all action oriented to social movement goals, rather than the action generated by movement organizations. It is important to note that if there is only one social movement in a society, the sector would be coterminous with the movement and countermovement.
2. In 1985 it is apparent that oligopoly and monopoly must be seen in their international context. Many industries that looked protected from the winds of competition just a decade ago, now seem fragile. For a recent critique of dual economy theory, see Hodson and Kaufman (1982).
3. For another interpretation of Italian trends, see Melucci (1981a, 1981b).

13

The Future of Social Movements

Mayer N. Zald

In our preoccupation with the social movements of the day, or of a particular movement, it is easy to miss the grand sweeping changes in the organization, tactics, and goals of social movement-like phenomena. Indeed, except for the writings of Charles Tilly, discussing the historical transformation of forms of collective action, and, in a different vein, Garner and Zald (chapter 12), the topic is rarely discussed. Here we briefly sketch the historical transformation of movements in America. We then use the recent past to project the future of social movement organizations, tactics, orientation, and sites. Our general theme is that in an organizational society the shape of social movements is closely tied to the technologies, forms, opportunities, and targets created by that society.

Historical Transformation

How to describe the transformation of movements? Think for a moment about the parallel transformation of large-scale organizations, both the profit making firm and public bureaucracy. Some fairly clear lines of development can be sketched. Organizations have gotten larger in size; they have developed new modes of internal management, moving from patrimonial and personal modes of control to bureaucratic systems with well-developed rule systems (Edwards, 1979). Firms changed their formal structures from those based on functional principles of delegation to divisional profit-center structures (Chandler, 1963; Chandler, 1977). Moreover, corporations have become increasingly multinational—although capital has always found ways to cross national borders, the growth of multinational firms that manage the combination of capital, labor, and facilities in many nations is a phenomenon of the last half century.

How would we sketch a parallel history of the transformation of social movements? One major trend in social movement transformation is represented by the growth of limited-purpose associations as formal organizations that are carriers of social movements. In the early part of American history, most social movements articulated with the major cleavages of society. Either loose networks of local notables (as in the Committees of Correspondence) interlinked to discuss grievances and to petition the authorities, or pamphleteers communicated with their constituencies. Of course, leaders emerged from their local communities, as in Shay's and Bacon's rebellion, to generate substantial collective actions.

In the early nineteenth century, social movement activity was linked directly to party politics. Although the abolitionist movement was tied to associations stemming from an evangelical tradition, it also penetrated party debate. The two-party system was not as well institutionalized, and new parties and splinter parties, especially at the local level, had a greater chance of success (Hesseltine, 1962). By way of contrast, modern SMOs and leaders maintain an independence from the established parties and find the third-party alternative risky. Although modern movement constituencies participate in politics, their related SMOs maintain a fair amount of institutional separation. Stated somewhat differently, sentiments for change are mobilized to support a social movement sector of many industries; at the same time, the sentiments for change penetrate ongoing political parties and structures.

It would be a mistake to argue that there was a sudden change in the associational capacity of the United States. After all, de Tocqueville had early seen the U.S. as *the* associational society. And Rosenthal et al. (1985) have recently documented the complexity of the associational field in which women reform leaders participated from 1840 to 1914. Yet as urbanization and industrialization proceeded, the ability of social movement entrepreneurs to capture resources for social movement purposes stands out. And by the turn of the century, the associational possibility had become a flood. Any examination of the organizational infrastructure in the Progressive Movement quickly reveals the growth of limited purpose, middle-class–based SMOs (Wiebe, 1967).

I suspect that the Progressive Movement also ushers in another aspect of organizational change that is a hallmark of later developments—full-time reformers, professionals of social change, if you will, make their appearance. There were two main threads of the Progressive Movement: the reform of urban government and the alleviation of the negative effects of poverty (i.e., child labor, housing and health, and safety codes). The reform of urban government leads to civil service, urban planning, and the use of expertise in assessing urban needs. The latter, aimed at alleviating the effects of poverty, led to the growth of social work as a reform agent—the settlement house movement, legislative lobbying, and the mobilization around specific legislative targets.

It is worth noting that two major types of social movement bases that are theoretically important can already be distinguished in the nineteenth century. On the one hand, movements based upon a *beneficiary* constituency can be seen in such movements as the early feminist movement and the labor movement. On the other hand, the abolitionist movement, the temperance movement, and the set of organizations and movements aimed at poverty alleviation in the first part of the nineteenth century represent movements largely based upon *conscience* constituencies.

Not only do we see the growth of middle-class–based "professional" movement organizations in the first part of the century, but we also see an enlarged role for the press—the growth of journalistic moral entrepreneurs. Such muckrakers as Lincoln Steffens and Ida Tarbell become key figures in defining issues. Their position is dependent upon the expansion of the mass circulation newspapers and weeklies, and the growth of a national audience.

There is one other aspect of the long-range transformation that deserves comment. In Gamson and Tilly's terms, some of the early movements are to gain access to the polity, to gain standing (e.g., voting rights, standing as legitimate members of the polity). But it is already the case for the movements based in the middle class that the issue is not polity membership, but policy influence and preferences. That is, individuals and groups have standing as citizens and right of access even when the issues they are concerned with have little credibility or legitimacy. Later I am going to argue that for modern social movements, the early issues of membership in the polity have largely receded.[1] The extension of the franchise to women, the elimination of racial barriers to citizenship, eliminate some of the historic issues of social movement mobilization. Moreover, the existence of discretionary resources and the growth of technologies that aid in their aggregation means that diverse interests are easily and continuously represented. As more groups are represented in the polity, on the one hand, and as groups that are well represented in the polity increase their tactical repertoire to include mobilizing the grass roots, on the other hand, the line between social movement analysis and pressure group analysis becomes increasingly blurred.

These broad trends—the growth of a relatively continuous social movement sector, the development of SMOs as enduring features of the society, the professionalization of movement leadership, and the transition from a search for membership in the polity, to the search for specific policy outcomes—shape the way in which social movements manifest themselves in modern society. What will be the specific and short-range trends of the next several decades? There would appear to be changes in the orientation of the social movement sector as the issues of an industrializing society transform into those of a postindustrial society. There are also changes in the technology of mobilization and representation. Finally, the organizational society creates the potential for social movement–like phenomena *within* organizations and professions.

Social Movement Orientation and Targets in a Postindustrial Society

As we have seen, over the decades the orientation of the social movement sector has changed, either as society changed, eliminating the social base and problems of the movement, or as the social movement and political process achieved changes, reducing the demands for potential social movements. The abolitionist movement, including the Civil War, led to the end of slavery. The labor unrest of the 1930s and first half of the century have given way to a somewhat institutionalized labor-management bargaining system. In both cases, although the social movements led to a transformation of the challenged institutions, underlying racial and class structures and antagonisms were by no means fully transformed. Class and racial balances were changed, "progress" was made, and surely, the new institutions eliminated the gross injustices of the prior scene. Yet underlying class and racial antagonisms remained and surfaced in new forms.

To predict the orientation of the social movement sector, the major goals of social movements, requires a juxtaposition of emerging social cleavage lines of class, race, religion, age, sex, and culture as they relate to the definition of actionable issues in the political system. Here I highlight the set of social movement potentials created by the changing nature of industrial society and changing demographic patterns that we are likely to see in the decades ahead.

Postindustrial Movements

We have already seen the growth of a cluster of movements that are reactive to the negative externalities of economic growth and the industrial production system. The environmental movement, the antinuclear power movement, local movements to control toxic wastes, and movements to regulate truck weights are all aspects of a set of reactions to the spinoffs of the complexities and conflicts over technical decisions (Nelkin, 1984). They are likely to be with us for a long time.

One might argue that the government had already responded to the threat through the creation of regulatory mechanisms at federal and state levels, such as the Environmental Protection Agency, Occupational Safety and Health Administration, and others. Haven't we institutionalized mechanisms for assessing risk and limiting dangers?

Two features of the underlying set of problems suggest that new outcroppings of the negative externalities of industrial society, and new groups and movements that no longer accept the costs will be part of the social movement landscape. First, negative externalities are created as unknown by-products of industrial processes and products (Mitchell, 1979). Only by preemptive and prohibitive research can the effects of all industrial processes and products be known before the damage occurs (Douglas and Wildavsky, 1982). At what point could the effect of acid rain be known? How does one control for long-term negative side effects of new drugs? Thus, the creation of issues for action is inevitable, though some risks can be avoided.

Second, the burden of costs of different negative externalities fall on different groups at different times. Catastrophes occur in specific instances as concatenations of normal processes that were designed to avoid catastrophe. Systems are not foolproof (Perrow, 1984). There is no way that the residents of the Love Canal area or of Three Mile Island can take steps beforehand to minimize the risk. Mobilization and community organization to cope with the fallout from these failures represents a movement entrepreneurial opportunity that will come often (see Walsh, 1981; Walsh and Warland, 1983). As new problems emerge, affecting new groups and communities, local movements, linked to circles of experts and professions, are likely to result.

One feature of these post-, or late, industrial movements is that their definition and resolution call for a heavy dose of expert opinion. Analysis of the interplay of causes, costs, consequences, and options requires extensive knowledge of esoteric subjects, unavailable to even relatively well-educated laymen. In modern society experts play a role in defining facts and issues for many movements—from issues of tax redistribution to the impact of pornography on behavior. Yet issues of technological fallout are peculiarly vulnerable to battles over technical definitions and complex, but often ill-defined, systems of causation and long-term effects. In this situation movements become battles over expert definitions, and the ability of parties to command expertise becomes an important part of the power equation (Molotch, 1970).

Many of the postindustrial social movements are "consumer" movements. They stem not just from the impact of specific products, but from the intersection of government policy, regulations, and law, as they bear on specific client-age-category groups. As the purview of the state has enlarged and penetrated a greater range of activities, the implications of state policy for discrete categories of users and producers carves up the political space. Each arena of state action—the labeling and testing of specific products (e.g., tobacco), the provision of specific services (e.g., remedial education)—creates the opportunity for political mobilization.

Client-consumer movements are likely to be a continuing feature of the landscape for two reasons. On the one hand, the penetration of state action into many areas of life seems to be ineluctable. (A regime may attempt to cut back its overreach, but in the United States, at least, citizens, politicians, and organizations will search out new venues in the decentralized system.) On the other hand, client-consumer movements are likely to be a continuing part of the social movement scene because of the transformation of social movement technology. Many, if not most client-consumer groups are made up of individuals affected by state action who are not members of solidary communities, usually a weak condition for mobilization. However, given that institutions often have a stake in creating groups for cooptation and support, given the possibilities of contingency fees in class-action suits, given the linkage of consumer issues to professional careers, given the rise of PMOs, client-consumer groups no longer have a large deficit of mobilization potential (McFarland, 1976).

Sociodemographic Bases

Changes in the structure of the labor force, in the structure of families, in the categorization and life opportunities of segments of the population do not automatically translate into social movement goals. Nevertheless, the existence of "at-risk" populations, those which, because of changing social relations and structures, experience major value deficits vis-à-vis other parts of the population, become grist for the social movement machine. Moreover, the mere growth in numbers of people in a social category at risk represents targets of opportunities for movements.

There are at least three major changes in sociodemographics of the American population that might have bearing on the development of political social movements: (1) the growing proportion of the population that is aged, (2) the changing racial-ethnic composition of the population, and (3) the growth of female-headed households combined with the high level of female participation in the labor force. These changes in sociodemographics and in social relations will vary in their impact on politics and social movements.

The growth of the aged population poses continuing policy and programmatic problems for our legislative bodies. Yet these problems are on the continuing political agenda. The aged vote, there are a well-developed set of institutional programs and legislative committees that cope with the changing needs of the elderly, and more sets of programs have been enacted to deal with facets of the concerns of the elderly. Writers on the welfare state, such as Harold Wilensky (1975), suggest a set of backlash political movements that attack the welfare state. And these are clearly in place. But, in fact, these backlash movements are more likely to be aimed at taxation levels, not the aged per se. It is, however, entirely possible that a prolonged economic decline could be accompanied by a set of antitax, antiwelfare social movements. Since our legislative process encourages the enactment of benefits more than the cutting off, or cutting back, of old programs, and since the center of political gravity has been to maintain programs, extreme reactions to the welfare state may well develop on the fringe of the Republican party and outside of it. But the main point is that the effects of a changing age distribution of the population are, I believe, well encapsulated in normal politics. Indeed, Samuel Preston (1984) has recently argued that the aged's income situation has been well protected as compared to children's in the period 1970-82. He attributes this income protection to the extensive political participation and influence of the aged. While there will be significant opportunities for policy change, as medical technology, mortality rates, and institutions create and cope with changes in the situation of the aged, the policy changes will work themselves out through normal politics.

The second aspect of demographic changes that might relate to social movements is the changing pattern of ethnicity and race in America. Demographic projections indicate a growth of the Hispanic population, and a continuing enlargement of the Asian-origin population. These changes in ethnic composition are already affecting the politics of Florida, New York, California, and Texas. They effect the politics of Chicago and Detroit as well. Here, too, citizenship rights are well established, the normal processes of political incorporation are already at work, and local and national party structures have begun to reflect the new constituencies.

The changing ethnic composition appears to me to have implications for social movements through two mechanisms: the creation of new coalitions and the redefinition of ethnicity and ethnicity at risk. The possibility of a "rainbow coalition" bringing together ethnic groups defined as "have-nots" and other "have-nots" as a significant entity could presage a significant shift in the control of party policy. It does not, I believe, portend a new Left social movement, since its advocates tend to operate largely in the arena of electoral politics. But it could press the Democratic party to the Left and could also press white supporters of the Democratic party to the Right (Petrocik, 1981). Social movement action would depend, I think, on the linkage of social democratic-populist ideology to the Rainbow Coalition (a hook-up between Jesse Jackson and Tom Hayden outside of the party).

Here, again, the actionable issues and the potential for mobilization emerge from the intersection of state policy and the situation of groups in society. Ethnicity is to some extent created by state policy. The disparate indigenous groups that make up the category "native Americans" and are impelled to act as a coalition and respond to similar policies would have no inherent unity without state policy. Similarly, Asian-Americans had (and have) little in common as Chinese, Japanese, Korean, Vietnamese, etc. But state policy may transform the utility of coalition and transformed identity (Nagel, 1982; Nielsen, 1985).

Although I am skeptical that trends in aging or in ethnicity will presage a new set of social movements, the prospects for social movements related to the feminist movement and the feminization of poverty are greater. First, the women's movement is in place and has not been incorporated into party alliances. The movement may lean slightly to the Democrats, but there has been a systematic attempt on the part of SMOs and their leaders to maintain some distance. Second, there is a unique constellation of issues related to the movement and to the feminization of poverty that challenge the social system on fundamental issues. The established political parties have trouble coping with these issues. Finally, the structure of the movement lends to permanence.

The three issues around which the women's movement may generate a more active movement program are defense policy and the antinuclear movement, the issue of equal pay, and the potential issue of child support and child-care policy for middle-class women. It is very clear that women are more likely to support the antinuclear power movement and to resist defense policies which threaten war (Brody, 1984). Secondly, the issue of equal pay for equal work, which has great moral claim and ideological resonance, is a direct threat to a fundamental ideological assumption of a capitalist system—the notion of a market price for labor. Third, the changing structure of the family and the feminization of poverty represent a potential policy agenda, far beyond where our current welfare state policies have led us.

It is not the case that this set of issues is unsolvable in our usual muddling through, incrementalist manner; but they each represent significant policy issues that can be combined into a women's movement agenda with far-reaching potential. None of them are easily accepted by major political parties. Each is costly. And the first two, the issues of equal pay and defense policy, represent direct threats to central postulates of entrenched elites.

Of the social movements on the current scene, a radicalized feminist movement represents the most likely candidate for domination of the movement sector. Since the movement has a number of single-issue items on the agenda with specialized organizations and constituencies (e.g., battered wives), the feminist movement would appear to have the best chances for continued high levels of mobilization and activity.

Cultural Movements: The Transformation of Class and Status

Aside from the sociodemographic trends discussed above, there are other changes in the distribution of the population by region, by class and occupation, and by religion that have implications for the social movement scene. The purported growth of "Yuppies" as a significant group, the growth of a new class of professionals and highly educated who are critical of established values, the movement to the Sun Belt and the economic growth of the Sun Belt, and the emergence of a large and relatively prosperous fundamentalist Protestantism all have implications for the social movement sector and the politics of the next several decades.

Part of the problem in assessing the implications of these trends for future social movements stems from definitional ambiguity. What, for instance, do we mean by "new class"? B. Bruce Briggs (1979) has published a useful collection of essays in which authors present alternative definitions and the implications of their alternatives for politics. Is the new class represented by the growth of people with college degrees? With advanced degrees? With professional degrees? With occupations in the media and human services? With degrees in the arts and social sciences? Moreover, occupation or occupational training does not make a social class. Steven Brint (1984) has attempted a systematic comparison of the definitions of a new class and an empirical test of differences in political attitudes of the groups identified under each definition. For the time period he studied (data sets collected from 1974 to 1980) there was a slight tendency for new entrants to the occupations and educational groups to be more critical of society than older members. More significantly for new-class theory, only people with cultural and social science backgrounds tend to be consistently critical of business when compared with other groups. Brint concludes that the strength and permanence of the new class has been exaggerated.

A somewhat different part of the problem in assessing the implications of these trends is that these groups do not represent classes or corporate groups with clear interests and organizational bases. For instance, the population of Houston, Texas, is diverse. In a period in which the oil industry was booming, its population had some interests in common with the growing Sun Belt. But in the period of economic retrenchment that occurred with the decline in oil prices in 1983 and 1984, their economic interests no longer coincided with that of the growing Sun Belt. Moreover, Kevin Phillips (1982) argues convincingly that the purported conservative drift of the Sun Belt exaggerates its permanence and unity. The migration and growth of the Sun Belt contributes to instability and change, but without clear direction. Phillips does show that some of the newly emerging occupational lifestyle communities have a distinctive political commitment. For instance, the high-tech/libertarian communities of Marin County or Palo Alto, or Denver, or suburban Boston do have a distinctive political style. In 1980, these were the lair of the supporters of John Anderson for president.

But in general, because the new class is amorphous, because Yuppies are distinguished more by age and family income pattern than by anything else, it is hard to believe that they represent a base for any substantial social movement. Instead, they are likely to be a base for expressive styles, not systematic policy and ideological program. Vic Tannys and aerobic dancing are not a basis for organizational mobilization.

On the other hand, the growth of the fundamentalist Protestant churches, with their strong communal base, married to modern social movement technology, does represent a trend that is likely to have deep social movement implications (see chapters 2 and 3). Movements such as the Moral Majority represent a political expression of a deep cultural split, a reaction to the trends of modernism, to secularism, to sexual and social libertarianism. Fundamentalism is not new. What is new is the size and wealth of the participants and the readiness of the denominational and church leaders to participate in political action (Harding, 1983, 1985).

The *orientation* of the social movement sector responds to underlying trends in social structure as they relate to political process and actionable issues. We have located the future orientation of the sector in demographic trends and emerging issues of postindustrial society. But the *volume* or size of the sector is also influenced by the organizational and mobilization technologies available to the society. So the future of social movements in the United States is partly an organizational and technological question.

Organizational Changes and Resource Mobilization

We have described in some detail the factors that eased the creation of social movement organizations (chapter 1, Appendix). Briefly, affluence creates discretionary resources that can be allocated for social movement causes, even when discretionary time is in short supply. Moreover, large numbers of people, especially college students, have discretionary time to allocate. The existence of marginal resources, gathered from many middle-class suppliers, or larger amounts of resources, gathered through churches, philanthropic organizations, government agencies, and labor unions, permits movement entrepreneurs to find an organizational niche even when a mass base of activists or mobilized marchers are difficult to find. Every cause can find an organizational vehicle—concern about air safety is quickly translated into "Aviation Consumer Action Project"—a Nader spinoff. The Children's Defense League, directed by Marian Wright Edelman, employs sixty people and has a $3 million a year budget.

Fund Raising and Organizational Development

There have been great strides in the techniques of mass fund raising. Social movement organizations share with political parties and "televangelism" the advantage of the computer revolution and mass mail marketing techniques. These include computer-personalized letters, carefully cleaned and targeted mailing lists, and the ability to reshape letters and appeals to a variety of audiences. Hadden and Swann (1981) describe how evangelical ministers meld television mailing lists, viewers, and letters into a television network based community. Social movements are at a disadvantage in this particular game, compared to evangelical religion, because they are less able to utilize television on a routine basis. Their audience is smaller and more episodic in its attention span.

On the other hand, social movements do have access to foundation and government agencies in a way that religious organizations do not. Craig Jenkins (forthcoming) traces the growth and shifts in philanthropic foundation support for social movement activity. Social movements are also aided by the general growth of voluntary association—community organization skills. The skills of networking, of meeting notification, of developing newsletters, have spread quite remarkably in the society. Networking, fund raising, and organizational techniques for utilizing the media are all transformed from techniques learned on the job to formally transmitted skills. Professional fund-raisers—pollsters, campaign managers—are guns for hire and it is extremely easy to learn the formal skills necessary for organizational development. Larry Sabato (1981, pp. 340-43) lists more than fifty political consultants who provide polling, fund-raising, and campaign management skills to political candidates. Some of these restrict their services to candidates from one or the other party and to social issues that are ideologically compatible. Richard Viguerie (1981), a key figure in fund raising on the Right, has been unique in his role as an ideologue as well as a fund-raiser.

The Representation of Groups

Earlier, I asserted that the modern system of mobilization now permitted most groups to be easily represented. In a sense, this is an assertion that basic access to the polity of societal members is easily achieved. Such an observation does not square with the obvious fact that groups may have access, but not be on the public agenda. Groups without resources or large moral claims continue to be isolated from political action. Our earlier arguments about the professionalization of movement mobilization can be used to shed light on the problem.

There are two major routes to gaining access to the policy agenda. First, beneficiary based movements can draw upon the infrastructure of support in a large interest category. While their mobilization process may depend upon, in part, a wider moral discourse, perceived grievances within the group and a broader agenda of communal action may sustain the mobilization of social movements, regardless of the support in the larger society. Second, groups that do not have citizenship status, or have weak citizenship status (e.g., children, animals, prisoners), or that have few resources (e.g., welfare mothers), can draw upon the moral discourse of the larger society.

Modern society makes it possible for weak groups to be represented because of two major characteristics. The existence of multiple subcultures in modern society, created and sustained by the enormous institutionalization of professions and associations, maintains a continuous dialogue about the core values of those differentiated institutions. Most weak and underrepresented groups are represented by conscience constituents tied to institutions and associations. Children, whales, and dogs, are the object of concern of foundations, voluntary associations, professional groups, and professional schools. These groups carry on a continuous dialogue and debate about the state and potential improvement in the lot of their objects of concern. For instance, one of the more vigorous movements of 1984 and 1985 involved the attempt to stop or limit the use of animals for medical research. The movement and its followers used a wide variety of tactics (e.g., rallies, lobbying, and the bombing of medical laboratories) to attempt to achieve its ends. It was not merely a movement of pet lovers, but developed a full-blown ideology about the relation of Homosapiens to other species.

That such representation occurs should not be taken to imply a strong representation. PMOs representing weak groups may be peculiarly dependent upon attaching their causes to broad social movements or to exploring windows of opportunity that open in the policy arena. As long as they are isolated from the broader movements, or from opportunities created by larger political events, coalitions, and processes, they may represent groups with little effect. But under the right conditions, PMOs can be major components of social change. Ronald Troyer and Gerald Markle (1983), for instance, have recently documented the extraordinary role of a PMO in changing American laws and regulations related to smoking tobacco. A PMO, ASH (Action on Smoking and Health), acted as a fulcrum and campaign manager as the evidence of the negative effects of smoking mounted.

Tactical Transformation

The organizational revolution represented by the growing ease of mobilization has also been accompanied by a tactical transformation. Over a decade ago, Michael Lipsky (1968) taught us that movement tactics must be seen as multivalent. Tactics may impose economic and political costs on authorities; they have effects upon the sympathies or antagonisms of local bystanding publics and referent elites, and, through the media, upon less immediately in-contact bystanders and referent elites; finally, they have impact upon the sympathies, readiness to act, and enthusiasm of adherents and constituents.

The tactical repertoire of any movement is dependent in the first instance upon the cultural-technological stock available to cadre and adherents. Boycotts, petitions, guerilla theatre, sit-ins, mass mailings to legislatures, class-action suits, voter registration drives, hijackings, assassinations, car bombings, marches, truck blockades, computer referenda, telethons, and political action committees are social inventions. They are mixtures of hard technology, legal constraints on behavior, and organizational resources. Each tactic is learned and can be transmitted. Each requires a particular combination of skills, personnel, and tools that may or may not be available to cadre. You cannot have a march with only five supporters. There is a *production function* for tactics.

Moreover, tactics occur in a stream of history. They take on meaning in specific situations and in relation to what has occurred before. Terrorism, for instance, is quite effective if the authorities are ambivalent about the legitimacy of their participation in a given setting, or if referent elites and mass publics are pressing for the withdrawal of authorities and their agents. Terrorism has opposite effects, in the short run at least, if authorities and referent elites are unified in opposition to the terrorists and their cause. Indeed, terrorist attacks on a unified authority and reference elite may only lead to the strengthening of authority response. Especially in the early stages of a movement, terrorism may signify to sympathizers the vitality and potential of suppressed movements. To bystanders it signifies the potential cost of not recognizing the legitimacy of the movement. Over time, however, repeated use of terror loses its shock-signifying value, and is assimilated to the flow of events.

When new tactics are introduced, cadre and adherents must gain experience in their use, so efficiency of deployment may increase over time. But tactics may decline in effectiveness as authorities and countermovements develop skills in responding or controlling them (see McAdams, 1984). If tactics are not followed by success, constituents may grow weary and despondent.

It is difficult to discuss trends in tactics without discussing the components of specific movements. The legitimation of tactics is not only a function of technological availability, but also of the basic commitments of adherents. The more a movement rejects the fundamental social order as embodied in the state, the more likely the use of terror and violence. On the other hand, even if the movement has narrower goals, if the enemy is seen as evil incarnate, more extreme measures are justified to some members of the movement. Pro-life supporters can bomb a Planned Parenthood office, but, so far, retirees do not bomb the Social Security Administration. More abstractly stated, tactical choice is part of a moral economy—what seems legitimate and appropriate to constituents and what seems legitimate to external audiences may vary.

Two tactical trends seem to be apparent. First, social movements in the United States quickly learn how to link local and national venues. An organization such as Common Cause, that begins as a national PMO, with only a mail membership, quickly learns the value of local chapters and activity as a means of building constituencies and as developing a source for local pressure on legislators and authorities (McFarland, 1984). Conversely, the existence of local groups concerned with local problems creates an opportunity for entrepreneurs to coordinate their action and represent their local interest on the national scene (e.g., the Civil Rights Leadership Conference, the Federation of Neighborhood Organizations). Note that I am using as "tactical" the very structure of organizations; that is, organizational structure is chosen as a technique to achieve social movement ends.

Parenthetically, it should be noted that established pressure groups and even corporations with local branches have adopted similar strategies. Thus, the coordinating associations for the electrical-power utilities developed local branches in order to support nuclear power. Firms like McDonalds and ARCO have also mobilized constituents to bring pressure on legislators. But our major point should be clear. In modern society, local groups can quickly develop a national presence, and groups that start at the national level can develop local arms.

A second tactical trend in the United States would seem to be a decrease in the use of violent methods over long periods of time. In part, I assume that large-scale conflict is prohibited both by the strength of the state and the ability of the state to repress conflict, *and* by the extent to which society has developed techniques for coopting and for incorporating groups and movements into the procedures. Writing on conflict and social movements from a world system's perspective, Edward Kick (1980) summarizes the matter nicely:

In the core, several factors combine to reduce conflict intensity. Strong states more effectively institutionalize conflict among internal parties (e.g., labor and management) by initiating and, if necessary, enforcing rules of the game. The state itself is unlikely to become a party to intensely violent mass conflict because its very strength and capacity for repression when necessary inhibit efforts to seize the government. Moreover, that capacity rarely needs to be fully activated since politics in the core is not a zero-sum game. The polyarchic political system, coupled with an increasing pool of resources, generates a fairly high probability that groups seeking recognition and/or material benefits will actually acquire them. Also, the economic ability to institute broad social welfare programs may constitute a general, rather than group specific, mechanism for reducing conflict. This type of opportunity, or cost structure, greatly encourages the formation of conflict groups with limited goals. . . . That is even more true from the perspective of the population at risk for recruitment into such groups. Given the class structure of core countries, there is a relatively large pool of persons who are unwilling to risk involvement in unlimited political conflict or in the governmental changes that such conflict may initiate.

What are the implications of these tactical and organizational trends for the future of social movements in the United States? First, that movements easily develop national-local linkages implies that pure "grass-roots" movements or national lobbying organizations can easily switch their forms. The availability of networks and organizations means that MOs are not restricted by their constituency bases. Although we may find pure "grass-roots" movements or pure national lobbying organizations which for *tactical* reasons do not develop into the other, increasingly it is a tactical choice.

Second, since groups easily gain legitimate status, and since the political structures of the U.S. are tied to legal and ideological roots prescribing openness and consultation, movements are easily brought into a ·participatory mode—the combination of an open electoral system and bureaucratic representation coopts movements. Indeed, violent tactics are as likely to be used between movements and countermovements, between branches of sects, as they are between movements and authorities.

Third, we can expect a continued evolution and refinement of the computer-television-personalized solicitation-lobbying interface. This technological organizational approach to fund raising and mobilization is a U.S. invention, now spreading to Western Europe. Leaders in the employment of this technology, such as Richard Viguerie, now have a European clientele, and political consultants such as Joseph Napolitan have clients in Latin America (Sabato, 1981).

Finally, the reformist character of modern American movements, coupled with the ease of organizing SMOs and the stability of the two-party system, implies the continuing pervasiveness of single-issue politics. SMOs in this electoral system focus on the marginal influence, rather than the seizure of power.

By no means does this analysis imply an end to large-scale conflict in which social movements mount major challenges to established institutions. Nor does it imply an end to the destruction of lives and property as part of the interaction of movements and authorities. It would be possible to develop a scenario of systemic economic decline that led in this direction. Our analysis *does* imply that, short of a major change in the direction of the social system, reformist and melioristic movements and contained tactics are more likely to be the mode.

The Situs of Social Movements

Our analysis has largely focused upon movements that express themselves through demands on the central political system, But in modern society much social movement activity in fact takes place in bureaucratic institutions and in the professions. For several decades, sociologists of the professions and organizations have recognized that social movement–like phenomena occur in organizations and professions (Bucher and Strauss, 1961; Weinstein, 1979; Zald and Berger, 1978). The growth of complex bureaucratic institutions, intersecting with professions as special-interest groups, suggests that much of social change and social movement phenomena occur not in political legislation but as reform and innovation movements connected to established agencies. It is impossible to evaluate the sheer quantity of such social movement–like activity, but let us give a few illustrations.

Over the last twenty years the hospice movement has spread rapidly (Paradis, 1985). It has been a social movement on the edge of the medical complex, led largely by medically related professionals. A prominent role has been taken by nurses and ministers related to medical settings. Although the institutionalization of the hospice movement has required changes in legislation and funding, a good part of the action has been involved in mobilizing local institutions. Another professional movement can be seen in the development of family therapy. It developed at the border of psychology, psychiatry, and clinical social work. It was at first frowned upon by the orthodox, but has had charismatic leaders, separate training institutions, and spread like wildfire before it became well institutionalized.

Other movements in professional settings include the transformation of city planning in the 1960s. The emphasis changed from formal physical planning to community development and organization. It developed a new recruitment base and led to conflict within agencies (Needleman and Needleman, 1974; Ross, 1975).

Our tools for the analysis of such movements are much weaker than our tools for the analysis of political movements. These movements often resemble "idea currents" carried by new generations of professionals. The events of the movements are less dramatic than police/demonstrator confrontations, or marches on Washington. And except in the case of organizational coup d'états, the media are unlikely to pay much attention to them. But in some cases these movements massively transform the territory of institutional operation. They occur at the frontier of the intersection of technological change, professional and normative challenges to established practices, and organizational change. They are likely to become a dominant part of social change in an increasingly bureaucratized and professionalized society.

Conclusion

I have sketched the trends in the organization of SMOs, transformation of tactics, the orientation of the social movement sector, and situs. This is a risky business. Who knows, tomorrow some new movement may emerge, totally unrelated to the current scene. "Speciism" as a social movement may dominate the headlines. On the other hand, short of major depression, war, or ecological catastrophe, I doubt that we will see a major reconstitution of the SM sector in advanced industrial society. Aside from the potential movements and countermovements around the feminist issues and the movements around fundamentalism that I discussed, no other movements on the current scene have much potential for social movement action.

But it should be clear that large-scale economic depression *is* possible; that ecological catastrophe in regions, or in nations, may occur. Such large-scale events would clearly reshape the social movement sector. Adam Przeworski and Michael Wallerstein (1982) have tried to sketch the mix of short-term and long-run considerations shaping working-class mobilization that might be affected by a large-scale downward change in the economy. It is clear that a prolonged depression could change the mobilization of the working class, upset the well-institutionalized balance of management-labor conflict and bargaining, and transform allegiance to political parties and the ongoing system. Finally, our analysis has been internal. We have treated the social movement sector as if it were isolated from a world political economy and the world currents of change. For most purposes this is appropriate. But in a period in which the United States is losing its hegemonic position and in which social movements and political change in other nations reverberate on our own politics and social movements, attention to these linkages will become more important.

Notes

Revision of a paper delivered to the Symposium on Community Organization and Administration, Council on Social Work Education, Detroit, Michigan, March 11, 1984.

1. It may be that in T. H. Marshall's (1965) terms, issues of political rights have receded, but a range of economic and civil rights denied to specific groups continue to be sources of social movement attack. The issue of political rights, however, has been central to a perspective on social movements that sees them as arising, in a sense, by societal members *outside* of the polity. I believe this perspective on social movements to be misguided. It starts the analysis of movements from below. Political social movements involve contests for power in which partisans believe routine access and a legitimate place on the agenda is inadequate. People of the Right and the Left, above and below, can believe the directions of the polity to be inadequate. They can believe that authorities do not represent their interests.

Appendix

The Trend of Social Movements in America: Professionalization and Resource Mobilization

John D. McCarthy and Mayer N. Zald

American sociologists have been intrigued with the phenomena of social movements. They have studied and analyzed movements ranging from those on the left wing aimed at overturning the social order to those on the right wing aimed at restoring an earlier order. But they have not neglected moderate movements with ameliorative goals or movements with no apparent political goals or implications (e.g., movements related to individual deviance such as alcoholism or to a belief in the end of the world). To understand the rise and fall of all of these movements—and their related movement organizations, which normally are the unit of analysis—sociologists have focused upon members. Leites and Wolf (1970) call this a "hearts and minds of the people" approach, which assigns primary importance to the state of consciousness of members and potential members. The development of group consciousness, the relation of a group's life situation to the formation of ideology and to social action, have been primary concerns of this study and analysis.

We stress a different approach. Our "resource mobilization" approach emphasizes the resources, beyond membership consciousness and manpower, that may become available to potential movements. These resources support the growth and vitality of movements and movement organizations. This view does not necessarily deny the existence of grievances. It stresses the structural conditions that facilitate the expresssion of grievances.

In the past, the resource mobilization approach has been characteristic of American right-wing political analysis. Conservatives, wishing to deny the validity of left radical and reform movements, have stressed the impor-

tance of "outside" resources. Right-wing analysts deemphasize felt grievances as the motor of social movements; they focus on concepts like
"outside agitators" and "the communist conspiracy," including especially
the charge of outside funding that creates the appearance of widespread
grievances.

We feel this view contains more than a kernel of validity, though we
reject much of this analysis. Serious analysis of social movements must, for
instance, recognize the similarity of the concepts of "outside agitator" and
"community organizer."

We have come to this view after realizing that few American social movement organizations have resembled the "classical" sociological model. The
picture of movements composed of aggrieved individuals banding together
to fight for their due seems to us seriously inadequate. We do not claim that
resource mobilization should replace the concerns of the "hearts and
minds" approach. Neither analytic approach is adequate by itself; we must
understand both the aggrieved group and the process of resource mobilization. In response to the "hearts and minds" bias of previous work, we stress
resource mobilization in this analysis.

Some may mistake our emphasis on the material bases of current social
movements for hostility to the aims of the movements. We harbor no such
hostility. Our discussion concerns the conditions that affect a movement's
potential for success, and these are as important to movement leaders and
supporters as they are to social scientists.

Introduction

Although our approach focuses upon the resources available to social
movements, we must explore the major alternative explanation for the
recent burst of social movement activity, the alleged increase in rates of
sociopolitical participation. In the 1960s, according to many scholars and
social critics, the American population greatly expanded its rate of participation in sociopolitical activities and will continue to do so. For example, in *The Public Interest*, Daniel Bell and Virginia Held note "that there
is more participation than ever before in American society, particularly in
the large urban centers such as New York, and more opportunity for the
active interested person to express his personal and political concerns"
(1969, p. 142). With respect to future prospects, James Q. Wilson writes,
"In fact participatory democracy has all along been the political style (if
not the slogan) of the American middle and upper class. It will become a
more widespread style as more persons enter into these classes" (1968, p.
120).

A participatory interpretation of events of the 1960s must inevitably raise a number of questions. The simplest to ask and possibly the most difficult to answer is whether the purported upsurge in sociopolitical participation is real. Remember, de Tocqueville, Martineau, and other observers of an earlier day were struck by the quantity of such participation in American society. Has there been an increase in the absolute amount of such participation?

There are, of course, numerous avenues for expressing sociopolitical concerns. One can throw a bomb or vote, join a social movement organization or write a letter to the local newspaper or to a congressman; one can argue with friends and neighbors or commit a major part of income to worthy causes; one can attend endless meetings of special purpose organizations or send a campaign contribution to a candidate of one's choice; one can choose a life career that expresses these concerns or advise one's children to do so. These many ways of expressing concern vary in their costs and consequences. Has the likelihood of action along each of these avenues increased? Or have observers generalized from the flamboyant manifestations? Have the rates of riots, pickets, and marches increased in comparison to those of 1880? 1920? If so, are these rates accurate indicators of trends in more traditional activities? If only certain forms of participation are increasing, while others remain stable or decline, what are the structural causes of the apparent independent variation?

On a more general and analytic level, what implications do changes in participation have concerning the assumptions and logic of accepted theories of social movements? Since it has been common for sociological theories to define social movements in terms of participation, questions about rates of participation and relevant causative factors are tied to questions about the future of social movements. Social movements are voluntary collectivities that people support in order to effect changes in society. Using the broadest and most inclusive definition, a social movement includes all who in any form support the general ideas of the movement. Social movements contain social movement organizations, the carrier organizations that consciously attempt to coordinate and mobilize supporters. In the traditional view, social movements are dependent upon their participating members.

Social movements range from those that are radical and all-embracing, aimed at totally changing the structure of society, to specifically focused reform attempts. They encompass idea movements aimed at changing the world by changing individual thought and movements tied to specific ideologies and tactics. At the level of social movement organizations they include in some degree radical and clandestine terrorist groups, retreatist sects that revalue the world, reform-oriented political action groups, and interest groups aimed at changing a law or policy to benefit its members.[1]

Despite this variety, the standard sociological view has been that social movement organizations are dependent upon their members for movement operation. Members provide all of the resources for the infrastructure of social movements. Organizations depend upon members for money, work (time and energy), sacrifice (death or prison), and leaders. And they are also dependent upon their members to demonstrate to elites that society must change to accommodate the movement. The "resource mobilization" approach leads us to raise two related questions here. First, have American social movement organizations been as typically dependent upon members as the "hearts and minds of the people" approach suggests? Second, do the ebbs and flows of social movement organizational activity over time directly reflect changing rates of sociopolitical participation within the population?

In the classical view member participation is tied to grievances and deprivation. But grievances ought to be inversely related to per capita income. If affluence leads to grievance satiation (the satisfaction of wants), would not the classical tradition of social movement analysis predict the decline of participation, and hence social movements, in a society whose per capita income has enormously increased since World War II? Even if one does not accept such a crude materialistic assumption about the motivation to participate in social movements, in predicting trends should one not consider the changing costs to participate, as well as the drives and benefits presumed to arise from participation?

Finally, what can be said of the long-range trends? Can what has been termed the "participatory revolution" be reversed by either historical forces or planned intervention? Does America in the 1960s and 1970s represent a relatively unique historical period where a confluence of specific issues—Vietnam, civil rights, women's liberation, environmental pollution—has galvanized and mobilized the population for a short historical moment? Or have structural changes made grievance mobilization more likely today than in earlier periods?

The view we will develop, speculatively and at some length, suggests that the rates of participation for many forms of sociopolitical involvement do var, somewhat independently in modern America. This variation is partially explained by the advent of social movement organizations unlike those treated by the traditional model. Our view substantially challenges the usual assumptions about participation and social movements in America. The functions historically served by a social movement membership base have been, we will argue, increasingly taken over by paid functionaries, by the "bureaucratization of social discontent," by mass promotion campaigns, by full-time employees whose professional careers are defined in terms of social movement participation, by philanthropic foundations, and by government itself. Moreover, an affluent society makes it possible for people devoted to radical change and revolution to eke out a living while pursuing their values. Modern society easily supports a large cadre of revolutionaries. For revolutionary and nonrevolutionary alike, modern American society makes it easy to pursue one's values in social movement activity.

The essay is divided into five parts. First, we weigh evidence for the claim that participation has in fact generally increased. Second, we describe the changes in factors to sociopolitical participation—affluence, leisure, and changes in discretionary time. In the third part we turn to changes at the institutional level, the funding patterns of foundations and churches and changes in participatory careers. The implications of these trends for a theory of social movements are addressed in the fourth part. At this point we counterpoise the traditional or classical model of social movements and a type of social movement organization, the professional movement organization, that is becoming more prevalent. In the last part we conclude with a discussion of the implications of social trends for the future of social movements in America. We also discuss whether the rate of social movements can be manipulated by authorities and elites.

Much of our argument will be inferential and speculative; at crucial points we must rely upon data and indicators that are only loosely connected with the concepts and problems we are examining. At times we are forced to rely on hearsay evidence. Whatever the particular weaknesses, however, we believe that our general interpretation is consistent with the available evidence and suggests serious rethinking of traditional modes of explanation.

Everyone a Participant?

Has there in fact been a participatory revolution? As we began our study we posed the following question to ourselves and colleagues: "If the Vietnam War ended next month and racial equality somehow appeared on the scene, would the present level of social activism decline?" The normal response was an emphatic "No!" or "Not very much." First of all, many other issues seemed to be waiting in the wings for a chance at center stage—the environment issue, population growth, rural poverty, women's liberation, and the starving children of Pakistan. Such issues seem more numerous today. Why so many more issues today than yesterday?

Rather than arguing the alteration of actual circumstances as the cause of the multiplication of issues, one might argue that the high rate of issue formation will continue because people are more willing to participate in social movements based on such sentiments. A larger proportion of the population may be willing to participate, because American society has become increasingly middle-class (as in the argument by Wilson above). Numerous studies show that the middle class participates in voluntary organizations and political activities more than the working class, although only tiny minorities at every level can be called "activists" (Hausknecht, 1962). Educational attainment and economic position both correlate positively with sociopolitical participation; therefore, the more America becomes a middle-class society, the higher the societal rate of participation in sociopolitical concerns.

First, we must concede that there is impressive consistency in the relationship between education and political participation.

> Perhaps the surest single predictor of political involvement is number of years of formal education. There are apathetic college graduates and highly involved people of very low educational level but the overall relationship of education and political interest is impressive. It is impossible to say with confidence why it is that formal schooling makes people more responsive to political stimulation. One may surmise that education tends to widen the scope of one's acquaintance with political facts, to increase capacity to perceive the personal implications of political events, or to enlarge one's confidence in his own ability to act effectively politically. Whatever the precise nature of the educational process, it has clear effects on political interest. (Campbell, 1962, p. 20)

But what of the mechanisms through which education produces such profound effects upon political behavior? A summary of findings from a five nation survey elucidates these mechanisms. Each of these findings is supported in all of the five nations of Great Britain, Germany, Italy, Mexico, and the United States. The chapter references are from *The Civic Culture* (Almond and Verba, 1963, p. 380-81).

1. The more educated person is more aware of the impact of government on the individual than is the person of less education (chap. 3).
2. The more educated individual is more likely to report that he follows politics and pays attention to election campaigns than is the individual of less education (chap. 3).
3. The more educated individual has more political information (chap. 3).
4. The more educated individual has opinions on a wider range of political subjects; the focus of his attention to politics is wider (chap. 3).
5. The more educated individual is more likely to engage in political discussion (chap. 4).
6. The more educated individual feels free to discuss politics with a wider range of people (chap. 4); those with less education are more likely to report that there are many people with whom they avoid such discussions.

7. The more educated individual is more likely to consider himself capable of influencing the government; this is reflected both in response to questions on what one could do about an unjust law (chap. 7) and in respondents' scores on the subjective competence (chap. 9).

The above list refers specifically to political orientations, which vary the same way in all five nations. In addition, our evidence shows that:

8. The more educated individual is more likely to be a member—and an active member—of some organization (chap. 11).
9. The more educated individual is more likely to express confidence in his social environment: to believe that other people are trustworthy and helpful (chap. 10).

Although education is related to political participation in all five countries in the Almond-Verba study, there is some evidence that this relationship is strongest in the United States and is mediated through organizational affiliation. That is, education leads to general involvement, leading to political involvement (Nie, Powell, and Prewitt, 1969a, 1969b).

Clearly we would expect an increasingly educated society to be an increasingly participatory one. The argument is plausible, but inferential. It requires demonstrating both that sociopolitical participation has increased and that the size of the highly participating middle class has increased. Then the link between the two trends must be demonstrated. Unfortunately, two or more surveys with similar questions about associational participation taken over long periods of time have not been done. However, Hyman and Wright have published one article comparing 1955 and 1962 survey data based upon similar national samples and closely similar question wording.[2] A summary of their evidence is reported in Table 1. Although the seven-year period resulted in some upward shift, still more than 50 percent reported no memberships. From Table 1 and other analysis Hyman and Wright reach the following major conclusions:

(1) Voluntary association membership is not characteristic of the majority of Americans (a finding originally from data in the 1950s, now confirmed by data from the 1960s). (2) A relatively small percentage of Americans belongs to two or more voluntary associations (another finding from the earlier study, confirmed by the new data). (3) There was a small but noteworthy increase in voluntary association memberships between the mid-1950s and the early 1960s. (4) The trend toward more membership in associations was not caused by the cohort who came of age during the period from 1955-1962, the two points in the study. (5) Membership is directly related to current socioeconomic position, as measured by a variety of indicators (a relationship established in the earlier study, confirmed by data from the 1960s). (6) The trend toward increase in associational memberships is not confined to the more well-to-do strata of the population, but occurs all along the line and especially among those of poorer economic means. (7) Current economic

situations appear to have more effect upon membership than does one's station of origin. (8) The trend toward increased membership applies to both Negro and White adults but is somewhat more evident among the former, thereby tending to reduce previous subgroup differences in membership. However, these findings are most tentative because of the small number of Negro respondents found in each sample. (Hyman & Wright, 1971, pp. 205-6)

We return to aspects of the Hyman and Wright analysis later. But let us turn to trends in specific types of social participation. There are two sources of data that measure trends in specific types of participation; extensive time series data on voting rates have been compiled, and for a recent sixteen-year period we have data on church attendance, union participation, and participation in political activity.

Table 2 presents the average percentage of voting-age population voting in presidential elections and in off-year elections for U.S. representatives, by decades. Clearly, the half-century from 1920 to 1968 shows a trend toward higher rates of participation. In the 1920s and 1930s, of course, much of the increase is usually attributed to an increase in voting by women. The off-year elections show a similar path of increasing rates of participation, 10-20 percent behind the presidential years. From our point of view the most interesting aspect of these data is the continuity of rates. In particular the voting rates of the 1960s are close (within 2 to 4 percentage points) to those of the 1950s. Furthermore, the rate of voting in the 1968 election was the lowest of the decade. No participatory revolution here. Even in the 1960s the absolute rate of voting turnout just began to reach the level of turnout in most national elections in Europe,[3] although Americans have been more likely to use informal means (such as letter writing and joining organizations) to influence politics.

However, these data do not directly indicate the effects of an enlarged middle class. For that evidence we turn to the relation of socioeconomic status and "reported" voting in the 1952-56 period and the 1968 period collected by the University of Michigan Survey Research Center.

One should remember that more people usually report having voted than actually did vote. Also, these data are not age-standardized, and we know that the group aged twenty-one to twenty-five, although more educated, tends to vote less because of mobility and other factors. Table 3 supports the relationship that has consistently emerged between education and political action; the more the education, the more likely the vote. The differences between the two time periods within each educational category are minor except for the group of respondents who have had some college and show a substantial decline in the reported voting rate. On the other hand, it can be observed that the relative size of the more highly educated

TABLE A.1

Percent Belonging to Voluntary Associations by Family Income

Family Income:	1955				1962			
	0	1	2	N	0	1	2	N
-$2,000	76%	17%	7%	385	69%	16%	14%	230
2,000-2,999	71%	17%	12%	304	62%	24%	14%	167
3,000-3,999	71%	18%	11%	379	70%	21%	10%	175
4,000-4,999[b]	65%	21%	14%	450	58%	26%	16%	183
5,000-7,499[b]	57%	22%	21%	524	56%	25%	20%	592
7,000 or more[b]	48%	22%	30%	328	45%	21%	35%	389
Total	64%	20%	16%	2379[a]	57%	22%	21%	1775[a]

[a]Total N differs from marginal N because of unknowns.

[b]In 1962 the break point on this category was above and below 8,000.

Source: Herbert Hyman and Charles R. Wright, "Trends in Voluntary Association Memberships of American Adults." American Sociological Review, 1971, 3:191-206.

TABLE A.2

Voters as Percentage of Voting-Age Population: Presidential and Off-Year House of Representatives Elections, by Decade, Since 1920

Presidential Elections		House of Representatives	
Year of Election	% Range	Year of Election	% Range
1920-24-28	43.5-51.9	1922-26	29.8-32.1
1932-36	52.5-57.0	1930-34-38	33.7-44.1
1940-44-48	51.3-59.2	1942-46	33.9-37.4
1952-56	60.1-62.6	1950-54-58	41.6-43.4
1960-64-68	61.8*-64.0	1962-66	46.3-46.7

*61.8 is the 1968 figure.

Source: Bureau of the Census 1970, p. 368.

groups has increased over this time period. This increase in size accounts for the slight increase in total reported voting between the two time periods, lending some support to an *embourgeoisiement* argument for increasing national rates of participation. The argument is weakened, however, by the decline in the rate of reported voting in the "some college" category.

One body of data does give us comparable evidence concerning several types of voluntary participation aside from voting. From 1952 on, the Survey Research Center has asked questions about church participation, union participation, and political participation. Table 4 presents this information for four points in time. The responses to these questions over time do not indicate increasing sociopolitical participation. Electoral participation outside of voting has not increased. Religious participation has shown a decline and, most notable, labor union membership has remained stable. These data, though limited in time span, certainly do not indicate a massive increase in social and political involvement.

It could be argued that we have missed the whole point of the participatory revolution, for the revolution is outside regular electoral political channels. Yet these data do bear on one interpretation of that supposed revolution: its relation to an enlarged middle class.[4] At the very least these data indicate no large increase in participation in general, nor greater participation by the broadly defined middle class. If nonelectoral participation has been increasing dramatically, it ought to be partially reflected in electoral and voluntary association participation, for numerous studies have shown them to be positively related (see Milbrath, 1965). Thus, our initial answer to the question of a participatory increase seems to be negative—some change, but not much. Yet the appearances leading us and other observers to such a view remain. To be sure, these data exclude, to a large extent, the student population. But are the appearances based exclusively upon the behavior of the student group? We think not, though student participation is important. In the following section we account for the appearances that are not reflected in these data.

Components of Participation: Social Structure and Individual Opportunities

The usual approach to explaining the higher rate of middle-class participation in organizations and politics is through cognition and motivation. On the one hand, education leads to greater awareness of political events and a greater awareness of the discrepancy between the observed world and values. On the other hand, higher status leads to higher self-esteem; high self-esteem leads to a sense of personal efficacy and the utility of participation. These approaches often ignore the costs of par-

TABLE A.3
Education and Reported Voting, 1952-1968

Education	1952-56[a]			1968[b]		
	N	% of Sample	% Voting	N	% of Sample	% Voting
Less than 8 years	635	19.6	57.2	149	10.7	53.0
8 years	478	14.8	63.6	140	10.1	65.7
9-11 years	648	20.0	68.8	272	19.6	69.1
High school graduate	905	28.0	82.0	433	31.2	83.8
Some college	322	10.0	8.8	206	14.8	79.1
College graduate	247	7.6	90.7	190	13.7	89.5
Total	3,235	100.0	73.1	1,390	100.0	75.9

[a]These figures are approximate and are a recomputation of figures presented in Table 14-1 of the American Voter (Campbell, Converse, Miller and Stokes 1964). The authors present only 1952 and 1956 combined.

[b]These figures are based upon the 1968 Survey Research Center Post-Election Survey.

TABLE A.4
National Trends in Political and Social Involvement, 1952-1968

Questions	1952[b]	1956[c]	1964[c]	1968[c]
"Do you belong to any political clubs or organizations?"	2%	3%	4%	3%
"Did you give any money or buy tickets or anything to help the campaign for one of the parties of candidates?"	4%	10%	10%	9%
"Did you go to any political meetings, rallies, dinners, or things like that?"	7%	7%	9%	9%
"Did you wear a campaign button or put a campaign sticker on your car?"	--	16%	15%	14%
"Does anyone in this household belong to a labor union?"	--	27%	24%	25%
"Would you say you go to church regularly, often, seldom, never?[d]"	--	60%	62%	52%

All of these figures are based upon Survey Research Center national post-election survey samples. Unless otherwise designated the percentage entry refers to the proportion of th total sample answering affirmatively.

[b]The 1952 figures are from Campbell, et al., 1964.

[c]The 1956, 1964, and 1968 figures are based upon data made available by the Survey Research Center, University of Michigan.

[d]These percentages refer to those who answered either "regularly" or "often."

ticipation. Participation requires some combination of money, leisure or discretionary time, and energy. The unequal command of such resources across the class structure, we believe, ought to bear importantly upon participation rates in addition to motivation and cognition. It is necessary, then, to examine trends in factors related to time and money expenditures for such behavior.

Affluence and Leisure

One argument for the alleged link between an enlarged middle class and an increase in participation is through a purported increase in leisure; the increase in leisure provides an opportunity for participation. But there is good reason to believe that an increase in leisure is mythical, especially among those segments of the population that are most likely to show high rates of sociopolitical participation (Wilensky, 1961).

First, over the last three decades the average work week in manufacturing has stabilized at around forty hours a week. Second, among white-collar and blue-collar workers, those in higher status occupations work longer hours than those in lower status occupations. A larger proportion of the incumbents of professional and managerial occupations than of clerical and sales occupations work more than forty-nine hours a week. Indeed, managers and officials in 1965 comprised 8.6 percent of the full-time workers but 18.2 percent of those working more than forty-nine hours a week (Carter, 1970). This is a complicated matter, and our example, though it captures the trend, exaggerates the picture. But the trend itself from 1948 to 1965 reflects an increasing proportion of the labor force working over forty-nine hours a week, from 13 percent to 20 percent. Since professionals and managers intrinsically tend to value work more highly than laborers and clerks, it is precisely the upper-middle class, it seems, that is more likely to opt for work over leisure, given the choice.

Two other trends blunt the implications of a leisure time argument for organizational participation—the labor force participation of women and the "costs of consumption." By now it is well known that there has been a massive increase in the labor-force participation of women. Each decade since 1900 has found an increasing proportion of women in the labor force. The trend is especially strong among women over thirty-five (Waldman, 1967, p. 32). A likely consequence is that both men and women must use available nonwork time for "service time" and household and physiological maintenance (e.g., cleaning of homes, care of possessions). Staffan Burenstam Linder (1970) argues briefly that as income increases, what he terms "consumption costs" increase. This thesis suggests another trend affecting the availability of leisure time. The sharp increases in per capita income have led to an increase in discretionary income that can be used to purchase consumer goods. But every new purchase, beyond the time spent making it, requires time for use and for service. (Linder distinguishes between work, personal work, and consumption or leisure.) Increased affluence leads to an increase in personal work. Since nonwork time on the average is not increasing (as shown above), there are increasing dollars competing for available nonwork hours. Furthermore, as the productivity of work increases, there is an increasing pressure to increase the utility yield of leisure time, for there is a strong tendency to balance utility yields in different sectors of activity. Linder argues that high-yield leisure activities will substitute for low-yield ones. Thus, motor boats supplant row boats, and physiological necessities as sex and eating lose ground in available-time allocations. We would add to Linder's list of low-yield leisure activities participation in social movement organizations. There are few ways of making these activities yield greater individual utility in a given time unit.

Episodically it may be exciting to attend a rally or "sit-in," but such activity grows boring. For low-yield social movement activities, Linder would predict a declining allocation of time.

Most of the argument presented above is inferential; a direct test would require trend data on time budgets by socioeconomic groupings. The middle class may get less sleep, for instance. But some evidence does exist on the relation of occupation and education to time allocation. As part of an international study of time budgets, the Survey Research Center studied time allocations of the U.S. population. They found, for instance, that the professional and semiskilled expend an average of two-tenths of an hour on organizational activities a day, whereas lower white-collar workers expend an average of three-tenths of an hour on such activities. The fact that semiskilled workers use mass media for an average of 2.6 hours a day and both professional and lower white-collar workers an average of 2.3 hours a day (Robinson and Converse, 1966, Table 6, p. 35), however, suggests both the low priority most Americans place upon organizational activities and at least the availability of a fair amount of nonwork time outside of "consumption costs."[5] The data on education parallel these findings. On the average, both college-educated persons and grade-school graduates spend less than 15 minutes a day in organization activities; there is little variation in average participation by educational attainment (Robinson and Converse, 1966, Tables 5 and 34).

The evidence and inference presented above strongly suggest that our affluent society is not creating an enlarged pool of leisured middle-class citizens who are potential organizational participants. This view is consistent with the trend of evidence on actual participation. Yet the appearance of more vigorous social activism remains. There are many ways, however, in which the affluent society does contribute to the creation of social movements besides time allocations.

Organizational Involvement and Social Status

The consistent positive association in American surveys between membership involvement and social status is well known. Yet our arguments have led us to expect, if any change, not an increasing but a decreasing proportion of nonwork time to be available for such involvements, at least in the last three or four decades. Two points need to be clarified. First, the association between status and involvement may well be a function of the way in which membership involvement is measured. Second, the fact that a small segment of the middle and upper class is in fact heavily involved in social-political concerns is partly a function of a "ladder process" of sociopolitical involvement.

If the members of the middle and working classes do not differ substantially in the amount of time available for participation, their differences in involvement may be a function of their allocation of money. The relation between class and involvement is normally demonstrated by differences in the number of organizational memberships. It is well known that many organizational memberships require nothing more than yearly dues. In particular we know that deductions for charitable and social contributions as a proportion of total income remain relatively constant at each income level. Higher rates of participation among the middle class may result from the fact that they have more money to join organizations.

As part of a study of the activities of foundations, the Treasury Department (*U.S. Treasury Department Report on Private Foundations*, 1965, p. 75) studied various trends in charitable giving, a form of social participation closely aligned, we assert, to the funding of political and social movements. This information reflects immense increases in absolute dollars of charitable giving—bequests, corporate gifts, and gifts of living individuals—between 1924 and 1960. In 1940, for instance, gifts of living individuals were estimated at little more than $1 billion, whereas in 1960 the estimate was close to $10 billion. Increases in bequests and corporate gifts are large, though not as dramatic during the same period.

The increase in giving of living individuals is related to the growth of personal income and the increase in the percentage of income allocated to contributions. From 1924 to 1962 adjusted gross income increased 650 percent, an advance far surpassing the rate of inflation and reflecting a massive increase in gross national product per capita. Over the period 1924-62 there was also an increase in the percentage of adjusted gross income given to charitable organizations. From 1924 to 1962 the ratio of contributions from the income of living individuals increased by 40 percent. The donor estimate and recipient estimate series, which includes corporate and estate contributions, does not increase as dramatically as the individual contributions ratio.

Now, with both per capita income and proportion contributed increasing, we would expect, as well, voluntary organizations to be gaining in contributions. That is, discretionary income can be allocated to organizations ranging from the church to educational institutions, from hospitals to politics. Important to our later argument, there is evidence to indicate that as discretionary income increases, citizens contribute to organizations further removed from their own personal experience. The *U.S. Treasury Department Report on Private Foundations* (1965, p. 78) also gives the total amount and rates of contributions of individuals deducted for specific types of purposes. In 1962 the higher the income class, the less the ratio of contributions for religious purposes. We assume that deductions for religious organizations are usually for church activities with which one is directly and closely affiliated.

Other evidence supports this interpretation, showing that the upper educational and income groups are more heavily overrepresented in organizations that pursue "public-regarding" (or, stated otherwise, non-self-regarding) goals.[6]

Table 5 presents the proportion of adult Americans who belong to different kinds of voluntary groups in 1953 and the proportion of upper and lower income and education groups in their membership. The top four types of groups are those in which people join largely for expressive and social relational benefits; the bottom four types tend to be those through which people pursue either occupational or public-regarding values, and they tend to deemphasize immediate personal benefits. These data reflect the general tendency of greater overrepresentation of upper socioeconomic status groups in civic and special purposes groups than in the more clearly expressive organizations. It is apparent that they are especially overrepresented in groups such as political clubs.

The general thrust of the above argument has been that affluence gives people resources to support their civic values; they can join and contribute widely to organizations. Such joining need not reflect an increase in leisure or of time committed to organizational activity. Instead it may reflect nothing more than an interest in the purposes of these organizations and discretionary resources to back up that interest.

The amazing funding potential of this state of affairs is illustrated in George McGovern's use of mailed solicitations for money to support his 1972 presidential bid. In April 1971 it was reported that "from 260,000 letters sent out at the time of the McGovern candidacy announcement in mid-January, a net total of $250,000, almost all in small amounts, has come in" (*Christian Science Monitor*, April 26, 1981, p. B6). Further, it was reported that 1,500 individuals pledged $100 a month to the campaign, and between 2,000 and 3,000 others are expected to do so. Such a response occurred at a time when Senator McGovern was preferred by approximately 5 percent of his party's supporters as a presidential prospect.

It is important to note that joining an organization may be a prelude to later involvement and activity. Joining is the lowest rung of the ladder of participation. Although our general argument has been that the population—in general—does not participate at a markedly increased rate now than it did several decades ago, the needs of organizations require them to co-opt members who might otherwise be more passive participants (see Long, 1958; Ross, 1954). A precondition to such co-option is visibility, and appearance on a membership list can be one of the important bases of visibility.

But the important conclusion from these last two parts is that even if actual volunteer time spent in social movement activity has not increased markedly, more people are in a position to join and contribute money.

TABLE A.5
Membership in Voluntary Organizations by Income and Education

Type of organization	Percent of adult population belonging*	Percent of members, some college or more	Percent of members, more than $5000/yr. income
Veterans, Patriotic	14.0	21.0	38.0
Fraternal	31.0	25.0	55.0
Church and Religious	25.0	23.0	38.0
Social and Recreational	16.0	27.0	47.0
Civic and Service	38.0	39.0	59.0
Political and Pressure	4.0	42.0	56.0
Economic and Professional	90.0	36.0	52.0
Cultural, Educational, and Alumni	40.0	50.0	42.0

*In 1953, when the data were collected, approximately 16.8 percent of the population had gone to college; 28 percent of the population earned more than $5,000 annually. Though the middle class is over-represented in each category, they are less heavily over-represented in "expressive" categories.

Source: Hausknecht, 1962, pp. 84, 89, 90.

Discretionary Time and Transitory Teams

Analysis of trends in leisure time and its usage suggests that in general there will not be a markedly increased amount of time available for sociopolitical and social movement activity. Even if more time has not become available, however, some occupations, we argue, allow one to arrange more flexibly the allocation of time to sociopolitical activities. Evidence suggests, as well, that the highly educated who enter these occupations carry their commitment to work and competence in work over into a commitment to active leisure (Wilensky, 1964). These occupations are a growing part of the labor force.

Three related propositions are advanced: (1) the growth of mass higher education creates a large pool of students whose discretionary time can be allocated to social movement activities; (2) as the relative size of the social service, administrative, and academic professions increases, more and more professionals can arrange their time schedules to allow participation in activities related to social movements; and (3) a relative increase in discretion over work-time allocation permits the emergence of transitory teams to engage in sociopolitical activities.

Student Involvement

Though students in general devote large amounts of time and energy to their academic obligations, they can increasingly rearrange their schedules to fit the needs of sociopolitical action. Traditional techniques of social control over college students have been relaxed. Dormitory hours have been reduced, and more students live outside of dorms. Class attendance requirements have been weakened, and the introduction of pass-fail grading and independent study produces increasing discretion over time schedules for larger proportions of the student population. Once class attendance is not required, a student can devote large blocks of time to social movement activities either on or off campus and make up his academic obligations afterwards. Such freedom over schedule has probably been more typical of graduate students in the past. That such transitory involvement does not necessarily detract from academic performance is suggested by many studies of student political involvement in which involved students have been shown, on the average, to receive better grades than noninvolved students (Kenniston, 1968, Appendix).[7] Except at examination time, and even then, too, if an issue finds widespread enough support, students are in an optimum position to rearrange time schedules to accommodate extracurricular interests. This interest need not be political, but when such freedom over time allocation intersects with sociopolitical sentiment, students may become the troops for social movement battles.

Indeed, one might argue that the connection between leisure and social movement activities holds for students as it does not for the adult population. Since their personal incomes tend to be low and task constraints weak, they do not face the money consumption problems discussed above. Since they are unmarried, family demands do not pull away from social movement activity. Furthermore, since they have not been heavily involved in political activity before, they are not issue-satiated. Each new cause leads to renewed involvement (Strickland and Johnston, 1970).

There are apparent empirical patterns to student availability. They are less available in the summertime, at least on campus. They may, however, be more available for concentrated mission tasks during the summer—e.g., Appalachia, Mississippi, specific volunteer programs. They are less available at the beginning of semesters and at finals. It is clear they are maximally available right after spring vacation. The weather is conducive, the hiatus in university-wide athletics, and the strain of a year of study show best then.

The periodicity of student availability may be affected by the degree of political activity in the off-campus community. Where many students and ex-students live year-round near the university in a quasi-bohemian state, a support organization for campus politics can develop, though the best studies of this kind of community suggest that a very small proportion of nonstudents maintain any continuous political involvement through organized groups (Watts and Whittaker, 1968; Lofland, 1970).

Two tendencies are important here. First, in an affluent society the person who rejects affluence by rejecting full-time employment and its related consumption costs can drastically increase his discretionary time. Although we know of no studies of the time and financial budgets of campus nonstudents, our assumption is that one or two days' work a week can support a meager lifestyle for a single individual. By sharing the cost of housing and food, an individual can maximize discretionary time, since he has no academic responsibilities. Second, if he works on or near campus, work time and social movement time can easily interpenetrate. Moreover, the existence of an off-campus ghetto supports other infrasrcuctre activities and settings that facilitate social movement organizational development, e.g., coffee houses, restaurants, and newspapers.

The combination of the lengthening of the student generation and the increasing size of student cohorts means that more people are available to participate within the constraints of the student role. Increased discretion over time allocation makes larger and more concentrated blocks of time available. As the off-campus nonstudent bohemian community expands, discontinuity in activities can be minimized and the accumulated experience base increased, allowing more efficient utilization of the available student manpower.

Discretionary Time and the Professionals

Earlier we noted that the upper occupational groups are not working fewer hours; indeed, they may be working more, though there are variations. For instance, the self-employed and selected managerial and professional categories exhibit this pattern, while employed engineers do not (Wilsensky, 1961). But many upper occupations do substantially free their members from time-space constraint, even though the decrease in self-employment over time may mean that greater numbers of the college-educated adult population find themselves subject to disciplined schedules. For instance, professors, lawyers, corporate divisional managers, and settlement house directors have freedom to "arrange" their schedules to fit their priorities. If their view of occupational responsibilities commits them to social movement engagements, at least for some time periods, they can arrange their schedules to accommodate such involvement. One of the most striking manifestations of this possibility occurred following the Cambodian invasion in the spring of 1970. Literally thousands of professors, from hundreds of campuses, canceled classes for two or three days to travel to Washington to express their discontent. (Note also that the costs of getting to Washington and arranging lodging and food were easily borne by these professors and their colleagues.) Any occupation whose members are not tied to specific and sharply delineated time and work spaces may arrange their work loads to increase participation in social movements. Though we have no systematic evidence here, we expect that such discretionary involvement is widespread. If discretionary time is widespread, it blunts somewhat the impact of occupational differences in nonwork time available.

Transitory Teams

Many social movements in modern society are composed of a small cadre and an amorphous though not unstructured collection of sympathizers and supporters. The existence of discretionary time and the increasing incomes of sympathizers make it possible for groups to be mobilized at relatively low cost for short periods of time. Students and professionals are especially available for such activities. The inability of sympathetic individuals from other occupational groups to participate in the recent antiwar moratoria illustrates these variations in constraints. Ad hoc committees are created, newspaper ads are financed, protests are arranged by groups of people with previous experience in organizational activity (reducing experience costs) who come together for specific events and maintain only loose ties after the event. Full-time organizers and cadres may relate to these groups, but these relations, too, may be transitory.

It is probably the case that social movements have always built upon transitory teams. Only the medieval Crusades, revolutionary wars, and full-time conspiratorial social movement organizations have dispensed or do dispense with transitory teams. The difference is that the relative coordination costs have gone down as discretionary income and time have increased and as experience with many organizations has increased. As the skills for mobilizing groups (whether the Boy Scouts or the Southern Christian Leadership Conference) become widespread, as people have money for travel or for taking out ads in newspapers, and as they have some free time to do what they wish, transitory teams are easily mounted.

In this part we have examined trends in modern society that would make available individual time and money to social movements. The idea that an increase in leisure time in general has recently made available more time for participation by individuals has been rejected. On the other hand, it has been demonstrated that changes in American society have encouraged individual participation in three basic ways. First, an increase in per capita income permits individuals to contribute money and join organizations that are compatible with their values. Second, student life in an affluent society permits a lifestyle and a network of contacts conducive to social movement involvement. Third, an increase in professional and managerial jobs leads to many more people being able to arrange their time schedules to participate episodically.

The data have not shown directly that individuals actually do use time for movement participation. For instance, it would be possible to use discretionary time or money for flower growing as well as social participation. Only the data in Table 5 directly bear on the question of middle-class participation in political and public-regarding activities. Although the middle class participates more than any other class in public-regarding activity, it is more likely to participate in cultural and other activities, as well.

The next section shows that the basic structure of institutions and careers has been changing in such a way as to facilitate an efflorescence of social movement activity.

Institutional Funding and Career Support

The 1960s was a period of increased social movement activity. It was also a period in which institutional support for social movement organizations became increasingly available and in which life careers in movements were more and more likely to be combined with established professional roles. Organizations not usually thought of as social movement supporters—for example, foundations, churches, business corporations—began to support social movement activities. At the same time established professions and government itself became bases for social movement activity.

Church and Foundation Support

Although charitable trusts and foundations are not unique to the United States, they have been encouraged to a greater extent here than elsewhere. The structure of estate tax laws had led capitalists to establish foundations. Foundations date back to the nineteenth century, and by 1967 there were some 18,000 of them. The major growth of foundations has come since 1940, however. Information gathered in 1962 about the establishment of foundations with assets over $100,000 shows that most of the foundations (88 percent) had come into existence since 1940 (*U.S. Treasury Department Report on Private Foundations*,1965, p. 82). It is also apparent that the larger foundations were, by and large, founded before 1950.

More important than the sheer number of foundations is the growth in foundation assets. The growth in assets determines the ability of foundations to support voluntary organizations including social movements. The massive increase (approximately 1,500 percent) in total assets of foundations between 1930 and 1962 has become a fertile source of social movement support.

The major purpose of foundations is to support worthy causes. Worthy causes are very broadly defined, from feeding the hungry to supporting the study of scholars. Their assets are not supposed to be used for the personal benefit of the founding contributors or their families, nor can they be used to finance political campaigns (although they are explicitly allowed to participate in voter registration campaigns), nor can they support illegal activities, such as blowing up banks, nor can they be used to finance profit-making activities. Beyond these restrictions their scope is wide.

How have foundations actually expended their funds? We have coded all grants listed in the *Foundation News* over the period 1963-70. Because this source reports items by three categories on a rotating basis, our data actually reflect many grants given as much as one year earlier. *Foundation News* also lists only grants of $10,000 or more and only those of which it is notified. We suspect that this evidence reflects the grants of the larger foundations more than the smaller ones. (It may also underreport a rise in social movements grants, which may not be publicized. We were informed of a large foundation grant of $60,000 to the first 1969 antiwar moratorium in Washington. We have not been able to trace this grant in published sources.)

This evidence shows an increase from $315 million to $667 million in foundation grants from 1962 to 1969. It also shows that education and international activities began to receive less support by the end of the decade. One must keep in mind that the apparent pattern may not reflect long-range trends, for they can be influenced by the year-to-year activities of single organizations (e.g., the Ford Foundation). The growth of social participation grants—for instance, grants to community groups working on open-housing legislation, and sometimes directly to major social movement organizations such as the National Association for the Advancement of Colored People (NAACP), the Congress of Racial Equality (CORE), the Student Nonviolent Coordinating Committee (SNCC), or the Sierra Club—is dramatic. These grants made up 1.1 percent ($3.7 million) of total reported grants in 1962 and 8.1 percent ($54.9 million) of such grants in 1969. The increases were especially large in the areas of race relations, urban problems, and poverty problems.

While it is difficult with these data to demonstrate the exact increase that is allocated to social movement organizations, our point is clear. Foundations have become an important factor in the funding of social movements.

At the same time that foundations have been increasingly involved in social movement funding, so, too, have churches. The involvement of the northern liberal clergy in social action is well known and documented (see, for instance, Hadden, 1969). It is not a new phenomenon. What appears a new departure are trends in social action–related projects for three of the more conservative Protestant churches, the Southern Baptist Convention, the Amercian Baptist Convention, and the Christian Church (Disciples of Christ). Attention to the 1963-69 period for these churches shows social action allocations increasing from $265,000 to $785,000. There is no question that evidence from the more liberal denominations would reveal an even more dramatic picture, in terms of both the absolute amount of money involved and the rates of increase. Again, the evidence does not directly demonstrate increased funding of social movements, but it strongly suggests dramatic increases in the possibilities of such funding.

Government Funding of Social Movements

The government itself has been involved in the business of supporting social movement organizations. While the federal government may be rapidly withdrawing such support, it is clear that its support was crucial in the latter half of the 1960s. Such support has been both direct and indirect. In terms of direct support the Community Action Programs of the Office of Economic Opportunity have been most important, as have been some of the Model Cities agencies. Other programs such as Volunteers in Service to America (Vista) and the legal service program for the poor indirectly have funded social movement staff. These programs provided the financial resources to support large staffs for social movement organizations at the local level. Many such organizations have had few members, though they have tried to cultivate the notion that they represent the interests (or desires) of a large group of citizens. The federal government's withdrawal from the encouragement and funding of these community movements is well documented (see Donovan, 1970).

The government also has funded social movement activities indirectly. Groups such as the National Welfare Rights Organization have been given program grants for manpower training programs and adult education. Although the funds are not directly for social movement activity, they provide a sustenance basis for a social movement cadre. Moreover, whenever the government funds a program with a staff likely to have strong commitments to social movement purposes, discretionary time and limited surveillance may lead to a situation in which government resources are diverted to social movement purposes. Mimeograph machines, meeting rooms, postage, and consultation by staff are available for allocation to groups and purposes related to, but formally outside of, agency goals (Gilbert, 1970).

Finally, there is a third and even more indirect way that government programs create social movement participation. By requiring bureaucratic consultation with citizen "representatives" on an ad hoc or permanent basis, these programs create a visible focus for the aggregation and articulation of grievances. In some cases government programs create funded citizens' groups. Even when operating program facilities and funds are not allocated for citizens' groups, a program contingent upon consultation creates the opportunity for social movement activity and the emergence of leaders.[8]

The increasing support of social movement activity by foundations, the churches, government, and individual donation has led, we believe, to a massive increase in "funded social movement organizations." Most of these organizations employ staff with varying degrees of commitment to movement goals.

Managerial and Staff Personnel

Traditionally three lines of analysis have dominated thinking about the origins of the leadership and staff of social movements. First, leaders might be charismatic members of the suffering group who have emerged to articulate group needs. Second, intellectual leaders emerge from different backgrounds and, by reason of personality and specific experience, come to identify with the oppressed or deprived groups. A third perspective is that as movements become routinized and oligarchical, leaders become more and more distant from the group whose interests they presumably represent.

None of these lines of analysis allows us to address the possibility of an institutionalization of social movement staff careers independent of specific movement organizations. Yet the changed funding patterns we have discussed have caused and have been accompanied by a change in the structure of staff careers and of career aspirations that facilitate the staffing of social movements on a part-time basis, for interim periods, and for life careers.

Part-Time Participation

Many corporations have traditionally encouraged their executive personnel to participate in community activities. Indeed, successful participation in community activities has been weighted into the criteria of evaluation for promotion (Ross, 1954). Moreover, lawyers and other professionals have often offered services free of charge. More and more corporations are encouraging participation in reforming organizations, as compared to the previous involvement in consensus philanthropic activities such as the YMCA, the local hospital board, or the Red Feather Drive. Business corporations have increasingly become "involved" both by direct financial support and staff involvement.

Jules Cohen reports an interview study of 247 of *Fortune* magazine's top 500 firms (1970). He found that 201, or 81 percent, of the firms had some type of program for social action. Only four of these programs were operating in 1965.

The programs focused on the "urban crises," which business saw as black ghettos, enclaves of poverty, unemployment, underemployment, and racial tension. The average amount granted by these corporations to local national groups was $175,000 each year. The study found that the organizations benefiting most from increased or redirected funding were the Urban Coalition, the National Alliance of Businessmen, the NAACP, the United Negro College Fund, and the Urban League. Twenty-five percent of the firms had added one of the last three to its donation list since 1967. Only three first contributed to CORE, SNCC, or the National Welfare Rights Organization, which businessmen considered to be more militant. Twenty percent of the firms indicated making a special effort to contribute to local grass-roots self-help programs. One San Francisco executive's feelings were "Let's contribute neighborhood-wise and avoid the kind of demonstrations that have hurt a few competitors." Twenty-seven companies indicated that they had sought out community groups to ask if they would accept donations.

Such funding reflects the behavior of the churches and foundations, but of particular importance here is the donation of staff time. Twenty-five percent of the firms studied donated staff and facilities under their programs. Many had one or more executives on a community board, working with the Urban Coalition, advising on an antipoverty council, working the Model Cities program, or helping black businessmen with management problems. Some taught and others led youth groups. About 40 percent of the companies encouraged their staff to help with community programs, and half of these firms allowed this work to be on company time. With some exceptions, community-based firms that need good local community relations tend more uniformly to make donations and be involved in community activities.

Whether businesses continue to donate personnel and money and have special training and hiring programs is partly dependent upon the incentives for doing so—the perception of success, the encouragement and tax benefits offered by government, and the like. One of the benefits accruing to some businesses will be their ability to attract managerial talent, though the relative tightness of the labor market ought to reduce such competition for talent. For instance, *Business Week* (March 1970, p. 107) reports that a group of graduate students at Stanford Business School had established an evaluation of what corporations were doing about social problems. Some students said they would consult the list before joining the firm.

It may seem fanciful to believe that corporate participation in social problems would be a major determinant of job choice of business school graduates, but it is less fanciful to believe that law students will take such considerations seriously. A report in *Fortune* (Zalaznick, 1969) indicates that young lawyers joining elite firms not only expect to be allowed to spend one paid day a week on social problem law, but they expect their senior partners to donate their efforts as well. Given (1) continuing concern with causes related to social movements and (2) a scarcity of top talent, corporations and law firms can expect to continue to be pressed both for movement involvement and for provision of some part-time staff personnel to such movements.

Though we do not have figures demonstrating increases in the allocations of church personnel to social movement activity, we suspect that this institutional sector has increased such allocations. The recent heavy involvement of priests and nuns in both full- and part-time capacities in movement-related activity, sometimes through church projects and sometimes through the outright allocation of personnel, has been much noted. Churches may face the same problem that law firms and corporations have had to face: The continued recruitment and retention of top talent may require more and more willingness to allow issue action on both a temporary and a full-time basis.

Temporary Full-Time Positions

A number of programs and positions have recently been developed in which individuals devote temporary periods up to two years to worthy causes. These programs include alternatives to military service, VISTA, and the Peace Corps. The goals of these programs do not require their participants to be activists, but their goals are often compatible with activist persuasions. Futhermore, the positions are often turned into activists adjuncts. It is our impression that many sponsoring local organizations maintain only loose control over these assignees, possibly because the organizations receive these services gratis. Two examples we have observed: (1) a technician fulfilling his alternative service in a local hospital, who is allowed to arrange his job schedule around his major commitment: fighting urban renewal and pollution, and (2) a conscientious objector fulfilling his alternative service with the Unitarian-Universalist Church, who is assigned full-time to a social movement organization working against "repressive legislation." The importance of such programs and positions is twofold. On the one hand, the positions swell the cadres of social movements (by some admittedly unknown factor). As important, the program becomes a mechanism for reinforcing the values and life commitments of participants.

VISTA had over 4,000 volunteers in the field in late 1970, and some 48 percent of those who had been enrolled for one year extended their stays, reenrolling for another year. A large proportion of VISTA alumni go into the helping professions or back to collegiate education. VISTA claims that, of those returning to school, roughly half participate in part-time volunteer work.

These temporary programs, as well as the many volunteer programs of universities, are important not only because they organize a large pool of manpower for current social movement participation but because they are a reinforcing and channeling mechanism for young adults whose unease with U.S. society has not formed into specific career choices and political ideologies. We suspect that such programs serve as a training ground for those who would make social movement activity a life career, while at the same time suggesting the possibility of such careers.

The many possibilities available for these temporary and part-time careers is reflected in a perusal of any issue of *Vocations for Social Change.*[9] Published bimonthly by a California commune, *Vocations* lists a wide variety of staff and line positions open in community and national organizations. The following sample of positions was advertised in a recent issue:

A community-elected corporation needs a program planner director.

SUDCIC (Syracuse University Draft Counseling and Information Center) is presently looking for a full-time *draft counselor* to run their draft counseling center at Syracuse U.

The World Without War Council has opening in the peace intern program. . . .

American Friends Service Committee. . . . *Interns* work in teams of two in specific communities in the New York City area. . . . Salary is $4500 per year. (*Vocations for Social Change*, 1970)

This institutionalization of employment information for social movement organizations probably will become more widespread, unless traditional channels of employment information step in to meet the demand for such service.

Full-Time Careers

Although the growth of university ghetto subculture, the emergence of communal living, and the growth of temporary programs such as VISTA all contribute to a manpower pool available for social movement activities, they do not reflect what may be the major change influencing the careers of social movement leadership: the growing institutionalization of dissent.

Briefly stated, as a result of the massive growth in funding, it has become possible for a larger number of professionals to earn a respectable income committing themselves full-time to activities related to social movements. To put this proposition in perspective, contrast the situation today with the 1930s. Then the liberal or radical college student could attempt to enter the labor movement (as, for example, Walter Reuther did), become a labor lawyer, or join a government agency. The labor question was the major social movement issue. We suspect that the actual number of college graduates joining the labor movement was really quite small. The Walter Reuthers were rare exceptions. To become a full-time advocate of social change, saintliness was required and vows of poverty would have reflected only reality.

We are not the first, however, to identify the growth in such career opportunities in post-World War II America. Wilensky (1956, 1964) has called attention to the "program professional," who is a highly competent expert in a particular social policy such as public assistance or race relations. This professional moves in and out of government agencies, private agencies, community organizations, foundations, and universities. His commitment is to specific programs and policies rather than to any specific organization. Program professionals have been able to pursue successfully such careers for some time. It is the recently expanding opportunities for such careers that we wish to note here.

A number of relatively well-financed occupations that support such social change commitments have emerged in modern America. Within law,
poverty law, consumer law, and civil rights law have each developed substantial funding claims. While most of the efforts of these lawyers are
devoted to specific cases, an important part of these agencies' functioning
involves making visible social problems and changing the structure and
operation of government. These lawyers have helped organize community
action groups, consumer cooperatives, housing groups, and so on. For
instance, the annual budget for legal services of the Office of Economic
Opportunity (OEC) increased from $25 million in 1966 to $42 million in
1969. In 1967, 1,200 lawyers were employed by this program (Levitan,
1969); there were roughly 2,000 in 1969. Possibly more important than the
numbers of lawyers are their educational backgrounds. Leading law schools
find that their best students are the most committed to activism.

Similar processes have occurred in the social work profession. Historically, social work has consisted of three major branches: community organization, casework, and group work. Other subdivisions, sometimes
cross-cutting the above, are administration and medical social work, psy-
chiatric casework, and so on. Community organization, however, has not
always attached itself to social change functions. It has been related predominantly to both community fund raising and interagency coordination. Social workers have traditionally been sympathetic to reform
movements, but the structure of the job opportunities has meant that
public assistance casework has been the dominant job category (Wilensky
and Lebeaux, 1965). In 1950, for instance, only 4 percent of American
social workers were categorized as primarily involved in community organization (U.S. Department of Labor, 1951). Even in 1956 only 2.5 percent of
the graduates of two-year schools in social work were placed in community
organization positions (*Statistics on Social Work Education*, 1956).

But in the 1960s, community organization was increasingly seen as a
viable professional route to social change—witness the recent trend in
community organization enrollments in schools of social work. Whether
you use a narrow or broad definition of community organization practitioners, between 1965 and 1969 there was well over a 300 percent absolute
increase and a 200 percent relative increase in the yearly supply of community organization practitioners graduating with master's degrees in social work (*Statistics on Social Work Education*, 1965-1969, Tables 254,
255). When finished with their training, these professionals might be employed in OEO Community Action Programs, Model Cities planning agencies, foundation-funded neighborhood projects, job training programs,
community-based delinquency programs, and the like. In one case with
which we are familiar, a white community organizer with a bachelor's

degree from an Ivy League school became the business advisor to the Vice Lords, a confederation of black youth gangs in Chicago.

Besides legal and community organization positions related to social movements, a variety of consulting organizations and established social action agencies have provided career options to activists. For example, an ex-Unitarian minister may become an American Civil Liberties Union (ACLU) development officer, an urban church may set up a community development center, a group of black college graduates may form a consulting firm to advise Model Cities groups and business corporations. It is impossible to estimate the number of positions involved. Many of these consulting firms seem to be short-lived, lasting a year or two at best.

We have investigated one source of evidence that may reflect this trend, though it is fraught with problems: staffing trends in different types of national nonprofit organizations listed in Gales' *Encyclopedia of Associations* (1964, 1969).[10] The major measurement problem here is that some of the movement organizations with which we are most concerned appear to be underreported in these volumes. Only national organizations are reported, and short-lived ones do not appear. We, therefore, would expect this source to underestimate any trend. Nevertheless, the evidence is instructive in two respects. First, besides the category of associations we have termed "task-related,"[11] the public affairs and the health, education, and welfare categories seem to be growing at the greatest rate in terms of absolute numbers of organizations. Second, the health, education, and welfare category exhibits a dramatic increase in average staff size, a far greater increase than in any other category. Those categories that are most likely to reflect social cause organizational proliferation show above-average increases in both number of organizations and staff size. Of course, not all staff in the social issue–related associations are social movement activists. Many are clerks, secretaries, and bookkeepers with only minimal attachment to organizational goals. In spite of their problematic nature, however, these data reveal a rather substantial growth in the absolute number of organization staff positions. This trend supports our observation that it is becoming increasingly possible for a committed individual to carve out a career of social issue–related movement leadership without financial sacrifice. Further, as these staff positions multiply, the necessity of linking a career to a single movement or organization is reduced.

Let us summarize our reasoning to this point. We have accepted the observation of an appearance of dramatic increases in sociopolitical and social movement activity. Though no dramatic increases in the level of time and energy participation among the general citizenry is apparent— the phenomenon, if it exists, is not general—we have continued to search for a way of accounting for appearances. We have looked at students and professionals in this light and concluded that they are relatively free for bursts of participation in the short run, whether or not they have increasing amounts of leisure time available in the long run. Finally, we have looked into the flow of resources from several large sectors of the society—especially the foundations, organized religion, and the affluent classes through discretionary personal income—and concluded that there has been a dramatic increase in both the direct and indirect flow of such resources to social movement organizations. This state of affairs has increased the possibility of both short- and long-range careers as social movement organization leaders.

To this point we have focused primarily upon changes in individual and institutional support for the growth of social movement organizations. In the following section we focus upon the way these changes influence modern social movements and the applicability of the classical model of social movements to the changed circumstances.

The Classical Model and Modern Social Movements

Scholars as disparate in conceptual focus as Smelser (1963), Turner and Killian (1957), and Zald and Ash (1966) have shared certain assumptions about the nature of social movements. These assumptions, about motivations to participate, the conditions favoring group formation, and the natural history of movements, we label the classical model. This model is classical in two senses: It summarizes a long tradition, and it is now seriously out of date.

The first assumption in traditional analysis of social movement organizations is that one begins with an analysis of a class, category, or group of individuals who have a common grievance or who are subject to common strains. Indeed, without such a mass the classical model could hardly conceive of a social movement's taking form. The mere existence of a social category with a common grievance, however, does not determine the birth of a social movement. Second, communication among the members of the group is seen as crucial to later common effort. Third, environmental factors impinge upon the group, molding the possibilities for effective communication of common grievances and the possibilities for group action. Literacy, residential patterns, the structure of working conditions, discontinuities in personal experience, and the existence of charismatic leaders are a few of the conditions that are important in determining the likelihood of communications and its effectiveness in mobilizing the members (Burks, 1961; Street and Leggett, 1961). Fourth, if communication is more or less effective, the group is more likely to take some concerted action to rectify the grievances. Fifth, in the early stages, however, the classical model teaches us to expect ill-organized, somewhat random responses designed to redress grievances. Sixth, only after a well-defined leadership emerges do we find well-defined group action. Seventh, as emergent leaders confront the common problems of the group, they help to define them and devise explanations for their occurrence—that is, they develop an ideology. The ideology helps to direct action toward specific targets and helps the leadership define legitimate organizational forms designed to make efficient use of the mass base.

Such an image of the genesis and development of social movement organizations makes several other assumptions, often implicit, which must be brought to the fore. Eighth, the membership or mass base provides the resources—money and manpower—that allow the movement to survive and carry out its program. Financial resources are needed to support the propaganda apparatus of the movement, to support organizers and leaders, and to procure equipment—from mimeograph machines to arms. The mass base may or may not provide manpower for the program of redress; often it does not provide the leadership cadres, but it must provide manpower for cells, and an army and the mass must be mobilizable for demonstrations and electoral participation.

Ninth, the size and the intensity of social movement organizations is thought to reflect the existence or nonexistence of grievances that must be dealt with by the political leadership of the society in question. Tenth, once the problems that formed the initial basis for concerted action have been solved, the mass base will be satiated, and the movement may disappear since the grievances upon which it was based have disappeared. Or, as more frequently happens, such a movement is transformed and institutionalized. Following the work of Weber (1947) and Michels (1949), modern analysis of social movements has been heavily focused upon such processes of institutionalization and the implications of such changes for goals, tactics, and the internal structure of movements.

An important characteristic of this model before transformation and institutionalization is its focus upon the psychological state of the member or potential member attempting to account for his motives for involvement. "Tension," "frustration," and "relative deprivations" are key terms in such an account. Even as the interdependence of the movement with environmental forces beyond its support base are analyzed, the psychological state of the support base remains crucial (Zald and Ash, 1966). Eleventh, the leadership of the movement must be sensitive to the membership as well. Since its ability to mobilize resources and energies for concerted action depends upon the feelings of the membership, its existence as a leadership presumably depends upon its ability to sense the membership's needs.

The utility of this model for the analysis of some movements cannot be questioned. However, for reasons related to the argument above, we believe that it does not accurately describe the genesis of many modern movements. Nor does it seem to present a valid picture of the genesis of many earlier movements.

The limits of the classical model can best be demonstrated by illustrating how leaders of many modern movements operate independently of a membership during the earliest stages of organizational growth. We will then examine an alternative model, the professional movement model, and document instances where it is applicable.

The Declining Functions of the Membership Base

To repeat, in the classical model the membership base provides money, voluntary manpower, and leadership. Modern movements can increasingly find these resources outside of self-interested memberships concerned with personally held grievances. Of course, membership base and beneficiary base (those who will personally benefit from movement success) have never been necessarily synonymous with movement organizations, though the classical model's stress upon self-interested action has tended to obscure this point. Early civil rights organizations, for instance, were heavily peopled by whites, whereas the prime beneficiaries of any successful civil rights action were black. One must remember this distinction in what follows, since we will argue both that the likelihood of disjunction between movement organizations and beneficiary bases has increased and that the meaning of membership for many movement organizations has been altered by the trends we have reviewed above.[12]

The Separation of Funding and Leaders from the Base

Because of the funding patterns described in the last part, it is increasingly possible that the financial support for a movement organization could be totally separate from its presumed beneficiaries. Consequently the base lacks any control over the leadership of the movement organization. The separation of funding from base probably increases the likelihood that the movement organization will survive beneficiary satiation. We would expect a movement organization leadership to have an interest in preserving the organization even after the aggrieved group has been satisfied.[13] If base and resources are sharply separated, the organization may survive without serious attempts to redefine its goals. (If the movement organization is funded by foundations, churches, and donors external to the presumed beneficiaries, then leaders, in lieu of goal transformation, may have to renew their moral credentials in the eyes of their financial supporters. A leader with unimpeachable dedication to cause does not have to resort to exotic means of demonstrating his leadership position. But when the leader has primarily emerged in a situation of separation between funding and beneficiary base, demonstration of credentials can take bizarre forms.)

Gordon Tullock (1966) has argued that the "efficient" altruistic agency is one that uses its resources to maximize donor utility. If the agency uses any funds actually to alleviate problems of the population, it does so only to insure credibility in the "eyes" of the donors. For instance, since donors cannot observe their largesse being given to the starving children of Pakistan, the most important product is before-and-after photographs (even if made in a New York studio). Tullock's cynical argument makes an important point: The growth and maintenance of organizations whose formal goals are aimed at helping one population but who depend on a different population for funding are ultimately more dependent upon the latter than the former. Outside financial support, indeed, means that a membership in the classical sense is almost dispensable. Outside funding allows a leadership to replace volunteer manpower drawn from the base with paid staff members chosen upon criteria of skills and experience.

Mass Media and Movement Organizations

Though we will not treat the use of mass media by modern movement organizations in any systematic detail here, we must mention several characteristics of this important fact of movement organization behavior. Since the invention of printing and the growth of widespread literacy, social movement organizations have employed mass communications to build membership commitment, to garner support for movement goals, and to influence decision makers. The advent of photogravure was an important development allowing the widespread portrayal of human suffering to viewers with no direct experience of distant events. Early efforts were restricted to pamphlets and newspaper coverage, but the modern era has seen the near-universal availability of radio and television. The tremendous communication potential of these new forms cannot be controlled directly by movement organizations in the same way that pamphlet content could be controlled. The universality and immediacy of these new forms, however, allow movement organization leaders to attempt to manipulate images of social problems with far greater impact. As well, these forms permit the mobilization of sentiment without direct personal contact. It is thus possible for a well financed movement organization to parlay a group's grievances into the appearance of seething discontent while bypassing the political processes of the classical model.

In the classical model the size and the amount of activity of a movement and its corresponding movement organizations are presumably a tip-off to a political elite that some action on its part is necessary, be it repressive or ameliorative. Size and amount of activity are likely to energize what Lipsky (1968) calls "reference publics" of elite decision makers—those groups to whom the decision makers are most sensitive. If these publics can be convinced of widespread grievances, they may act on elite decision makers directly in favor of the goals of the movement. But the public's perception of a movement's intensity of action may reflect media coverage rather than the actual membership strength or the scope and intensity of grievances. A movement may appear to command a large membership in the classical sense, while in fact the membership may be nonexistent or exist only on paper. If such a state of affairs can mobilize reference publics sympathetic to movement goals, we may speak of manipulating the elite's perception of the necessity for action.

Attempts to manipulate elite perceptions of the necessity of action occur in two stages. The first addresses sectors of the elite who are most involved in funding movement organizations. Such financial support depends upon a perception by some funding source of a disparity between present reality and the proper state of the world. Once funding is secure, the movement organization can focus upon imparting this same sense of disparity to political decision makers and their reference publics. (Though these two stages can be separated analytically, in practice they are not always distinct.)

Television is well suited to portraying disparities between real and ideal conditions. First, few American homes lack a television set. In 1969, 95 percent of American homes had a television set (*Final Report of the National Commission on Causes and Prevention of Violence*, 1970). Second, the scope of coverage and the immediacy of dissemination mean that events in any area of the nation are directly observable. Occurrences on the streets in Selma, Alabama, and Roxbury, Massachusetts—indeed, anywhere on the globe—can be seen almost as they happen. This state of affairs would not necessarily affect perceptions of real-ideal disparities, since coverage could be restricted to tornadoes, murders, religious observances, and the latest in clothing styles; but for one reason or another social movement activity based on real-ideal disparities receives extensive coverage on television—this material is good copy. Television has clearly created new opportunities for social movement leaders (Hubbard, 1968). By knowing which events make good television copy, movement organization leaders have used the medium to create the impression of widespread activity and grievance.

Many recent movement leaders have utilized the media in this manner. For instance, Stokely Carmichael, who during his "black power" phase was always good copy, received widespread coverage. The impression he clearly sought to impart was "spokesman for the Amercian black community."

The movement that he headed at the time, the Student Nonviolent Coordinating Committee, never possessed a large membership and did not attempt to recruit one (Zinn, 1964). Further, the majority of a representative sample of black respondents apparently did not approve, or were unaware, of Carmichael's views (Marx, 1967). But by becoming good copy Carmichael was able to gain extensive coverage and therefore appear to be speaking for a broad constituency. Of course, elites and authorities are sophisticated; they listen to the people back home, read their mail, keep an ear open to their constituencies (Lindblom, 1968). Thus, television by itself hardly controls the images that elites perceive. It may have more effect upon elites indirectly through reference publics.

But at the same time that television communicates an impression of the state of the world to elites and policymakers, it also affects social movement mass support and opposition. Involvement, pro or con, becomes less dependent upon personal experience and immediate situational context and more dependent upon image and impression, which are, in great part, filtered through the medium. At the same time that the media shape perception, they select the events and problems to be defined (Warner, 1971). What a radical or college professor believes is the problem, the media may reject. The mass media present news and problems that they define as of interest to the masses. It is possible that some issues that ought to generate social movements get short-changed in the process.

The Growing Trend to Inclusive Organizations

Because television can involve in a problem people who do not have direct contact with the events or problems, a larger pool of potential supporters is created. (Television news can be seen as advertisements for social causes.) Combined with increasing disposable income and the use of mailed requests for funds, the inclusive form of social movement organizations is likely to characterize newly formed organizations.

Some writers, using the classical model of social movement organizations, assume what has been termed "exclusive membership." That is, membership is seen as reflecting a strong commitment to the organization as the sole agency for rectifying problems. Inclusive membership, on the other hand, means partial commitment and relatively little in the way of membership requirements (cf. Zald and Ash, 1966). Inclusive membership is not new. It has characterized churches, unions, and most voluntary associations in the United States for decades. The ACLU is an inclusive organization. The large bulk of the membership participates in the activities of the organization only through its contributions. A large number of the recent antiwar groups have functioned as inclusive organizations, in the same manner as did many of the earlier civil rights organizations. The

NAACP demands little more of members than regular contributions. Anyone who has contributed funds to such an organization knows how widespread the phenomenon of mailed requests for such funds has become. The growth of a middle class with disposable income and ideological commitment activated through the portrayal of real-ideal disparities is all that is necessary to guarantee the growth of such movement organizations. The donor to such a movement has little control over the movement leadership short of withholding funds. Withholding funds, however, does insure some control if other funding sources are lacking and requires that a leadership properly gauge and mold donor grievances. A classic illustration is provided by the different response of the Southern Christian Leadership Conference (SCLC), CORE, and the NAACP to charges of anti-Semitism. Both the SCLC and the NAACP have been closely tied to Jewish financial support, and both have responded to protect their lines to the Jewish community. CORE, which has attempted to be a more militant social movement organization, has been more ready to play to its mass base rather than its supporters. The important point, however, is that as more and more organizations that are at the same time inclusive and heterogeneous develop, they will become less dependent upon any single base of support. As will be seen below, movement organizations based upon inclusive membership contributions may represent mixed forms displaying characteristics of both classical and modern forms.

Professional Social Movements

The rise of professional social movements results from changed funding patterns and resulting changed career patterns of social movement leaders. Movement leaders in this matrix become social movement entrepreneurs. Their movements' impact results from their skill at manipulating images of relevance and support through the communications media. The professional social movement is the common form of recent movements and represents a sharp departure from the classical model. Although movement entrepreneurs have always existed and some earlier movements closely resemble the professional movement (namely, the social movement organizations making up the Progressive movement), modern conditions bring them to the fore.

Daniel Patrick Moynihan (1969) coined the phrase "the professionalization of reform," to describe the extent to which the Kennedy-Johnson "War on Poverty" was conceived and implemented by the government and foundations. The War on Poverty represents a case of political issue entrepreneurship. Its only partial link to the classical model was its connection to the civil rights movement. Our analysis goes beyond Moynihan's, we think, in making explicit the departures from the classical model.

Professional social movements are characterized by: (1) a leadership that devotes full time to the movement, with (a) a large proportion of resources originating outside the aggrieved group that the movement claims to represent; (2) a very small or nonexistent membership base or a paper membership (membership implies little more than allowing name to be used upon membership rolls); (3) attempts to impart the image of "speaking for a potential constituency"; and (4) attempts to influence policy toward that same constituency.

As we noted earlier, we do not believe that the existence of professional social movements is a new phenomenon; such an organizational form has existed in the past. It is the widespread nature of the phenomenon that characterizes the modern era. Earlier periods of intense social movement activity have spawned many similar organizations.

For instance, while the Progressive movement apparently possessed a substantial sentiment base, there is some evidence that Progressive social movement organizations had difficulty in recruiting active memberships. And even though memberships were small in such organizations, "only a small part of the membership did more than pay their yearly dues or make more generous contributions to their favorite organizations" (Yellowitz, 1965, p. 77). "In general, the regular activities of the organizations were performed by a small staff of paid employees, while the general membership made up the governing boards, did some of the committee work, and paid expenses" (Yellowitz, 1965, p. 77). Finally, "Most of the reform organizations depended upon a small group of wealthy patricians, professional men, and social workers for their financial support and leadership. Wealthy women, including some from New York City society, were indispensible to the financing and staffing of the Consumer's League" (Yellowitz, 1965, p. 71).

Lacking large membership bases, these organizations relied heavily upon the media to mobilize sentiment bases in order to influence elite decision makers directly and indirectly. As Smith observes, "The basic method utilized by Progressive movement organizations was to publicize investigations undertaken by themselves or by government agencies. Simply worded leaflets described in muckraking style the conditions discovered by these investigations and proposed a specific piece of legislation to deal with the problem. Extensive use of photographs, cartoons, graphs, etc., illustrated the "Evil" produced by the excesses of the industrial system" (Smith, 1968, p. 21).

The ferment accompanying the Depression and New Deal era also produced movements at odds with the classical mold. Huey Long's Share Our Wealth Society is such an early departure. The funding of the society came from Long's personal reserves, deriving ultimately from his Louisiana organization. Membership in local Share our Wealth clubs required no dues, and at its peak, in 1935, the society claimed a membership of between four million and seven million members. Through national radio broadcasts, again funded by Long, he encouraged the formation of clubs, and a large national staff of organizers and office workers was employed to aid this process. The national office of the society provided organizational material and propaganda for the local clubs. Long made all of the important decisions concerning the policies of the society and liked to "boast that the Share Our Wealth clubs represented a powerful national movement, 'an active crusading force' that someday would sweep into control of the government" (Williams, 1970, p. 735).

At about the same time, Father Charles E. Coughlin founded the National Union for Social Justice. Concerning this organization McCoy says, "It should be emphasized that instead of offering encouragement and guidance to a spontaneous organization of the discontented by the discontented, Coughlin offered them a ready-made organization and ideology. Throughout the existence of the National Union, any real participation by the membership in decision-making processes seemed to be lacking" (McCoy, 1958, p. 119).

Membership in these organizations was inclusive and implied little more than support for the founders' stated aims. Indeed, both organizations were developed to demonstrate that widespread support existed. Since membership implied neither activity nor much in the way of financial support, the membership could not have been expected to have a serious voice in policy formation of the organizations.

An excellent modern example of the phenomenon outlined above is the Citizen's Board of Inquiry into Hunger and Malnutrition in the United States (Brown, 1970). The Citizen's Board was originally organized by the Citizen's Crusade Against Poverty, an antipoverty organization drawing its financial support from a private foundation. The Citizen's Board drew upon a highly trained professional staff who employed the media effectively as a rallying device against hunger. The potential mass base of hungry Americans was never involved in this movement. Hungry Americans did not provide the resources employed by this organization. Financial support was drawn from the "Citizen's Crusade Against Poverty, the United Auto Workers, and six foundations" (Brown, 1970, p. 119). The media cooperated by giving broad coverage to the board's activities and the final report issued by the board. The media also produced a television documentary dealing with the issue raised by the board (CBS, "Hunger in America"). We do not imply that the board misrepresented the needs or desires of hungry Americans or that hungry Americans would not have become involved in such a movement if they had been given a chance or were needed to effect policy. The point is that the organization functioned without mass involvement.

A somewhat different example of a professional social movement is the National Council of Senior Citizens for Health Care through Social Security (NCSC). It was possibly more typical of professional social movements in that it arranged to appear as a classical movement, of the inclusive type, whereas it was clearly professional in its operating orientation. Its major source of funding was the AFL-CIO (Rose, 1967, p. 423). The professional staff of the organization conducted rallies around the country in support of health care for the elderly and encouraged mass petitioning. Such funding also allowed professional expertise to be made available to smaller groups, which were encouraged and aided in holding hearings in support of health care for the aged. The staff also wrote press releases that were used across the country by constituent groups, and the media responded by publicizing the organization. "By the close of 1961 [NCSC] claimed a membership of 400,000 elderly persons and 900,000 supporting members of all ages" (Rose, 1967, p. 433).

The example of the NCSC deviates from our characteristics of a pure professional social movement in that it possessed a large membership base. That membership base, however, was created after the fact. If the Citizen's Board of Inquiry into Hunger and Malnutrition in the United States had desired to develop a loosely organized membership in this fashion, one suspects, it could have. The decision by a professional staff to devote resources to this method of image manipulation will vary from situation to situation. The NCSC was pushed in this direction by the contention of the American Medical Association that the aged did not lack medical care and that existing health insurance schemes adequately met the needs of the elderly (Rose, 1967).

A more recent example of a professional social movement is Common Cause, headed by John W. Gardner, former secretary of the Department of Health, Education, and Welfare. This organization has assembled a professional staff of about 30 and has "managed to build a respectable financial base of about $1.75 million with $15 in dues from each of its members, plus seed money from such contributors as John D. Rockefeller III, the Ford Motor Company, and Time, Inc." (Halloran, 1971). The organization claims a membership of 108,000 citizens. Observations of the scale of the advertising and mailing campaigns launched by the organization suggests that a major financial investment was required to enlist the membership, and the New York Times reported initial funding of $250,000 from a group of wealthy backers (Halloran, 1971).

Several points are worth noting about Common Cause. First, many of the staff members have been involved in other professional movement organizations. Indeed the president and chief executive officer of Common Cause in 1971, Jack Conway, was involved in the hunger campaign discussed above through his involvement in the Child Development Group of Mississippi. Conway had also been employed by the AFL-CIO in a political action role. Second, members of the organization have no serious role in organizational policymaking short of withholding membership dues. The professional staff largely determine the positions that the organization takes upon issues. In general, the membership seems to relate to the organization primarily through the mails and the media, though the staff attempts to activate the membership for pressure campaigns upon decision makers—thereby making membership constitute something more than a financial contribution. Furthermore, Common Cause develops other groups and helps start pilot projects in various states. By 1972 Common Cause had developed a variety of mechanisms for building local groups.

Let us conclude our discussion of modern professional social movement organizations with a brief look at the highly publicized set of organizations developed by Ralph Nader. Though this set of organizations has been continually expanding, in 1971 three organizations represented the core of Nader's activities: the Center for the Study of Responsive Law, the Public Interest Research Group, and the Center for Auto Safety. While the three organizations have continued to operate, specific issue groups have been formed for short periods of time. Issue groups, normally termed "Raiders" by the press, work closely with the Center for the Study of Responsive Law, which sponsors the reports of their inquires (McCarry, 1972).

The source of funds for the various activities of these organizations varies from the proceeds of published reports, Nader's speaking fees, and foundation and private donations. In 1970, for instance, the Midas International Foundation gave Nader's various projects $100,000 of the more than $500,000 contributed by foundations and private donors (McCarry, 1972). In 1971, Public Citizen, Inc. was developed to solicit small donations from a broader base through mailed requests for funds. "From June through October 1971, Public Citizen collected $100,000" (McCarry, 1972, p. 210). The Center for Auto Safety in 1971 received two-thirds of its funds from Consumers Union and Public Citizen, Inc. (Marshall, 1971).

This complex of organizations illustrates very clearly the staffing trends we have outlined above. Reliance upon both full-time professional staff and episodic student volunteer manpower is the mode. The core organizations depend primarily upon full-time professionals who are paid at subsistence wages—a lawyer for the Public Interest Research Group, for instance, receives $4,500 a year. Members of the full-time staff organize the use of summer student volunteers.

Each organization claims to represent and fight for an unorganized constituency. It is only through Public Citizen, Inc., though, that any direct support tie to such a purported constituency has been attempted. Beyond Public Citizen, Inc., none of the organizations is in any sense a membership organization. Professional competence rather than broad citizen action characterizes these organizations, with a heavy use of the media as a critical component of utilizing this competence as a lever for social change.

It is not that professional movement organizations in Machiavellian fashion manufacture pseudoproblems, though this remains a possibility. There are always grievances at large among the citizenry. But for many such grievances the individual rewards for organizing to solve individual problems, if in fact they are soluble, are likely to be less than the energy and resource expenditure required.[14] If vehicles are provided, however, for attacking such grievances and participation is essentially costless, minimal levels of citizen participation are an increased likelihood. Professional social movement organizations can provide such vehicles. (Indeed, professional movements might actually pay members to participate in the name of citizen identification, much as War on Poverty groups paid the poor to represent the poor.) These organizations do not necessarily manufacture grievances—they do make it more likely that such grievances will receive a public hearing and policy action. Even minimal levels of citizen participation are dispensable, though, as professional movement organizations may be effective in their absence.

The process of the definition of strain and grievance is altered by the advent of professional movement organizations and the conditions that favor their birth. We suggest that the definition of grievances will expand to meet the funds and support personnel available, and the criterion for the existence of such a personnel may be a foundation's willingness to believe a professional entrepreneur's characterization, rather than the perception of strain in the minds of the potential constituency. If large amounts of funds are available, then problem definition becomes a strategy for competing for them, and we would expect more and more sophisticated attempts at problem definition. Those intellectuals who engage in such problem definition will not normally have been subject to the odious conditions they seek to allay, and their definitions will depend upon disparities between general value commitments and the realities of social organization. Many of the supporters of such organizations, as well, will base their support upon such disparities rather than upon personal experience.

Government agencies, as well, are many times involved in the early stages of grievance manufacture. Agency involvement is not always reactive to issues defined by external groups. Issuing reports and calling public attention to problems may serve to build a favorable environment for the development of social movement organizations around an issue. The facilitation of apparent grass-roots concern, of course, is ample evidence that agency appropriations be increased to attack the problem at hand. The recent attempts of the Department of Health, Education, and Welfare to increase the representation of female faculty in American universities illustrate this pattern. This action has encouraged campus feminist groups to organize and press for change supporting the agency's case that grievances requiring affirmative action exist.

Finally, we may carry our argument even further away from the classical model by positing the distinct possibility of the development of professional social movement organizations that create rather than mobilize grievances.[15] We have assumed to this point that movement organizations engineer the appearance of grievances in good faith. But it is entirely likely that the creation of the appearance of grievances by such an organization will bear no relationship to any preexisting grievance structure. In such an event movement entrepreneurs can be thought of as representing no one but themselves in such pursuits unless their efforts lead to the development of actual feelings of grievance among a target population. Success in such manufacture will be seen as leadership, whereas failure will be seen as hucksterism. In any case, movement origins will occur outside of the mass.

Stability and Change in the New Careers and Organization

Earlier we argued that there has been a marked increase in the number of career positions in organizations related to social movements. People commit their lives to working in organizations related to their change-oriented values. These careers are contingent upon organizational opportunities and upon the survival of the social movement industry and of particular movement organizations. The next part examines the ways in which the infrastructure processes we have discussed shape the overall size and direction of the industry. Here, however, we need to ask how particular professional movement organizations and full-time social movement careers are affected by the vicissitudes of their relationships to media, to funding sources, and to membership and beneficiary bases.

The New Careers

Ministers, community organizers, public relations directors, membership and development specialists, lawyers, doctors, and engineers are some of the occupations from which the professional movement organization attracts its cadres. They are distinguished from their colleagues in these professions largely by their rejection of traditional institutional roles, careers, and reward structures. One consequence, we suspect, is a lower commitment to professionalism per se. That is, they define their opportunities less in terms of the use of professional skills and more in terms of social change objectives. Of course, traditional professionals are not strictly tied to professional settings for their careers. For instance, lawyers often take jobs as business executives or in government agencies, and engineers become administrators. But most professionals commit themselves to professionally related settings.

If professional movement organizations exhibit stability and elongated hierarchical organization, careers in movement organizations may come to resemble those in other professional settings, but one of the characteristics of these organizations is that their funding is unstable. As there is an ebb and flow of foundation support, as individual contributors change interests, and as society passes on to new issues, sectors of movement support are likely to dry up and new ones to expand. A likely consequence is that personnel will switch from organization to organization and move among locales. As personnel shift from organization to organization, a national network of personnel relations develops. Some movement organizations may routinize their funding sources, however, as community consensus develops around their goals. The Planned Parenthood Association exhibits this pattern where in many locales it has come to be funded by the United Givers Fund.

Also, many of these movement organizations will probably intersect with traditional institutions that have some relation to particular issue sectors. Just as personnel go between the Defense Department and the defense industries, so we may expect movement personnel to flow back and forth among movement organizations, foundations, and the government agencies and professional schools that maintain a tie to the policy issue at stake. Lawyers flow in and out of law schools and government. A community organizer is attached to a metropolitan housing authority one year and to a neighborhood action group the next. A state health department loses a middle-level bureaucrat to a health action council, and the health action council loses an executive to a comprehensive health center. A "guerilla administrator" with the Department of Housing and Urban Development takes a job with a Fair Housing organization, and so on. For some of the movement professionals, one of the steps leads into a traditional career setting, even though it builds upon the expertise he has acquired. The overall direction and rate of flow between traditional and untraditional settings depends upon the overall growth of traditional versus new careers.

Several recent developments support a view of the rationalization of social movement organization careers. The first is the beginning of routinized training for such positions in the form of training institutes for social movement personnel. The most notable examples of such institutes are those sponsored by the Industrial Areas Foundation, the Citizens College Organizing Committee, and the Southern Christian Leadership Conference. The second is the growth of a literature that attempts to systematize the knowledge required for success at such activity. Some recent examples of the growth of this literature are Michael Walzer's *Political Action: A Practical Guide to Movement Politics* (1971), Si Kahn's *How People Get Power* (1970), Saul Alinsky's *Rule for Radicals* (1971), Lakey and Oppenheimer's *Manual for Direct Action* (1965), and *The Organizer's Manual* (O.M. Collective, 1971). Though these manuals in general focus upon what is termed "grass-roots" organizing à la classical model, several of them advise how the potential organizer goes about exploiting the infrastructure of social movement organization support we have outlined. For instance, *The Organizer's Manual* explains in detail how to apply for foundation grants. Presumably, the next step in the process is the founding of a social movement organizers' association and the institution of formal credentialing procedures.

Product Diversification Change in Movement Organizations

One line of analysis of classical movement organizations suggests that they have a strong tendency to perpetuate themselves and to develop oligarchic and bureaucratic features. In doing so they moderate their goals and institutionalize careers. Zald and Ash (1966) argue that this tendency is dependent upon a routinization of resource flow. Many movement organizations will fail or shrivel if they cannot define a relationship to a support base. Some of the movement organizations that we are discussing easily transform themselves into service institutions. A poverty law firm routinizes its relationship with the government, and as long as it does not transgress political boundaries, its chances of survival are increased. Obviously, shifts in political control can lead away from movement goals.

Other movement organizations are more clearly focused upon policy changes, upon political action that is more difficult to transform into services. What happens to them? Needless to say, the less the movement organization is tied to enduring cleavages or issues, the less likely it is to survive. It is hard to imagine inclusive organizations like the ACLU or the NAACP going out of business, because they relate to enduring issues. The NAACP relates to a basic racial-status cleavage in the society, the ACLU an abstract value that can never be fully attained. Both may have to shift programs to meet the competition for their support base provided by other movement organizations, but they can do so merely by shifting program definitions and personnel. On the other hand, narrowly defined organizations such as an organization for day-care centers or Citizens for Clean Water may find themselves without an issue.

In this regard an organization like Common Cause is especially interesting. It is a "conglomerate" of the ameliorative social movement industry, for it speaks for reform in general, allying with many special interest groups. On the one hand, as it loses some supporters when it takes on issues outside of or opposed to their interests, it picks up others. On the other hand, as a problem or reform is achieved, it switches to a new issue. Its growth and stability depend upon picking up a new product line for social action. Its diversity of change goals also protects it against the faddishness of issue definition. As long as the media focus upon it and foundations and individuals contribute some resources to it, it is able to maintain or protect its less popular causes. Much as a conglomerate or diversified manufacturer, in comparison with a single-line producer, is better able to invest in a product that has long-range potential, a diversified social movement organization can invest in projects that have long-range change potential, even though current definitions of the important issue would not lead it to invest in them.

Professional Social Movements in Modern America: Does the Piper Call the Tune?

A fundamental conclusion of the analysis is that we have recently witnessed a major increase in professional social movement activity and that this phenomenon has been interpreted by many as a participatory revolution. This so-called revolution is, we believe, the result of several secular trends—in funding, through foundations and personal income, the increased importance of television and other communication devices, in discretionary time, and in career alternatives. We are not convinced that the increased size of the middle class in modern America has produced dramatic increases in the time and energy devoted to social movement organizations by private citizens. Nor do we believe that the increasing number of social arrangements defined as problematic reflects an increase in "objective" problem incidence. Besides, it is problem perception, not objective problem incidence, that is relevant to our arguments here. Man may or may not be closer to doom today than at the time of the Black Plague. For our purposes what is important is how a society channels and perceives that "objective problem" (Blumer, 1971).

How permanent are the trends we have described? If increases in the size of the middle class have produced the so-called revolution, then it ought to be rather permanent. Indeed, we would expect more of the same as the middle class grows in size, both relatively and absolutely. If an increase in the objective incidence of problems has produced it, the satiation element of the classical model explaining the rise and fall of social movements would direct us to base predictions of permanence, short of actual revolution, upon the willingness and ability of the political elite to deal with the problems. The political elite, those in positions to act upon grievances and change social policies, are, in the classical model, the gatekeepers of social movements; they either respond or fail to respond to demands, and in those responses membership motivations are either satisfied or frustrated. On the other hand, if the apparent revolution is the result of the trends outlined above, an analysis of the permanence of these specific trends permits an assessment of the permanence of this revolution and its ideological directions.

Social Control and Social Movements Analysis

Sociological analysis of social movement organizations has focused primarily upon the internal dynamics of specific organizations. Even attempts to focus upon the relationship between such organizations and the broader environment have tended to ignore the social control attempts of authorities directed toward movements and organizations.[16] We too are influenced by this tradition. We have focused upon techniques by which professional social movement organizations can influence elites and upon the internal dynamics of such movements, but we have paid little attention to the other side of the coin—the processes by which elites, in and out of government, attempt to exercise social control over professional social movement organizations. Such processes are no doubt operative with what we have termed classical social movement organizations. However, the potentialities of control by elites are highlighted by a focus upon professional social movement organizations when the question of permanence and direction are considered.

We would expect elite groups, especially when they are in government, to take a rather jaundiced view of social movement organizations with publicly stated radical goals. We would not expect established institutions— i.e., foundations, established churches, corporations, and above all the federal government—to support such movements vigorously. If one assumes that social control is perceived as necessary, there are two very general approaches that authorities can take toward the sort of participatory revolution we have outlined above. Elites may enter by attempting to control the direction of dissent (the quality issue), thereby molding the implications of it, or they may respond by attempting to minimize dissent, thereby molding the quantity of it. Let us address these two possibilities as they might affect the participatory revolution we have outlined.

Does the Piper Call the Tune?

One reason why we have stated that professional social movements highlight the potentialities of elite social control is the dependence of professional movement organizations on elites for funds. We noted the independence from a mass support base that is implied in such funding procedures, but clearly this independence implies another dependence. If it is displeased, a source controlling major amounts of organizational funds can destroy a social movement organization overnight. Though mistakes might be made, we would not expect established institutional sectors to support radical professional social movement organizations for any length of time. Foundations, churches, and government agencies are involved in a web of institutional controls that prohibit them from getting too far out of line. Consequently, though it may appear obvious, we believe that the bulk of the institution-backed participatory revolution is ameliorative rather than radical in intent. Even the charge of "radical" against organizations funded through these sources is likely to produce pressure upon the organizations to soften both rhetoric and behavior. Goulden's (1971) accounts of the behavior of the Ford Foundation in several "politically charged" instances illustrate the point.

The effects of established institutions' involvement in the backing of professional social movement organizations should have the broader implication of directing organized dissent into legitimate channels. That student energies can be diverted into legitimate channels by flourishing professional social movement organizations remains a distinct possibility. By applying large amounts of resources, then, in ameliorative directions, elites may have the effect of diffusing the radical possibilities of dissent in general.

Such an argument does not hinge upon the motives of the elite groups. Whether or not their motives are sincere concern or social control, their actions are likely to have the same general effects. Action, however, that supports the massive infrastructure of dissent may provide some indirect support for social movement organizations with radical goals. The resources available in the ameliorative sphere may easily, we believe, be diverted to radical organizations. For instance, the publication facilities of ameliorative organizations are regularly made available to almost any movement organization (see *The Organizer's Manual,* O.M. Collective, 1971), regardless of its tactics and goals. Legal representation has been provided to members of radical social movement organizations as a result of the existence of ameliorative organizations. Our own view is that the interstices of the massive ameliorative movement[17] sponsored by elite sectors provides more in the way of resources for the radical segment of the movement than would be available without it. And when the well-funded sources dry up, the radical movement organization moves to less well-funded ones. From government agencies it falls back on the churches.

Minimization of Dissent: Surviving the Piper's Demise

If the political elite decided to attempt to minimize the scope and quantity of dissent in U.S. society in the 1970s, could it? This question suggests two related ones. First, how would withdrawal of support for social movement activity affect the trends we have outlined as affecting professional social movement organizations? Second, would the massive elite involvement we have outlined have any lasting effect upon the level of movement activity following such withdrawal?

The institutional funding patterns we have discussed are highly vulnerable to change. The federal government has already begun to cut back its support of social movement organizations through its Community Action Program agencies of the Office of Economic Opportunity. Though possibly it could, the government has by no means, however, cut back all such programs. The funding by the churches and foundations is also vulnerable in that rules governing funding by such agencies can be changed. Indeed, legislative action has been interpreted by some foundations as having already moved toward restriction upon grants (see Goulden, 1971). Further, foundation boards of directors and church constituencies could press for an end to such funding. We believe that the trends in funding for such activity could be reversed very rapidly by a determined federal administration. But such determination would require an attack upon tax laws and the institutional independence of the churches and foundations beyond informal pressure. This action would require a major confrontation and, in our view, is highly unlikely.

The media's willingness to trade in citizen grievances and hence aid professional social movements in their activities is also vulnerable, given federal control over television broadcasting. The reality of this control makes the possibility of threat and innuendo by administration figures a real force. It is obvious from the U.S.S.R. example that an industrial society can systematically control the dissemination of information and hence grievance accumulation. Similarly, competing for mass audiences seems to lead the media away from serious issues that have low current interest. But it is unlikely, short of a fascist regime in the United States, that all of the grievances portrayed by the media could be suppressed.

Several of the trends we have discussed, however, are not as vulnerable to short-run action on the part of a political elite committed to decreases in movement activity. These factors tend to be related to the general level of prosperity in the society. Though they should be sensitive to economic recessions, mailed donations to movement organizations are probably likely to continue.

The ability of youth with intense value commitments to survive on subsistence incomes probably means continued periods of involvement in social movement activity for many members of this group (see Kenniston, 1968). However, as the relative proportion of youth decreases, as it is likely to in the future, this source of energy and involvement should also tend to decrease in importance. Whether a period of intense involvement during youth implies that individuals will continue heavy outlays of energy and resources in later life to movement activity seems an open question to us, unless funding allows career involvement.[18] There is no doubt that we have seen increased involvement during youth.

Whether the intense value commitments leading to action will continue to characterize youth, we cannot say. Introspection does appear to be a serious competitor to action. Indeed, a clear result of the triumph of Charles Reich's "Consciousness III" (Reich, 1970) would be a withdrawal from movement activity of the sort we have focused upon. Whether self-examination can have structural consequences is beyond the scope of our remarks here. Social movement analysis is not very instructive on this point. It does not point to the structural solution of alienation, anomie, and breast beating in general.

We are led to conclude that some portion of the increase in professional social movement activity could quite rapidly be reversed if the political elite were determined to bring about such a change. On the other hand, if prosperity continues, there are several factors that would lead an observer to expect a proportion of the increase in such activity to remain. Higher and higher standards of living, through these factors, would lead to an expectation of future increases in spite of the actions of political elites directed specifically at movement activity. Whereas the classical model of social movements predicts less activity in prosperous times, our analysis predicts just the reverse.

If one accepts our analysis of the development of a massive social movement industry in modern America, then it follows that the industry will act as a powerful source of pressure in behalf of its own lines of support. Representatives of this industry and its supporting institutions will be likely to resist pressures to cut off resource flows and even attempt to expand them. In this regard the House Ways and Means Committee held hearings in May of 1972 to consider changes in the Internal Revenue Service Regulations "controlling the tax exempt status of nonprofit organizations which attempt to influence legislation" (*Nashville Tennessean*, 1972, p. 8). During these hearings the National Council of Churches argued very strongly for liberalization of regulations as they affect the activities of church groups. If such a change were to occur, we would expect more resources to become available to professional social movement organizations.

Finally, the ability of specific professional social movement organizations to convert to classical social movement organizations through time would seriously qualify the effects of elite withdrawal.[19] If there is a high likelihood of such an occurrence—by a telescoping of the early organizational and interest articulation phases—then the short-run effects of elite withdrawal from the support of movement activity would be blunted. That is, the withdrawal of foundation and institutional support would have little effect. Only longitudinal case studies of professional social movements could suggest the likelihood of such occurrences and hence the importance of this dimension to an overtime prediction of the general societal level of movement activity. We tend to believe that movement organizations based upon deep interest cleavages are more likely to be able to utilize elite support for the construction of viable classical social movement organizations than multi-interest and soluble issue movement organizations are. A professional movement organization can become a classical social movement organization by attaching itself to a major social cleavage and developing a unified membership support base. If this is so, the extent to which movement organizations are based on such cleavages will determine the elite's ability to throttle movement activity.

One question mentioned above demands fuller attention as we attempt to predict the future of social movements in modern America: What is the relationship between Consciousness III, the value counterculture, and the future of social movements? Our analysis has focused upon the infrastructure of costs and organizational facilitation created by some of the secular trends of affluence. We have ignored, or treated only in passing, the values and attitudes that motivate individual social movement participation.

Our references to the enduring potential of the civil rights movement were based upon a perception of how the racial cleavage and value disparities based upon that cleavage create an enduring base for a social movement. Is there a similar potential to serve as an enduring base for social movements in the culture/counterculture cleavage? An answer seems based upon several contingencies.

An enduring social cleavage is based upon differences in status, position, and belief that are relatively irreconcilable by "normal relations" in the short run. (The short run is defined in terms of the time perspective of those who are trying to change status, position, and belief differentials.) To the extent that the counterculture leads its members to encounter the larger culture as an enemy, the counterculture can be seen as self-reinforcing of an important cleavage and specific issues based upon it. As long as contacts with the police, schools, families, and work institutions maintain a negative quality, reinforcing the distinction, then membership in the counterculture will be likely to continue to lead to some form of social movement activity—whether of a retreatist, reformist, or revolutionary type.

On the other hand, the dominant culture may react by partial incorporation, taking over some of the values and behaviors of the counterculture.

The relaxation of marijuana laws, sympathetic police officers, and the relaxation of dress and hair codes in many institutional settings may all contribute to a deemphasis of the culture/counterculture cleavage. Insofar as the cleavage is based upon style and belief, then, partial incorporation is likely to moderate the effects of the cleavage. Such an argument leads us to doubt that this cleavage will persist.

There is also the fact that the counterculture is based on a transient role, that of young persons, whereas the civil rights/black power and labor movements are based on relatively permanent roles. A brief hiatus in civil rights activity still leaves numerous experienced black organizers around to socialize newcomers. An interruption in a "youth movement" can lead to a situation in which later cohorts may experience the same problems as earlier ones, but lack role models and interpreters of their experience. There is an absence of movement "tradition" in the counterculture—no one thinks of himself as an extension of the Beat Generation or sees rock as equivalent to jazz in terms of social position. Nonstudent pacifists and blacks, however, have a relatively strong sense of a movement past.

Conclusion

Our analysis has stressed two subjects: secular trends in modern society affecting social movements and the theoretical analysis of social movements. Possibly the most important point that needs to be made in conclusion is the following: Classical analysis has had too much in common with "bleeding-heart liberal" analysis focusing upon the life situation of the oppressed. We make such a statement at the risk of being thought cynical men without sympathy for the oppressed. But a vision of the future runs the risk of remaining just a vision if it does not confront the sources and weaknesses of movement activity aimed at bringing it about. Social analysis must confront the infrastructure of social movement funding, supply and demand of labor, the media, and the interaction of movements and elites before it can be of much utility in the grievance proceedings of modern society.

Notes

1. As an aside, it is worth noting that political scientists use the phrase "interest groups" and sociologists write about "social movement organizations" without acknowledging their overlapping functions and processes. See Lowi (1971) for a recent attempt to combine these previously separate traditions of analysis.
2. The 1955 questions: "Do you happen to belong to any groups or organizations in the community here? Which ones? Any Others?" The 1962 questions: "Do

you belong to any groups or organizations here in the community? Which ones? Any others?"

3. See Burnham (1965) for a review of the factors involved in the U-shaped curve of voting participation from the 1840s until 1960.

4. *Some* readers will insist that the real participatory revolution is missed because it has occurred among the blacks and the poor. Although the civil rights movement effloresced in the 1960s, it is not at all clear that Negro social participation changed that much. Myths of nonparticipation to the contrary, several studies have shown that at each class level blacks belong to associations as much or *more* than whites of the same income-education group. See Orum (1966) for a review of this literature. Moreover, a study of the Office of Economic Opportunity Community Action Agencies (CAAs) in several large cities concludes that "CAA's seem unable to produce or create participation where it doesn't exist and unable to increase it very much where it already does exist" (Vanecko 1969).

5. Watching television could be considered a "consumption cost"—a $500 investment in a color television set *must* be utilized. If organizational participation is in high-priority competition for the time allocated to tube gazing, consider the participatory implications of an America with no television. By increasing the wasteland content of TV, revolutionaries could mobilize more activists from among the bored.

6. See Edward Banfield and James Q. Wilson (1963, pp. 234-40) for a discussion of how readiness to note and support activities that do not appear to have a direct payoff to oneself or one's own groups varies by class and ethnicity.

7. The brighter students might get even better grades if they were not so involved in social movement organizations activity.

8. Note that the political trials of the Nixon administration have served a similar function. Several observers have remarked that there was no conspiracy in 1968 but that there was after the trial.

9. V.S.C., Inc., Box 13, Canyon, California 94516.

10. The first edition of this encyclopedia was published in 1959. It seemed clear to us that the 1959 volume was quite incomplete as a result of nonreporting of organizations. The 1964 edition appeared to reflect more comprehensive coverage, and so we examined the 1965-69 time period rather than the 1959-69 period, which we would have preferred.

11. Horticulture, Hobby and Avocational, and Athletic.

12. We may overstate the meaning of membership for the classical model. The often hazy distinction between social movement and social movement organization in this literature may cloud an understanding of the term "membership." Certainly much of the individual behavior discussed within the framework of the classical model is episodic, exhibiting only minimal commitment. Traditional analysis appears to assume that the only qualification for membership in a social movement is sentiment sympathy. Organizational membership seems to be another matter but, as we will argue, may require no more.

13. See David L. Sills (1957) for an illustration of this process, normally termed "goal succession," for The National Foundation for Infantile Paralysis. Success in eradicating infantile paralysis required the development of new goals to justify continued organizational life.

14. See Mancur Olsen, Jr. (1965) for an analysis that sharply challenges the assumptions of interest group theorists that people will devote time, money, and

energy to collective causes that promise only small personal rewards. Olsen would argue that individuals are more likely to be "free riders" on these causes. Our analysis, however, substantially deflects the *importance* of Olsen's argument, since, as we have argued, individual citizen participation may be unimportant to movement vitality. We accept the validity of Olsen's analysis, but its central importance rests upon its pessimistic conclusions about the possibility of organized action to rectify citizen grievances. Furthermore, outside funding allows the possibility of easily offering what Olsen terms "by-products" for citizen involvement in movement organizations; by-products could be low-cost loans, aid in gaining welfare benefits, transportation to agencies, or even outright payment for membership. See Leites and Wolf (1970) for an analysis parallel to ours that stresses the dispensability of citizen participation given outside resource supply in the context of guerilla warfare. Social movement organizations will probably feel called upon to conceal their material by-products; the moral rhetoric of social movements is tarnished by making self-interest an explicit rationale for membership. This is, in fact, one important difference between "interest groups" and "professional social movements." See Edelman (1967) for an analysis of the differences in rhetoric of social movements and narrow, self-regarding interest groups.

15. We are indebted to Gary Long for bringing this implication of our arguments to our attention.

16. Smelser (1963) is a notable exception to this generalization. See also Gamson (1968).

17. Let us note that the interstices of modern society in general support social movement organizations. Earlier we noted how easy it is for individuals to get by if they want to commit themselves to a life in social movement activity. "Quickie" organizations can also get by; they can get telephones installed and rent office space and not pay the bills. Since our corporation laws are loose and social movement organizations are often of short duration, some short-lived social movement organizations resemble fly-by-night businesses in their style of operation.

18. See Greene (1970) for a discussion of withdrawal from action by many leaders of the Berkeley Free Speech movement following the taking on of family and job responsibilities.

19. Students for a Democratic Society (SDS), which was originally sponsored by adult labor radicals (the League for Industrial Democracy) but broke away from them.

References

Aaron, D., Ed. 1952. *America in Crisis: Fourteen Crucial Episodes in American History.* New York: Knopf.

Abendroth, W. 1972. *A Short History of the European Working Class.* London: NLB.

Aberle, D. 1966. *The Peyote Religion Among the Navaho.* Chicago: Aldine.

Abraham, D. "State and Classes in Weimar Germany." *Politics and Society* 7(3) (1977): 229-66.

Adams, R.L. "Conflict over Charges of Heresy in American Protestant Seminaries." *Social Compass* 17(2) (1970): 243-60.

Alexander, C.D. 1965. *The Ku Klux Klan in the Southwest.* Lexington, KY: University of Kentucky Press.

Alidoost, Y. "Religious Revolutionaries: An Analysis of the "Religious Groups's Victory in the Iranian Revolution of 1978-79." Ph.D. dissertation, University of Michigan, Ann Arbor, 1981.

Alinsky, S. 1971. *Rules for Radicals.* New York: Random House.

Allen, M.P. "The Structure of Interorganizational Elite Cooptation: Interlocking Corporate Directorates." *American Sociological Review* 39 (June 1974): 393-404.

Almond, G.A., & Verba, S. 1963. *The Civic Culture.* Princeton, NJ: Princeton University Press.

Althusser, L., ed. "Ideology and Ideological State Apparatuses." In *Lenin and Philosophy.* London: NLB, 1971.

Ashmore, H. 1982. *Hearts and Minds: The Anatomy of Racism from Roosevelt to Reagan.* New York: McGraw Hill.

Atomic Industrial Forum, Inc. *Annual Washington Report, 1979,* Washington, DC.

_____. *Nuclear Information.* Newsletter No. 143, May 1980.

Auclaire, P.A. "Public Attitudes toward Social Welfare Expenditures." *Social Work* 29 (March-April 1984): 139-45.

Aveni, A.F. "Organizational Linkages and Resource Mobilization: The Significance of Linkage Strength & Breadth." *Sociological Quarterly* 19 (Spring 1978): 185-202.

Bailis, L. 1974. *Bread and Justice.* Springfield, MA: Heath-Lexington.

Bain, J.S. 1959. *Industrial Organization.* New York: Wiley.

Bandiera, A.R. "The Portuguese Armed Forces Movement: Historical Antecedents, Professional Demands, and Class Conflict." *Politics and Society* 6(1) (1976): 1-56.

Banfield, E. 1958. *The Moral Basis of a Backward Society.* Glencoe, IL: Free Press.

Banfield, E., & Wilson, J.Q. 1963. *City Politics.* Cambridge, MA: Harvard University Press.

Barkan, S.E. "Strategic, Tactical, and Organizational Dilemmas of the Protest

Movement Against Nuclear Power." *Social Problems* 27 (September 1979): 19-37.

Barnes, S. 1977. *Representation in Italy.* Chicago: University of Chicago Press.

Barth, F. 1969. *Ethnic Groups & Boundaries.* Boston: Little, Brown.

Bartley, N.V. 1969. *The Rise of Massive Resistance: Race & Politics in the South During the 1950s.* Baton Rouge, LA: Louisiana State University Press.

Becker, H., & Strauss, A. "Careers, Personality, and Adult Socialization." *American Journal of Sociology* 52 (November 1956): 253-63.

"Behind the Palace Revolt at Ford." *Business Week* (September 20, 1969): 138-41.

Bell, D. 1964. *The Radical Right.* New York: Doubleday.

———. "The Background and Development of Marxian Socialism in the United States." In *Socialism in American Life,* ed. Donald D. Egbert & Stow Persons. Princeton, NJ: Princeton University Press, 1952.

Bell, D., & Held, V. "The Community Revolution." *Public Interest* 16 (1969): 142-79.

Ben-David, J. "Professions in the Class System of Present Day Societies." *Current Sociology* 12(3) (1963-64).

Bennett, L., Jr. 1966. *Confrontation, Black and White.* Baltimore, MD: Penguin Books.

Bensman, J., & Vidich, A. 1971. *The New American Society: The Revolution of the Middle Class.* Chicago: Quadrangle Books.

Benson, J.K. "Organizations: A Dialectical View." *Administrative Science Quarterly* 22(1) (1977): 1-21.

Berg, I. "The Nice Kind of Union Democracy." *Columbia Forum* 5 (Spring 1962): 18-23.

Berger, B.M. "Sociology and the Intellectuals: An Analysis of a Stereotype." *Antioch Review* 17 (Fall 1957): 275-90.

Berger, J. 1977. *Nuclear Power: The Unviable Option.* New York: Dell.

Berger, M. "Organization Coup d'Etat: The Unexpected Social Movement for Succession." Xerox. Nashville, TN: Vanderbilt University, Department of Sociology, 1975.

Bergerson, F.A. 1980. *The Army Gets an Air Force: Tactics of Insurgent Bureaucratic Politics.* Baltimore: Johns Hopkins University Press.

Bernstein, P.W. "A Nuclear Fiasco Shakes the Bond Market." *Fortune Magazine* (February 22, 1982): 100-112.

"The Big Board's New Mr. Big." *Newsweek* (May 10, 1976): 85-86.

Blackmer, D., & Tarrow, S., Eds. 1975. *Communism in Italy and France.* Princeton, NJ: Princeton University Press.

Blake, J. "Abortion and Public Opinion: The 1960-1970 Decade." *Science* 171 (1971): 540-49.

Blake, J., & Del Pinal, J.H. "Negativism, Equivocations, and Wobbly Assent: Public 'Support' for the Pro-Choice Platform on Abortion." *Demography* 18 (August 1981): 309-20.

Blake, J.A. "A Case Study of Resistance in 'Total Institutions': The American Military During the War in Vietnam." Paper presented at the meeting of the Southern Sociological Society, April 9, 1976, Miami, FL.

Blumer, H. "Social Problems as Collective Behavior." *Social Problems* 18 (1971): 298-305.

———. "Social Movements." In *Principles of Sociology,* ed. A. M. Lee. New York: Barnes & Noble, 1955, pp. 99-220.

_____. "Public Opinion and Public Opinion Polling." *American Sociological Review* 13 (October 1948): 542-49.

_____. "Collective Behavior." In *A New Outline of the Principles of Sociology,* ed. A. M. Lee. New York: Barnes & Noble, 1946, pp. 167-219.

Bonacich, E. "Advanced Capitalism and Black/White Race Relations in the United States: A Split Labor Market Interpretation." *American Sociological Review* 41(1) (February 1976): 34-51.

Bord, R.J., & Faulkner, J.E. 1983. *The Catholic Charismatics: The Anatomy of a Modern Religious Movement.* University Park, PA: Pennsylvania State University Press.

Bottomore, T. 1979. *Political Sociology.* New York: Harper & Row.

Bowen, D., Bowen, E., Gawiser, S., & Masotti, S. "Deprivation, Mobility and Orientation Toward Protest of the Urban Poor." In *Riots and Rebellion: Civil Violence in the Urban Community,* ed. L. Masotti and D. Bowen. Beverly Hills, CA: Sage, 1968, pp. 187-200.

Bowles, S., & Gintis, H. 1977. *Schooling in Capitalist America.* New York: Basic Books.

Boyte, H.C. 1980. *The Backyard Revolution.* Philadelphia: Temple University Press.

Bradburn, N., & Caplowitz, D. 1964. *Reports on Happiness.* Chicago: Aldine.

Braverman, H. 1975. *Labor and Monopoly Capital.* Monthly Review Press.

Breton, A., & Breton, R. "An Economic Theory of Social Movements." *American Economic Review. Papers and Proceedings of the American Economic Association* 59(2) (May 1969).

Brint, S. "'New Class' and Cumulative Trend Explanation of the Liberal Political Attitudes of Professionals." *American Journal of Sociology* 90 (1) (May 1984): 30-71.

Britt, D., & Galle, O. "Industrial Conflict and Unionization." *American Sociological Review* 37(1) (1972): 46-57.

Brody, C. J. "Differences by Sex in Support for Nuclear Power." *Social Forces* 63 (1) (September 1984): 209-28.

Bromley, D., & Shupe, A. D., Jr. "Repression and the Decline of Social Movements: The Case of the New Religions." In *Social Movements of the Sixties and Seventies,* ed. J. Freeman. New York: Longman, 1983, pp. 335-47.

_____. 1981. *Strange Gods.* Boston, MA: Beacon Press.

_____. "Financing for the New Religions: A Resource Mobilization Approach." *Journal for the Scientific Study of Religion* 19 (1980): 227-39.

Bromley, D., Shupe, A.D., Jr., & Busching, Bruce C. "Repression of Religious 'Cults.'" In *Research in Social Movements, Conflict, and Change,* Vol. 4, ed. L. Kriesberg. Greenwich, CT: JAI Press, 1981, pp. 25-45.

Brown, L. "Hunger U.S.A.: The Public Pushes Congress." *Journal of Health and Social Behavior* 11 (June 1970): 115-25.

Brown, W. "NAACP Votes to Strip Name from Longtime Civil Rights Ally." *Washington Post* (June 26, 1979): A5.

Bruce-Briggs, B. 1979., Ed. *The New Class?* New York: McGraw-Hill.

Bucher, R., & Strauss, A. "Professions in Process." *American Journal of Sociology* 66 (December 1961): 325-34.

Bupp, I.C., and Derian, J. 1978. *Light Water: How the Nuclear Dream Dissolved.* New York: Basic Books.

Burawoy, M. "Consciousness and Contradiction: A Study of Student Protest in Zambia." *British Journal of Sociology* 27(1) (March 1976): 78-98.

Bureau of the Census. *The Statistical Abstract of the U.S.* Washington, DC: U.S. Department of Commerce, U.S. Government Printing Office, 1970.

Burks, R.V. 1961. *The Dynamics of Communism in Eastern Europe.* Princeton, NJ: Princeton University Press.

Burnham, D. "Pronuclear Groups Seek Citizen Action." *New York Times* (December 26, 1979): 1.

Burnham, W.D. "The Changing Shape of the American Political Universe." *American Political Science Review* 59(1) (1965): 7-38.

Burns, T. "The Reference of Conduct in Small Groups: Cliques and Cabals in Occupational Milieux.'" *Human Relations* 8 (November 1955): 467-86.

_____. "Micro-Politics: Mechanisms of Institutional Change." *Administrative Science Quarterly* 3 (December 1961): 257-81.

Burstein, P. "The Sociology of Democratic Politics and Government." *Annual Review of Sociology* 7 (1981): 231-319.

Business Week. (March 1979): 107.

Cable, Sherry. "Professionalization in Social Movement Organization: A Case of Pennsylvanians for Biblical Majority." *Sociological Focus,* 17 (October 1984): 287-304.

Campaign for Political Rights. *Organizing Guide* (pamphlet). Washington, DC, 1979.

Campbell, A. "The Passive Citizen." *Acta Sociologia* 6 (1962): 9-21.

Campbell, A., Converse, P.E., Miller, W.E., & Stokes, D.E. 1960. *The American Voter.* New York: Wiley.

Cantril, H. 1941. *The Psychology of Social Movements.* New York: Wiley.

_____.1965. *The Pattern of Human Concern.* New Brunswick, NJ: Rutgers University Press.

Cardoza, T. "Agrarian Elites and the Origins of Italian Fascism: The Province of Bologna, 1901-1922." Ph.D. dissertation, Department of History, Princeton University, 1975.

Carey, C.M. n.d. *YMCA Boards and Committee of Management.* New York: Association Press.

_____. "Perspectives for YMCA Growth in the 1960s." In *1959 YMCA Year Book.* New York: Association Press.

Carey, C.M., & Reece, S.M., Eds. 1962. *1962 YMCA Year Book and Official Roster.* New York: Association Press.

Carroll, M. "Revitalization Movements and Social Structure: Some Quantitative Tests." *American Sociological Review* 40(3) (June 1975): 389-401.

Carter, H., III. 1959. *The South Strikes Back.* Garden City, NJ: Doubleday.

Carter, R. "The Myth of Increasing Non-Work U.S. Work Activities." *Social Problems* 18(1) (1970): 52-66.

Chalmers, D.M. 1965. *Hooded Americanism.* New York: Doubleday & Co.

Chandler, A.D., Jr. 1977. *The Visible Hand: The Managerial Revolution in American Business.* Cambridge, MA: Harvard University Press.

_____. 1962. *Strategy and Structure: Chapters in the History of the Industrial Enterprise.* Cambridge, MA: MIT Press.

Chapin, F.S., & Tsouderos, J. "The Formalization Process in Voluntary Organizations." *Social Forces* 34 (May 1956): 342-44.

Chirot, D., & Hall, T.D. "World-System Theory." *Annual Review of Sociology* (8) (1982): 81-106.

Christian Science Monitor (April 26, 1971): B6.

Cicchetti, C.J., Freeman, A.M., III, Haveman, R.H., & Knetsch, J.L. "On the Economics of Mass Demonstrations: A Case Study of the November 1969 March on Washington." *American Economic Review* 61 (4) (September 1971): 719-24.

Cicourel, A., & Kitsuse, J. 1963. *The Educational Decision-Makers.* Indianapolis, IN: Bobbs-Merrill.

Clark, B. "Organizational Adaptation and Precarious Values: A Case Study." *American Sociological Review* 21 (June 1956): 327-36.

Clark, P.B., & Wilson, J.Q. "Incentive Systems: A Theory of Organizations." *Administrative Science Quarterly* 6 (September 1961): 129-66.

Clymer, A. "Nuclear Freeze Issue Puzzles U.S. Politicians." *International Herald Tribune* (July 7, 1982): 1.

Cohen, J. "Is Business Meeting the Challenge of Urban Affairs?" *Harvard Business Review* 48(2) (1970): 68-82.

Cohen, R.L. "Understanding a Trillion-Dollar Question." *National Review* (February 20, 1979): 10-15.

Coleman, J. 1961. *The Adolescent Society.* Glencoe, IL: Free Press.

Collins, R. 1982. *Sociological Insight.* New York: Oxford University Press.

Committee for Energy Awareness. *Energy Action* (pamphlet). Washington, DC, 1980.

Connolly, W.E. 1969. *The Bias of Pluralism.* New York: Atherton.

Conover, P.J., & Gray, V. 1983. *Feminism and the New Right: Conflict Over the American Family.* New York: Praeger.

Converse, P.E. "Of Time and Partisan Stability." *Comparative Political Studies* 2 (2) (July 1969): 139-71.

Cook, C.E. 1980. *Nuclear Power and Legal Advocacy.* Lexington, MA: Heath.

Cook, R. "Memo to Nuclear Energy Women." Mimeograph. Washington, DC: Nuclear Energy Women, 1979.

Coser, L.A. 1970. *Men of Ideas.* New York: Free Press.

_____. 1956. *The Functions of Social Conflict.* New York: Free Press.

Crawford, A. 1980. *Thunder on the Right.* New York: Pantheon Books.

Crawford, T.J., & Naditch, M. "Relative Deprivation, Powerlessness, and Militancy: The Psychology of Social Protest." *Psychiatry* 33 (May 1970): 208-23.

Critical Mass Bulletin, Vol. 1. University of Tennessee, 1973-74.

Cronin, J.E. 1980. *Industrial Conflict in Modern Britain.* London: Croon Helm.

Crouch, C., & Pizzorno, A. 1978. *The Resurgence of Class Conflict in Western Europe Since 1968,* Vol I. *National Studies,* Vol. II, *Comparative Studies.* London: Macmillan.

Crozier, M. 1964. *The Bureaucratic Phenomenon.* Chicago: University of Chicago Press.

Culver, D.W. 1963. *Negro Segregation in the Methodist Church.* New Haven, CT: Yale University Press.

Curtis, R.L., Jr., & Zurcher, L.A. "Stable Resources of Protest Movements: The Multi-Organizational Field." *Social Forces* 52 (1973): 53-61.

Cyert, R., & March, J. 1963. *A Behavioral Theory of the Firm.* Englewood Cliffs, NJ: Prentice-Hall.

Dahl, R., Ed. 1966. *Political Oppositions in Western Democracies.* New Haven, CT: Yale University Press.

Daniels, A.K., & Kahn-Hut, R., Eds. 1970. *Academics on the Line.* San Francisco: Jossey-Bass.

Dedmon, E. 1957. *Great Enterprises: 100 Years of the YMCA of Metropolitan Chicago*. Chicago: Rand McNally.

"Defense: Ernest Fitzgerald RIF." *Newsweek* (November 17, 1969): 106-8.

Del Sesto, S.L. 1979. *Science, Politics, and Controversy: Civilian Nuclear Power in the United States, 1946-1974*. Boulder, CO: Westview.

Demerath, N.J., III, Marwell, G., & Aiken, M. 1971. *Dynamics of Idealism*. San Francisco: Jossey-Bass.

Dodgett, L.L. 1896. *The Founding of the Association, 1844-1855. History of the Young Men's Christian Association*, Vol. I. New York: International Committee of Young Men's Christian Association.

Dollard, J. 1957. *Caste and Class in a Southern Town*. New York: Doubleday.

Domhoff, G.W. 1974. *The Bohemian Grove and Other Retreats*. New York: Harper and Row.

Donovan, J.C. 1970. *The Politics of Poverty*. Indianapolis: Pegasus.

Douglas, M., & Wildavsky, A. 1982. *Risk and Culture: An Essay on the Selection of Technological and Environmental Dangers*. Berkeley, CA: University of California Press.

Downs, A. "Up and Down with Ecology—the Issue Attention Cycle." *Public Interest* 28 (Summer 1972): 38-50.

———. 1957. *An Economic Theory of Democracy*. New York: Harper & Bros.

Draper, H. 1966. *The New Student Revolt*. New York: Grove Press.

Draper, T. 1957. *The Roots of American Communism*. New York: Viking Press.

Dubofsky, M. 1969. *We Shall Be All*. Chicago: Quadrangle Books.

Dulles, F.R. 1940. *America Learns to Play: A History of Popular Recreation 1607-1940*. New York: D. Appleton-Century.

Dunn, J. 1979. *Western Political Theory in the Face of the Future*. Cambridge: Cambridge University Press.

Dunne, J.G. 1967. *Delano*. New York: Farrar, Straus & Giroux.

Duverger, M. 1954. *Political Parties*. London: Methuen & Co.

———. 1963. *Political Parties*. New York: Wiley.

Edelman, M. 1967. *The Symbolic Uses of Politics*. Urbana, IL: University of Illinois Press.

Edelstein, J.D., & Warner, M. 1975. *Comparative Union Democracy: Organizations and Opposition in British and American Unions*. New York: Halstedt.

Edsall, T.B. 1984. *The New Politics of Inequality*. New York: W.W. Norton.

Edwards, P.K. 1981. *Strikes in the United States: 1881-1974*. Oxford: Basil Blackwell.

Edwards, R. 1979. *Contested Terrain: The Transformation of the Workplace in the Twentieth Century*. New York: Basic Books.

Encyclopedia of Associations, 4th and 5th eds. Detroit: Gale Research, 1964 and 1969.

Engelmann, L. 1979. *In Temperance: The Lost War Against Liquor*. New York: Free Press.

Epstein, I. "Specialization, Professionalization, and Social Worker Radicalism: A Test of the Process Model of the Professions." *Applied Social Studies* 2(3) (October 1970): 155-63.

Etzioni, A. 1961. *A Comparative Analysis of Complex Organizations: On Power, Involvement, and Their Correlates*. Glencoe, IL: Free Press.

———. 1968. *The Active Society*. New York: Free Press.

Evan, W. "Superior-Subordinate Conflict in Research Organizations." *Administrative Science Quarterly* 10(1) (1965): 52-64.

_____. Ed. 1978. *Inter-Organizational Relations: Selected Readings.* Philadelphia: University of Pennsylvania Press.

Faltermeyer, E. "Nuclear Power after Three Mile Island." *Fortune Magazine* (May 7, 1979): 114-22.

Faubert, E.F. "Mr. YMCA Secretary." Mimeograph. 1961.

Fendrich, J., & Tarlau, A.T. "Marching to a Different Drummer: Occupational and Political Correlates of Former Student Activists." *Social Forces* 52 (December 1973): 245-53.

Final Report of the National Commission on Causes and Prevention of Violence: To Establish Justice, to Insure Domestic Tranquility. New York: Bantam Books (1970).

Fireman, B., & Gamson, W.A. "Utilitarian Logic in the Resource Mobilization Perspective." In *The Dynamics of Social Movements,* ed. Mayer N. Zald & John D. McCarthy. Cambridge, MA: Winthrop, 1979, pp. 8-44.

Firey, W. "Informal Organization and the Theory of The Schism." *American Sociological Review* 13 (February 1948): 15-24.

Foundation News. Foundation Library Center, Baltimore, MD.

Frank. R. "Media Taught Public to 'Revolt' Over Taxes." *San Diego Business Journal* (May 24, 1982a): 3.

_____. "The Tax Revolt as a Social Movement: Professionalization in Resource Mobilization." Unpublished paper Southwestern College and University of California, San Diego, C.A., 1982b.

Frankel, G. "Common Cause Racked by Conflict in Reorganization." *Washington Post* (November 2, 1979): A-31.

Freeman, J. "Resource Mobilization and Strategy: A Model for Analyzing Social Movement Organization Actions." In *The Dynamics of Social Movements,* ed. Mayer N. Zald & John D. McCarthy. Cambridge, MA: Winthrop, 1979, pp. 167-69.

Fuchs, V.R. 1968. *The Service Economy.* New York: National Bureau of Economic Research.

Gale, R. "Social Movements and The State: The Environmental Movement and the Evolution of Natural Resources Bureaucracies." Unpublished manuscript, Department of Sociology, University of Oregon, 1982.

Gallup Opinion Index. *Religion in America, 1976,* Princeton, N.J. 1976 Report No. 130, p. 8.

Gamson, W.A. 1975. *The Strategy of Social Protest.* Homewood, IL: Dorsey.

_____. 1968. *Power and Discontent.* Homewood, IL: Dorsey.

_____. "Coalition Formation at Presidential Nominating Conventions." *American Journal of Sociology* 68 (September 1962): 157-72.

Garfinkle, A.M. 1984. *The Politics of the Nuclear Freeze.* Philadelphia: Foreign Policy Research Institute.

Garner, L., & Garner, R. "Problems of the Hegemonic Party: The PCI and the Limits of Structural Reform." *Science and Society* 45 (Fall 1981): 257-73.

Garner, R. 1977. *Social Movements in America.* Chicago: Rand McNally.

Gerlach, L., & Hine, V. 1970. *People, Power, and Change: Movements of Social Transformation.* Indianapolis, IN: Bobbs-Merrill.

Germond, J.W., & Witcover, J. 1980. *Blue Smoke and Mirrors: How Reagan Won and Why Carter Lost the Election of 1980.* New York: Viking Press.

Gerstl, J., & Jacobs, G. 1976. *Professions for the People: The Politics of Skill.* New York: Wiley.

Gerth, H.J., & Mills, C.W., Eds. 1946. *From Max Weber: Essays in Sociology.* New York: Oxford University Press.

Gilbert, N. 1970. *Clients or Constituents: Community Action in the War on Poverty.* San Francisco: Jossey-Bass.

Gitlin, T. 1980. *The Whole World is Watching: Mass Media in the Making and Unmaking of the New Left.* Berkeley, CA: University of California Press.

Glock, C.V., & Ringer, B.B. "Church Policy and the Attitudes of Ministers and Parishioners on Social Issues." *American Sociological Review* 2 (April 1956): 148-55.

Goldsmith, C. "The Student Peace Union." Unpublished manuscript, University of Chicago, 1965.

Goldsmith, M.W., & Shants, F.B. "Dealing with Site Occupations: A Viewpoint and Practical Recommendations." Mimeographed paper of the Atomic Industrial Forum, Washington, DC, 1978.

Goodman, R. 1982. *The Last Entrepreneurs.* Boston: South End Press.

Goodwin, R.K., & Mitchell, R.C. "The Implications of Direct Mail for Political Organization." Unpublished manuscript, Resources for the Future, Washington, DC, 1983.

Gorz, A. 1967. *Strategy for Labor.* Boston: Beacon Press.

Goulden, J.C. 1971. *The Money Givers.* New York: Random House.

Gouldner, A.W. "Metaphysical Pathos and the Study of Bureaucracy." *American Political Science Review* 49 (June 1955): 496-507.

――――. "Attitudes of Progressive Trade Union Leaders." *American Journal of Sociology* 52 (March 1947): 389-92.

Granberg, D., & Denny, D. "The Coathanger and the Rose: Comparison of Pro-Life Activists in Contemporary U.S." *Society* (May 1982).

Green, W. "Where are the Savios of Yesteryear?" *New York Times Magazine* 12 (1970): 6-9, 35-37.

Grinker, R. "Mentally Healthy Young Males." (Homoclites). *Archives of General Psychiatry* 6 (June 1962): 405-53.

――――. n.d. Personal conversation.

Gundelach, P. 1982a. "The New Middle-Layers, Grass-Roots Organizations and Alternative Values." Institute of Political Science, University of Aarhus, Aarhus, Denmark.

――――. 1982b. "Grass-Roots Organizations, Societal Control, and Dissolution of Norms." *Acta Sociologica* 25 (supplement): 57-65.

Gurr, T.R. 1970. *Why Men Rebel.* Princeton, NJ: Princeton University Press.

――――. 1972. *Politimetrics: An Introduction to Quantitative Macropolitics.* Englewood Cliffs, NJ: Prentice-Hall.

Gusfield, J. "Historical Problematics and Sociological Fields: American Liberalism and the Study of Social Movements." *Research in Sociology of Knowledge* 1 (1978): 121-49.

――――. 1969. *Symbolic Crusade.* Urbana: University of Illinois Press.

――――. "Social Movements and Social Change: Perspectives of Linearity and Fluidity." In *Research in Social Movements, Conflict, and Change*, Vol. 4, (1981) ed. L. Kriesberg. Greenwich, CT: JAI Press, pp. 317-39.

――――. "Functional Areas of Social Movement Leadership." *Sociological Quarterly* 7 (1966): 137-56.

――――. "The Problems of Generations in an Organizational Structure." *Social Forces* 35 (May 1957): 323-30.

Gyorgy, A., & friends. 1979. *No Nukes: Everyone's Guide to Nuclear Power*. Boston: South End Press.

Hadden, J.K. 1969. *Gathering Storm in the Churches*. New York: Doubleday.

Hadden, J.K., & Swann, C.E. 1981. *Prime Time Preachers: The Rising Power of Televangelism*. Reading, MA: Addison-Wesley.

Halloran, R. "The Idea That Politics Is Everybody's Business." *New York Times* (March 7, 1971): sec. 4, p. 3.

Handler, J. 1978. *Social Movements and the Legal System*. New York: Academic Press.

Hannan, M.T. "The Dynamics of Ethnic Boundaries in Modern States." In *National Development and the World System*, ed. J.W. Meyer & M.T. Hannan. Chicago: University of Chicago Press, 1979.

Harding, S. "World Consuming Rhetoric: The Movement Behind the Moral Majority." Unpublished manuscript, University of Michigan, Department of Anthropology, Ann Arbor, MI: 1985.

_____. 1983. *Reverend Jerry Falwell and the Moral Majority: Origins of a Movement*. Unpublished manuscript, University of Michigan, Department of Anthropology, 1984.

Harrington, M. 1968. *Toward a Democratic Left: A Radical Program for a New Majority*. New York: Macmillan.

Harrison, P.M. 1959. *Authority and Power in the Free Church Tradition*. Princeton, NJ: Princeton University Press.

Hausknecht, M. 1962. *The Joiners*. New York: Bedminster Press.

Heard, J. "Friends of the Earth Give Environmental Interests an Activist Voice." *National Journal* (August 8, 1970): 1712-18.

Heberle, R. "Types and Functions of Social Movements." In *International Encyclopedia of the Social Sciences*, Vol. 14, ed. David Sills. New York: Macmillan, 1968, pp. 438-44.

_____. 1951. *Social Movements: An Introduction to Political Sociology*. New York: Appleton-Century Co.

_____. 1945. *From Democracy to Nazism: A Regional Case Study on Political Parties in Germany*. Baton Rouge, LA: Louisiana State University Press.

Heilbroner, R. 1974. *An Inquiry into the Human Prospect*. New York: W.W. Norton.

Heirich, M. "Change of Heart: A Test of Some Widely Held Theories about Religious Conversion." *American Journal of Sociology* 83 (November 1977): 653-80.

_____. 1971. *The Spiral of Conflict: Berkeley, 1964*. New York: Columbia University Press.

Helfgot, J. "Professional Reform Organizations and the Symbolic Representation of the Poor." *American Sociological Review* 39(4) (1974): 475-91.

Hentoff, N. 1963. *Peace Agitator: The Story of A.J. Muste*. New York: Macmillan.

Herbers, J. "Women Turn View to Public Office." *New York Times* (June 28, 1982): A-1.

Hesseltine, W.B. 1962. *Third-Party Movements in the United States*. Princeton, NJ: Van Nostrand.

Hibbs, D.A., Jr. "On the Demand for Economic Outcomes: Macroeconomic Performance and Mass Political Support in the United States, Great Britain, and Germany." *Journal of Politics* 44 (May 1982): 426-62.

_____. "Political Parties and Macroeconomic Policy." *American Political Science Review* 71 (December 1977): 1467-87.

_____. "On the Political Economy of Long-Run Trends in Strike Activity." *British Journal of Political Science* 8 (April 1978): 153-75.

_____. "Industrial Conflict in Advanced Industrial Societies." *American Political Science Review* 70 (December 1976): 1033-58.

_____. "Long-Run Trends in Strike Activity in Comparative Perspective." Monograph. Center for International Studies, Massachusetts Institute of Technology (August 1976): 72 pp.

_____. "Economic Interest and the Politics of Macroeconomic Policy." Monograph. Center for International Studies, Massachusetts Institute of Technology (1975): 88 pp.

Hickson, D.J., Hinings, C.R., Lee, C.A., Smeck, R.E., & Pennings, J.M. "A Strategic Contingencies Theory of Intraorganizational Power." *Administrative Science Quarterly* 16 (June 1971): 216-29.

Hirsch, E. "Chicago Radicals." Ph.D. dissertation, University of Chicago, 1979.

Hirschmann, A.O. 1982. *Shifting Involvements: Private Interests and Public Actions.* Princeton, NJ: Princeton University Press.

_____. 1970. *Exit, Voice, and Loyalty: Responses to Decline in Firms, Organizations, and States.* Cambridge, MA: Harvard University Press.

"His Master's New Voice." *Newsweek* (November 17, 1975): 79-81.

Hobsbawm, E.J. 1965. *Primitive Rebels: Studies in Archaic Forms of Social Movement in the 19th and 20th Centuries.* New York: W.W. Norton.

_____. "Labour Traditions." In *Labouring Men.* New York: Basic Books, 1964.

Hodson, R., & Kaufman, R.L. "Economic Dualism: A Critical Review." *American Sociological Review* 47 (December 1982): 727-39.

Hofstadter, R. 1963. *Anti-Intellectualism in American Life.* New York: Knopf.

_____. 1955. *The Age of Reform.* New York: Random House.

Hoge, D.R. 1968. *Division in the Protestant House.* Philadelphia: Westminster Press.

Hoge, D.R., Potvin, R.H., & Ferry, K.M. 1984. *Research on Men's Vocations to the Priesthood and Religious Life.* Washington, DC: United States Catholic Conference.

Hoge, D.R., & Roozen, D.A. 1979. *Understanding Church Growth and Decline, 1950-1978.* New York: Pilgrim Press.

Hopkins, C.H. 1950. *History of the YMCA in North America.* New York: Association Press.

Hough, P. "How the Directors Kept Singer Stitched Together." *Fortune* (December 1975): 100.

Hubbard, H. "Five Long Hot Summers and How They Grew." *Public Interest* 12 (Summer 1968): 3-24.

Hyman, H., & Wright, C.R. "Trends in Voluntary Association Memberships of American Adults." *American Sociological Review* 3 (1971): 191-206.

Ikle, F.C. 1971. *Every War Must End.* New York: Columbia University Press.

Info June, 1980, 143 "Suit Filed Against Seabrook Protestors" Washington, D.C.: Atomic Industrial Forum.

Jackson, K.T. 1967. *The Ku Klux Klan in the City, 1915-1930.* New York: Oxford University Press.

Jaffe, F.S., Lindheim, B.L., & Lee, P.R. 1981. *Abortion Politics: Private Morality and Public Policy.* New York: McGraw-Hill.

Jenkins, C.J. Forthcoming. *Patrons of Social Reform: Private Foundations and the Social Movement of the 1960s and 1970s.* New York: Russell Sage.

_____. "Socio-Political Movements." In *Handbook of Political Science*, ed. Samuel Long. New York: Plenum Press, 1981.

_____. "Radical Transformation of Organizational Goals." *Administrative Science Quarterly* 22 (December 1977): 568-86.

Jenkins, C., & Perrow, C. "Insurgency of the Powerless: Farm Workers Movements (1946-72)." *American Sociological Review* 42(2) (1977): 249-67.

Jonas, G. 1971. *On Doing Good: The Quaker Experiment*. New York: Charles Scribner's Sons.

Kahn, S. 1970. *How People Get Power: Organizing Oppressed Communities for Action*. New York: McGraw-Hill.

Kanter, R.M. 1977. *Men and Women of the Corporation*. New York: Basic Books.

_____. 1972. *Commitment and Community: Communes and Utopias in Sociological Perspective*. Cambridge, MA: Harvard University Press.

Kaslow, F., & Sussman, M., Eds. 1982. *Cults and Families*. New York: Haworth Press.

Katz, H. 1974. *Give! Who Gets Your Charity Dollar?* Garden City, NJ: Doubleday.

Kearns, K.D. "Citizen Action: A Key in the Nuclear Controversy." Mimeographed paper of Water Reactor Division, Westinghouse Electric Corporation, Pittsburgh, n.d.

Kelman, S. 1970. *Push Comes to Shove: The Escalation of Student Protest*. Boston: Houghton Mifflin.

Kenniston, K. 1968. *Young Radicals*. New York: Harcourt, Brace & World.

Kerr, C., & Siegel, A. "The Interindustry Propensity to Strike: An International Comparison." In *Industrial Conflict*, ed. Arthur W. Kornhauser, Robert Dubin, & Arthur M. Ross. New York: McGraw-Hill, 1954, pp. 189-212.

Kick, E. "World System Properties and Mass Political Conflict Within Nations: Theoretical Framework." *Journal of Political and Military Sociology* 8(2) (Fall 1980): 175-90.

Killian, L. "The Significance of Extremism in the Black Revolution." *Social Problems* 20 (Summer 1972): 41-48.

King, C.W. 1956. *Social Movements in the United States*. New York: Random House.

Klanderman, B., & Oegema, D. "Mobilizing for Peace: The 1983 Peace Demonstration in The Hague." Paper presented at the Annual Meeting of the American Sociological Association, 1984, San Antonio, TX.

Kohn, H. "The National Rifle Association." *Rolling Stone* 343 (May 14, 1981): 19-25.

Kolko, G. 1963. *The Triumph of Conservatism? A Reinterpretation of American History, 1900-1916*. Glencoe, IL: Free Press.

Kornhauser, W. 1962. *Scientists in Industry: Conflict and Accommodation*. New York: Wiley.

Krause, E.A. 1971. *The Sociology of Occupations*. Boston: Little, Brown.

Kriesberg, L. 1982. *Social Conflicts*, 2nd ed. Englewood Cliffs, NJ: Prentice-Hall.

Krueger, T.A. 1967. *And Promises to Keep: The Southern Conference for Human Welfare, 1938-1948*. Nashville: Vanderbilt University Press.

Kuhn, J.W. 1962. *Bargaining and the Grievance Process*. New York: Columbia University Press.

Kurtz, L.R. "The Politics of Heresy." *American Journal of Sociology* 88 (May 1983): 1085-1115.

Kyvig, D.E. 1979. *Repealing National Prohibition*. Chicago: University of Chicago Press.

Lacouture, J. 1968. *Ho Chi Minh.* New York: Vintage Books.

Lader, L. 1973. *Abortion: Making the Revolution.* Boston: Beacon Press.

Lakey, G., & Oppenheimer, M. 1965. *Manual for Direct Action.* Chicago: Quadrangle Books.

Lammers, C.J. "Tactics and Strategies Adopted by University Authorities to Counter Student Opposition." In *The Dynamics of University Protest,* ed. Donald W. Light. Chicago: Nelson Hall, 1977.

_____. "Strikes and Mutinies: A Comparative Study of Organizational Conflicts Between Rulers and Ruled." *Administrative Science Quarterly* 14 (December 1969): 558-72.

Lanctôt, C.A., M.C. Martin and M. Shivandan, eds. 1984. *Natural Family Planning: Development of National Program.* Washington, DC: International Federation for Family Life Promotion.

Landsman, G. "Comment on Carroll, ASR, June 1979, The Ghost Dance, and the Policy of Land Allotment." *American Sociological Review* 44 (February 1979): 162-66.

Lane, D.A. 1984. *Foundations for a Social Theology.* New York: Paulist Press.

Lang, K., & Lang, G. 1961. *Collective Dynamics.* New York: Thomas Crowell.

Lawson, R. "He Who Pays the Piper: The Consequences of Their Income Sources for Social Movement Organizations." Paper delivered at the Annual Meeting of the American Sociological Association, 1978, San Francisco, CA.

Leeds, R. "The Absorption of Protest: A Working Paper." In *New Perspectives in Organizational Research,* ed. W.W. Cooper, H.J. Leavitt, & M.W. Shelly II. New York: Wiley, 1964, pp. 115-35.

Leites, N., & Wolf, C., Jr. 1970. *Rebellion and Authority.* Chicago: Markham.

Lenin, V.I. 1929. *What Is To Be Done?* New York: International Publishers.

LeRoy Ladurie, E. 1979. *Montaillou.* New York: Vintage Books.

Levine, S., & W., P.A. "Exchange as a Conceptual Framework for the Study of Interorganizational Relationships." *Administrative Science Quarterly* 15 (1961): 583-601.

Levitan, S.A. "Community Action Programs: A Strategy to Fight Poverty." *Annals of the American Academy of Political and Social Science* 385 (1969): 63-75.

Levy, S. "The Psychology of Political Activity." *Annals* 391 (September 1970): 83-96.

Lieberson, S., & O'Connor, J.F. "A Study of Large Corporations." *American Sociological Review* 37 (April 1972): 117-240.

Liebman, R.C. "Mobilizing the Moral Majority." In *The New Christian Right: Mobilization and Legitimation,* ed. R.C. Liebman & R. Wuthnow. New York: Aldine, 1983.

Lin, N. "The McIntire March: A Study of Recruitment and Commitment." *Public Opinion Quarterly* 38 (Winter 1974-75): 562-73.

Lindblom, C.E. 1968. *The Policy-Making Process.* Englewood Cliffs, NJ: Prentice-Hall.

Linder, S.B. 1970. *The Harried Leisure Class.* New York: Columbia University Press.

Linenwebber, C. "Working Class Communities." Paper delivered at the annual meeting of Society for Study of Social Problems, 1980, New York.

Lipset, S.M. 1960. *Political Man.* New York: Doubleday.

_____. 1959. *Agrarian Socialism: The Cooperatiive Commonwealth Federation in Saskatchewan: A Study in Political Sociology.* Berkeley: University of California Press.

Lipset, S.M., & Altbach, P.G., Eds. 1969. *Students in Revolt*. Boston: Houghton Mifflin.

Lipset, S.M., & Dobson, R.B. "The Intellectual as Critic and Rebel: With Special Reference to the United States and the Soviet Union." *Daedalus* 101 (Summer 1972): 137-98.

Lipset, S.M., & Ladd, C.E., Jr. "College Generations—from the 1930s to the 1960s." *Public Interest* 25 (Fall 1971).

_____. "And What Professors Think." *Psychology Today* 4 (November 1970): 49-51.

Lipset, S.M., & Raab, E. 1970. *The Politics of Unreason: Right-Wing Extremism in America, 1790-1970*. New York: Harper & Row.

Lipset, S.M., Trow, M., & Coleman, J. 1956. *Union Democracy: The Inside Politics of the International Typographical Union*. Glencoe, IL: Free Press.

Lipsky, M. "Protest as a Political Resource." *American Political Science Review* 62 (December 1968): 1144-58.

Litwak, E., & Hylton, L. "Interorganizational Analysis: A Hypothesis on Coordinating Agencies." *Administrative Science Quarterly* 6 (1962): 395-420.

Lo, C.Y.H. "Countermovements and Conservative Movements in the Contemporary U.S." In *Annual Review of Sociology* 8. Palo Alto, CA: Annual Reviews, Inc., 1982, pp. 107-34.

Lofland, J. "The Youth Ghetto." In *The Logic of Social Hierarchies*, ed. E.O. Laumann, P.M. Siegel, and R.W. Hodge. Chicago: Markham, 1970.

Long, E.N. "Politics as an Ecology of Games." *American Journal of Sociology* 64 (November 1960): 251-61.

_____. "The Local Community as an Ecology of Games." *American Journal of Sociology* 64 (1958): 251-61.

Lowi, T.J. 1971. *The Politics of Disorder*. New York: Basic Books.

Luker, K. 1984. *Abortion and the Politics of Motherhood*. Berkeley: University of California Press.

Luttwak, E. 1969. *Coup d'Etat: A Practical Handbook*. New York: Knopf.

Lyng, S. G., & Kurtz, L.R. "Bureaucratic Insurgency: The Vatican and the Crisis of Modernism." *Social Forces* 63 (June 1985): 901-22.

Mallet, S. 1975. *Essays on the New Working Class*, ed. and translated by Dick Howard & Dean Savage. St. Louis: Telos Press.

_____. 1969. *La Nouvelle Classe Ouvrière*. Paris: Edition du Seuil.

Management Consultant Report to the Chicago YMCA, Chicago, IL. n.d.

Mandel, E. 1978. *Late Capitalism*. London: NLB.

Mann, J. "Hard Times for the ACLU." *The New Republic* 178 (15) (April 15, 1978): 12-15.

Marshall, E. "St. Nader and His Evangelists." *The New Republic* 165 (1971): 13-14.

Marshall, T.H. 1965. *Class, Citizenship, and Social Development*. Garden City, NY: Doubleday.

Martin, G.T. "Organizing the Underclass: Findings on Welfare Rights," Working Paper No. 17. Human Side of Poverty Project, Department of Sociology, State University of New York at Stony Brook, 1971.

_____. "Welfare Recipient Activism: Some Findings on the National Welfare Rights Organization." Paper presented at the annual meeting of the Midwest Political Science Association, April 26, 1974, Chicago, IL.

Martin, J.B. 1954. *Break down the Walls—American Prisons: Present, Past, and Future*. New York: Ballantine.

Marx, G.T. "External Efforts to Damage or Facilitate Social Movements: Some

Patterns, Explanations, Outcomes, and Complications." In *The Dynamics of Social Movements, Resource Mobilization, Social Control & Tactics*, ed. Mayer N. Zald & John D. McCarthy. Cambridge, MA: Winthrop, 1979, pp. 94-125.

_____. "Thoughts on a Neglected Category of Social Movement Participant: The Agent Provocateur and the Informant." *American Journal of Sociology* 80 (September 1974): 402-42.

_____. "Issueless Riots." *Annals* 391 (September 1970): 21-33.

_____. 1967. *Protest and Prejudice*. New York: Harper & Row.

Marx, G.T., & Useem, M.M. "Majority Involvement in Minority Movements: Civil Rights, Abolition, Untouchability." *Journal of Social Issues* 27 (January 1971): 81-104.

Marx, G.T., & Wood, J. "Strands of Theory and Research in Collective Behavior." *Annual Review of Sociology* 1 (1975): 363-428.

Mattick, H.W. n.d. Personal communication.

Mayer, A. 1971. *Dynamics of Counterrevolution in Europe, 1870-1956: An Analytic Framework*. New York: Harper & Row.

Mazur, A. 1981. *The Dynamics of Technical Controversy*. Washington, DC : Communication Press.

McAdam, D. "Tactical Innovation and the Pace of Insurgency." *American Sociological Review* 48 (December 1983): 735-53.

_____. 1982. *Political Process and the Development of Black Insurgency, 1930-1970*. Chicago: University of Chicago Press.

McAdam, D., & McCarthy, J.D. "The Professional Project: The Invention of Work Through Collective Action." Paper presented at the annual meetings of the Society for the Study of Social Problems, 1982, San Francisco.

McCarry, C. 1972. *Citizen Nader*. New York: Saturday Review Press.

McCarthy, J.D., & Hoge, D.R. "Mobilizing Believers: Toward a Model of Religious Recruitment." Paper delivered at the annual meeting of the American Sociological Association, 1978, San Francisco, CA.

McCarthy, J.D., & Zald, M.N. "Resource Mobilization and Social Movements: A Partial Theory." *American Journal of Sociology* 82 (May 1977): 1212-41.

_____. "Tactical Considerations in Social Movement Organizations." Paper delivered at the annual meeting of the American Sociological Association, August 1974, Montreal.

_____. 1973. *The Trend of Social Movements in America: Professionalization and Resource Mobilization*. Morristown, NJ: General Learning Press.

McCoy, D.R. 1958. *Angry Voices*. Lawrence, KS: University of Kansas Press.

McFarland, A.S. 1984. *Common Cause: Lobbying in the Public Interest*. Chatham, NJ: Chatham House.

_____. "The Complexity of Democratic Practice Within Common Cause." Paper delivered at the annual meetings of the American Political Science Association, 1976, Chicago, Il.

_____. 1976. *Public Interest Lobbies: Decision Making on Energy*. Washington, DC: American Enterprise Institute.

McIntosh, W.A., Alston, L.T., & Alston, J.P. "The Differential Impact of Religious Preference and Church Attendance on Attitudes Toward Abortion." *Review of Religious Research* 20 (Spring 1979): 195-213.

McMillen, N.R. 1971. *The Citizens' Council: Organized Resistance to the Second Reconstruction, 1954-64*. Urbana, IL: University of Illinois Press.

McNeil, K., & Thompson, J.D. "The Regeneration of Social Organizations." *American Sociological Review* 36 (August 1971): 24-37.

Meier, A., & Rudwick, E. 1973. *CORE: A Study in the Civil Rights Movement, 1948-1968.* New York: Oxford University Press.

_____. "Attorneys Black and White: A Case Study of Race Relations Within the NAACP." *Journal of American History* 62 (March 1976): 913-46.

Melucci, A. "Ten Hypotheses for the Analysis of New Movements." In *Contemporary Italian Sociology,* ed. D. Pinto. Cambridge: Cambridge University Press, 1981a, pp. 173-94.

_____. "New Movements, Terrorism, and the Political System: Reflections on the Italian Case." *Socialist Review* 56 (March-April 1981b): 97-136.

Messinger, S. "Organizational Transformation: A Case Study of a Declining Social Movement." *American Sociological Review* 20 (February 1955): 3-10.

Methodist Church. 1964. *Doctrines and Disciplines of the Methodist Church.* Nashville, TN: Methodist Publishing House.

Methodist Layman's Union. 1959. *A Pronouncement.* Southern Metropolis: Methodist Layman's Union.

Michels, R. 1949. *Political Parties.* Glencoe, IL: Free Press.

Milbrath, L.W. 1965. *Political Participation.* Chicago: Rand McNally.

Miller, N. "Formal Organizational Schismozenesis." Unpublished manuscript, Department of Sociology, University of Chicago, 1963.

Miller, W.D. 1974. *A Harsh and Dreadful Love: Dorothy Day and the Catholic Worker Movement.* Garden City, NJ: Image Books.

Miller, W.E., & Levitin, T.E. 1976. *Leadership and Change: The New Politics of the American Electorate.* Cambridge, MA: Winthrop.

Mills, C.W. "The New Left." In *Power, Politics, and People,* ed. Irving Louis Horowitz. New York: Ballantine Books, 1962, pp. 247-59.

_____. "The Social Role of Intellectuals." In *Power, Politics, and People,* ed. Irving Louis Horowitz. New York: Ballantine Books, 1962, pp. 292-304.

_____. 1951. *White Collar: The American Middle Class.* New York: Oxford University Press.

Mitchell, D., Mitchell, C., & Ofshe, R. 1980. *The Light on Synanon.* New York: Wideview Books.

Mitchell, R.C. "We are a Minority: People's Identification with Right to Life and Prochoice Positions in NARAL Foundation Surveys." Unpublished manuscript, Washington, D.C., Resources for the Future 1981.

_____. "National Environmental Lobbies and the Apparent Illogic of Collective Action." In *Collective Decision Making,* ed. C. Russell. Baltimore: Johns Hopkins University Press, 1979, pp. 87-135.

Mitchell, R.C., & Davies, C.J., III. "The United States Environmental Movement and Its Political Context: An Overview," Discussion Paper D-32. Washington, DC: Resources for the Future, 1978.

Mitchell, R.C., McCarthy, J.D., & Pearce, K. "The National Abortion Rights Action League Report on a Membership Survey." Unpublished report, Washington, DC, 1979.

Modigliani, A., & Gamson, W.A. "Thinking about Politics." *Political Behavior* 1 (June 1979): 5-30 Resources for the Future.

Molotch, H. "Oil in Santa Barbara and Power in America." *Sociological Inquiry* 40 (1970): 131-44.

Montgomery, W.D., & Quirk, J.P. "Cost Escalation in Nuclear Power." In *Perspec-*

tives on Energy, 2nd ed., ed. L.C. Ruedisili, and M.W. Firebaugh. New York: Oxford University Press, 1982.

Moore, W. 1967. *Order and Change*. New York: Wiley.

Morgan, J.N., Dye, R.F., & Hybels, J.H. 1975. *A Survey of Giving Behavior and Attitudes: A Report to Respondents*. Ann Arbor, MI: Institute for Social Research.

Morris, A.D. 1984. *The Origins of The Civil Rights Movement: Black Communities Organizing for Change*. New York: Free Press.

_____. "Black Southern Sit-In Movement: An Analysis of Internal Organization." *American Sociological Review* 46 (December 1981): 744-67.

_____. "The Pace of Insurgency: A Critique." 1985 Unpublished manuscript, University of Michigan, Ann Arbor.

Morris, B. "Consumerism Is Now a Luxury Item." *Washington Star* (October 28, 1975): 1-7.

Morrison, D.E. "Some Notes Toward Theory on Relative Deprivation, Social Movements, and Social Change." *American Behavioral Scientist* 14 (May-June 1971): 675-90.

Mottl, T.L. "The Analysis of Countermovements." *Social Problems* 27 (June 1980): 620-35.

Moynihan, D.P. 1969. *Maximum Feasible Misunderstanding: Community Action in the War on Poverty*. New York: Free Press.

Mueller, C. "In Search of a Constituency for the New Religious Right." *Public Opinion Quarterly* 47 (1983): 213-29.

Mueller, E. "A Test of a Partial Theory of Potential for Political Violence." *American Political Review* 66 (September 1972): 928-59.

Muench, M. "The American Socialist Movement: Organization and Adaptation." 1962 Unpublished manuscript, Department of Sociology, University of Chicago.

Mullaney, T.E. "6 on Genesco Board Plan Action Today to Oust Chairman." *New York Times* (January 3, 1977).

Nagel, E. 1961. *The Structure of Science: Problems in the Logic of Scientific Explanation*. New York: Harcourt, Brace & World.

Nagel, J. "Collective Action and Public Policy: American Indian Mobilization." *Social Science Journal* 19 (January 1982): 37-45.

Nagel, J., & Olzak, S. "Ethnic Mobilization in New and Old States: An Extension of the Competition Model." *Social Problems* 30(2) (December 1982): 127-43.

Nashville Tennessean. (May 5, 1972): 8.

Needleman, M., & Needleman, C.E. 1974. *Guerillas in the Bureaucracy: The Community Planning Experiment in the United States*. New York: Wiley.

Negandhi, A.R. 1969. *Interorganization Theory*. Kent, OH: Kent State University Press.

Neitz, M.J. "Slain in the Spirit." Ph.D. dissertation, University of Chicago, 1981.

Nelkin, D. 1984. *Controversy: The Politics of Technical Decisions*, 2nd ed. Beverly Hills, CA: Sage.

_____. 1982. *The Creationist Controversy*. New York: Norton.

Nelkin, D., & Pollak, M. 1981. *The Atom Besieged: Extraparliamentary Dissent in France and Germany*. Cambridge, MA: MIT Press.

Nelsen, H.M. "The Black Churches as a Politicizing Institution." *Sociological Inventory*, Trial Issue (April 1979): 30-31.

_____. "Social Movement Transformation and Pre-Movement Factor-Effect: A Preliminary Inquiry." *Sociological Quarterly* (Winter 1974): 127-42.

New York Times. "Social Action Hit by Financial Woes" (November 8, 1974): sec. 1, p. 20.

Nickel, H. "Talking Back to the Anti-Nukes." *Fortune Magazine* (January 28, 1980): 108-110.

Nie, N., Powell, G.B., & Prewitt, K. "Social Structure and Political Participation: Part I." *American Political Science Review* 63 (1969a): 361-78.

_____. "Social Structure and Political Participation: Part II." *American Political Science Review* 63 (1969b): 808-32.

Niebuhr, H.R. 1929. *The Social Sources of Denominationalism.* New York: Holt.

Nielsen, F. "Toward a Theory of Ethnic Solidarity in Modern Societies." *American Sociological Review* 50 (2) (April 1985): 133-49.

O.M. Collective. 1971. *The Organizer's Manual.* New York: Bantam Books.

Oberschall, A. 1973. *Social Conflict and Social Movements.* Englewood Cliffs, NJ: Prentice-Hall.

O'Connor, J. 1973. *The Fiscal Crisis of the State.* New York: St. Martin's.

Olson, M., Jr. 1965. *The Logic of Collective Action.* Cambridge, MA: Harvard University Press.

Olzak, S. "Contemporary Ethnic Mobilization." *Annual Review of Sociology* (1983): 355-74.

Orum, A.M. "A Reappraisal of the Social and Political Participation of Negroes." *American Journal of Sociology* 72 (1966): 32-46.

Orum, A.M., & Wilson, K.L. "Toward a Theoretical Model of Participation in Political Movements, I: Leftist Movements." Unpublished manuscript, Department of Sociology, University of Texas at Austin, 1975.

Osgood, C., & Tannenbaum, P. "The Principle of Congruity in the Prediction of Attitude Change." *Psychological Review* (1955): 42-55.

Paige, J. 1975. *Agrarian Revolution: Social Movements and Export Agriculture in the Underdeveloped World.* New York: Free Press.

Paradis, L.F. "The American Hospice Movement: A Resource Mobilization Perspective." Paper delivered at annual meetings of the Southern Sociological Society, 1985, Charlotte, NC.

Park, R.E. 1952. *Human Communities.* Glencoe, IL: Free Press.

Pearce, K. "Pro-Choice Organizational Structure: 1973-1980." Unpublished manuscript, Department of Sociology, Catholic University, Washington, DC, 1982a.

_____. "Survey Results from the South Dakota Right to Life Committee." Unpublished manuscript, Department of Sociology, Catholic University, Washington, DC, 1982b.

Perrow, C. 1984. *Normal Accidents: Living with High-Risk Technologies.* New York: Basic Books.

_____. 1972. *Complex Organizations: A Critical Essay.* Glenview, IL: Scott, Foresman.

_____. "Members as Resources in Voluntary Organizations." In *Organizations and Clients,* ed. W.R. Rosengren & M. Lefton. Columbus, OH: Merrill, 1970a, pp. 93-116.

_____. "Departmental Power and Perspectives in Industrial Firms." In *Power in Organizations,* ed. Mayer N. Zald. Nashville, TN: Vanderbilt University Press, 1970b, pp. 58-59.

_____. "Goals in Complex Organizations." *American Sociological Review* 26 (October 1961): 859-66.

Peterson, B. "ERA Leaves in Wake Potent Political Force Set for New Battles." *Washington Post* (June 27, 1982a): A-2.

_____. "Backers of Legalized Abortion, in Switch, Adopt Hardball Tactics." *Washington Post* (August 24, 1982b): A-2.

Peterson, R.E. 1968. *The Scope of Organizational Student Protest in 1967-68.* Princeton, NJ: Educational Testing Service.

Peterzell, Jay "Nuclear Power and Political Surveillance." *CNSS Report*

Petrocik, J.R. 1981. *Party Coalitions: Realignments in the Decline of the New Deal Party System.* Chicago: University of Chicago Press.

Pettigrew, A. 1973. *The Politics of Organizational Decision-Making.* London: Harper & Row.

Pfeffer, J. 1978. *Organizational Design.* Arlington Heights, IL: AHM Publishing Company.

_____. "Size and Composition of Corporate Boards of Directors: The Organization and Its Environment." *Administrative Science Quarterly* 16 (June 1972): 218-28.

Pfeffer, J., & Salancik, G. "Organizational Decision Making as a Political Process: The Case of the University Budget." *Administrative Science Quarterly* 19 (June 1974): 135-51.

Phillips, K.S. 1982. *Post-Conservative America: People, Politics and Ideologies in a Time of Crisis.* New York: Random House.

Pinard, M. 1971. *The Rise of a Third Party.* Englewood Cliffs, NJ: Prentice-Hall.

Piven, F.F. "The Social Structuring of Political Protest." *Politics and Society* 6 (3) (1976): 297-326.

Piven, F.F., & Cloward, R.A. "Social Movements and Societal Conditions: A Response to Roach and Roach." *Social Problems* 26 (December 1978): 172-78.

_____. 1977. *Poor People's Movements: How They Succeed, How They Fail.* New York: Vintage.

Polsby, N.W. 1983. *Consequences of Party Reform.* New York: Oxford University Press.

Pombeiro, B.G. "Recession Cripples Social Aid Groups." *Philadelphia Inquirer* (October 12, 1975): 1-2.

Pondy, L.R. "Budgeting and Intergroup Conflict in Organizations." *Pittsburgh Business Review* 34 (April 1964): 1-8.

Portes, A. "Political Primitivism, Differential Socialization, and Lower Class Leftist Radicalism." *American Sociological Review* 36 (5) (1971): 820-34.

Preston, S.H. "Children and the Elderly: Divergent Paths for America's Dependents." *Demography* 2 (4) (November 1982): 435-56.

Princeton Religion Research Center. *Emerging Trends* 4 (6) (1982): 5.

Przeworski, A. "Social Democracy as a Historical Phenomemon." *New Left Review* 122 (July-August 1980): 27-58.

Przeworski A., & Wallerstein M. "The Structure of Class Conflict in Democratic Capitalist Societies." *American Political Science Review* 76 (June 1982): 215-38.

Quarantelli, E.L., & Hundley, J.R. "A Test of Some Propositions About Crowd Formation and Behavior." In *Readings in Collective Behavior*, 2nd ed., ed. R.R. Evans. Chicago: Rand McNally, 1975, pp. 317-86.

Ramirez, F. "Comparative Social Movements." *International Journal of Comparative Sociology* 22 (1-2) (1981): 3-21.

Rapoport, A. 1960. *Fights, Games, & Debates.* Ann Arbor, MI: University of Michigan Press.

Ready, T., Tyson, B., & Pagnucco, R. "The Impact of the Nobel Peace Prize on the Work of Adolfo Perez Esquivel." Unpublished manuscript, Department of Anthropology, Catholic University, Washington, DC, 1985.

Reich, C.A. 1970. *The Greening of America.* New York: Random House.

Reitman, J.I., & Greene, J.S. 1972. *Standard Education Almanac.* Orange, NJ: Academic Media.

"Revolt of the Admirals." *Time* (October 17, 1949): 21-23.

Rimlinger, G.V. "The Legitimation of Protest: A Comparative Study in Labor History." In *Protest, Reform, and Revolt: A Reader in Social Movements,* ed. J.R. Gusfield. New York: Wiley, 1970, pp. 363-76.

Roach, J., & Roach, J. "Mobilizing the Poor: Road to a Dead End." *Social Problems* 26 (December 1978): 160-71.

Robbins, T. "Marginal Movements." *Society* 21 (May-June 1984): 47-52.

Roberts, S.V. "Foes of Abortion Meet with Reagan." *New York Times* (January 23, 1982): 1.

Robinson, J.A.O. 1981. *Abraham Went Out: A Biography of A.J. Muste.* Philadelphia: University of Pennsylvania Press.

Robinson, J.P., & Converse, P.E. 1966. *Summary of United States Time Use Survey.* University of Michigan Survey Research Center, Institute for Social Research, Ann Arbor, MI.

Robinson, M. "Television and American Politics: 1956-76." *Public Interest* 48 (Summer 1977): 3-39.

Roche, J.P. 1963. *The Quest for the Dream: The Development of Civil Rights and Human Relations in Modern America.* New York: Macmillan.

Rose, A. 1967. *The Power Structure.* New York: Oxford University Press.

Rosenberg, T. "How the Media Made the Moral Majority." *Washington Monthly* 14 (May 1982): 26-34.

Rosenthal, N., Fingrutd, M., Ethier, M., Karant, R., & McDonald, D. "Social Movements and Networks Analysis: A Case Study of Nineteenth-Century Women's Reform in New York State." *American Journal of Sociology* 90 (5) (March 1985): 1022-54.

Ross, A.D. "Philanthropic Activity and the Business Career." *Social Forces* 32 (1954): 274-80.

Ross, D.K. 1973. *A Public Citizen's Action Manual.* New York: Grossman.

Ross, R.J. "Generational Change and Primary Groups in a Social Movement." Unpublished manuscript, Clark University, Worcester, MA, 1975.

――――. "Advocate Planners and Urban Reform." Ph.D. dissertation, Department of Sociology, University of Chicago, 1975.

Sabato, L.J. 1984. *PAC POWER: Inside the World of Political Action Committees.* New York: W.W. Norton.

――――. 1981. *The Rise of Political Consultants: New Ways of Winning Elections.* New York: Basic Books.

Sale, K. 1973. *SDS.* New York: Random House.

Salisbury, R.H. "An Exchange Theory of Interest Groups." *Midwest Journal of Political Science* 13 (February 1969): 1-32.

Samuelson, P. 1964. *Economics: An Introductory Analysis.* New York: McGraw-Hill.

Scharf, L. 1980. *To Work and to Wed: Female Employment, Feminism, and the Great Depression.* Westport, CT: Greenwood Press.

Schattschneider, E.E. 1960. *Semisovereign People: A Realist's View of Democracy in America.* Hinsdale, IL: Dryden Press.

Scherer, R.P. 1980. *American Denominational Organization: A Sociological View.* Pasadena, CA: William Carey Library.

Schuman, H., & Presser, S. "The Attitude-Action Connection and the Issue of Gun Control." *Annals* 455 (May 1981): 40-47.

Schumpeter, J.A. 1947. *Capitalism, Socialism, and Democracy.* New York: Harper & Bros.

Schwartz, M. 1976. *Radical Protest and Social Structure: The Southern Farmer's Alliance and Cotton Tenancy, 1880-1890.* New York: Academic Press.

Schwartz, M.A. "Politics and Moral Causes in Canada and the United States." *Comparative Social Research* 4 (1981): 65-90.

Selznick, G.J., & Steinberg, S. "Social Class, Ideology, and Voting Preference: An Analysis of the 1964 Presidential Election." In *Structural Social Inequality,* ed. Celia S. Heller. New York: Macmillan, pp. 216-25.

Selznick, P. 1957. *Leadership in Administration.* Evanston, IL: Row, Peterson.

_____. 1949. *TVA and the Grass Roots.* Berkeley: University of California Press.

_____. "Foundations of the Theory of Organization." *American Sociological Review* 13 (February 1948): 25-35.

_____. "An Approach to a Theory of Bureaucracy." *American Sociological Review* 8 (1) (1943): 47-54.

Serrin, W. 1973. *The Company and the Union: The "Civilized Relationship" of the General Motors Corporation and the Automobile Workers.* New York: Knopf.

Sewell, W.H., Jr. "Ideologies and Social Revolutions: Reflections on the French Case." *Journal of Modern History* 57 (March 1985): 57-85.

Sheets, K.R. "Is Nuclear Power Finished in the U.S.?" *U.S. News and World Report* (March 29, 1982): 59-60.

Shils, E. "From Periphery to Center: The Changing Place of Intellectuals in American Society." In *Stability and Social Change,* ed. Bernard Barber & Alex Inkeles. Boston: Little, Brown, 1971.

Shoenherr, R.A., & Sorenson, A. "Social Change in Religious Organizations: Consequences of Clergy Decline in the U.S. Catholic Church." *Social Analysis* 43 (1983): 123-52.

Shupe, A.D., Jr., & Bromley, D.G. 1980. *The New Vigilantes: Deprogrammers, Anti-Cultists, and The New Religion.* Beverly Hills, CA: Sage.

_____. "The Moonies and the Anti-Cultists: Movement and Countermovement in Conflict." *Sociological Analysis* 40 (Fall 1979): 325-34.

Shupe, A.D., Hardin, B.L., & Bromley, D.G. "A Comparison of Anti-Cult Movements in the United States and West Germany." In *Of Gods and Men: New Religious Movements in the West,* ed. Eileen Barker. Macon, GA: Mercer University Press, 1983, pp. 177-94.

Sills, D. 1957. *The Volunteers.* New York: Free Press.

Sinclair, W. "Political Consultants: The New King-Makers Work Their Magic." *Washington Post* (June 5, 1982): A-6.

Singelmann, J. 1978. *From Agriculture to Services: The Transformation of Industrial Employment.* Beverly Hills, CA: Sage.

Singelmann, J., & Browning, H. 1973. *The Service Sector.* Austin: University of Texas.

Singh, B.K., & Leahy, P. "Contextual and Ideological Dimensions of Attitudes Toward Abortion." *Demography* 15 (August 1978): 381-88.

Skocpol, T. "Cultural Idioms and Political Ideologies in the Revolutionary Reconstruction of State Power: A Rejoinder to Sewell." *Journal of Modern History* 57 (March 1985): 86-96.

_____. "France, Russia, China: A Structural Analysis of Social Revolutions." *Comparative Studies in History and Society* 18 (April 2, 1976a): 175-210.

_____. "Old Regime Legacies and Communist Revolutions in Russia and China." *Social Forces* 55 (December 1976b): 284-315.

Smelser, N.J. 1963. *Theory of Collective Behavior*. New York: Free Press.

Smith, R.A. "The Progressive Movement: A Sociological Interpretation." *Center for Social Organization Studies*, Working Paper No. 121, University of Chicago, 1968.

Snow, D.A., Zurcher, L.A., Jr., & Ekland-Olson, S. "Social Networks and Social Movements: A Microstructural Approach to Differential Recruitment." *American Sociological Review* 45 (October 1980): 787-801.

Snyder, D. "Institutional Settings and Industrial Conflict: Comparative Analysis of France, Italy, and the United States." *American Sociological Review* 40 (June 1975): 259-78.

Snyder, D., & Kelly, W. "Strategies for Studying Violence and Social Change: Illustrations from Analyses of Racial Disorders and Implications for Mobilization Research." In *The Dynamics of Mobilization: Resource Mobilization, Tactics, and Social Control*, ed. Mayer N. Zald & John D. McCarthy. Boston: Winthrop, 1979, pp. 212-37.

Snyder, D., & Tilly, C. "Hardship and Collective Violence in France." *American Sociological Review* 37 (October 1972): 520-32.

Social Science Information, Vol. 13 (1974). Paris; International Social Science Council.

_____. Vol. 14 (1975).

Solzhenitsyn, A.I. 1973. *The Gulag Archipelago, 1918-1956: An Experiment in Literary Investigation*. 2 vols. New York: Harper & Row.

Spaulding, C.B., & Turner, H.A. "Political Orientation and Field Specialization Among College Professors." *Sociology of Education* 41 (Summer 1968): 245-62.

Stallings, R.A. "Social Movements as Emergent Coalitions: An Interorganizational Approach," Working Paper No. 14. School of Public Administration, University of Southern California, 1977.

_____. "Patterns of Belief in Social Movements: Clarifications from Analysis of Environmental Groups." *Sociological Quarterly* 14 (Autumn 1973): 465-80.

Standard Industrial Classification Manual 1972, Washington, D.C.: Executive Office of the President, Office of Management and Budget.

Statistics on Social Work Education, 1956. New York Council on Social Work Education, 1956.

Steinhoff, P.G., & Diamond, M. 1977. *Abortion Politics: The Hawaii Experience*. Honolulu: University of Hawaii Press.

Stern, R. "Fighters and Switchers: Alternating Forms of Industrial Protest." Mimeograph. Ithaca: New York State School of Industrial and Labor Relations, Cornell University, n.d.

Stevens, A. "AFNE Made the Difference." *The Nuclear Advocate* (September 1980): 3.

Stever, D.W. 1980. *Seabrook and the Nuclear Regulatory Commission: The Licensing of a Nuclear Power Plant*. Hanover, NH: University Press of New England.

Stinchcombe, A.L. "Agricultural Enterprise and Rural Class Relationships." *American Journal of Sociology* 67 (1967): 165-76.

_____. "Social Structure and Organizations." In *Handbook of Organizations*, ed. James March. Chicago: Rand McNally, 1965, pp. 142-93.

_____. 1964. *Rebellion in a High School*. Chicago: Quadrangle Books.

Stobaugh, R., & Yergin, D. 1979. *Energy Future: Report of the Energy Project at the Harvard Business School*. New York: Random House.

Stockton, B., & Janke, P. "Nuclear Power: Protest and Violence." *Conflict Studies*, No. 102. London: The Institute for the Study of Conflict, 1978.

Stoner, C., & Parke, J.A. 1977. *All God's Children*. New York: Penguin Books.

Stouffer, S. 1955. *Communism, Conformity, and Civil Liberties*. Garden City, NY: Doubleday.

Street, D., & Leggett, J.C. "Economic Deprivation and Extremism: A Study of Unemployed Negroes." *American Journal of Sociology* 67 (1961): 53-57.

Strickland, D.A., & Johnston, A.E. "Issue Elasticity in Political Systems." *Journal of Political Economy* 78 (September-October 1970): 1069-92.

Stroops, W., Copland, R., & Sieminski, A. 1979. *Nuclear Energy: Dark Outlook*. Washington, DC: Washington Analysis Corporation.

Swanson, G.E. "An Organizational Analysis of Collectivities." *American Sociological Review* 36 (August 1971): 607-24.

_____. 1967. *Religion and Regime: A Sociological Account of the Reformation*. Ann Arbor: University of Michigan Press.

Takayama, K.P. "Strains, Conflicts, and Schisms in Protestant Denominations." In *American Denominational Organization: A Sociological View*, ed. R.P. Scherer. Pasadena, CA: William Carey Library, 1980, pp. 298-329.

Takayama, K.P., & Cannon, L.W. "Formal Polity and Power Distribution in American Protestant Denominations." *Sociological Quarterly* 20 (Summer 1979): 321-32.

Takayama, K.P., & Darnell, S.B. "The Aggressive Organization and the Reluctant Environment: The Vulnerability of an Inter-Faith Coordinating Agency." *Review of Religious Research* 20 (Summer 1979): 315-34.

Talar, C.J.T. "Paradigm and Structure in Theological Communities: A Sociological Reading of the Modernist Crisis." Unpublished dissertation. Catholic University of America, Washington, DC, 1979.

Tannenbaum, A. "Control in Organizations: Individual Adjustment and Organizational Performance." *Administrative Science Quarterly* 7 (2) (1962): 236-57.

Tatalovich, R., & Daynes, B.W. 1981. *The Politics of Abortion*. New York: Praeger.

Tedrow, L.M., & Mahoney, E.R. "Trends in Attitudes Toward Abortion: 1972-1976." *Public Opinion Quarterly* (1979): 181-89.

Temples, J.R. "The Politics of Nuclear Power: A Subgovernment in Transition." *Political Science Quarterly* 95(2) (1980): 239-60.

Therborn, G. "The Rule of Capital and the Rise of Democracy." *New Left Review* 103 (May-June 1977): 3-41.

Thibaut, J., & Kelley, H. 1959. *The Social Psychology of Groups*. New York: Wiley.

Thieblot, A.J., Jr., & Cowin, R.M. 1972. *Welfare and Strikes: The Use of Public Funds to Support Strikers*. Philadelphia: Industrial Research Unit, Wharton School.

Thomas, J.M. 1981. *Revolutionary Russia, 1917*. New York: Charles Scribner's Sons.

Thomas, G.M., & Meyer, J.W. "The Expansion of the State." *Annual Review of Sociology* 10 (1984): 461-82.

Thompson, J.D. 1971. *Organizations in Action*. New York: McGraw-Hill.

_____. "Organizational Management of Conflict." *Administrative Science Quarterly* 4 (March 1960): 389-409.

Tilly, C. "Useless Durkheim." In *As Sociology Meets History*. New York: Academic Press, 1981, pp. 95-108.

_____. "Social Movements and National Politics," Working Paper No. 197. Center for Research on Social Organization, University of Michigan, Ann Arbor, 1979.

_____. 1978. *From Mobilization to Revolution*. Reading, MA: Addison-Wesley.

_____. "Revolution and Collective Violence." In *Macro Political Theory. Handbook of Political Science*, Vol. 3, ed. G. Greenstein & N. Polsby. Reading, MA: Addison-Wesley, 1975, pp. 483-555.

_____. "Does Modernization Breed Revolution?" *Comparative Politics* 5 (April 1973): 425-47.

Tilly, C., Tilly, L., & Tilly, R. 1975. *The Rebellious Century: 1830-1930*. Cambridge, MA: Harvard University Press.

Topolsky, M. "Common Cause?" *Worldview* 17 (April 1974): 35-39.

Touraine, A. 1981. *The Voice and the Eye: An Analysis of Social Movements*, trans. A. Duff. New York: Cambridge University Press.

Trow, M. 1972. *The Expansion and Transformation of Higher Education*. Morristown, NJ: General Learning Press.

Troyer, R.J. "Saving the Nation and Nonsmokers' Rights: Professionalization and Antismoking Movements." Unpublished manuscript, Department of Sociology, Drake University, Des Moines, Iowa, 1980.

Troyer, R.J., & Markle, G.E. 1983. *Cigarettes: The Battle Over Smoking*. New Brunswick, NJ: Rutgers University Press.

Tufte, E.R. 1978. *The Political Control of the Economy*. Princeton, NJ: Princeton University Press.

Tullock, G. "Information Without Profit." In *Papers on Non-Market Decision Making*, ed. G. Tullock. Charlottesville: Thomas Jefferson Center for Political Economy, University of Virginia, 1966, pp. 141-60.

Turner, R.H. "Determinants of Social Movement Strategies." In *Human Nature and Collective Behavior: Papers in Honor of Herbert Blumer*, ed. Tamotsu Shibutani. Englewood Cliffs, NJ: Prentice-Hall, 1970, pp. 145-64.

_____. "The Public Perception of Protest." *American Sociological Review* 34 (December 1969): 815-31.

_____. "Collective Behavior and Conflict, New Theoretical Frameworks." *Sociological Quarterly* 5 (Spring 1964): 122-37.

Turner R.H., & Killian, L. 1957. *Collective Behavior*. Englewood Cliffs, NJ: Prentice-Hall.

_____. 1972. *Collective Behavior*, 2d ed. Englewood Cliffs, NJ: Prentice-Hall.

U.S. Department of Labor, Bureau of Labor Statistics. 1951. *Social Workers in 1950*. American Association of Social Workers. Washington, D.C.

U.S. Treasury Department. *Report on Private Foundations*. Washington, DC: U.S. Government Printing Office, 1965.

Useem, B. "Center-Periphery Conflict: Elite and Popular Involvement in the Boston Anti-Busing Movement." In *Research in Social Movements, Conflict and Change*, ed. Richard Radcliff. Greenwich, CT: JAI Press, 1984, pp. 271-93.

Useem, B., & Zald, M.N. "From Pressure Group to Social Movement: Organizational Dilemmas of the Effort to Promote Nuclear Power." *Social Problems* 30 (December 1982): 144-56.

Vaillancourt, J.G. 1981. *Papal Power: A Study of Vatican Control over Lay Catholic Elites.* Berkeley, CA: University of California Press.

Vanecko, J.J. "Community Mobilization and Institutional Change: The Influence of the Community Action Program in Large Cities." *Social Science Quarterly* 50 (1969): 609-30.

Van Voorst, L.B. "The Churches and Nuclear Deterrence." *Foreign Affairs* 16 (Spring 1983): 827-52.

Vidich, A., & Bensman, J. 1960. *Small Town and Mass Society: Class Power and Religion in a Rural Community.* Garden City, NY: Doubleday Anchor Books.

Vigurie, R.A. 1981. *The New Right: We're Ready to Lead.* Falls Church, VA: Caroline House Publishers.

Vocations for Social Change, No. 22 (1970).

Von Eschen, D., Kirk, J., & Pinard, M. "The Organizational Substructure of Disorderly Politics." *Social Forces* 49 (June 1971): 529-44.

_____. "The Disintegration of the Negro Nonviolent Movement." *Journal of Peace Research* 3 (1969): 216-34.

Wagner, J.R. "Friends of the Earth Staff Members Organize New Environmental Lobby." *National Journal* (February 5, 1972): 246.

Waldman, E. "Marital and Family Characteristics of Workers, March 1966." *Monthly Labor Review* 4 (1967): 39-96.

Walker, J.L. "The Origins and Maintenance of Interest Groups in America." *American Political Science Review* 77 (June 1983): 390-406.

_____. "Setting the Agenda in the U.S. Senate: A Theory of Problem Selection." *British Journal of Political Science* 7 (October 1977): 423-45.

Wallerstein, I. 1980. *The Modern World System II: Mercantilism and the Consolidation of the European World Economy.* New York: Academic Books.

_____. 1976. *The Modern World System.* New York: Academic Press.

Walsh, E.J. "Resource Mobilization and Citizen Protest in Communities Around Three Mile Island." *Social Problems* 29 (October 1981): 1-21.

Walsh, E., & Warland, R.H. "Social Movement in the Wake of a Nuclear Accident." *American Sociological Review* 48 (December 1983): 764-80.

Walzer, M. 1971. *Political Action: A Practical Guide to Movement Politics.* Chicago: Quadrangle.

Wamsley, G.L., & Zald, M. 1973. *The Political Economy of Public Organizations.* Lexington, MA: Heath Lexington Books.

Warner, M. "Organizational Context and Control of Policy in the Television Newsroom: A Participant Observation Study." *British Journal of Sociology* 12 (3) (1971): 283-94.

Warren, R.C. "Comprehensive Planning and Coordination: Some Functional Aspects." *Social Problems* 20 (Winter 1973): 355-63.

Wasserman, H. 1979. *Energy War: Report from the Front.* Westport, CT: Lawrence Hill.

Watts, W.A., & Whittaker, D. "Profile of a Non-Conformist Youth Culture: A Study of Berkeley Non-Students." *Sociology of Education* 41 (1968): 178-200.

Weber, Max. 1947. *The Theory of Social and Economic Organizations.* New York: Oxford University Press.

Weingast, B.R. "Congress, Regulation, and the Decline of Nuclear Power." *Public Policy* 28 (2) (1980): 231-35.

Weinstein, D. 1979. *Bureaucratic Opposition.* New York: Pergamon.

West, G. 1981. *The National Welfare Rights Movement.* New York: Praeger.

White, O.K. "Mormons for ERA: An Internal Social Movement." Paper presented at the annual meeting of the Association for the Sociology of Religion, 1981, Toronto, Ontario.

Wicker, T. 1975. *Scientific Sociology: Theory and Method.* Englewood Cliffs, NJ: Prentice-Hall.

Wiebe, R.H. 1967. *The Search For Order.* New York: Hill and Wang.

Wilensky, H. 1975. *The Welfare State and Equality: Structural and Ideological Roots of Public Expenditures.* Berkeley, CA: University of California Press.

_____. "The Professionalization of Everyone?" *The American Journal of Sociology* 70 (2) (1964): 137-58.

_____. "The Uneven Distribution of Leisure: The Impact of Economic Growth on 'Free Time.'" *Social Problems* 9 (1961): 32-56.

_____. 1956. *Intellectuals in Labor Unions.* Glencoe, IL: Free Press.

Wilensky, H.L., & Lebeaux, C.N. 1965. *Industrial Society and Social Welfare.* Glencoe, IL: Free Press.

Wiley, S.W. 1944. *History of YMCA-Church Relations in the United States.* New York: Association Press.

Wilkinson, P. 1971. *Social Movements.* New York: Praeger.

Williams, H. 1970. *Huey Long.* New York: Bantam Books.

Williams, R. 1960. *Culture and Society, 1780-1950.* Garden City, NY: Doubleday.

Wilsnack, R. "Explaining Collective Violence in Prisons: Problems and Possibilities." In *Prison Violence,* ed. Albert K. Cohen, George F. Cole, & Robert G. Bailey. Lexington, MA: Lexington/Heath, 1976, pp. 61-78.

Wilson, B. 1961. *Sects and Society.* Berkeley: University of California Press.

Wilson, J. 1973. *Introduction to Social Movements.* New York: Basic Books.

Wilson, J.Q. 1973. *Political Organizations.* New York: Basic Books.

_____. "Why Are We Having a Wave of Violence?" *New York Times Magazine* 19 (1968): 23-24, 116-20.

_____. 1966. *The Amateur Democrat.* Chicago: University of Chicago Press.

Wilson, K.L., & Orum, A.M. "Mobilizing People for Collective Action." *Journal of Political and Military Sociology* 4 (Fall 1976): 187-202.

Wilson, M.B. "Energy and Its Implications on Social Progress." Speech before the Second National Conference on Energy Advocacy: Energy for the Eighties, June 29, 1980, Chicago, IL.

Wise, J.A. "The Coup d'Etat at Interpublic." *Fortune* (February 1968): 134.

Wittner, L.S. 1984. *Rebels Against War: The American Peace Movement, 1933-1983.* Philadelphia: Temple University Press.

Wolfe, B. "The Nuclear Expert and the Debate." Speech before a meeting of the Atomic Energy Industrial Forum, April 19, 1978, Atlanta, GA.

Wolfe, B. 1955. *Three Who Made a Revolution.* Boston: Beacon.

Wood, J.R. 1981. *Legitimate Leadership in Voluntary Organizations: The Controversy Over Social Action in Protestant Churches.* New Brunswick, NJ: Rutgers University Press.

_____. "Authority and Controversial Policy: The Churches and Civil Rights." *American Sociological Review* 35 (December 1970): 1057-69.

_____. "Protestant Enforcement of Racial Integration Policy: A Sociological Study in the Political Economy of Organizations." Ph.D. dissertation, Vanderbilt University, 1967.

Wood, J.R., & Zald, M.N. "Aspects of Racial Integration in the Methodist Church:

Sources of Resistance to Organizational Policy." *Social Forces* 45 (December 1966): 255-65.

Wood, M., & Hughes, M. "The Moral Basis of Moral Reform: Status Discontent vs. Culture and Socialization as Explanations of Antipornography Social Movement Adherence." *American Sociological Review* 49 (February 1984): 86-99.

Wood, R.C. "When Government Works." *Public Interest* 18 (Winter 1970): 39-51.

Woodward, C.V. 1963. *Tom Watson*. New York: Oxford University Press.

Wootton, G. 1970. *Interest Groups*. Englewood Cliffs, NJ: Prentice-Hall.

Worsley, P. 1968. *The Trumpet Shall Sound*. New York: Schocken Books.

Wright, E.O. "Class Boundaries in Advanced Capitalist Societies." *New Left Review* 98 (July-August 1976): 3-41.

Wright, E.O., Costello, C., Hachen, D., & Sprague, J. "The American Class Structure." *American Sociological Review* 47(6) (December 1982): 709-26.

Wright, J.D. "Public Opinion and Gun Control: A Comparison of Results from Two Recent National Surveys." *Annals* 455 (May 1981): 24-39.

Wright, J.D., Rossi, P.H., & Daly, K. 1983. *Under the Gun: Weapons, Crime, and Violence in America*. New York: Aldine.

Wuthnow, R. "Religious Movements and Countermovements in America." In *New Religious Movements and Rapid Social Change*, ed. J.A. Beckford. Paris: UNESCO, 1984.

_____. "The Political Rebirth of American Evangelicals." In *The New Christian Right: Mobilization and Legitimation*, ed. R.C. Liebman & R. Wuthnow. New York: Aldine, 1983, pp. 168-87.

_____. "World Order and Religious Movements." In *Studies of the Modern World-System*, ed. A. Bergesen. New York: Academic Press, 1980, pp. 57-75.

Yablonsky, L. 1967. *Synanon: The Tunnel Back*. Pelican Books.

Yellowitz, I. 1965. *Labor and the Progressive Movement in New York State, 1897-1916*. Cornell University Press.

Yinger, J.M. 1957. *Religion, Society, and the Individual*. New York: Macmillan.

Zalaznick, S. "Small World of Big Washington Lawyers." *Fortune* 80 (1969): 120-25.

Zald, M.N. 1971. *Occupations and Organizations in American Society: The Organization-Dominated Man?* Chicago: Markham.

_____. 1970a. *Organizational Change: The Political Economy of the YMCA*. Chicago: University of Chicago Press.

_____. 1970b. *Power in Organizations*. Nashville, TN: Vanderbilt University Press.

_____. "Who Shall Rule: A Political Analysis of Succession in a Large Welfare Organization." *Pacific Sociological Review* 8 (1) (1965): 52-60.

_____. "Organizational Control Structures in Five Correctional Institutions." *American Journal of Sociology* 68 (November 1962): 335-45.

Zald, M.N., & Ash, R. "Social Movement Organizations: Growth, Decline, and Change." *Social Forces* 44 (March 1966): 327-40.

Zald, M.N., & Berger, M.A. "Social Movements in Organizations: Coup d'Etat, Insurgency, and Mass Movement." *American Journal of Sociology* 83 (January 1978): 823-61.

Zald, M.N., & Denton, P. "From Evangelism to General Service: On the Transformation of the YMCA." *Administrative Science Quarterly* 8 (June 1963): 214-34.

Zald, M.N., & Jacobs, D. "Compliance/Incentive Classifications of Organizations: Underlying Dimensions." *Administration and Society* 9 (4) (February 1978): 403-24.

_____. "Symbols into Plowshares: Underlying Dimensions of Incentive Analysis." Unpublished manuscript, Vanderbilt University, 1976.

Zald, M.N., & McCarthy, J.D. "Social Movement Industries: Cooperation and Competition Among Movement Organizations." In *Research in Social Movements, Conflict and Change*, Vol. 3, ed. L. Kriesberg. Greenwich, CT: JAI Press, 1980, pp. 1-20.

_____. "Organizational Intellectuals and the Criticism of Society." *Social Service Review* 49 (September 1975): 344-62.

_____. "Notes on Cooperation and Competition Amongst Social Movement Organizations." Unpublished manuscript, Vanderbilt University, 1974.

Zald, M.N., & Useem, B. "Movement and Countermovement: Loosely Coupled Conflict." Paper presented at the annual meetings of the American Sociological Association, September 8, 1982, San Francisco, CA.

Zinn, H. 1964. *SNCC: The New Abolitionists*. Boston: Beacon Press.

Zipp, J.F., & Smith, J. "A Structural Analysis of Class Voting." *Social Forces* 6 (3) (March 1982): 738-59.

Index

Aaron, D., 247
Abendroth, W., 300
Aberle, D., 76
Abolitionist movement, 71, 82, 321-22
ACTION, 262
Action on Smoking and Health (ASH), 330
Adams, Robert, 79, 86, 188
Adherents, 23-25, 30, 199, 257
Ad hoc committees, 52, 176, 357, 361
Admirals' revolt, 186, 201
Advertising, 30-32, 39, 50, 54, 61
Affinity groups, 5-6
Affirmative-action offices, 36
Affluence, 20, 34, 328, 349-53
AFL-CIO, 18, 37, 176, 273, 377-78
AID, 90
Alcoholics Anonymous, 294
Alexander, C.D., 71
Alinsky, Saul, 15, 382
Allende, Salvador, 303
Alliances, 2, 57, 110, 175-78
Almond, G.A., 295, 342-43
Altbach, P.G., 188
Althusser, L., 299
American Baptist Convention, 360
American Cancer Society, 152
American Civil Liberties Union (ACLU), 52, 128, 167, 172, 367, 373, 382
American Enterprise Institute, 114
American Family Institute, 73
American Federation of Teachers, 170
American Friends Service Committee (AFSC), 22, 31, 74-75, 365
American Life Lobby (ALL), 52, 61
American Medical Association (AMA), 18, 377
American Nuclear Energy Council, 276
American Revolution, 303
Americans for Democratic Action (ADA), 21
Americans for More Power Sources (AMPS), 263

Americans for Nuclear Energy, 262, 282
Americans United for Life (AUL), 52
Amin, Samir, 88
Anderson, John, 328
Antiabortion movement. *See* Pro-life movement
Anticult groups, 78
Antinuclear movement, 245-46, 274-88, 322, 326; definition of, 275
Antipoverty movement, 107-8, 112
Antiprohibition movement, 254
Anti-Saloon League, 71
Antiwar movement, 76, 112, 207, 284
Apathy, member, 122, 131, 133, 137, 219
ARCO, 332
Armed Forces Movement of Portugal, 312-13
"Articulating leadership," 137-38
Ash, Roberta (now Garner, Roberta), 1, 4, 6, 28, 109, 119-20, 161, 178, 248, 273, 280, 291, 312, 319, 368-69, 373, 382
Ashmore, H., 253
Association Against the Prohibition Amendment (AAPA), 260
Associational density, 207-8, 211
Assumption extremes, 18
Atomic Energy Commission (AEC), 276
Atomic Industrial Forum, 262, 276-79, 283-84, 287
At-risk populations, 324-25
Auclaire, Philip, 114
Autonomy, 81, 149, 297-98

Bacon's Rebellion, 320
Bailis, L., 25, 28, 56
Bain, J.S., 22
Bandiera, A.R., 313
Banfield, E., 295
Baptist Church, 177
Bargaining, 19
Barkan, S.E., 259, 285